THE OLD UNITED EMPIRE LOYALISTS LIST

With a New Introduction

by

MILTON RUBINCAM, F.A.S.G., F.N.G.S., F.G.S.P.
Honorary Vice-President
Ontario Genealogical Society

CLEARFIELD

Originally Published As
*Centennial of the Settlement of Upper Canada
By the United Empire Loyalists
1784-1884*
Toronto, 1885

Reprinted with a New Introduction
Genealogical Publishing Co., Inc.
Baltimore, 1969

Reprinted with a New Introduction (Revised)
Genealogical Publishing Co., Inc.
Baltimore, 1976, 1984, 1993

Reprinted for
Clearfield Company, Inc. by
Genealogical Publishing Co., Inc.
Baltimore, Maryland
2003

Library of Congress Catalogue Card Number 69-17131
International Standard Book Number: 0-8063-0331-X

Made in the United States of America

Copyright © 1976
Genealogical Publishing Co., Inc.
Baltimore, Maryland
All rights reserved

Made in the United States of America

THE CENTENNIAL

OF THE

SETTLEMENT OF UPPER CANADA

BY THE

UNITED EMPIRE LOYALISTS,

1784–1884.

THE CELEBRATIONS AT ADOLPHUSTOWN, TORONTO AND NIAGARA,

WITH

AN APPENDIX,

CONTAINING A COPY OF THE U. E. LIST, PRESERVED IN THE CROWN LANDS DEPARTMENT AT TORONTO.

PUBLISHED BY THE CENTENNIAL COMMITTEE.

> " Stern was the test,
> And sorely pressed
> That proved their blood best of the best,
> And when for Canada you pray
> Implore kind Heaven
> That, like a leaven,
> The hero-blood which then was given
> May quicken in her veins alway."
> —*Le Roy Hooker.*

Toronto:
ROSE PUBLISHING COMPANY.
1885.

New Introduction

By MILTON RUBINCAM, F.A.S.G., F.N.G.S., F.G.S.P., C.G

Honorary Vice-President, Ontario Genealogical Society

Canadians hold the Loyalists, those colonists who remained steadfast in their allegiance to King George III, in the same high honor that Americans regard the patriots who had the courage to rebel against Great Britain's oppressive measures and declare their independence. Called Tories on this side of the border, they suffered the humiliation of being tarred and feathered, and they endured imprisonment and confiscation of their properties. At the close of the Revolutionary War thousands of families and individuals emigrated to the British Isles and Canada, in the latter country settling in the provinces of Nova Scotia and New Brunswick (created in 1784) and Upper Canada (now Ontario) after it was opened for settlement in 1791.

His Majesty's Government was not insensible of the sufferings of the Loyalists. For seven years, from 1783 to 1790, a commission interviewed thousands of claimants and their witnesses, compiled data on lost properties in all of the thirteen States, and weighed the evidence. After the commission had completed its task, the payments came slowly to the successful claimants. The original Loyalist memorials, petitions, and supporting papers are in the Public Record Office, London, in the Audit Office 12 and 13 classes. Microfilm reproductions are in the Manuscript Division of the Library of Congress, Washington, D. C., and the Genealogical Society of the Church of Jesus Christ of Latter-day Saints, Salt Lake City, and perhaps elsewhere. The original notes of the Loyalist Commissioners came in the last century to the Smithsonian Institution and were eventually transferred to the Library of Congress where, in the Manuscript Division, they are preserved in thirty-six bound volumes and two boxes. They were published, not entirely accurately (due to the difficult handwriting of the Commissioners or their clerks), in the 1,436-page *Second Report of the Bureau of Archives for the Province of Ontario*, 1904. Transcripts of the Loyalists' papers, prepared at the turn of this century, are in the New York Public Library, 42nd Street and Fifth Avenue, New York City.

Sir Guy Carleton, Lord Dorchester, Governor-General of Canada, wishing to honor those persons in his provinces who had remained loyal to Great Britain, proposed to the Executive Council on 9 November 1789 that "a Marke of Honour" should be put on "the families who had adhered to the Unity of the Empire, and joined the Royal Standard in America before the Treaty of Separation in the year 1783." The Council concurred, and registers of persons falling into this category were prepared. From Lord Dorchester's words, "unity of Empire," came the name "United Empire Loyalists."

There are numerous Loyalist lists. In the 1969 reprint of this volume we were misled by a statement in *The Encyclopedia of Canada* to assert categorically: "The 'Old U.E.L. List', as it is called, with additions down to 1798, is the official register of persons who are entitled to the appellation of United Empire Loyalists. . . . In spite of attempts to do so, no additions can be made to it." This is false, as shown by an examination of Wilfrid Campbell's *Report on Manuscript Lists in the Archives Relating to the United Empire Loyalists, With Reference to Other Sources* (1909), a copy of which was kindly provided this writer by Mrs. Audrey L. Kirk, Streetsville, Ont., an authority on the Loyalists, and A. Phillips Silcox (now deceased), President of the Ontario Genealogical Society. The Public Archives of Canada at Ottawa has the Executive (or Privy) Council List, which Mr. Campbell described as "the only official U. E. list" for Upper Canada "which we have. It was, without doubt, made from the Original District Rolls of Upper Canada, which are referred to in its pages."

The "Old U.E.L. List" is known as the Crown Lands Department List, since it was preserved in that Department. The original list seems to have disappeared. There are two copies in the Lands Administration Branch, Ontario Ministry of Lands and Waters, which the writer examined in Toronto in November 1975. The older copy was made about 1850, perhaps some years before, and we were informed at the Archives of Ontario that it was from this list the present publication was initially made in 1885. A close study shows that in addition to people who were undoubtedly Loyalists, it includes soldiers from disbanded German regiments who had fought for Great Britain during the Revolution and settlers who came in search of cheap land—not necessarily because of an attachment to the Sovereign.

A succinct but excellent account of "Loyalist Migrations," by Robert F. Kirk, and a good bibliography by Mr. and Mrs. Kirk, were published in the *Bulletin of the Ontario Genealogical Society*, Vol. 8, No. 3 (Summer 1969), pp. 49-57. The Loyalist holdings of the Library of Congress are described in *Manuscript Sources in the Library of Congress for research on the American Revolution*, by John R. Sellers, Gerard W. Gawalt, Paul H. Smith, and Patricia Molen van Ee of the American Revolution Bicentennial Office (1975), pp. 106 (no. 497, Loyalist Commissioners' Proceedings, or notes), 194 (no. 1143, 18 volumes of photostats of Loyalist regimental muster rolls), 284-285 (nos. 1559-1560, microfilms of the Loyalists' claims, Audit Office 12 and 13 classes), etc.

Although not all persons on the Old U.E.L. List are Loyalists, it contains a tremendous amount of information on the people included, their service, if any, with the Provincial Forces, the British Army, and the German Regiments, and the general location of their homes in Upper Canada (such as Home District, Fredericksburgh, Adolphus Town, etc.). As a result of his studies of the Loyalists' claims for compensation for their losses, the writer was able to identify many of them on the List. And it was through this List that he was able to determine the regiment in which his own Loyalist ancestor, Laurence Johnson (p. 198) served—the Loyal American, commanded by Col. Beverley Robinson.

W. Hyattsville, Md.

January 1976

INTRODUCTION.

WHEN the American Colonies revolted in 1776, and declared their Independence, there was a very large number of the Colonists who vehemently opposed the movement, and aided the Imperial troops in the war that ensued. Those who took up arms for the Crown, fought for a United Empire, that was their rallying cry, they wished to see the English race united under a common flag and under the same sovereign. They deplored the dismemberment of the Empire, and during the long struggle maintained a sturdy adherence to their principles. They were known as the United Empire Loyalists or as has become a familiar phrase on this continent, the U. E. Loyalists.

On the conclusion of the war, and the severance of the old Colonies from the Mother Country, these U. E. Loyalists abandoning all they possessed, moved into what is now New Brunswick and Nova Scotia, in 1783, and in 1784 a large number of them moved up the St. Lawrence and settled in the then unbroken wilderness of Upper Canada. Many also moved from the United States through the wilderness, to the Niagara River, where they crossed into British Territory and made the first settlement in that district in the same year. A very large proportion of the present population of Upper Canada can trace their descent from these early pioneers, who settled this Province by reason of their unyielding loyalty to a great principle. This volume records the Celebration of the Centennial of the arrival of the U. E. Loyalists in Ontario. The demonstrations originated in the following manner :

Some time in the summer of 1876, at a meeting of the York Pioneers, held in Toronto, the late Mr. Richard H. Oates suggested that as the United States were celebrating the centennial of their Declaration of Independence, it would be but right for the descendants of the United Empire Loyalists to hold a celebration in honour of the gallant efforts of their fathers to maintain the unity of the Empire, and in grateful recognition of the sacrifice made by them in founding this Province, as a British community.

Dr. Wm. Canniff pointed out to the society that the settlement of Upper Canada began in 1784, by the arrival of the Loyalists, and that 1884 would be the proper date for holding the centennial celebration in Ontario. Mr. Oates coincided with the view, and was looking forward to taking part in it with much anticipation, when death overtook him. This seems to have been the inception of the idea of a U. E. Loyalist demonstration.

On the twenty-ninth of October, 1880, Mr. Canniff Haight, in the Toronto *Daily Mail*, suggested " an Exhibition, or some other demonstration in honour of the men who, through privation and toil, laid the foundation of this free and prosperous Province." This suggestion was noticed by the Picton, Belleville and Kingston papers.

Nothing further was done in the matter until 1882, when the following letter was addressed to the Mayor of Toronto, by Dr. Wm. Canniff—

"ST. JAMES' SQUARE,
"TORONTO, 14th Dec., 1882.
" *To His Worship the Mayor* :

" DEAR SIR,—I am greatly interested in the proposed semi-centennial celebration of the Incorporation of Toronto, and beg to congratulate you on having conceived the idea of such a demonstration. But my object in addressing you is to call your attention to the fact that 1884 will be the centennial of the first settlement of Upper Canada, when the pioneers—U. E. Loyalists, took possession of their lands along the St. Lawrence, from Kingston westward along the shores of the Bay of Quinté, and on the Niagara frontier. It has occurred to my mind that perhaps it might be possible, and deemed advisable to widen the basis of the commemoration and celebrate at the same time the centennial of the settlement of the Province. Of course, to do this it would be necessary to procure the co-operation of the other cities and the towns of the Province. There has been something said in the eastern papers about observing the centennial, and Kingston was mentioned as the place most suitable for the purpose. But as there is some doubt about the matter, perhaps the centennial of the Province, and the semi-centennial of the capital might be appropriately held in Toronto. This proposition may not be deemed feasible, but it seems to be a question not unworthy of consideration, and is, therefore, respectfully submitted to you for consideration.

" I am, respectfully yours,

" WM. CANNIFF."

In accordance with the above suggestion, the Toronto Semi-Centennial Committee set apart one day for the U. E. Loyalist demonstration, and Mr. Wm. B. McMurrich chairman of the Committee, placed the whole matter of the Toronto celebration in the hands of Dr. Canniff. A meeting was called by Dr. Canniff, and a U. E. Loyalist Centennial Committee was appointed, and circulars were sent to all the Wardens of counties and Mayors of cities, asking their co-operation. These circulars, which were also sent to the newspapers of the Province, attracted public attention to the matter, and at Adolphustown and Niagara, where the early settlements actually took place, the descendants of the U. E. Loyalists decided to hold local celebrations. The Adolphustown celebration was fixed for the sixteenth of June, 1884. The first landing of the Loyalists at that point having taken place on the sixteenth of June 1784. The Toronto celebration was fixed for the third of July, and the Niagara one for the fourteenth of August.

The Appendix contains a copy of the Order-in-Council of the 9th November, 1789, ordering a record to be preserved of the U. E. Loyalist settlers, and also a copy of the U. E. List preserved in the Crown Lands Department, at Toronto, with all the notes and remarks in it complete. This list, which has never been published before, contains the names of the many thousands of U. E. Loyalist settlers who founded the Province of Upper Canada.

The following pages contain accounts of the three celebrations in the order in which they came off.

CONTENTS.

ADOLPHUSTOWN CELEBRATION.

	PAGE		PAGE
FIRST DAY—		Address by G.E Henderson Esq.,Q.C	41
Address by Lewis L. Bogart, Esq.	11	" S S. McCuaig, Esq., and	
" A. L. Morden, Esq.	12	Parker Allen, Esq.	42
" Dr. Wm. Canniff	14	" Rev. C. E. Thompson	42
" Sir Richard Cartwright	24	" Lieut. Gov. J. B. Robinson	43
" Rev. D. V. Lucas	29	" D. W. Allison, Esq., M.P.	45
SECOND DAY—		THIRD DAY—	
Address to the Lieutenant Governor	35	Address by Wm. Anderson	47
Address by Chief Sampson Green	38	" Robert Clapp	48
" Capt. Grace	40		

TORONTO CELEBRATION.

	PAGE		PAGE
Toronto Celebration	49	Address by Lt. Col. George T. Denison.	67
Address by Dr. Wm Canniff, Chairman.	53	Poem Loyalist Days," by Mrs. Kittson	74
" Hon. George W. Allan	54	Address by the Bishop of Niagara	75
Poem by Rev. Le Roy Hooker	62	Reception at Government House	76
Address by Chief Green	65		

NIAGARA CELEBRATION.

	PAGE		PAGE
Niagara Celebration	79	Address by Wm. Kirby, Esq	104
Address by R. N. Ball, Esq., Chairman.	82	" Chief Hill	116
Prayer by the Rt Rev. Thomas Brock Fuller, Bishop of Niagara	84	" Chief A. G. Smith	117
Address by the Lieutenant Governor	84	" James Hiscott Esq	119
" The Lord Bishop of Niagara	85	" W. H Merritt, Esq	120
" Hon. J. B. Plumb	87	Poem "U. E. Loyalists," by William Kirby, Esq	122
" Lt Col. George T. Denison	95		

APPENDIX.

	PAGE		PAGE
Appendix A., copy of Order-in-Council 9th November, 1789	127	Appendix B., copy of old U. E. List preserved in the Crown Lands Department at Toronto	129

ADOLPHUSTOWN CELEBRATION COMMITTEE.

L. L. BOGART,
President.

J. J. WATSON,
Cor. Secretary.

J. B. ALLISON,
Secretary.

L. L. Bogart,
Parker Allen,
A. L. Morden,
D. W. Allison,
J. J. Watson,
J. B. Allison,
A. C. Davis,
P. D. Davis,
L. W. Trumpour,
Thos. Trumpour,
Paul Trumpour,
H. H. Allison,
S. W. Ruttan,
E. Ruttan,
J. W. Dorland,
Redford Dorland,
Geo. German,
J. H. Trumpour,
E. Clapp,
Geo. Ham,

Dr. Ruttan,
Dr. Canniff,
W. R. H. Allison,
S. S. McCuaig,
Sampson Green,
Robert Clapp,
S. M. Conger,
John Prinyer,
Hy. Huff,
J. B. Diamond,
S. Wright,
W. H. Ingersoll,
N. W. Mallory,
C. A. Roblin,
Jno. H. Roblin,
Jacob Roblin,
Wm. Peterson,
D. Griffifth,
Geo. Harrison,
H. Rikely.

UNITED EMPIRE LOYALISTS.

CENTENNIAL CELEBRATION

AT

ADOLPHUSTOWN,

June, 16th, 17th and 18th, 1884.

IN connection with the celebration, and as preliminary thereto, the corner stone of the Methodist U. E. L. Memorial church was laid on Saturday 14th June with peculiarly interesting ceremonies. There were present, Rev. D. V. Lucas, B. A., of Montreal; Rev. J. J. Leach, of Odessa; Rev. M. L. Pearson, of Napanee; Rev. Adams, of Bath; Rev. Briden, of Newburgh; Rev. M. I. Bates, of Tamworth; and Rev. Mr. Gibson. All these participated in the proceedings. The ceremony of laying the corner stone was performed by Mrs. Joseph Allison, one of the few remaining ones of the first generation succeeding the U. E. Loyalists. This lady having been for nearly three-fourths of a century a faithful and consistent member of the Methodist church, and being the daughter of one of the Loyalist Pioneers, it was peculiarly fitting that she should perform this office. The stone having been laid, refreshments were served, when an adjournment was had to the gospel tent, which had been erected across the road, where

Rev. Mr. Lucas delivered an admirable address appropriate to the occasion. He predicted a brilliant future for Canada so long as she continues her loyalty to Methodism and Great Britain. A few brief words from Revs. Leach and Gibson, and the proceedings were brought to a close by singing "God save the Queen." On Sabbath, Rev. Mr. Lucas preached three sermons in the tent to large audiences, his addresses being marked by power, force and a practical application to present circumstances and requirements. Seldom has it been the privilege of the people of this section to listen to three such effective discourses in one day. The financial outlook for this undertaking is most encouraging, as indeed it should be, located as it is in the heart of a large Methodist community and in the richest section of this fair country.

On Sunday, 15th June, a sermon was preached at St. Paul's church, Adolphustown, and St. Paul's church, Fredericksburg, by the Rev. C. E. Thompson, M. A. Incumbent of Carlton, Diocese of Toronto, from Ezekiel, xxxvi, 28, "And ye shall dwell in the land that I gave to your fathers; and ye shall be my people, and I will be your God."

The preacher is a grandson of the late Sheriff Ruttan, one of the United Empire Loyalists. The sermon was replete with historical facts in relation to the Loyalists. A highly eloquent discourse terminated with a reference to the wild idea of independence. He gave six months as the time the independence craze would continue.

The usual Sunday quietude of the front was much changed by the presence of the 15th battalion, which arrived from Belleville in the morning at daybreak. The battalion, under the command of Col. Lazier, was camped near by the place of celebration on the shores of the bay, and the red coats gave an additional amount of beauty to the scene.

The regiment had Divine service on the United Empire Loyalists burying ground in the afternoon. Rev. Mr.

Forneri preached an eloquent sermon. He held up the Christian loyalty of the sires of Canada as a pattern to modern Canadians.

On Monday, the 16th of June, the celebration commenced. From early dawn carriages began to arrive; all Adolphustown and adjacent places were well represented. The day was most auspicious. By noon a number of boats from Belleville on the west and Kingston on the east arrived with decks crowded from all the intervening oints. The Picton troop of cavalry under Major Fred White was among the arrivals. Three bands discoursed sweet music at frequent intervals, the fine band of the 15th battalion, the band from Picton, and the band of Kingston. The military display was very fine.

The proceedings were opened by the playing of the National Anthem and a public invocation of Divine blessing on the day's festivities and those taking part in them. In the afternoon the people were summoned about the speakers' stand, and addresses were delivered. Above the speakers' heads floated the handsome flag of the Native Canadian Society, of Belleville. The programme was opened by the playing of the National Anthem, and the invocation of the Divine blessing and returning thanks for the prosperity which has attended the U. E. Loyalists and their descendants, and the nation which they founded.

The President, LEWIS L. BOGART, who is over eighty years of age, and who was selected for the position because he is the oldest living male representative of the U. E. Loyalist band, came forward and delivered the following brief but pointed address:

LADIES AND GENTLEMEN—I can assure you that it affords me very great pleasure to see so many present to do honour to our fathers and forefathers who landed at this place a century ago to-day. If we go back in our imagination to that time when the little company who had left their all for the love of king and country, and came here to hew out for themselves new homes in this vast primeval forest, and then as we look around us to-day, contrasting the past with the present, and behold a beautiful land, beautiful homes, a country free from famine and pestilence, where the pure bright sunlight of God's love shines down upon a prosperous, contented and happy people, who enjoy the blessings of peace on every hand and good will toward man, we would be very ungrateful indeed did we not appreciate the sacrifices and labours of our pioneer ancestors in procuring for us so goodly a heritage. I can only say that my father and grandfather were among that company; and I rejoice that I have been spared to see this grand centennial celebration in their homes. Although I feel incompetent for the duty assigned me, I desire to thank you for the honour you have conferred upon me in choosing me to preside on this occasion.

A. L. MORDEN, Esq., vice-president, was then introduced, and delivered an admirable address, of which the following is a brief synopsis:

The present is an occasion of no ordinary interest. The people of Adolphustown and those associated with them in the enterprise have put on foot this celebration in order, to use the words of that grand old man, Dr. Ryerson, "to do at least a modicum of justice to the memory of a Canadian ancestry, whose heroic deeds and unswerving Christian patriotism form a patent of nobility, more to be valued by their descendants than the coronets of many a modern nobleman." To-day the people of Adolphustown witness the beginning of that for which many of them for some time past have ardently toiled and hoped. To-day, Adolphustown extends a cordial welcome to the descendants of every U. E. Loyalist, and every loyal citizen of Canada, on these beautiful grounds. If Adolphustown be a small township, it is small only in its acreage, but it has standing ground enough for every Loyalist descendant in the Province of Ontario, and the people have hearts large enough to give them a hospitable welcome to this historic ground. When the Roman dominion was at its best, when the city sitting upon her seven hills from her throne of beauty ruled the world, when the Romans from their lofty civilization and culure dictated laws for all succeeding ages, *Civis Romanus sum*, was the proud boast in which the citizens claimed participation in all the greatness, the glory and the protection of Roman citizenship. It is ours to-day to be able in saying, ' I am a British subject." to utter a prouder boast than the Romans. It is largely due to the effort of those pioneers who, one hundred years ago to-day landed upon this spot, that this fair and fertile Province, and we who live in it, are British territory and British subjects. We do well to-day to take thought, for a little time, and congratulate ourselves upon our heritage, one which the lamented General Brock called upon our fathers in 1812, " Not to give their children cause to reproach them for having too easily parted with the richest inheritance on this earth—a participation in the name, character and freedom of Britons." It is said we are a young country and have no history, but I have not read of any country which, during the last one hundred years, has a more glorious history. If our forefathers for their fervent loyalty to Britain, lost every thing but their honour, and bravely bore the hardships and privations of first settlers, what feelings should animate our breasts to-day, when with our attachment to British laws, institutions, traditions, rights and liberties, there is added the intensity of our attachment to the sovereign. Never had British subjects such reason for inviolable attachment to the ruler as have we to-day for Her Most Gracious Majesty, Queen Victoria. Thirty years ago the poet Laureate prophesied that our children's children would say of Her :

" She wrought her people lasting good,
Her court was pure, her life serene,
God gave her peace, her land reposed,
A thousand claims to reverence closed
In her as mother, wife and queen."

To-day this forecast is abundantly verified. But, ladies and gentlemen, it is not proper for me to further occupy your time. I am only here to extend to you a cordial welcome to our celebration, to break the ice, as it were ; the orator of the day is our cherished friend, the historian of the Bay Quinté Loyalists, Dr. Canniff. Thanking you for the kind hearing you have given me, I will conclude with some words of Dr. Ryerson, uttered at a meeting of Loyalists at Brock's monument :—" May Loyalty ever be the characteristic trait of Canadians, may freedom ever be our possession, and may we ever have cause and heart to say God Save the Queen."

DR. CANNIFF then delivered the following address.

LADIES AND GENTLEMEN,—Two hundred years ago or more, at a seaport town in Holland, was to be seen on a certain day, a sea-going vessel, around which was the usual activity and bustle incident to the final preparation for a voyage. As the work of taking in supplies and putting the ship in sailing order was going on, a somewhat motley crowd of on-lookers regarded the scene with a lazy, listless air of indifference. Suddenly the attention of all was quickened by a remarkable occurrence. The doleful tolling of a church bell, heard now and again above the din of numerous voices, had passed unheeded by those collected on the shore. Now, however, as there appears a procession slowly wending its way toward the place, the solemn peals suggest the thought of death. Leading the procession walks a venerable looking man, whose garb and mien betoken a dominie or minister of the Gospel. After him came a young couple in the first years of vigorous manhood, and the fresh bloom of womanhood, walking hand-in-hand. They are clothed in holiday attire, and have the appearance of a newly wedded husband and wife. Following them are a man and woman, whose grey heads and bent forms speak of advanced years. Next is another couple, also in the decline of life. Then walk two and two men, and women, boys and girls of all ages. They all wear the habiliments of woe, and the procession moves with a slow and solemn tread, as if following a loved one to his grave. All that is wanting to complete a funeral train is the hearse with its nodding plumes, or coffin containing the body of one dead. The spectators, hushed to silence, gaze on the line of mourners, and wonder and watch to see its course and destination. With measured steps the dominie is followed to the vessel, and over its side. Then they gather in a group upon the deck around the young man and wife. A silence falls upon the assembled mourners as the man of God opens the Bible and reads from the inspired Book such words as give comfort and support to those who are bereaved. Now his voice is raised in prayer to God, and his prayer reveals to all who hear, the cause and reason of this strange scene. First, he prays that the aged parents may have Divine help in this their hour of trial in losing their dear children, and that they might still be happy in their earthly pilgrimage, be received hereafter into God's kingdom, and finally re-united to their children. He then commits to Him, who controls the winds and the waves, the young couple. He implores that they may be in His gracious care and keeping—these dear ones, who to-day set out at once on the journey of married life, and to cross the wide ocean, parting forever in this life from their parents and friends, and who are, as it were, to be buried in the far away New World. Words of counsel follow to the young pair, sympathy to the parents of each is duly given. Finally, amid emotions which cannot be depicted, the mourners at last tear themselves from the voyageurs, who cling to each other in this hour of sore trial. The stricken parents have looked upon their children for the last time; they, in turn, shall see their parents' faces no more in this world.

This is a picture from real life presented at the period of time I have mentioned. Having determined to seek new homes in America, this young man and woman knew, in making this choice, they would leave parents and homes, with no possibility of seeing them again. Crossing the Atlantic then was a far different matter from what it is to-day, with rapid steam navigation. The name these young emigrants bore is one well known in Adolphustown. It was found among those who accompanied Major VanAlstine when he landed on this spot one hundred years ago to-day. And, pardon me for adding, I can claim to be, on my mother's side, one of the descendants of that pair, and there are not a few present who can make the same claim, and whom I am proud to know as kinsmen. The story was often told me by my venerated mother many years ago. I have presented it to you to-day, not merely for personal gratification, but to show the stern courage which characterized the first settlers in America. Many nations of Europe contributed equally bold and intrepid men and women to people the Atlantic coast of this continent. England, Ireland, Scotland, Wales, Germany, and Holland gave their most vigorous sons, and the Huguenots of France formed a rich quota to lay the foundation of the United States and Canada.

It was mainly the descendants of these hardy pioneers of the seventeenth century, who a century later became exiles from their fathers' homes, and who penetrated to the wilderness of Upper Canada to plant the noble Province of Ontario. Why was it they left the comfortable homes their fathers had made, and the place which by their labour, energy, and enterprise had from a wilderness blossomed into a goodly fruitful land? This is not the time to fully discuss the events attending the great American rebellion of 1776. This is not the place to weigh the controlling motives which caused a portion of the British Americans at that time to take up arms against the Mother Country, nor the abiding principles which impelled another portion of the same people to stand true

CENTENNIAL CELEBRATION. 17

to the flag under which they had been born, under which they had prospered, and under which they had fought and conquered French Canada. They were willing to sacrifice and did sacrifice everything to uphold British power in America. But, while I may not to-day, place in the balance the motives which influenced the two parties —the Whigs and the Tories—of that day, I do maintain whatever reason the Whigs may have had for the course they took, the Tories, the Loyalists were actuated by a noble sense of duty, of patriotism, of Christian fidelity to the Crown. They could not discover a sufficient reason for raising the standard of revolt and engaging in civil strife.

Neither is this the time to consider the reasons why the rebellion commenced in 1776 became a revolution, why rebels became heroes, and the British empire became dismembered. At the commencement of the hostilities the rebels were in a minority throughout the thirteen colonies. In New England they predominated, but many of the other colonies, especially New York, from which so many of the Bay of Quinté settlers came, were largely against the rebellion. I know exception may be taken to this statement on the ground that the war terminated in a revolution. But it must be remembered that the war continued for seven years, during which time the loyalists were continually leaving the country. Then there was a large number who were indifferent as to the result, and stood ready to embrace the cause which succeeded. There were even a considerable number of Whigs who, at first were averse to independence, and who were forced into accepting it. England was already engaged with European complications. Then the mistakes and ignorance of the country on the part of the British officers in command in America, led to disaster and discouragement among the Loyalists. Finally, and which turned the scale, France gave substantial assistance, and at last the surrender of Cornwallis practically terminated the struggle. The end had come. England recognized the independence of the Colonies, and the loyal Americans found themselves without homes, and aliens to the land of their birth. They were not only homeless and aliens, but they were subjects of persecution. Many would have accepted the changed condition and have become reconciled, but they were deprived of their property and their lands were confiscated. How the Loyalists departed—some driven away, and some because they would not live under any but the British Flag, and how they found their way into the wildernesses of Nova Scotia, New Brunswick and Canada, is a sad and touching story, a story which has never been fully told. Says an American writer, speaking of his countrymen: "Our writers of history have been almost silent upon this topic, and it is not impossible that some persons have read books devoted exclusively to an account of the revolution without so much as imagining that a considerable part of the force employed to suppress the rebellion was composed of our countrymen." But why has not the story been told by the U. E. Loyalists themselves? The words of the same writer gives the answer. He says: "Of the reasons which influenced, of the hopes and fears which agitated, and of the miseries and rewards which awaited the Loyalists of the American revolution but little is known. The most intelligent, the best informed among us confess the deficiency of their knowledge. The reason is obvious. They, who like the Loyalists separate themselves from their friends and kindred, who are driven from their homes, who surrender the hopes and expectations of life, and who become outlaws, wanderers and exiles—such men leave few memorials behind them. Their papers are scattered and lost and their very names pass from human recollection." To this may be added the statement that the pioneers of any country, struggling to create a home and procure the necessaries of life, have no time to devote to writing history or recording events. The consequences have been that while the Americans for a century have been engaged in writing up the Revolution from their point of view, the history of the American Loyalists has received but little attention, and many of the facts relating to their history have been irretrievably lost.

No wonder then that the U. E. Loyalists are not only mostly forgotten, but have had their conduct, their motives, and their character misrepresented by partisans. The efforts made by that noble and patriotic Canadian, that grand descendant of the U. E. Loyalists—I refer to the late Rev. Dr. Ryerson—to place before the world a more accurate estimate of the Loyalists, and the attempts by others, in later years, to rescue from oblivion facts honourable and praiseworthy relating to them, have been received, even by the Canadian public, with almost incredulity, when not with cold indifference. During the hundred years that the Loyalists have been engaged in converting the wilderness into comfortable homes, the press of the United States has occupied itself, the thousands of Americans abroad have been assiduously at work educating the world to the effect that the American Tories of 1776 were the offscourings of the land, the vilest of the vile, worthy only of being execrated by mankind. Not only the daily and weekly press has been thus engaged, but the school books used by the young in the United States, and sometimes in Canada, have contained the most outrageously partial accounts of the struggle and the participants on either side. Never was history so perverted, never did misrepresentations so effectually deceive. Not only have the children of the United States been imbued with hatred towards the Loyalists, but the modern Englishman, Scotchman, not to say Irishman, has accepted the teachings of partisan American writers. Even Canadians may be found who have nothing but praise for the rebels of 1776, and nothing but obloquy for those who did not think rebellion was a justifiable act. British statesmen and the press of Great Britain have seemingly vied to see which could offer to the screaming goddess the most profound adulation. It would be amusing were it not humiliating to see Canadians so-called, shall I say bastard Canadians, especially those by adoption, endeavouring in a feeble way to cast discredit upon the U. E. Loyalists. With the most superficial knowledge of the subject, they undertake to instruct native Canadians respecting their fathers. They mostly set out on the supposition that the Loyalists had no love of liberty, that they were willing to be almost, or quite, serfs or slaves, and to pay taxes to the Imperial treasury without Parliamentary representation. But nothing could be more at variance with the truth. In the first place, a vast number of those who ultimately sided with the rebels were indifferent about the question of liberty. A great many joined the insurrectionists simply to advance their personal interests, and could their interests have been equally served they would have been found on the side of the Loyalists. With not a few it was only a struggle for office and power. On the other hand there were a very large number of Loyalists who recognized all the evils which really did exist in the relationship between England and America. They were not blind to the injustice which, in many ways, was evinced by the Crown toward the colonies. But they did not and could not see a sufficient grievance to justify rebellion; at least they desired to seek redress by peaceful means. And those acquainted with the conflict of opinion among British statesmen at that time as to the rights of America know that, had peaceful means been pursued, all the complaints would, in time, have been removed. Then it must not be forgotten that Britain had given money and blood to conquer French Canada in the interests of the colonies.

It is submitted, as adequate proof of the statement, that the U. E. Loyalists were not without a love of liberty, that the subsequent history of the British provinces, settled by them, presents a steady and healthy development in liberal government; and to-day Canada has more

CENTENNIAL CELEBRATION. 21

liberty and the government of the people is really more democratic than the United States. The sapient writers I have referred to, are wont to assert that the contest for responsible government in Canada was between the Loyalists, joined together in a family compact, and somebody else; but whom has never been made quite clear. But as a matter of fact it was the general mass of the U. E. Loyalists who obtained the benefits of responsible government. The "Family Compact" represented only a fragment of the U. E. Loyalist element, and was by no means composed exclusively of that class. The love of liberty was manifested by the Loyalist settlers of Upper Canada in many ways. In the Declaration of Independence of the colonies it is stated that "all men are born free and equal." How far this principle was carried out by the United States, history tells us in words no one can misunderstand. As a matter of fact it was not until 1865, and after a bloody war in which hundreds of thousands of lives were sacrificed, that slavery was abolished, and the words I have quoted really stated the condition of the people of the United States. The proclamation of President Lincoln, made necessary by the exigencies of the war, was made 70 years after the U. E. Parliament of Upper Canada had passed an "Act to prevent the further introduction of slaves, and to limit the time of contract for servitude within this province." And during this period Canada was the asylum of the down-trodden of the United States. Again, in the treatment of the native Indians, how differently they have fared in Canada than they have in the United States! While cruelty and injustice have attended the footsteps of the frontier men in the latter, in the former, the aboriginal owner of the soil has been, like the African, treated as a man and a brother. His rights have been respected; and treaty obligations with them, faithfully observed; with the result, that, while bloody Indian wars have marked the history of our neighbours, we have had peace in our borders. There is, therefore, abundant reason for maintaining that the U. E. Loyalists were not wanting in the essential principles of liberty; liberty broad and deep, which embraces all mankind, irrespective of race, or colour.

But ladies and gentlemen, in drawing a comparison between our U. E. Loyalists' fathers and the fathers of the republic, I have no desire to belittle people of that generation. Any such attempt on my part would be puny indeed. While 1 honestly endeavour to eulogize the U. E. Loyalists, I do not desire to ignore all that is good and noble in our kinsmen over the border. The bitterness of last century is all buried. As Canadians to-day, we entertain toward them no feeling but that of good will, and we wish them God-speed. We even hope that their destiny may be as great as we believe ours is sure to be. As an elder offspring of Old England we cannot avoid being influenced by her examples. But while that nation and the Canadian nation are advancing on parallel lines in growth and development, the lines cannot come together.

I am tempted to draw a comparison between the descendants of the rebels and Loyalists of 1776 as we find them to-day, but time will not permit. However, I hesitate not to say that the sons of Canada—children of the Loyalists, have physical and mental qualities which will bear any comparison.

Ladies and gentlemen, we are assembled to-day to celebrate the settlement of this province—the Province of Ontario. But we do so with no narrow feeling of sectionalism. We are here as Canadians above all. No pent-up Utica contracts our power and feelings of patriotism for the whole Dominion. The whole breadth of the continent—from Newfoundland to Vancouver's Island—is ours to hold and to cultivate. We take in our maritime brethren, who also are descendants of the Loyalists. We do not exclude the French of Lower Canada, notwithstanding their disposition to keep isolated, for we remember how they stood firmly by the side of our fathers in the fight for Old England in 1776 and 1812. We embrace the vigorous sons of Manitoba and the North-West, many of whom have the U. E. Loyalist blood in their veins; and we extend a brother's hand to the loyal Canadians of the Pacific coast. Looking east, west, and north over our rich heritage, we say Canada one and indivisible for ever—Canada for the Canadians, and Canadians only.

As Dr. Canniff concluded his address, the 15th Battalion headed by their band, came down from the camp and made their way towards the spot where one of the genial events of the day was to take place, the laying with Masonic honours of the corner-stone of the new monument to the U.E. Loyalists. Thither the people filed. The Masons also formed in line and proceeded to the spot in a body. The stone, which was lying on the ground, just at the edge of the plot used for the burial ground, was soon surrounded twenty deep by people anxious to witness the ceremony. All being ready, R. W. Bro. Arthur McGuinness, D. D. G. M., acting as G. M., made a brief address, in the course of which he eulogized the Loyalists, and said that the only reason why such men had not already had some such tribute as was now proposed to be erected to their memory, must be found in the fact that such acknowledgments of the people's love and gratitude must come when there was time for the cultivation of the arts and wealth to accumulate. He and his brethren deemed it an honour to lay this corner-stone, as a monument to the memory of men who had sacrificed so much for their allegiance to the British flag. The mystic rites having been duly solemnized, a prayer was offered by Worshipful Bro. Rev. R. J. Craig, as Grand Chaplain, and the stone was duly declared laid. The conclusion of the ceremony was announced by the National Anthem by the band, followed by a grand salute by the 15th Battalion, "B" Band, Kingston, and the Picton Silver Cornet Band, which had arrived on the grounds early in the afternoon, played some lively selections near the speaker's stand.

The addresses from the grand stand were then resumed.

Mr. D. W. ALLISON, M. P. for Lennox, was called to the chair. He announced as first speaker,

SIR RICHARD CARTWRIGHT, who came forward amid applause. After greeting the audience, among whom he recognized many old friends, he proceeded : I do not believe you could be assembled for a more laudable or patriotic purpose than that which has brought you together to-day. We are here for the purpose of doing what honour we can to the memory of men to whom we owe it that not merely Ontario, but onehalf the continent of North America, remains to-day under British rule. It is desirable, too, that we should endeavour to understand the magnitude of the sacrifice made by the noble band who a hundred years ago drew up their batteaux on the shores of Adolphustown. These men were not inconsiderate youths ; they were men, most of them of mature years, and some advanced in life, who won for themselves comfortable independence in a country south of us. At what they conceived to be the call of duty, they were ready to sacrifice everything that men commonly hold dear; resign the wealth they had accumulated, forfeit their prospects—their own and their children's—for sake of their loyalty to the flag under which they had served, and under which many of them had fought and bled. That was not an ordinary act, and men who performed it were cast in no ordinary mould. Nowadays it is far too common to judge a man's acts by the standard of mere material success. These men had something nobler and loftier before them. Had it been worldly prosperity they looked for they would have cast their lot in with the Republic to the south of us ; had they blenched from the trials before them; had they been frightened away from their task of carving a home in the wilderness—a very few years would have passed before the Amercan flag would have waved over the whole of this continent. Here the men who did these things possessed the courage of their convictions. Where they thought they were right, they were not afraid of being in the minority. They were prepared to fight. and if need be to suffer and die for their convictions. It is of such men the salt of the earth is made, and we in Canada have good right to be proud that we can look back to such ancestors. You may deem these men foolish in their enthusiasm, but if you are worthy to be their descendants, you will agree with me in saying that they dared greatly, and succeeded greatly, and they have left behind lessons which we will do well to follow. We ought, on an occasion like this, to understand what induced our grandfathers to make the sacrifice they did. You must look back a little to see America during the course of the eighteenth century. Beginning in 1700 and ending in 1775, a great struggle was going on, waged in different parts of America between tbe two greatest nations of Europe. In that struggle these men had many of them borne a part. The struggle was to decide whether England or France was to rule this great continent. Those who look back and consider how far the French pioneers had advanced, what their exertions were, how much blood and treasure England and France had spilled in the struggle, will understand in some degree why it was our forefathers desired not to show themselves ungrateful for the great sacrifice which the parent country had made. The other day I came across a strange letter from the distinguished French General Montcalm, who fell in the great battle which finally decided the fate of North America. I find that Montcalm, who was not only a great general but a very able statesman, put on record a prediction of his own fall, declaring he would be defeated, and that he would not survive the loss of North

B

America. He predicted also that ten years after Canada was conquered, the other colonies would assert their independence. As you know, who have paid attention to history, that was fulfilled almost to the hour and day. Canada was ceded to Great Britain in 1763, and within twelve years thereafter the first blood was drawn in the struggle which resulted in the independence of the United States of America. The letter first predicts that if General Wolfe understands his trade that Montcalm must be defeated; and declares that as this defeat means the total loss of North America, he will not survive.

"I console myself, nevertheless, for the prospect of my own defeat, and of the loss of the colony, by my firm conviction that this defeat will prove in the long run better than a victory for France, and that the conqueror, England, will find a tomb in her own conquest. This may appear a paradox, but a little reflection and a glance at the political situation in North America will prove the correctness of my opinion. A large portion of the English colonists are the children of men who left England during the period of the civil war, and betook themselves to America to find a country where they might live and die in freedom and independence. I know them thoroughly, not by hear-say, but by means of sure information and correspondence which I have arranged myself, and which if my life had been prolonged, I had meant to turn to the advantage of France. In fact all the English colonists would have shaken off the yoke long ago, and every one of them would have become a little independent republic had it not been for the fear of France at their doors. As between two masters they preferred their own fellow countrymen to foreigners, taking care, meanwhile, to render no more obedience than they could help; but if Canada is conquered, and if the Canadians and the English Colonies become one people the very first occasion on which England will appear and interfere with their interests, do you suppose the Colonists will obey her? What have they to fear if they do revolt? I am so perfectly certain of the truth of what I have written that I will only allow ten years after the conquest of Canada to see my predictions accomplished. Now you see the reason which consoles me as a Frenchman for the imminent danger France is incurring of seeing Canada lost forever."

Most of the Loyalists whom we honour to-day had fought for the supremacy of Great Britain and of the British race in North America, and they thought after such great sacrifices that had been made they were bound to see that the English race was not robbed of the price of the sovereignty of this continent. Remember when in 1775, the Colonies decided to break off their allegiance this struggle was of very recent date; that many of the men served under British generals in the armies which conquered Canada and took Quebec. There were men of different classes among the Loyalists. Some were impelled simply by honest and laudable instinct of loyalty to the flag to which they had owed allegiance, and they were prepared to make sacrifices for that loyalty. I would have you all to make sacrifices where necessary for your convictions; but besides these there were others among that band. These men, as their name United Empire Loyalists showed, thoroughly appreciated the enormous future which awaited the English race in North America. It would be a mistake to suppose that they wholly approved of the course of the British Government. As their correspondence shows, they objected, as Burke and Chatham objected, but they felt it would be a thousand pities and a disgrace to the race, that after all that had passed, the English race should allow itself to be split into fragments, and we have numerous proofs of how powerfully these men's acts and feelings affected the whole destiny of this country. Gentlemen, the Loyalists builded better than they knew. They came a handful of men, perhaps four or five thousand souls, to the Province of Ontario, and yet they have given to a very great extent impulse and direction to the feelings and destiny of four or five millions who now inhabit the Dominion. But for the effect of the example and traditions they left behind them, I believe you would not see yonder flag float from this ground to-day. If there be here, as possibly there may be, a few of those veterans who recollect the war of 1812 and 1815, they will tell you how powerfully the example of the Loyalists strengthened their hands for the desperate struggle to preserve Canada to the British Crown.

Look to history and you will not find a case in the whole range in which a handful of men maintained themselves successfully against desperate odds, which reflects more lustre on the people who did it, than the struggle of our fathers in that war. America placed along the frontier 20,000 men, a greater number than the whole male population of the Province capable of bearing arms at that time. All the aid the British Government could send during the first year was four companies of regulars. She sent us also Brock, who alone was worth an army. Brock with eighteen hundred men reduced three thousand Americans to capitulation. In the face of the great European wars, the deeds of heroism on the frontier of Canada were lost sight of, but it is not for any patriotic Canadian to forget them. I have said elsewhere and I now repeat that the colony of Ontario has a proud pre-eminence among the colonies of Britain for this reason. All the other colonies have been founded by men who sought to better their condition, or were founded by the Government of Britain, or obtained by conquest, but Ontario stands alone as the colony founded by men making great sacrifices to maintain their allegiance to Great Britain. I know of but one community in America, or elsewhere perhaps—that founded by the Puritan fathers in New England. I am not going to make a political harangue, but I have ventured in another place to point out how I thought we, descendants of the U. E. Loyalists, might best act in the spirit of our forefathers. Bear in mind that what these men sought to prevent was a division which France sought to foster between the great portions of the English race. I believe the Loyalists, and the people of Canada who derive their inspiration from them, can best do justice to the spirit of their forefathers by doing what they can to bring together in a union all the English-speaking races in the world. I state as a man loyal to Britain and to British institutions. I believe I know whereof I speak when I say no such service can be rendered to the people of Great Britain and of the whole world than to remove all chance of hostility between the two great branches of the English race. As a descendant of a loyalist, I say it would be a work to which any man might be proud to consecrate his life. It is the part of wisdom for us to do what we can to fulfil the object for which our forefathers sacrificed so much ; to bring together as a united people, if not under one Sovereign, at any rate in one alliance offensive and defensive, two great nations, which, to the misfortune of the world, have been severed and alienated. You may call this a dream—Cavour was called a dreamer when he hoped for a united Italy ; Bismarck was condemned as a visionary when he saw in the future a German Confederation. The English speaking people are not inferior to the Italians and Germans, when the real welfare of their race is at stake. In closing, he urged upon the Canadians to imitate the heroism of their ancestors, because the nation could never become great, unless some citizens were willing to sacrifice themselves for the general good, and Canada at the time needed such men.

The REV. D. V. LUCAS, Montreal, then addressed the meeting as follows :

MR. CHAIRMAN, LADIES AND GENTLEMEN.—I esteem it a very great privilege indeed to be permitted to join with the distinguished statesman who has just addressed you, and with you all in doing honour to those worthy people who, one hundred years ago, landed upon the spot where we are now assembled, to lay in this Province the foundations of civilization. We are carried back in our thoughts to those days. Few of us know anything of the hardships through which these "pilgrim fathers" of Canada had to pass. Pushing one's way into a new country to-day, by means of our railways and other modern facilities is not what it was a century ago.

However much we may admire their courage and fortitude in braving the rigours of Canadian winters, and the difficulties of making homes for themselves and their posterity in the Canadian forests, we have met to-day more particularly to admire the spirit which brought them hither, and if possible to catch something of their devotion to principles which through the medium of the British Constitution, Heaven itself, in their estimation, had bestowed upon them.

We go back in thought a little farther, to those days when the older Colonies of Britain on this continent, decided to dishonour the flag, under whose ægis they had received all that is excellent in their present political system. I do not stop now to question the motives of those who excited the colonists to rebellion. It is enough for the present to say that, the men whom Canada delights to honour, regarded the course of the insurgents as a most unrighteous one, and rather than give it their consent and aid, chose to begin anew in this northern part of our great continent, where even amid cold and poverty and hardships of various kinds they might still live under the free flag of Britain, and enjoy the blessings of which that flag is the emblem.

When we consider the present progress of our native land to which our honoured fathers directed their steps, and the excellence of our political institutions, and the grand future which is evidently before our beloved Dominion, we feel that these noble men of a hundred years ago, built " better than they knew." They honoured the flag of England and the principles which that flag represented, and we have met to honour them. I trust, Sir, that while we are less worthy than they, those who come after us will at least respect us for assembling on this, the first centennial anniversary, to do honour to those noble and devoted fathers of our Canadian Dominion.

It might not be unprofitable, Mr. Chairman, to go still farther back and remind ourselves of the growth of liberty in England, and of the British Constitution. Somehow, more than among other nations of Europe, there seems to have been in the English Isle, from the earliest ages, an intense desire for liberty. The great Alfred had said that it was his desire that the people of England should be as free as the air they breathed. Through centuries, most of those wars, aside from those associated with the conquests, were simply a long struggle between the despotism of kings on the one hand, and the inherent love of liberty on the other.

The constitution of England as we now know it, was of slow growth, but each century found it more in accord with the will of the people. The last great element of liberty may be said to have been introduced into the constitution when William III. and his queen signed the memorable Bill of Rights on their accession to the throne, after the abdication of James II. America had by this time been brought more fully to the notice of the people of the old world, and it was hoped that those grand principles, for which the English people had so long struggled, would find scope and development on this continent, such as might not be accorded them where there still lingered considerable sympathy with royal ambition and ecclesiastical conservatism. Though it is hard to find excuse for the arbitrary spirit of George III. and his advisers, and a majority of his parliament, yet as has been clearly shown by Dr. Ryerson, the difficulty between the Home Government and the Colonies might have been adjusted without secession on the part of the latter, and, as the same distinguished writer has shown, would have been in harmony with the general wish of the Americans, if it had not been for a few ambitious leaders urging the people on to, as our fathers thought, an unjustifiable rebellion, and somehow we cannot divest our minds of the thought that our fathers were right.

The long history of the struggle on the part of their ancestors for constitutional freedom was deeply engraven on their minds. They loved that history and were proud of it. Their fathers had fought to make the grand old flag of England the emblem of all that was good politically. If it could have been shown that there was still lacking some element of pure constitutional liberty, they were willing to labour to secure it, but to tread both flag and constitution in the dust, looked to them not only as an insult to Him who had so helped their fathers, but an insult to the cherished memory of their fathers as well.

Be that as it may, we rejoice when we remember their loyalty, not merely because we admire the principle itself, but because of the blessings which their loyalty has brought to us.

Look at our widely-extended country, with its great fertility, its salubrious atmosphere, its broad acreage of arable land, its lofty mountains, magnificent rivers, rich minerals almost incalculable in extent, with its valuable forests and fisheries—a country almost as large as the whole of Europe—and remember that because of the devotion and loyalty and self-sacrifice of those men whom we to-day commemmorate, all the principles of British constitutional liberty are ours by birthright.

The British Constitution, modified in some of its details to meet our colonial requirements, without in any sense changing any of its general principles, becomes to us the highest type of political freedom, and offers us the easiest political yoke borne by any people under Heaven.

Talk of annexation to the United States. That is im-

CENTENNIAL CELEBRATION. 33

possible. The institutions of the two peoples are too diverse to admit of a political amalgamation. Our ideas of sovereignty differ so widely from those of our neighbours that we could never, even for one hour, consent to surrender the power which constitutes us the sovereign people. With our education and experience, politically, we never could give up our rights in this matter to the head of the nation and his chosen advisers.

Talk of independence in the sense of separation from the old land! This is quite as impossible with the Canadian people. For this is our pride and our boast, we are a part of the great British Empire. Like that angel which John saw standing in the sun, I see standing in the earth a mighty giant, made mighty by the King of Heaven. Upon his head are those wonderful and glorious British Isles, his feet resting on the golden sands of Australia; his left arm, India, now being redeemed from the wheels of the Juggernaut and the superstitions of past ages; his right arm, Canada, now being redeemed from the growl of the wild beast and the war whoop of the savage. When I think, sir, of the vast millions who may, and who surely will, yet dwell in our great dominion, all educated under the great influence of British political institutions, and lovers of the flag which to-day waves over us, and of those principles which that flag represents, I think of the future of this vast empire, exercising in the earth its influence for the elevation of mankind, as the mighty power of God making itself felt through the instrumentality of human government.

As Canadians, this is our boast, we are a part, and we hope no insignificant part, of the British Empire, and our prayer is that nothing may ever occur, to the end of time, to sever those ties which bind our favoured and happy country to the motherland. Our loyalty is too strong, and we trust our children's loyalty will be equally so, to admit of any action which implies and involves dismemberment of that mighty empire of which we are justly proud.

THE SECOND DAY.

ADOLPHUSTOWN, June 17.—The second day of the U. E. Loyalist celebration was marked by fine weather and a very large attendance of visitors. All the steamers plying on the Bay of Quinté brought crowds of people. The first event this morning, though not down as a part of the celebration under the auspices of the Committee, was an interesting and important one, no less than the laying of the corner-stone of the Memorial Church by Lieutenant-Governor Robinson. The Rev. R. S. Forneri, B.A., Pastor of the Anglican Church, here, has since he took this charge worked earnestly in promoting this object, and the present celebration gave him the best opportunity of having the work of the actual building inaugurated with becoming ceremonies.

The Lieutenant-Governor arrived from Napanee this morning by private yacht, about eleven o'clock. He was met at the wharf by a guard of honour of the 15th Battalion, Argyle Light Infantry, under command of Adjt.-Captain T. C. Lazier, and conducted to St. Paul's Church, the present Anglican Church of Adolphustown.

Rev. R. S. Forneri, rector of Adolphustown, has every reason to feel gratified by the marked success attending his indefatigable efforts to bring this enterprise to a successful issue. The new church edifice, which has been named St. Alban's, is to be a handsome structure of the modern Gothic style, capable of seating about 250 people. It will have a neat bell tower seventy-two feet high. The main entrance will be at the side of the building, and will have an open porch with doors of iron work. The nave is $32 \bowtie 50$ feet and the chancel $26 \bowtie 24$ feet. The interior is to be decorated with a number of memorial tablets to leading members of the pioneer band who landed on the shores of Quinté 100 years ago. The site is one of the most commanding along the bay front and was liberally donated for the purpose by J. J. Watson, Esq. After a short service at the church by the Archdeacon, the pro-

CENTENNIAL CELEBRATION. 35

cession was re-formed, and singing an appropriate hymn marched to the site of the new edifice. The ceremony throughout was most impressive, the Ven. Archdeacon leading and the people joining heartily in the responses. At the proper time a beautiful silver trowel, suitably engraved, was handed to the Lieutenant-Governor, with which he laid on the cement, saying:

"We lay this stone of foundation to the honour and glory of God, and in memory of the United Empire Loyalists, who one hundred years ago laid the corner-stone of our Province in peace and righteousness and in loyalty to the British Crown and Empire."

Among the clergymen present were the following:— Dean Lyster, of St. George's Cathedral, Kingston ; Rural Dean Kirkpatrick, of Kingston ; Rev. J. W. Burke, of Belleville ; Revs. C. E. Cartwright, of Kingston; Cook, Kingston; R. S. Forneri, Incumbent of Adolphustown ; Rural Dean Baker, Tyendinaga ; Rev. Mr. Cook, Oshawa; Revs. Carey, Roberts, Stanton, D. F. Bogert, and Thompson.

The Lieutenant-Governor was presented with an address which was gorgeously illuminated, and of which the following is a copy :

To His Honour John Beverley Robinson, Lieut.-Governor of the Province of Ontario.

MAY IT PLEASE YOUR HONOUR—

On behalf the Rector and members of the Church of England in the Parish of Adolphustown and Fredericksburg, and sundry other persons interested in commemorating the important historical event of the arrival there of British subjects known as UNITED EMPIRE LOYALISTS, by the erection of a new church near the spot on which landed the "worthy band of refugees" in 1784, this address is respectfully presented.

Most cordially and gratefully we bid your Honour welcome to Adolphustown on this occasion, when after the lapse of one hundred years, we would raise a sacred edifice in memory of many brave men, who not only sacrificed everything in obedience to the divine command, "Honour the King," but who were equally ready to recognize the paramount duty to "Fear God."

The U. E. Loyalists were, we believe, religious as well as loyal men, and wherever they settled in Canada they laid the foundation not alone of patriotism but also of piety. Therefore we, their descendants and devoted admirers, have deemed the erection of a HOUSE OF PRAYER a significant and appropriate memorial embodying these two great principles, which the sons of the ancient Church of England have been ever foremost and steadfast in upholding—principles we would endeavour to inculcate in our children, and transmit to future generations in this country, viz. : that along with the duty we owe to ourselves in maintaining civil and religious freedom, we are no less bound to be faithful in discharging what is due by loyal men to their Sovereign, and by Christian men to their God.

It is an auspicious coincidence that on this day, 17th June, the Church of England commemorates in her calendar England's Proto-Martyr, St. Alban, the first man who on Britsh soil sealed with his life-blood his testimony as a loyal subject of his Heavenly King, our Lord Jesus Christ. May his name, under which the memorial church is to be dedicated to God, ever unite our affections to the dear old mother land, and inspire us all to follow the example of one who held not his life dear for the cause of Christ.

Animated by such sentiments, we have undertaken this pious work, which, we rejoice to know, has received the warm approval of your Honour as Lieutenant-Governor of the Province, and as yourself, an illustrious member of a famous U. E. L. family. We have asked you, Sir, to put to it the first hand in laying the corner stone, and we tender our very grateful acknowledgements for your kind compliance with our request. We beg to assure you that it is to us a matter of the most lively satisfaction and congratulation that the Chief Magistrate of our Province

CENTENNIAL CELEBRATION. 37

of Ontario, representing Her Gracious Majesty, should honour us with his presence and co-operation on this occasion. For in whatever other respects we may have degenerated from the noble U. E. Loyalists of 1784, we may fain hope we may justly claim to be their rivals in firm attachment both to the THRONE under which it is our happiness to live, and to that great EMPIRE of which we fervently pray that the Dominion of Canada may long constitute an integral portion.

As we conclude this address, we cannot forget the fact that the honour of being a descendant of U. E. Loyalists is shared by your own gracious and accomplished lady, a daughter of the distinguished house of Hagerman, and we venture to join her name with that of your Honour as we most sincerely wish you both the enjoyment of many years of happiness and prosperity in your public and private life.

Signed on behalf of the General and Local Building Committee,

RICHARD SYKES FORNERI,
Rector of Adolphustown.
T. BEDFORD-JONES, LL.D.,
Archdeacon,
Chairman of Committee.

ADOLPHUSTOWN, June 17th, 1884.

The Lieut.-Governor replied briefly, expressing his cordial thanks to the clergy and building committee for their invitation to take part in the proceedings of this memorable occasion, and re-echoing all the sentiments contained in the address. Brief speeches were made by a number of the clergy, that of Dean Lyster being particularly appropriate.

The ceremony completed, the Lieut.-Governor and a large party were invited to the residence of J. J. Watson, Esq., where lunch was served.

The Lieut.-Governor paid a visit to the camp of the 15th Battalion, and was right royally entertained at the officers' mess. Chief Sampson Green was the first introduced to deliver an address, on "The Union of the Six Nations." He appeared in full Indian costume and was accompanied by other members of his band in full war paint and feathers. He first expressed the great pleasure it afforded him to take part in this important gathering, in honour of that patiotic and heroic band of refugees, who freely gave up their all as a sacrifice to their loyalty. He reviewed the traditional history of the Indians of America and especially of the Six Nations, of which he is a representative. He claimed that the Indians are the original Americans, and he felt proud of being a descendant of the aboriginal inhabitant of this continent. He also felt a pride in the fact that, in the day of trial, when the majority rebelled against British rule, his people remained firm in their allegiance, and fought, bled and died beside the pale face in defence of the Union Jack, to uphold its sway on this continent. He explained how the Six Nations came into existence by an alliance of six smaller tribes against the oppression of the doughty, powerful and bloodthirsty Iroquois. He explained their system of government, by which all legislation originated with the Mohawks; after being approved it was then sent to another tribe and considered, adopted or amended as the case might be, until at last it reached Onondagas, or firekeepers, but the Mohawks were possessed of the power of veto. The Onondagas were called the firekeepers because they always started the fire at the Great Council, kept it burning, and finally extinguished it when the Council was completed. At the present day, instead of lighting and extinguishing the fire, they make the opening and closing speeches. Finally the Iroquois themselves sued for admittance to the confederation, but their application was rejected. The tribe to which he belonged came from the Mohawk flats, remained at

Lachine a short time and then came on to Tyendinaga, which spot was selected by Captain John. The reserve was named after the great Chief Tyendinaga, who led the Mohawks to Canada. When Christianity was proposed to the Six Nations it was considered, and four accepted, but two rejected the Christian faith, and to this day two of the tribes are Pagans. Although these tribes are Pagans, they may be fairly termed religious. They believe in the existence of a Supreme Being, but instead of worshipping God in solemn exercises, they return thanks to the Great Spirit for pure water, an abundance of berries, the full corn in the ear, and all the blessings of peace and plenty, by dancing and other rejoicings. Their religion does not permit of stealing or lying, but they have no scruples in regard to Sunday work. He stated his conviction that the only way in which these tribes could be Christianized would be first to educate them and then place the Bible in their hands. What they can read they will accept, but what is told them by missionaries is received with diffidence or suspicion. He again referred to the loyalty of the Indians on many occasions when their adherence was severely tested. In 1812 many of the Indians fought with the British troops, and in 1837 the speaker's father went to the front with his band, and returned with one scalp which was erected on a staff opposite the church, and a tree planted in honour of the event which is to be seen to this day. In 1866, with 17 others, the speaker went to the front to assist in driving back the Fenian invaders, and in the future, as in the past, he was assured that his band would be found ever faithful to the old flag, and ever ready to shed their blood in its defence. The Mohawks, when they landed, consisted of fifteen families; they now number over 1,000 souls. They at first owned the whole township of Tyendinaga, but they had sold a portion, and the money, $127,000, is invested with the government to provide schools and religious instructors. They have now four good schools and two churches. He thanked the committee for the invitation to participate in this gathering, which he considered a great honour to himself and his people.

The next speaker was CAPT. GRACE of Lindsay. He said,

MR. PRESIDENT, LADIES AND GENTLEMEN,—It is rather a matter of good fortune for me that the Lieut.-Governor is not here at present, and thus an opportunity is afforded me of expressing to you all my feelings, which I think are those of all gathered here, and in this my endeavour I crave your indulgence. The deeds which were the first causes of this settlement about us were those of men to whom principles and loyalty were nature's inspiration; were men, who to us have shown examples worthy of imitation; were men who by the sacrifice of home comforts and luxuries have left their images of force of will and self denial. This morning's ceremony was a matter of gratification to all, and to us it was a bounden duty to commemorate the memory of those dear ones of old, with fitting tribute as far as the outward world is concerned; but one cannot help thinking of those brave men, who, one hundred years ago, landed here to the right, leaving happy homes, wealth and comforts, to seek out a new home for themselves in nature's forest, apart from monuments of stone and mortar, and appreciating them by those feelings which emanate from the inspiration of our mothers, and we cannot help thinking of those good old men of yore, as Shakespeare did when he suggested by words, which in substance meant the folly of endeavouring to commemorate intrinsic worth in stone and mortar. Our country, a rich branch of the mother tree which springs from the Atlantic and casts her shadows to all quarters of the globe, it should be our bounden duty to sustain in proper relation to that mother tree, defending her interests by all in our power, which defence is but what we owe.

It was with pleasure I listened to the various speeches of yesterday, and however dampened the love of our

CENTENNIAL CELEBRATION. 41

country might have been by the suggestion of one speaker, that dampening must have been removed by the next speaker, who in feeling terms related the story of the good old woman who said " We shall go and leave everything, and go to that country where we can breathe easily beneath that flag which is floating on our left."

And as often as any defence of the country has been required, so often have the good men of the U. E. Loyalist blood and connection been ready and shared their parts, and it is no small pleasure for me to be the great grandson of the man who had the first Militia Battalion along these shores, and that zeal and that ardour, which seem at least intuitive, have not yet died out, as the young man who is now addressing you has the honour of a Captain's Commission in the Militia at present.

It is an extreme satisfaction to me to be able to undergo a trip of even a hundred miles to meet so many friends, all of whom must necessarily feel the common tie which links us all; and before closing, I must to Dr. Canniff, express my feeling of thankfulness and sympathy for his untiring efforts in the U. E. Loyalist cause. I am sure it was not without a very great deal of trouble he wrote his book, in which are pictured many proper examples for the youngest of us to bear well in mind.

And now Mr. President, ladies and gentlemen, being under an obligation to you for your indulgence I beg to retire.

MR. G. E. HENDERSON, Q. C., Belleville, County Crown Attorney, said that while they must not forget men who had come from over the sea and their descendants, surely they had the right to honour the memory of their Loyalist fathers. These men had chosen a magnificent country, and had put its prosperity upon a grand foundation. He had had the opportunity of viewing the greater part of Europe, and he could assure them that nowhere was there a grander country than this. This Bay of Quinté was as beautiful a sheet of water as any of the
C

famed lakes of Switzerland. Canadians had a right to be proud of their land, and by no other means than by loving it and honouring it could they make it a great country. Without patriotism people were a mere collection of individuals, but if joined by a common bond of love of country, they became an irresistible power. Here every man was free; here every man has the opportunity to carry on the great responsibilities that rested upon him in building up this country. They did not want to be joined to the United States. Canadians were anxious to live at peace with them. Glad of their successes and proud of their advance, but Canadians could show a country whose prosperity was greater than that of the States. They had here a magnificent country, with schools and every advantage and luxury. In Europe he found people called farmers who worked day and night for their lords, who lived in walled cities. They lacked in education and almost every form of enlightenment, and he himself had seen women harnessed along with cows drawing a load on the public highway near Rome. He advised them to remain loyal to this grand country, and to the Empire under whose fostering care it had grown to its present state.

MR. J. S. McCUAIG, ex-M.P. for Prince Edward County, congratulated the people upon the large assembly, and made a brief speech dwelling upon the great work which the Loyalists had accomplished.

MR. PARKER ALLEN dwelt upon the hardships suffered by the U. E. Loyalists as contrasted with the comfort enjoyed by the people he represented. It was necessary that the Committee should have money to procced with the monument, and he asked that liberal subscriptions be given.

The REV. C. E. THOMSON, M. A., Incumbent of St. Mark's Church, Carlton West, added a few words. He said in substance, that it gave him great pleasure, as the grandson of William Ruttan, one of the U. E. Loyalist settlers in Adolphustown, to be here on this occasion, and to help in doing honour to the memory of these noble men. He could not say much beyond what had been already said, but would exhort them to be true to the traditions of their forefathers, and to maintain, unbroken, their connection with the great and glorious empire for whose integrity their ancestors had so greatly suffered. He would remind them that on this day they were passing through the anniversary of that great final struggle, whereby, on the field of Waterloo, the valour and endurance of the British army were so gloriously shown. Surely to have a share in such a magnificent achievement as this ought to make us most highly value the privilege of being British subjects. The time for speaking was short and he would now call on them to welcome him who was about to address them—himself a Canadian born—the grandson of a United Empire Loyalist, the son of one whom Canada was proud to number among her brilliant array of lawyers and judges, and the husband of a lady whose grandfather shared in the privations and toils of the first settlers in this very neighbourhood—a gentleman, who had come here as the Lieutenant-Governor of the Province to do honour to their celebration, to join with them in paying respect to the Loyalists of 1784 and to inaugurate the erection of well deserved monuments to their memory.

LIEUT.-GOVERNOR ROBINSON having arrived, was now introduced. He expressed regret at the delay that had occurred, but claimed that he was hardly responsible as the hospitality of the clergy and citizens, and afterward that of the militia had prevented him from appearing sooner. He considered it a duty for the Lieut.-Governor to show on every occasion his appreciation of the volunteer militia and acknowledge the great things they had done for Canada. In 1776 when the militia was 'tampered with they stood staunch to the old flag. In 1812 they had been equally brave in manifesting their allegiance, and on other occasions they had given proof of their valour and loyalty, and it was therefore a plain duty he should express his appreciation of their organization and their services. While he was pleased to meet and receive the hospitality of the militia, he was equally well pleased to meet such a large gathering on an occasion so important to all Canadians. An American once discussing the various forms of government claimed that the Canadian was the best in existence, for while the people paid all the expenses the Governor had all the fun. Part of his fun was to receive the hospitalities of to-day, to see so many good looking ladies and gentlemen, and to know they were all intent on one laudable purpose—doing honour to the memory of those who had suffered everything for their loyalty. Up to a certain point the acts of the English Government in reference to the thirteen colonies were oppressive. U. E. Loyalists did not uphold that oppression, but when it came to revolt, and they saw something more than redress of the grievances was to be demanded, they, through years of war, showed heroism and devotion to their convictions seldom equalled in the history of any country. He recognised old names, having heard them from his youth. They were the names first known here by the arrival of the heroic band who landed on this point one hundred years ago. If we had a grand country we owed it to them. He had heard the question discussed as to whether the time has come when our political status should be changed; it was not for him, as Lieut.-Governor, to discuss these matters, but he would say to Loyalists that while others, be they gentlemen of the press or politicians, discuss that question—the descendants of Loyalists can afford, knowing what they knew of old times, to mark time and listen to the discussions. They must recollect that if the medicine is given hurriedly, the physician must take good care that the death of the patient does not follow. He hoped that the young people would mark this day, and that when fifty, or sixty, or seventy years hence they went over memory's records, they would think that this great celebration took place in the *regime* of Governor Robinson. Knowing the blessings we have received under the British Constitution we can afford to remain some time longer at any rate without changing our position. He regretted that he had not before visited the lovely scenes through which he passed to-day. He regretted that he had not before had the opportunity of making the acquaintance of the people of this district, but he hoped this would not be his last visit. He hoped they would make this day a grand and permanent success. He hoped they would testify in a substantial way their regard for the Loyalists by subscribing liberally to the monument to be raised to their memory.

Mr. D. W. ALLISON, M.P., though suffering from temporary illness, consented, at the earnest request of many, to address the meeting. He dwelt with feeling on the scene which this point had witnessed a hundred years ago yesterday, when the pilgrim band of Loyalists landed at the outskirts of an unbroken wilderness, which Ontario was, and contrasted that with the scene of life and luxury which the place presented to-day. He dwelt also upon the strong contrast between the condition of the Loyalists and of their descendants of to-day. The first were victims of persecution, leaving all for the sake of their loyalty to their country and to duty, braving hardships and privations that they might have the flag they loved float over them. Their descendants possess the land which they had redeemed from the encumbering forests, and in that land peace and plenty reigned, so that even the poorest enjoy advantages which the best of their forefathers could not hope to secure. The colonists of these days, instead of coming in the face of all hardships, had colonial roads and railways provided in advance of them in the wilderness. The first apples grown here were from seed brought over by the first party when they came. When the first crop was ripe the man who grew them called all the people of the settlement—men, women and children —together, and the apples were shared equally. Had that been in this day, the man who had the apples would have been governed by the law of supply and demand, and would have sold the apples to his neighbours at the highest price. It had been stated that there was settlement at Kingston before here, but those people did not leave the States till after Independence was declared, and the date given for the Kingston settlement was too early for that. He contended this was the first settlement, and that the first line of this township of Adolphustown was the first line ever run by a surveyor in Ontario. He closed by expressing pleasure at the large turn out to do honour to the memory of Loyalists.

Mr. J. J. Watson, Secretary of the Celebration Committee read a letter of regret from the Hon. G. A. Kirkpatrick, Mr. A. F. Wood, M. P.P., and others, who had expected to be present, but were unable to do so. He explained also Sir John Macdonald's absence by stating that he had a letter from the Premier stating that owing to ill health and press of work at home he would be unable to attend. This concluded the afternoon proceedings.

THIRD AND CLOSING DAY.

The main feature of to-day's proceedings were speeches under the shade of the trees, and over the graves where the U. E. Loyalists lie buried.

Mr. D. W. Allison, M.P., first occupied the chair, but he afterwards gave place to Mr. Parker Allen. Both are Vice-Presidents of the Celebration Association, but Mr. Allison claimed priority for Mr. Allen. The principal speaker of the day was Dr. J. H. Sangster, of Port Perry. Dr. Sangster followed in the footsteps of the former speakers in contrasting the prosperity and comfort of to-day with what the Loyalists found when they landed, and what they obtained for years after. He elaborated the idea far more, however, and caused not a little amusement by going into the details of daily life, contrasting, for instance, the young lady of to-day at her organ or piano, with her grandmother whose humble art was confined to the music of the wash-board. He drew a brilliant picture of the future of Canada, the result of her mighty extent of fertile soils. The aristocracy of England proudly traced their lineage back to the uncultured invaders who came with William of Normandy. Much more proudly could the descendants of the Loyalists boast of their ancestry. He recognized the fact that Canada would some day be independent; but separation from the mother country could not come except in the natural way without straining or undue haste. Canada had not only a soil-bracing climate, but God-fearing earnest men and women, and he urged all Canadians to do what they could to make the future of the country commensurate with its possibilities. Above all, he spoke to the descendants of the Loyalists to show their zeal in Canada's cause. He called upon them because there was an intelligent pride of birth, of ancestry, which ennobled those who were moved by it and had a mission to promote the arts of peace, and to give to the world the highest standard of national honour. He recognized the difficulties in the way, and the most pressing and important of these was the bitterness of party spirit. He urged upon the politicians of both parties to devote more attention to national, and less to party advantages.

MR. WM. ANDERSON, Warden of Prince Edward county, was then called upon. He stated that some of those who were here yesterday found fault with the carrying out of the arrangements. He thought that the committee had done all that men could do, and they deserved the thanks of the community for having given so many the opportunity to celebrate the noble deeds of the U. E. Loyalists. He commended the people here for having begun these ceremonies by the laying of the corner-stone of the church. He did not agree with Dr. Sangster in the fear that party rancour would ultimately wreck the ship of State. He believed very strongly that party feeling was less bitter now than it formerly was, and with the ameliorating Christian influences everywhere at work this improvement must continue. He dwelt upon the great work begun by the Loyalists, and contended that the Dominion, which they had founded, was the first country in the world to-day. An American speaking with him had boasted of the fact that the States had gained their independence, that they were free, but their liberty was based upon the principles recognized in Britain, the benefit of which the people in Canada enjoyed, and their system of government, like that of Canada, was almost a copy of the British form.

MR. ROBT. CLAPP, of Prince Edward county, spoke on behalf of that county, assuring the people of Adolphustown that they had the sympathy of all in their commemoration of the U. E. Loyalist centenary.

Mr. J. J. WATSON, secretary of the committee, presented an excuse from Mr. W. A. Reeve, Toronto, who was to have addressed the meeting.

The people soon after began to leave the grounds, and the Adolphustown U. E. Loyalist Centennial Celebration was over.

CENTENNIAL CELEBRATION
AT
TORONTO,

3rd July, 1884.

COMMITTEE OF MANAGEMENT.
(RESIDING IN TORONTO)

WM. CANNIFF, ESQ., M.D. . . . . CHAIRMAN.

His Honour, Lt.-Gov. JOHN BEVER-
LEY ROBINSON
Lt.-Col. George T. Denison
Hon. Alex. Morris, M.P.P.
Hon. George W. Allan
A. McLean Howard
Rev. Dr. Withrow
D. B. Read, Q.C.
Salter J. Vankoughnet
J. F. Byan
Dr. James Baldwin
Dr. J. H. Richardson
W. H. Merritt
His Honour Mr. Justice Rose
Dr. Geo. S. Ryerson
Alderman Fred Denison
James H. Morris
Rev. Dr. Rose
Canniff Haight
Rev. Hugh Johnston, M. A., B. D.
Rev. Dr. Caven
Rev. Canon Scadding, D.D.

Hon S. C. Wood.
Dr. Daniel Wilson
Rev. Prof. Gregg
Dr. J. S. King
Rev. S. S. Rice, D. D.
Rev. E. H. Dewart, D. D.
John Playter
John J. Withrow
His Honour Judge Macdougall
Chas. F. McDonald
D'Alton McCarthy, Q.C.
Mayor Boswell
Dr. S. D. Hagel
Rodney Moore
Rev. Septimus Jones
Rev. D. J. Macdonnell, B.D.
J. C. Dent
A. N. Gamble
W. A. Foster
Wm. Roaf
J. R. Roaf
D. W. Clendennan

C. EGERTON RYERSON, SECRETARY-TREASURER.

SEPTIMUS A. DENISON, ASSISTANT SECRETARY.

GENERAL COMMITTEE.

The Right Rev. T. B. Fuller, D.D., D.C.L., Lord Bishop of Niagara
Hon. George Kirkpatrick, Speaker of the House of Commons
Sir Alexander Campbell, Ottawa
Hon. A. S. Hardy, Provincial Treasurer
Major Robert Z. Rogers, Grafton
Rev. Bishop Carman, D. D., Belleville
His Honour Judge Jones, Brantford
His Honour Judge Dean, Lindsay
Rev. S. S. Nelles, D.D., LL.D., President Victoria University
Rev. Dr. McNab, Bowmanville
Robert D. Rogers, Ashburnham
J. G. Pense, Waterdown
Rev. Le Roy Hooker, Kingston

Captain Moberly, Collingwood
Rev. Dr. Williams, St Catharines
Rev. Dr. Grant, Principal of Queen's University, Kingston
Rev. Dr. Jeffers, Belleville
D. W. Allison, M.P., Adolphustown
Dr. C. E. Hickey, M.P., Morrisburg
Rev. Dr. Ryckman, London
Wm. Kirby, Niagara
G. D. Hawley, M.P.P., Bath
Rev. W. R. Parker, M.A., Chatham
J. J. Watson, Adolphustown
Dr. W. Harris, Brantford
Rev. R. S. Forneri, B.D., Adolphustown
C. H. Ross, Barrie
Henry Thompson, Penetanguishene
Samuel Chrysler, Penetanguishene

GENERAL COMMITTEE.

Rev. J. Langford, Hamilton
G. H. Hale, Orillia
W. F. Casey, Napanee
Parker Allen, Adolphustown
J. W. Nelles, Guelph
T. Merritt, Cayuga
Frank Ball, Q.C., Woodstock
Rev. John Gemley, Simcoe
E. Clapp, Adolphustown
Rev. S. A. Anderson, Penetanguishene
Alex. Robertson, M.P., Belleville
Dr. Playter, Ottawa
Col. Macpherson, Ottawa
Alex. Servos, Niagara
R. N. Ball, Niagara
Col. Duncan Macfarlane, Niagara
Angus Kilburn, Beamsville
James Hiscott (Warden of Lincoln) Niagara
Col. F. A. B. Clinch, St. Catharines
Dr. Willoughby, Colborne
Sheriff Burk, Bowmanville
Levi Van Camp, Bowmanville
Arthur Craig, Craighurst
William Switzer, New Lowell
Dr. Bogart, Whitby
Dr. P. H. Spohn, Penetanguishene
J. E. Robson, Newcastle
W. Cuthbertson, Deseronto
P. S. Van Wagner, Stony Creek
Dr. Hillier, Bowmanville
His Honour Judge Carman, Cornwall
Thos. Cowan, Ingersoll
Col. Bantam, Cookstown
Dr. Robertson, Ex-M.P.P., Peel
D. B. Solmes, Northport
William Lount, Barrie
George Walker, Beamsville
John Miller, Brougham
John Dryden, Booklard
L. D. Raymond, Welland
Rev. C. E. Thompson, Weston
R. R. Loscombe, Bowmanville
Philip Secord, St. David's
Johnston Butler, St. David's
Dr. Burdette, Belleville
Joseph Rymal, Waterloo
Moses Springer, Waterloo
Dr. McCammon, Kingston
Dr. Shaver, Stratford
David Dunn, Warden of Simcoe
Rev. Dr. Hodgson
W. Hill, Colborne

John Monro, Ex-M.P., Aultsville
J. J. B. Flint, Belleville
Hon. Billa Flint, Belleville
Henry Jeffrey, Whitby
F. F. McArthur, Bowmanville
Walter Kerr, Drummondville
Iram Bender, Niagara Falls
I. Bender, Niagara Falls
J. P. Wilson, Welland
John Allen, Picton
S. M. Conger, Picton
Captain Cook, Cookstown
D. L. Sanson, Orillia
O. J. Phelps, Phelpston
Noah Assance (Chief of Mohawk Indians), Penetanguishene
C. S. Wilson, Picton
J. Jordon, Rosseau
Wm. Buchner, Fort Erie
Wm. Cryderman, Hampton
Jesse Trull, Oshawa
Wm. J. Hill, Shannonville
James Cryderman, Darlington
Rev. E. Loucks, Picton
Thomas Claus, Tyendenaga
T. S. McCuaig, Picton
Rev. E. H. M. Baker, Rector of Chippewa Indians, Deseronto
Grant Powell, Ottawa
Alex Burritt, Ottawa
A Keefer, Ottawa
Deputy-Sheriff E. D. Sherwood, Ottawa
T. H. Kirley, Ottawa
Wm. Pennock, Ottawa
J. F. Pennock, Ottawa
John Pennock, Ottawa
Wm. Sherwood, Brockville
Samuel Keefer, Brockville
Dr. Hurlburt, Ottawa
Hon. Wm. Macdougall, Ottawa
Frank Macdougall, Ottawa
J. Cuppage, Orillia
John W. Ryerson, Simcoe
P. F. Canniff, London
Dr. Oronhyatekha, London
Dr. A. S. Bristol, Napanee
Dr. H. S. Griffin, Hamilton
H. Ouderkirk, Uxbridge
Henry Belcher, Uxbridge
C. S. Grace, Lindsay
M. K. Lockwood, Brighton
Rev. A. L. Gee, Brantford
Duncan Chisholm, Oakville

UNITED EMPIRE LOYALISTS.

CENTENNIAL CELEBRATION

AT

TORONTO,

Thursday, July 3rd, 1884.

THE United Empire Loyalist Centennial Celebration in Toronto was commenced on the morning of Thursday, July 3rd, 1884, in the Horticultural pavilion, the gathering taking the form of a public meeting, interspersed with musical selections. For a morning meeting the attendance was exceptionably good, the hall being about filled. There were a few Indians present, descendants of those who accompanied the Loyalists to Canada in 1784. In the rear of the platform hung the old flag presented in 1813 to the 3rd regiment of York Militia, by the ladies of the county. Dr. Canniff, City Medical Health Officer, presided, and with him on the platform were His Worship the Mayor, the Lord Bishop of Niagara, Hon. Senator Allan, Lieut.-Col. G. T. Denison, Rev. Dr. McNab (Bowmanville), Rev. Leroy Hooker (Kingston), Rev. Dr. Scadding, Rev. Dr. Rose, Rev. Arthur Baldwin, Rev. Dr. Dewart, Rev. S. A. Anderson (Penetang.), Rev. R. S. Forneri (Adolphustown), Rev. Dr. Withrow, Chief Green (Tyendinaga), Ald. F. C. Denison, Messrs. W. Kirby (Niagara), A. McLean Howard, D. B. Read, S. J. Vankoughnet, J. H.

CENTENNIAL CELEBRATION. 53

Morris, C. Haight, C. Egerton Ryerson, S. A. Denison, John Playter, Rodney Moore, J. Graham, A. N. Gamble, E. W. Clendenan, Chiefs Hill and Cross (Tyendinaga), Dr. Hillier (Bowmanville), and others.

The Chairman said:—Ladies and Gentlemen—One hundred years ago the foundation of this province, the Province of Ontario, was laid by a band of pioneers known as the United Empire Loyalists. We meet to-day to commemorate the event. In appearing before you as chairman of this representative and brilliant gathering, it is only appropriate that I should briefly state why it is that I, so poorly qualified for the duties, should occupy so distinguished a position. It so happens that the Semi-Centennial of the incorporation of the city of Toronto is the centennial of the settlement of the province. When my friend, Mr. W. B. McMurrich, while mayor of the city, inaugurated the scheme for the celebration of the Semi-Centennial of Toronto, it occurred to my mind that it would be a fitting thing to combine with the Semi-Centennial of the capital of the province a celebration of the centennial of the province itself. The idea having been suggested to the Semi-Centennial Committee, it was decided to set apart Thursday of the Semi-Centennial week as the U. E. Loyalists' day. Mr. McMurrich having intimated to me that I should take the initiative in making the necessary arrangements for this day, I took steps to convene a meeting of those living in Toronto interested in the matter. Among those present at that meeting was His Honour the Lieutenant-Governor, a distinguished descendant of a distinguished United Empire Loyalist. The Lieutenant-Governor did me the honour to nominate me as permanent chairman of the committee, and I was consequently elected to the position. The next step in the matter was a convention of delegates from different parts of the province. At this convention my appointment as chairman was unanimously confirmed. I need not say that I esteem it a great honour to fill the position. The first duty resting upon me is on behalf of the committee to welcome the representatives of the U. E. Loyalists who are assembled here, and the gentlemen who have honoured us, and the ladies who grace the occasion. Our celebration differs from the city's in this respect—that it is held under the auspices of the Provincial Government. While the substantial aid afforded by a Government grant is thankfully recognized, the great gratification is that the worthy U. E. Loyalist pioneers of the province were officially recognized. In so doing the Government honours itself no less than the pioneers of the province. I am heartily glad to inform you that I do not feel called upon to occupy your time in speaking upon the subject which is foremost in our thoughts. I have already, on another occasion and at another place, said all I might have wished to say on the subject relating to the U. E. Loyalists, but in any case I should prefer to leave the matter in the hands of the gentlemen who are to speak—gentlemen well known for their eloquence—who will do ample justice to the occasion. The pleasing duty now devolves upon me of carrying out the programme placed in your hands.

Mr. Sims Richards sang "Rule Britannia" in a manner which evoked great enthusiasm, each verse being greeted with a round of applause.

Hon. G.W. Allan next addressed the meeting. He said: Mr. Chairman, Ladies and Gentlemen—This is surely a week which will long live in the memories of the citizens of Toronto. It has been devoted to rejoicing, such as may most fittingly commemorate the fiftieth anniversary of the incorporation of our city, and he must surely possess but a dull and inimpressible soul, who has not caught something of the spirit and enthusiasm which have characterized the proceedings of the last few days. This morning, however, we are met here to commemorate an event which concerns more or less not only the citizens of Toronto, not only the people of Ontario, but all Canadians from the Atlantic to the Pacific, for in every part of this wide Dominion may still be found some of the descendants of that noble band of whom a Canadian poet has so worthily sung, that they—

> "Loved the cause
> That had been lost ; and scorned an alien name,
> Passed into exile, leaving all behind
> Except their honour and the conscious pride
> Of duty done to country and to King."

As the chairman has reminded us, just one hundred years ago did the Loyalists of America, abandoning home, property, every worldly gain and advantage, rather than forego their allegiance to the British Crown, and in the face of hardships and trials, such as might have daunted less brave and resolute hearts, come to what was then a wilderness, and become fathers and founders of what we now so proudly call the Dominion of Canada. It concerns us not, upon this occasion, to inquire into the merits of that unhappy quarrel which cost Great Britain the American colonies. Ample justice has been done by the writers and historians of that day, and down to the present time, to the motives and actions of the successful revolutionists. More than justice, in fact, for too many of the chroniclers of these events have not been satisfied with exalting the actors on the one side, and ascribing to them every virtue, but have most unjustly and ingeniously depreciated and misrepresented those whose greatest crime was that they were "loyal and true to their sovereign, and willingly sacrificed every worldly possession rather than sever their connection with the Empire." The United Empire Loyalists of one hundred years ago valued liberty as much as the revolutionists, but they would have secured the redress of their grievances by other means than by severing the tie which bound them to Great Britain, and when the party of revolution became the stronger and the die was cast, and the ultimate appeal made to the sword, then they drew it for the king, and never sheathed it until the struggle was over, when, rather than preserve land or possessions, or secure an immunity from persecution and ill-treatment by the abandonment of their principles, they determined upon that grand exodus which we commemorate this day, and manfully set their faces toward the wilds of New Brunswick, Nova Scotia, and Canada, to become the first founders of what is yet, thank God, an integral part of the Empire, the fairest jewel in Britain's Crown. The history of the cruel persecution and unjust legislation of which the loyalists were made the subjects in most of the States of the American Union after the close of the struggle and the establishment of the Republic, were it only more generally known, would astonish those even among our own countrymen who have so much admiration to bestow upon the successful revolutionists, and but little sympathy for the heroism and endurance of those who remained faithful to the cause, as they believed it to be, of loyalty and honour. Undoubtedly the revolution, owing to the bitter animosities engendered by the struggle, frequently led to cruel reprisals and deeds of bloodshed on both sides; but that could not justify the cruelty and persecution with which hundreds were visited who had taken no active part in the strife, or the expatriation of the many thousands whose only crime had been their refusal to renounce their allegiance to their king. In a work called "Loyalists of America and their Times," written by that distinguished man, the late Rev. Egerton Ryerson, himself the son of a U. E. Loyalist, there occurs the following passage :—" At the close of the war, instead of witnessing, as in the case of all other civilized nations at the termination of a civil war, however rancorous and cruel, a general amnesty, and the restoration of all parties to the rights and property which they enjoyed at the commencement of the strife, the Loyalists found themselves exiled and impoverished, and their enemies in possession of their homes and domains. It is true about three thousand of the Loyalists were able to employ agents, or appear personally to apply to the English Government and Parliament for compensation for their losses and suffering in maintaining their fidelity to the Mother Country ; but these three thousand constituted not one-tenth of the Loyalists who had suffered losses and hardships during the civil war. Upwards of thirty thousand of them were driven from the home of their birth into what was then an almost untrodden wilderness." Of these latter who found their way to Upper Canada and the sister provinces, many had fought stoutly for the royal cause all through the war, and many were the hairbreadth escapes, many the hardships they endured before they reached British ground in safety. Others had taken no active part in the contest, but were proscribed and banished because their sympathies were known to have been with the losing side. Others there were who, while the struggle lasted, had taken what they considered the side of duty and loyalty, but when hostilities were over and England had recognized the Independence of the States, were prepared to submit to the inevitable, and take their place as citizens of the Republic. But the cruel and vindictive treatment to which they were subjected, and the penal legislation enacted against them, drove them forth also to swell the ranks of those who were to become the founders of a loyal British American Confederation, side by side with the Republic which had cast them out. The hardships which the Loyalists endured in making their way to Canada, and the suffering and privations experienced by many of them for years after their first settlement in the country, were far more severe than anything experienced by the Pilgrim Fathers during the first years of their settlement in Massachusetts. From whatever point they came, long and weary was the journey which the refugees had to perform before they reached British territory. The majority of them travelled on foot ; others who were better off carried their little effects and young children on pack-horses, sometimes bringing their cattle with them. Many bands made

D

their way to Canada by Whitehall, Lake Champlain, Ticonderoga, and Plattsburg, and then, turning southward, proceeded to Cornwall, thence ascending the St. Lawrence, along the north shore of which many of them settled. Some among the earliest of the refugees had sailed round the coast of New Brunswick and Nova Scotia, and up the St. Lawrence to Sorel, wintering there, and the following spring prosecuting their voyage in boats, until they reached their destination at Kingston, then called Cataraqui. But the most common route from New York and that part of the States taken by the Loyalists was on the Hudson River to Albany, then up a branch of the Hudson called the Mohawk, and by a branch of that river, called Wood creek, to Oneida lake, and from Oneida lake to Lake Ontario by the Oswego River. Flat-bottomed boats, built or purchased by the Loyalists for the purpose, were used for their journey, and some idea may be formed of the arduous nature of that journey when we remember that the boats themselves had to be hauled and all their contents carried over the various portages, which are stated to have amounted altogether, on the whole journey, to more than thirty miles in extent. From Oswego some of the Loyalists coasted along the eastern shore of Lake Ontario to Kingston, and then up the Bay of Quinté; others went westward along the south shore of the lake to Niagara and Queenston; some pursued their course to the head of the lake at Burlington; others made their way up the Niagara river to Queenston, conveyed their boats over the portage of 10 or 12 miles to Chippewa, thence up the river and into lake Erie, and settled in what was called the Long Point country, now the County of Norfolk. As you all know, in order to reward the loyalty and to relieve the present necessities of the Loyalists and their families, as well as to provide for their future subsistence, the British Government made liberal grants of land in Upper Canada. The Bay of Quinté was, I believe, among the first to be surveyed and

CENTENNIAL CELEBRATION. 59

settled, and the settlement of what was then called the Midland District commenced in the summer of 1783. The new settlers were provided with farming implements, building materials, and provisions, and some clothing for the first two years. And to quote from Dr. Ryerson's admirable work again—"In order to put a mark of honour, as the Order in Council expressed, 'upon the families who had adhered to the unity of the Empire, and joined the Royal standard in America before the treaty of separation in 1783,' a list of such persons was directed in 1789 to be made out and returned, to the end that their posterity might be discriminated from future settlers. From these emphatic words, the Unity of the Empire, it was styled the United Empire List, and they whose names were entered upon it were distinguished as United Empire Loyalists." And now one hundred years have passed away since that honour roll was drawn up—the Loyalists of that day have passed to their rest, but far and wide throughout the Dominion their descendants may still be found glorying in the name and the traditions they have inherited, and by our gathering here to-day we desire to show that, as did our fathers in those days of old —so do we desire to preserve the unity of the Empire, and shall ever honour the memory of those who cheerfully risked every worldly gain or advantage, aye, even life and liberty, to preserve unbroken the ties which bound them to the Motherland. Nor can we forget, on an occasion like the present, how nobly the old Loyalist spirit showed itself when Canada subsequently became the battlefield during the war between Great Britain and the United States. It has been well remarked that the true spirit of the Loyalists of America was never shown with greater force than in the conduct of their descendants during the war of 1812-14. As their fathers willingly risked life and fortune to maintain their connection with the Empire, so the sons were ready at the first trumpet call to leave wives and little ones' come forth from their homesteads, and acquit themselves like men in resisting the invaders who strove to wrest their adopted country from the British Crown. Sir, it is a just subject of pride to us Canadians that, thanks to the loyalty and the pluck of the militia and volunteers of those days, without distinction of class or nationality, the Canadas, with a frontier of more than 1,000 miles, and aided only by a few regiments of regular soldiers, resisted the whole military power of the United States for two years, at the end of which not one inch of Canadian soil was in possession of the invaders. Behind us hangs a flag [here the speaker turned and pointed to it] which I thought would not be an uninteresting relic to be displayed on the present occasion. That flag was presented by the ladies of York in 1813 to the third regiment of York Militia. In some old manuscripts now deposited in the library of the Dominion Parliament, called the Coventry papers, and relating to the early history of Canada, and especially to the war of 1812, there is contained an account of the presentation of this flag, on behalf of the ladies of York, by Miss Powell, daughter of Chief Justice Powell, its consecration by Dr. Strachan, afterwards so well known as the venerable Bishop of Toronto, the reception of the colours by Major Allan, commanding the regiment on that day, and who afterwards became its colonel, and the committal of the colours to the charge of Ensigns Charles Denison and Edward Thompson. The records of those days show what good service the flank companies of this regiment did at the capture of Detroit and the glorious battle of Queenston Heights. And the old chronicler in the papers I have referred to goes on to speak of "the devotion and gallantry of those who had been so lately called away from the enjoyment of every peaceful blessing to defend their property and rights, and the safety and glory of this highly favoured portion of the British Empire." Mr. Chairman, I am persuaded that the same spirit that characterized the Canadian militiamen and volunteers in 1812 and the Loyalists of 1784, breathes in their descendants now, and that my countrymen would be ready and prepared now, as then, if occasion should unhappily require, to defend not only "their rights and property," but the "safety and glory of this Dominion, as one of the most highly favoured portions of the British Empire." True, we do find a certain class of writers in our midst attempting to decry loyalty to the Crown and attachment to Imperial connection as inconsistent with true patriotism and pride in our country as Canadians. I yield to no one in my love for my native country. The very soil of Canada is dear to me. I love her lakes and forests, her mighty rivers, her broad and fertile fields. I am proud of the past history of my country, of the wonderful progress it has made not only in material prosperity, but in all that contributes to the higher life of a nation; its advancement in education and culture, the fitness our people have displayed for free and constitutional government, and that observance of law and order which is the noblest characteristic of the Anglo-Saxon race. But all this is entirely consistent with a deep and abiding love and attachment to the Motherland, whose glorious traditions we inherit, and which are the common property of every subject of the empire. Is there anything servile or unpatriotic in the feeling which makes the pulse beat more quickly and the heart swell, as we recall the glorious deeds of Britain's heroes on land and sea—whether in the old days of Wellington and Nelson, Waterloo and the Nile, or, coming down to our time, to Balaklava or Inkerman; or but yesterday, as we read of the rush of the Highlanders upon the foe at Tel-El-Kebir? Is there anything servile or unpatriotic in that feeling of reverence and affection for all that is great and noble in the lives and characters and works of the long array of statesmen, philosophers and poets, of men of mark in Church and State, that have made Britain's history the proud and glorious one that it is? Is there anything servile or unpatriotic in that sentiment of deep and chivalrous loyalty to the sovereign which takes out of self and makes men dare to do and die from the highest motives of faith and duty? Sir, are not all those feelings which elevate and ennoble a people? And if it is good for us to recall to-day the loyalty and patriotism, the bravery and endurance of our Loyalist forefathers, shall we abandon the rich heritage of centuries, and cut ourselves and our children adrift from the glorious memories and associations which now belong to us Canadians as members of the one great United Empire? I am persuaded of better things of my countrymen. The old Loyalist spirit is not extinct. It may not babble as loudly of its loyalty as some do of their independence, but the stream runs deep, though noiselessly, and that time, I trust, will never come when Canada will cease to be a part of the Empire, and when we shall cease to bear the proud name of British Canadians. "Home, Sweet Home" was then sung by Miss K. C. Strong, after which Mrs. Charlotte Morrison recited the following original poem, specially written for the occasion by the Rev. LeRoy Hooker, of Kingston:—

THE UNITED EMPIRE LOYALISTS.

In the brave old Revolution days,
  So by our sires 'tis told,
King's-men and Rebels all ablaze
    With wrath and wrong,
    Strove hard and long ;
  And, fearsome to behold,
O'er town and wilderness afar,
O'er quaking land and sea and air,
All dark and stern the cloud of war
  In bursting thunder rolled.

Men of one blood—of British blood,
  Rushed to the mortal strife ;
    Men, brothers born,
    In hate and scorn
  Shed each the other's life.
Which had the right and which the wrong
  It boots not now to say :

CENTENNIAL CELEBRATION.

But when at last
The war-cloud passed,
Cornwallis sailed away;
He sailed away, and left the field
To those who knew right well to wield
The powers of war, but not to yield,
Though Britons fought the day.

Cornwallis sailed away, but left
Full many a loyal man,
Who wore the red,
And fought and bled
Till Royal George's banner fled
Not to return again.

What did they then, those loyal men,
When Britain's cause was lost?
Did they consent,
And dwell content
Where Crown, and Law, and Parliament
Were trampled in the dust.

Dear were their homes where they were born;
Where slept their honoured dead:
And rich and wide
On every side
The fruitful acres spread;
But dearer to their faithful hearts
Than home, or gold, or lands,
Were Britain's laws, and Britain's crown,
And Britain's flag of long renown,
And grip of British hands.

They would not spurn the glorious old
To grasp the gaudy new.
Of yesterday's rebellion born
They held the upstart power in scorn—
To Britain they stood true.

With high resolve they looked their last
On home and native land;
And sore they wept,
O'er those that slept
In honoured graves that must be kept
By grace of stranger's hand.

They looked their last and got them out
Into the wilderness,
The stern old wilderness!
All dark and rude
And unsubdued;
The savage wilderness!

Where wild beasts howled
And Indians prowled;
The lonely wilderness!
Where social joys must be forgot,
And budding childhood grow untaught;
Where hopeless hunger might assail
Should Autumn's promised fruitage fail
Where sickness, unrestrained by skill,
Might slay their dear ones at its will;
Where they must lay
Their dead away
Without the man of God to say
The sad sweet words, how dear to men,
Of resurrection hope. But then
'Twas British wilderness!
Where they might sing,
God save the King!
And live protected by his laws,
And loyally uphold his cause.
'Twas welcome wilderness!
Though dark and rude
And unsubdued;
Though wild beasts howled
And Indians prowled;
For there their sturdy hands,
By hated treason undefiled,
Might win from the Canadian wild
A home on British lands.

These be thy heroes, Canada?
These men of proof, whose test
Was in the fevered pulse of strife
When foeman thrusts at foeman's life;
And in that stern behest,
When right must toil for scanty bread,
While wrong on sumptuous fare is fed,
And men must choose between;
When right must shelter 'neath the skies,
While wrong in lordly mansion lies,
And men must choose between;
When right is cursed and crucified,
While wrong is cheered and glorified,
And men must choose between.

Stern was the test,
And sorely pressed,
That proved their blood best of the best.
And when for Canada you pray,
Implore kind Heaven
That, like a leaven,
The hero-blood which then was given
May quicken in her veins alway;
That from those worthy sires may spring,
In number as the stars,

Strong-hearted sons, whose glorying
Shall be in Right,
Though recreant Might
Be strong against her in the fight,
And many be her scars ;
So, like the sun, her honoured name
Shall shine to latest years the same.

KINGSTON, Ont.

The Chairman then announced that Judge Dean, of Lindsay, who was to have delivered an address, was unable to be present. His place would be taken by Chief Green, one of the descendants of the well-known warrior Brant—who had fought side by side with the U. E. Loyalists who came into the wilderness a hundred years ago.

CHIEF GREEN, a Mohawk Indian of Tyendinaga, then came forward, and was received with loud applause. He said it gave him great pleasure to meet there the descendants of the U. E. Loyalists, assembled to commemorate one of the greatest events in the history of the country. The old Loyalists had chosen to sacrifice everything in a country where they were prospering, and came out to the Canadian wilderness rather than be untrue to their king. He felt that they had chosen in favour of the right. There was a time when the whole continent of North America was occupied by the race he represented. They often fought among themselves. One day a very wise head among the Mohawks suggested a scheme for the consolidation of several tribes for mutual protection—a scheme which was adopted, and led to the organization of the Six Nation Indians, whom he now represented. In the course of time England and his nation made a treaty, which his tribes had since loyally observed. In fact, when the rebellion took place, his nation removed from New York State, and sacrificed their territory, in order to accompany their white Loyalist brethren to this country. They did more than this; for they took up arms and fought and died for England. The United States gained their independence, but his forefathers remained under British connection. The Six Nation Indians were all Christians, belonging to the Church of England, which they loved. They formed a settlement on the shores of the Bay of Quinté, and built a church there. He here remarked that a communion service on the platform had been presented to his forefathers by Queen Anne. He proceeded to say that of late years his people had made much progress in civilization and Christianity. They had to-day two churches, one of which had cost $7,000, and the other $3,500. They had four good schools in the reservation, and two white lady teachers. In 1879 he went to England and made an appeal to the people there on behalf of one of the schools. He succeeded in his mission, and found the English the kindest people under the sun. He found them as his forefathers had represented them to be—ladies and gentlemen of the first rank. He obtained a grant in England to carry on the work for twenty years. He was proud to be there to associate with the descendants of the U. E. Loyalists, even as his forefathers had associated with their forefathers. He believed Canada ranked with any nation on the globe acccording to its age.

Mr. Warrington then sang in splendid style the well-known patriotic song, " If England to Herself be True," and in answer to an enthusiastic *encore*, sang " Who's for the Queen ? " with equal spirit.

The Chairman here exhibited the Communion set presented to the Mohawk Indians in 1711. During the rebellion the Indians buried them to preserve them, and dug them up again after the war. He then, in introducing Lieutenant-Colonel G. T. Denison, said the Denison family in old times had done good service on the borders. In the war of 1812 and 1837 they were found at their post of duty. They took an active part in securing the country to the Canadians. The Denison family were not only soldiers, but descendants of the U. E. Loyalists, and the United States lost a good deal when they lost this famliy.

LIEUTENANT-COLONEL GEORGE T. DENISON said—Mr. Chairman, ladies, and gentlemen, we meet to-day in honour of the U. E· Loyalists who a hundred years ago came here and founded this province. Their coming was the result of their loyal adherence to a great principle. It was not so much a question of what is called loyalty as devotion to a particular type of government.

The great question fought out in the United States, in 1776, was whether they should be ruled by a republic or a monarchy, and when the U. E. Loyalists were defeated in the States they came here, and established this province upon monarchical institutions. In 1812, an attempt was made to annex this country by the people of the United States, and to make us a republican people. This was a repetition of the struggle between the two forms of government. At that time Upper Canada was a sparsely settled community, and we had about 80,000 of a population, almost altogether consisting of U. E. Loyalists and their descendants, while the United Sates had a population of something like ten millions. The odds were enormous, infinitely greater than they would be to-day. Fortunately we had at that time the right kind of a man at the head of affairs, General Brock. He was one of the great men of all history. He called together the volunteers of this city, told them what they would have to encounter; told them what odds were against them, and asked them to follow him to the front. Every one of them responded. Invasion followed invasion, and although the odds were always against us, the fortune of war was with us. Of the victories over the invaders we all know. At the end of the fight we had not lost a single inch of Canadian territory while we had the State of Michigan, and had burned the capital city of our enemies.

This was the lesson we should teach our children, and keep it ever freshly remembered as a ground of hope for us, to give us confidence in the future. The U. E. Loyalists deserved the greatest credit for the gallant stand they made in 1776 for monarchical institutions, but they deserve ten thousand times more credit because, when the odds were against them, they maintained their rights, and handed them down unimpaired to us. The people of Canada live in the freest country on the face of the globe, and must appreciate what the U. E. Loyalists have done for them in preserving it for their descendants.

Let us compare the position of Canada to-day with that of the United States. We have every liberty to do what is right, but we have no license to do what is wrong. Our laws are honestly administered. Life and property are safe in this country. In everything which affects the individual, this is the freest and the best country. In the State of Kentucky, in ten years, there have been 700 murders, and yet there has been in that time only one hanging by process of law. There were 1,500 convictions for murder across the line in 1883, and only 93 hangings, while 118 people were lynched. The chances of a murderer escaping after he is convicted in the United States are sixteen to one. The number of murders in England amount to 237 per annum in each ten millions; in the United States they are 820, or three times as many. Are we not better off than the people of a country where they carry deadly weapons with impunity; where lax divorce laws have shaken the sanctity of the marriage tie; where the principal, if not the sole test of respectability is wealth, and where lynch law spasmodically attempts to remedy the lax administration of justice by the regular courts, and for the fact that we are living under a better and freer system, we have to thank the U. E. Loyalists, who saved us from annexation.

Again, our system of government is simpler, cheaper and more dignified. Our neighbours have never considered what it costs them to elect the head of the State every four years. I was told by a prominent gentleman connected with one of the party organizations in one of the States, that the expenses of his party in that State alone amounted to $600,000 for the Presidential election. Counting the expenditure for all the States and for both parties, it would seem that the cost of an election was $40,000,000, or at the rate of $10,000,000 a year. That sum would pay the whole expense of maintaining the Royal houses of England, Austria and Germany. And with all the expense, they had at the head of the States simply the representative of a faction, and very often only of the wire-pullers and tricksters of that faction. Without expense, without labor, worry or anxiety, we Canadians have a sovereign respected by all political parties, and by all the world. For this we have to thank the United Empire Loyalists.

In talking of loyalty to the Queen, I speak of her as the Queen of Canada. I am as loyal to Canada as any man upon its soil, and it is because of that loyalty to Canada, and Canada alone, that I am loyal to the Queen, believing that living under the institutions of which the Queen is the representative, Canadians will become a better and a greater race of people.

There is another point to be considered in reference to this great question of republicanism and monarchy. The great objection to a republican form of government is that it is very uncertain and unreliable. If we look at the republics of the world we shall find that these republics have rarely, if ever, been a success, except among poor, sparsely settled countries. The republican form of government is liable to lead to constant civil war. That is the experience of history. The republics of South America and of Mexico have had civil wars and bloodshed every few years. Ever since they destroyed the legitimate monarchy in France, they have had revolution and bloodshed about every fifteen years. But it might be said that that is not the case in the United States. I think that the same thing is beginning there. In 1830 —before which date they did not have the same time to give to politics—when General Jackson was elected President, there was a narrow chance of parties breaking out in civil war; but a vigorous man being at the head of affairs that was prevented. In 1860, when the Democratic party was defeated, the country was visited by one of the most terrible civil wars known in history, one which loaded their country with debt, and drenched their fields with blood. In 1876 there was another great risk of war, which certainly would have taken place had the late war not occurred so recently. Twenty years will not pass without civil war again breaking out in that country, and if Canadians know what is good for them they will have nothing to do with them, or their form of government.

I wish to say a few words about independence. This is the same old question under another form. It is the Republican idea, as opposed to the Monarchical, and it is not the first time it has come up in this country. It came up in 1776, when Arnold and Montgomery came here and tried to annex the country. But the lately-conquered French stood by the Crown, and the scheme was defeated. In 1812 the same question was up, and by the lavish shedding of Canadian blood our rights and liberties were preserved. In 1837 a rebellion was begun, headed by a stranger, a new-comer, but the loyalists of that day came out in defence of the constitution. It is true there were then many grievances to be remedied. The government was by an irresponsible executive. There really were grievances, but the descendants of the Loyalists knew that no matter what the grievances were they were nothing compared with what they would have had to submit to in a republic. The Loyalists turned out *en masse* and the rebellion was put down. In 1849, a few prominent politicians, a little annoyed about some political matter, signed an annexation manifesto, but instantly the feeling of the Canadians was shown to be so strongly against them that it dropped at once. In 1871, the Canada First movement began. I was a member of that party, and had a good deal to do with it, because I consider Canada before any other country in the world. But one gentleman made the mistake of believing that some of the members were in favour of independence, and speaking in that spirit killed the thing with a breath. Many gentlemen left it, feeling that their action was likely to be misunderstood.

From whom comes this cry for independence? Not from the real Canadians, but from a few hangers on of the newspaper press—a few wanderers and Bohemians—men who have lived indifferently in Canada and the States, and have never been satisfied anywhere— men without an atom of stake in the country. And do you think that the people of Canada are going to submit themselves to the guidance of such men? Never. The independence party in Canada can almost be counted on one's fingers and toes. The movement did not amount to anything, and the moment the people of Canada thought it did, the real feeling of the country would manifest itself. I would like to ask these gentlemen whether they thought it fair and honest of strangers to come here to air their theories, trying to interfere with a prosperous, happy, and contented people—a people who have no grievances they cannot easily remedy themselves. What these men want, goodness only knows. If Canadians are not an independent people, I do not know where such a people can be found.

I have read their arguments, and they do not amount to anything. They say, " If we were independent we could have an officer of our force in command of our militia." The law which requires an officer of the British Army was passed by the representatives of the Canadian people, and can be repealed by the same power. They find fault because we have the Privy Council as a Court of final appeal. I look upon it as a great blessing that Canadians have a tribunal so learned and impartial, so free from all bias through party squabbles, to adjudicate on points of difference. Independent nations often refer questions of difference to foreign tribunals, yet they do not forfeit their freedom by so doing.

There is not a single point in which we are not as well off as our neighbours. But we have this also, we belong to the greatest empire the world has ever seen. We have all the credit and respectability attached to being connected with so great an empire, and our ambition should be to become the most powerful part of that empire. They say a Canadian cannot hold his head up because he does not belong to an independent nation—that if he did he would be a great fellow. They try to appeal to our vanity. If we were independent, would we be any greater a people than we are to-day. Take Brazil, an independent empire, with about the same territory, twice the population, and three times the revenue of Canada, and who would not rather be called a Canadian than a Brazilian? Who would not rather be a Canadian than a Mexican? The whole of their arguments were fallacies. The reason we are proud of being Canadians is that Canada is not only one of the finest countries on the face of the globe, and going to have as fine a population as can be found anywhere, but also that it is a part of the great empire to which we are proud to belong.

I have endeavoured to show that every attempt to bring about independence in the past had been put down by the Canadian people by bloodshed, and there could not be any attempt to bring Republican institutions into this country without bloodshed. I ask these wanderers, these Bohemians, therefore, whether it is right of them to come here and interfere with us, when they have the opportunity of going to the United States, where they can get a Government exactly as they want it—where they can find a similar climate, and a people speaking the same language. They have no excuse to remain here, for when they can so easily get what they want they should go to the United States, and leave us alone.

We do not want them, and we can get on very well without them.

It must not be forgotten that all the advantages we have to-day we owe to our ancestors, the U. E. Loyalists, and the sacred trusts handed down by them should be passed on intact and unimpaired to our children. That is the duty of this generation, and it is to the descendants of the Loyalists that we must look to see that this is done. I wish to quote to you some words written by Mr. Haliburton, of Nova Scotia, son of the celebrated author of " Sam Slick " : " Whenever we lower those we love into the grave, we entrust them to the bosom of our country as sacred pledges that the soil that is thus consecrated by their dust shall never be violated by a foreign flag or the foot of a foe, and whenever the voice of disloyalty whispers in our ear, or passing discontent tempts us to forget those who are to come after us, or those who have gone before us, the leal, the true, and the good, who cleared our forests, and made the land they loved a heritage of plenty and peace to us and to our children, a stern voice comes echoing on through thirty centuries; a voice from the old sleepers of the pyramids; a voice from a mighty nation of the past that long ages has slumbered on the banks of the Nile. ' Accursed be he who holds not the ashes of his fathers sacred, and forgets what is due from the living to the dead.' "

Let our energies be devoted to building up our country, improving our commerce, strengthening our defences, increasing our confidence in ourselves and in each other, and it will not be many years or generations before Canada will hold a place in the British Empire as the most important and principal part of it. To the United Empire Loyalists and their descendants we must look to see that this is done. I can not sit down without quoting those admirable words of the Rev. Mr. Leroy Hooker :—

" Stern was the test,
And sorely pressed,
That proved their blood best of the best,

And when for Canada you pray
 Implore kind Heaven
 That, like a leaven,
The hero-blood which then was given
May quicken in her veins alway ;
That from those worthy sires may spring,
 In number as the stars,
Strong-hearted sons, whose glorying
 Shall be in Right,
 Though recreant Might
Be strong against her in the fight,
 And many be her scars ;
So like the sun, her honoured name
Shall shine to latest years the same."

Miss Foster, of Guelph, then sang a "A Loyalist Song," a beautiful production, the beauties of which were fully brought out by Miss Foster. She was loudly applauded, and the people insisting on a recall. She came back and repeated the first verse. Mrs. Morrison then gave another reading, "Loyalist Days," commemorative of the traits and deeds of the United Empire Loyalists, which was loudly applauded. The author is Mrs. Kittson, of Sorel, P. Q. Thus it runs :—

LOYALIST DAYS.

In Memory of the United Empire Loyalists. Dedicated to their descendants.

The earliest ages claim immortal heroes.
 Among the stars great conquerors' names are found.
The hosts of Israel sing, " Arise, Jehovah,"
 The dust they trod is consecrated ground.
Greece is one shrine of earth's anointed warriors,
 Our souls are with their self-devotion thrilled ;
A thought of Regulus lights up the grandeur
 Which lingers round the city seven hilled.

The last "Adieu" of Rowland's silvery bugle
 Is heard amid the snowy Pyrenees ;
A voice floats from the rugged slopes of Sempach
 On every waft of mountain-hallowed breeze.
The heavens bow with majesty of triumph,
 The ocean winds those sounds of victory keep,
The muffled drums of armaments are rolling,
 The sea-kings hear the clarions of the deep.

O'er pathless cliffs and storm-emblazoned ramparts,
 Above the flow of an impetuous tide,

The banners of rich sunset cloud saluted
　The *fleur-de-lis*, the New World's virgin bride.
The dawn mist hung around the plains o Abraham,
　The tears of war dropped swiftly, brightly red ;
When conquest left the death roll on the altar
　The morning light its purest halo shed.

The river gleams with monumental marble,
　While, foaming round the battle crested rock,
The regal waves, beneath the heights of Queenston,
　In every ripple write the name of Brock.
Has Laura Secord any living homage ?
　When strife's tornado burst upon our shores,
Through lines of sentry and through Indian forests
　That soldier's wife her timely warning bore.

Has history crowned the staunchly bold defenders,
　Who nobly braved the conflict's darkest hour—
The men who for the heritage of Britons
　Left brightning spheres of stately wealth and power ?
They fought, to live beneath the Old Flag's shadow,
　The sceptr'd lion's foremost sons were they,
Who halted not at breastworks formed of bayonets,
　Through gates of fire they held their onward way.

The U. E. Loyalists were never vanquished,
　Though many sleep in their blood-sprinkled ground,
As true as steel by battle lightnings tempered,
　As true as steel, they " unto death were found."
Their swords were in their own brave keeping buried.
Else from their scabbards they would leap in flame
　To hear the words by recreant statesmen uttered,
Who would defile the Royalty of Fame.

The vast Dominion from each frontier summons
　A mighty host with memories of the past ;
The U. E. Loyalists unfold their banners,
　And rouse the echoes with a trumpet blast.
Sons of the brave, remember your forefathers,
　Shine kindly words from every warrior grave,
Shreds of the Union Jack, in battle cloven,
　O'er hero dust your glorious records wave.

Mr. E. W. Schuch sang in splendid style, and with great feeling, the well-known Canadian patriotic song, "The Maple Leaf for Ever."

THE BISHOP OF NIAGARA said he had felt that they had not recognized, as fully as they ought to have done on that occasion, that the Loyalists were as a body imbued with a true religious spirit, and they had been told that more by their red brother that morning than by their white brethren. He could not help feeling deeply that what Chief Green had said was perfectly true, and therefore he asked the privilege of concluding the service by giving them, with God's permission, the apostolic benediction. His Lordship pronounced the benediction, after which the gathering dispersed.

His Honour Lieutenant-Governor Robinson gave a reception at Government house during the afternoon between the hours of three and five o'clock. There was a large and representative gathering of descendants of U. E. Loyalists from all over the Province. Captain Merritt, G.G.B.G., acted as A.D.C. in place of Capt. Geddes, who was unavoidably absent from the city. Following is a list of those present :—

Col. R. B. Denison, Deputy-Adjutant General; Col. G. T. Denison, Col. Alger, Col. Shaw, Col. Acton, Col. Graveley, Major F. Denison, Bishop and Mrs. Fuller, Niagara, Rev. Dr. Scadding, Rev. Foreman, Rev. Johnston, Rev. Dobies, Rev. Thomas Cullen and wife, Rev. Leroy Hooker, Dr. and Mrs. Hogart, Hon. Mr. Allan, S. Denison, A. Denison, Mrs. E. Ryerson, F. Wooten, A. W. Smith, J. Playter, N. A. Gamble and wife, S. Secord, T. Horner, E. Field, Dr. and Mrs. Beatty, Cobourg; Judge McDougall, C. B. Stephens, H. J. Medaw, Mrs. H. Frazer, G. Gamble, Mr. and Mrs. Brynes, Mrs. J. S. Ryerson, E. J. Beaty, Mrs. Boldins, K. and H. Chisholm, T. H. Condill, C. E. Macdonald, Canniff Haight and wife, Mrs. J. Cormock jr. and Miss Fanny Harding, Mr. Racey, Mr. Leach and wife, Mr. Sutherland and wife, and Mr. McDonald, of Philadelphia; Ald. Brandon, Ald. Walker, J. Osborne, P. Peterson, J. N. Stephenson and wife, R. Moore, Mr. Meek, R. T. Watson, Miss Beard, Mr. Birmington, wife and daughter, Miss Thomas, T. H. Drinkwater, J, Pearson and wife, Mrs. Stephenson, S. Jarvis, J. A. Hunter, Mr. Pettit, Mr. Biggar, Mr. Haskitt, S. M. Sanford, Mr. Grainger, H. Burns, W. Greeve, Mr. and Mrs. Vaudusen, sr., Mr. and Miss Davis, Mr. Peter, A. A. Davis, Mr. Coppige, R. Holmes, the

Misses Cornish and Miss Armstrong, W. Medland, W. Anderson, T. W. Elliott, Mr. Raymond, Mrs. Vanwagner, J. C. Campbell, Mr. Wallace, J. F. Day.

The band of the 10th Royal Grenadiers was present and played for some time in the beautiful grounds, outside the conservatory. Several interesting addresses were delivered, his Honour being the first to speak. He began by saying that he had just returned from hearing speeches that did justice to heroic men. He was glad to welcome the descendants of those heroes at Government House, and would like the people of Ontario to know that there is at least one place in this Province where politics do not intrude, and where all were welcome. He referred to his being a descendant of a U. E. Loyalist, and was only sorry that he could not do full justice to their memory. No words could adequately describe the loyalty and devotion of the heroes who shed their blood to defend the grand old flag that now floated above Government House. Sons of such sires could not forget their deeds, and looking back through the long vista of a hundred years we see them forsaking the land that had been theirs, to carve their way through the forests of Ontario. They left their broad acres and the graves of their fathers through their love for Britain and British institutions. It gave him pleasure, he said, to welcome the American gentlemen present. He had smoked the pipe of peace with them, and hoped that none but the most friendly relations would ever exist between Canada and the American Republic. He had been in New York when they were celebrating Evacuation Day. At the reception which he attended the health of the Queen was drunk with the greatest enthusiasm, and he would never forget the remarks made by the chairman on that occasion. Said he : " When I look around and see with what enthusiasm the health of the Queen of England has been received, I cannot but think that after all the evacuation so far as we are concerned was not a thorough success. It was really a dismal failure, for although we succeeded in getting rid of a few Englishmen then, they have come back in overwhelming numbers, and thousands of English vessels carry our commerce round the world, and we could but ill afford to lose them." Although a reverse was sustained by England in that desperate struggle of a century ago it has not been without lasting benefit. It has founded the supremacy of the English race, and it was his prayer that it might ever continue. The labour demonstration of the previous day had shown what Canadians were doing. They have a great heritage, thanks to their noble ancestors, and he was glad that all classes were trying to appreciate it. Numbers do not make a country, but the enterprise, intelligence, and loyalty of its inhabitants.

His Honour then called upon Mr. Leroy Hooker, who commenced by saying that though not a descendant of a U. E. Loyalist he was as every Canadian should be, a United Empire Loyalist, one who believed in Canada, and in the great bright future that is opening for it. Mr. Hooker was followed by Mr. Kirby, of Niagara, a gentleman widely known in Western Ontario. He spoke of the settlement in Upper Canada by the U. E. Loyalists, and gave a short account of some of the stirring incidents that occurred during the war.

Lieutenant-Governor Aikins, of Manitoba, was the next speaker. He paid a glowing tribute to the U. E. Loyalists, who gave up everything for king and country, and said that but for them the map would not show such a large extent of country on this continent under the flag of Britain as it does.

The Rev. Mr. Anderson, who has been among the Canadian Indians almost from childhood, followed. Of the Indian Loyalists who fought side by side with their white brothers, he spoke in the most favourable terms. But for them the tide of battle would often have turned against us, and a debt that can never be fully paid is due to the aborigines who fought for us.

His Honour Lieutenant-Governor Robinson then made a few additional remarks, and the visitors withdrew.

CENTENNIAL CELEBRATION
AT
NIAGARA,
AUGUST 14th, 1884.

GENERAL COMMITTEE.

His Honor J. B. Robinson, Lieut.-Governor of Ontario.
The Warden, Reeves and Deputy-Reeves of the County of Lincoln.
R. H. Smith, Mayor of St. Catharines.
H. S. Garrett, Mayor of Niagara.
Rt. Rev. T. B. Fuller, Bishop of Niagara.
Hon. W. H. Dickson, ex-Senator.
Hon. J. B. Plumb, Senator.
Hon. J. R. Benson, Senator.
J. C. Rykert, M.P.
S. Neelon, M.P.P.
Dr. Ferguson, M.P.
Col. Moran, M.P.P.
L. McCallum, M.P.
R. Harcourt, M.P.P.
D. Thompson, M.P.
J. Baxter, M.P.P.
T. R. Merritt, St. Catharines.
J. P. Merritt, do
Col. Macdonald, do
R. Lawrie, do
Thos. Keyes, do
Jas. Seymour, do
J. A. Woodruff, do
W. Kirby, Niagara.
J. G. Dickson, do
R. Dickson, do
Col. Clench, do
Dr. Anderson, do
Dr. Canniff, Toronto.
C. E. Ryerson, do
Col. G. T. Denison, Toronto.
D. B. Reed, do
J. Playter, do
R. B. Miller, do
J. C. Kirby, do
Rev. Dr. Withrow, do
G. A. Clement, Toronto.
Ven. Archdeacon McMurray, Niagara.
A. Hill, Chief of Mohawks, Bay of Quinté.
S. Green, Chief of Mohawks, Bay of Quinté.
H. Paffard, Niagara.
J. W. Ball, Niagara Township.
W. A. Thompson, do
J. Cooper, do
Joe Clement, do
J. Butler, do
R. N. Ball, do
Alex. Servos, do
Peter Whitmore, do
Rev. Dr. Scadding, Toronto.
Dr. Ruttan, Napanee.
D. W. Allison, M.P.
Rev. R. S. Forneri, Adolphustown.
Archdeacon Dixon, Guelph.
Rev. W. S. Ball, Elderton.
W. A. Campbell, Chatham.
Jas. Ingersoll, Woodstock.
Jas. Davis, sr., Hamilton.
E. Servos, Hamilton.
T. Davis, Winona.
John D. Servos, Niagara.
J. B. Secord, Niagara.
S. Secord, Louth.
Rev. J. A. Anderson, Penetanguishene.
I. P. Wilson, Welland.
Rev. W. Walsh, Fonthill.
Richd. Miller, St. Catharines.
P. H. Ball, Thorold.
F. L. Walsh, Simcoe.
G. Whitmore, Niagara Township.
Rev. LeRoy Hooker, Kingston.

UNITED EMPIRE LOYALISTS.

CENTENNIAL CELEBRATION

AT

NIAGARA,

August 14th, 1884.

ON the 14th of August, 1884, at Niagara, on historic ground, in a glade of the Oak Grove, a short distance from the ruins of Fort George, on the scene of the first Parliament of Upper Canada, and in a neighbourhood watered by the blood of their forefathers, the descendants of the United Empire Loyalists, assembled to hold the final centennial celebration of the arrival of the Loyalists in this country. A large platform, thirty-six by twenty-four feet square, was erected for the committee and speakers. A tall flag-staff, in the centre of the platform, displayed the Union Jack, and at each of the four corners rose tall flag-staffs supporting British ensigns.

In front was a large painting of the Royal arms, and around the platform were hung graceful festoons of oak and maple. Some tablets were on the sides and front containing the names of men and officers of the Lincoln militia who fell during the war.

Shortly after one o'clock there assembled representatives from all parts of the Province interested in the day's proceedings, Among them were His Honour the Lieutenant-Governor, the Lord Bishop of Niagara, the Archdeacons of Niagara and Guelph, Rev. Dr. Barclay, Toronto, Rev. Dr. McNab, Bowmanville, Hon. J. Burr Plumb, Colonel Denison, D. A. G, Colonel G. T. Denison, Major F. C. Denison, Chief Green and Chief Hill, Bay of Quinté Reserve, Chief Johnson, Colonel McFarland, Mr. Garrett, Mayor of Niagara, Rev. Charles Campbell, Mr. S. Neelon, M. P. P., Hon. J. G. Dickson, Niagara, Mr. J. Hiscott, Warden of Lincoln, Mr. J. H. Morris, Toronto, Mr. A. Whitmore, Niagara, Lieutenant W. H. Merritt, Toronto, who was acting aide-de-camp to the Lieutenant-Governor, Mr. Wm. Keys, Grantham, Mr. F. Lefroy, Mr. D. B. Read, Mr. W. Kirby, Niagara, Rev. Mr. Anderson, Penetanguishene, Mr. W. H. Doel, J. P., Toronto, Mr. C. N. Ball, Judge Senkler, St. Catharines, Dr. Clark, Messrs. John Elliott, J. T. Gilkison, A. Cleghorn and W. Griffin, Brantford, Dr. Rolls, Sheriff Woodruff, Mr. W. R. Pattison, St. Catharines. Mr. I. P. Wilson, County Clerk of Lincoln, Mr. L. D. Raymond, County Attorney, Mr. J. M. Dunn, and many others. The York Pioneers were well represented, and there was also in attendance a delegation of 48 Chiefs and Warriors from the Grand River reserve, headed by Chief A. G. Smith, official interpreter. Of this delegation two of the Chiefs were survivors of the war of 1812. They were Captain John Smoke Johnson, in his 93rd year, who was present at the battles of Queenston, Lundy's Lane, Black Rock, and other engagements on the Niagara frontier, and Chief John Tutelle, in his 91st year. The Tuscarora Indian band was also present and played some delightful selections during the afternoon. Around the platform about 2,000 persons were assembled.

R. N. BALL, Esq., of Niagara, occupied the chair, and opened the proceedings. He said:—

MY FRIENDS,—The time has arrived when we should begin the proceedings of the day. I am much pleased to see so large a gathering of the descendants of the U. E. Loyalists on this classic ground, to do honour to the memory of those noble men and women who, rather than live under an alien rule, left all the comforts and luxuries of their well filled homes that they might found in the then wilderness of Canada a new home, where the British flag might still wave over, and British laws still govern them. This decision, on their part, brought with it many hardships and disadvantages. But the result has fully justified the wisdom of their choice, and we, their descendants, now reap the benefits of their sacrifices in the possession of this noble Canada of ours, whose fertile acres reach from the Atlantic to the Pacific, and containing within its bounds all the elements of a great and prosperous nation. A country of lakes and rivers, of noble forests and almost boundless prairies. A country that every descendant of the U. E. Loyalists will be proud to acknowledge as the land of his birth, and be willing to defend to the best of his power. Many a time, in my early youth, I have listened with wrapt attention as my grandmother told me the story of the capture of Fort Wyoming by Butler and Brant (in which she was detained as belonging to a loyal family), of the long journey from the Mohawk river to Oswego, through the then almost unbroken forest, traversed only by an Indian trail ; how, on arriving at Oswego, she and others embarked in an open boat for Fort Niagara ; how they were nine days on the lake and five days without food except the hips of the wild rose which they gathered on shore, and how an Indian woman was sent ahead for supplies, which came in the form of hard cakes, strung on a pole, and carried by two swift Indians, but which came none too soon. These and many incidents of savage cruelty, and unavoidable hardships, made me look with wonder at the kindly old face, as she told me the tales of olden times. As Chairman, it is out of place for me to make a long speech, especially as our time is limited, and there are many present, who are better qualified than I am to do justice to the occasion. I will, therefore, now call upon the Lord Bishop of Niagara to open the proceedings with prayer.

THE RIGHT REVEREND THOMAS BROCK FULLER, Lord Bishop of Niagara, then made the following prayer:—

"O Almighty everliving God! who in the inscrutable ways of Thy providence didst permit the early settlers of this fair land to be driven from their comfortable properties in the revolted colonies; from their farms, their mills and their stores, out of pure attachment to the British throne; and after enduring many and grievous hardships and sufferings Thou didst bring them to this glorious land to hew out for themselves new homes in the wilderness; grant, we beseech thee, O Lord, that the descendants of those noble parents may ever carry out the principles by which those who settled here an hundred years ago were guided; may be loyal and devoted servants of the Crown; faithful servants of God; honest and industrious members of society and good neighbours; continually striving to adorn the doctrine of God, their Saviour, in all things, through Jesus Christ our Lord.—Amen."

LIEUTENANT-GOVERNOR ROBINSON was called upon as the first speaker. He thanked the chairman and the audience for their kind reception of him. This was the third time he had been called upon to greet the descendants of the U. E. Loyalists gathered together to celebrate the deeds of their ancestors. At Adolphustown, on the shores of the beautiful Bay of Quinté, thousands had gathered to do honour to the noble dead, and but a few weeks ago he had had the pleasure of meeting representatives of the U. E. Loyalists from all parts of the Province, at Government House. The spot where they now stood was historic ground. Here in this old town of Niagara the first Parliament of Canada assembled, and they then passed the jury law, and an act declaring that from that time there should be no slavery in Upper Canada. Those were great and good laws, and the fact that they were so early passed was a just cause of pride to Canadians. Col. Littlehales, one of the staff of Governor Simcoe, made the first trip through the interior of this Province, of which there was any record. Part of that record was to the effect that before going to rest at a station near the site of the present city of London they sang " God Save the King," and now a hundred years after, at every public meeting held in any of the fine halls in which the people assemble they hear the strains of "God Save the Queen." He dwelt upon the heroism of the men of the Revolutionary War, and of the war of 1812, as an incentive to the people to cultivate the same spirit. He eulogized the Indians, representatives of whom he saw present. If above our heads floated the British flag to-day, they had to thank the Six Nation Indians in large measure for it. Some undertook to sneer at the feeling of loyalty, of which they were proud. But those men could not understand this feeling, but they, who were moved by it, felt that the spread of it among all people would be to the benefit of the country. The current literature of England showed that the fact was being recognized that the colonies were almost of as much value to the empire as was the empire to the colonies. If this feeling was carried to its final outcome the result would be largely due to the bravery and loyalty of the United Empire Loyalists, who have saved to the British Crown this finest unoccupied part of the world.

The Venerable BISHOP OF NIAGARA next spoke. He said : I am not the son of an U. E. Loyalist, in the strictest sense of the term, though my mother's father, Capt. England, of the 47th Regiment British army, lost blood at Bunker's-hill, on the right side, (laughter) ; and after the war settled at Kingston, Upper Canada. I have ever admired the noble body of men who sacrificed their all— their comfortable farms and every thing they had accumulated for a principle, that of loyalty to the British

Crown. There are other colonies in the British Empire whose first settlers were convicts, viz., Botany Bay and Van Dieman's Land; but such was not the case with our country. It was settled by men of high principle—by men of education. There are men, little removed from the beast that perishes—who have no principle, who are satisfied to live under any government so long as their bodily wants are satisfied. Such were not the early settlers of Upper Canada—such were not the men who settled in the Niagara district—the Butlers, the Balls, the Swayzes, the Scroopes, the Whitmores, the Woodruffs, the Stalls, the Lampmans, the Rykerts, the Merritts, the Dureetes, the Gregories, the Nelleses, the Pettits, the Lundys, the Kerbys, the Warrens, the Macklems, the Rykmans, the Ryersons, and the thousands of U. E. Loyalists. He felt that many now enjoying the glorious privileges of British subjects in Ontario, did not realize what they owe to these men and women, who landed on these shores a hundred years ago. Many of them here had heard but little of what the first settlers had sacrificed out of principle, what they had endured in coming here, to prepare the Province for their occupation, and therefore they do not appreciate this noble band of men as they deserve. Many of the settlers, who had fought valiantly in the revolutionary war as young men, fought again as men well advanced in years under Generals Brock and Riall and under Colonels Harvey and Bishopp, and other noble soldiers, who led them to victory, when this peaceful Province was invaded in 1812 by a body of men who thought that they had only to show themselves on our shores to pluck this glorious Colony from the British Crown. But they were mistaken—they found that those who had endured hardships in the revolutionary war, were ready to endure the same in defence of their wives and children and their new homes in the wilderness. After doing their best to conquer Canada, the invaders were glad, in 1815, to sue for an inglorious peace, without having secured an acre of our soil! The Bishop said, that he was thankful to have been spared by a gracious God to have seen that day. He was an old man—had thankfully watched the growth of this country for nearly seventy years. He said that he was "an old man," but Canadians often lived to be *very* old men. He had then living an uncle, who had entered on his 97th year on the 13th January last. He was, at last accounts, in the enjoyment of good bodily health, a full General of the Royal Artillery, and the oldest officer in the British army, and, like the speaker, he was a native Canadian. In conclusion, the Bishop remarked, that he hoped that his fellow-countrymen, with such glorious examples before them, would emulate the virtues of their fathers, improve the laws of the land, love God and honour the Queen.

SENATOR PLUMB'S SPEECH.

The chairman then called upon the Hon. J. B. Plumb, Senator of the Dominion, who was received with applause.

MR. PLUMB said that as a resident of the Town of Niagara and a member of the Reception Committee, he desired to unite with the chairman in extending a cordial and hearty welcome to all who were here on this memorable occasion. He was deeply gratified to find so large an assemblage, and to know that a great proportion of those who composed it were descendants of the early settlers of the country, and that they were here to do honour to the memory of their loyal and brave forefathers. The chairman himself was a representative descendant of a worthy U. E. Loyalist family, an inheritor of the lands granted by the Crown to his ancestors, who cleared them from the primeval forest, lands which are now teeming with the products of the field, of the orchard, and of the vineyard under the practical and successful cultivation which has made the name of their present owner widely and favorably known as an agriculturist and fruit-grower.

He (Mr. Plumb) could not claim to be here by virtue of such a descent. It was well known that his earlier life had been passed in the neighbouring Republic of which he was a native, but his forefathers had held positions of trust and honour under the Crown prior to the Revolution both in civil and military life, and when, upon mature reflection, he decided to take the oath of allegiance, he resolved to the best of his ability to do his duty as a loyal subject.

Conspicuous among those who were with us to-day are deputations of chiefs of the Iroquois, who come from their reservations on the Grand River and the Bay of Quinté to join in this celebration. They were entitled to special greeting and honour. The alliance of the Six Nations strengthened the British power in its struggle with the French for the mastery of this continent and largely contributed to its triumph.

When the Revolution began, they refused to break the covenant chain and at the hazard of their homes and their hunting grounds in the State of New York, at the risk of the destruction of their ancient league of the Long House, they joined the forces of the King, led by Brant, whose grandson, chief of the Mohawks of the Bay of Quinté, is with us to-day. They served the Royal cause with unswerving fidelity and indomitable courage until the war was ended, and by its fortunes their great possessions were lost to them forever. The treaty of 1784 left them homeless and unprotected exiles, "To dig unable and to beg ashamed," but the British Government soon made them amends by large grants of territory on the Bay of Quinté and on the Grand River. While the sons may look back with regret to the days when their fathers held supremacy over the greater part of the continent, east of the Mississippi and north of the Gulf States, they may compare their position with that of such of their brethren as stood neutral or took part with the colonists and depended on their promises. They were driven before the white settlers, the Oneidas and the Cayugas were utterly dispossessed, and the Onondagas, Senecas and Tuscaroras were confined within the narrow limits of reservations that have been sacrificed piece-meal to the greed of land-jobbers till scarcely a foothold remains.

Three dim-eyed feeble old warriors who are now upon this platform, one of them a chief of high rank, have passed four score and ten, and were perhaps among the firstborn of those who took possession of their new home on the Grand River. The eldest of the three, Chief Johnson, whose Indian name is Sakayondagwaraton, or the "Dissolving Mist," is ninety three years of age. He held the important office of Speaker of the Council and his familiarity with the mnemonic language of the wampum records, by which all the transactions of the League are preserved, enabled him last year to perform a prodigious feat of memory in reading the belts several hours each day for three days in succession.

Mr. Horatio Hale, whose "Book of Rites" is a late and important contribution to Indian history says of him " His eloquence was noted even among a race of orators, I can well believe what I have heard of its effect, as, even in his old age, when an occasion has for a moment aroused his spirit, I have not known whether most to admire the nobleness and force of his sentiments and reasoning, or the grace and flowing ease, with which he delivered the stately periods of his sonorous language." All these veterans served with distinction and bravery in the war of 1812, and their spirit survives in the young men of the League, many of whom form companies in the volunteer battalions of Haldimand and Brant, and are praiseworthy for soldierly appearance, discipline and drill.

Our Iroquois are to be greatly commended for improvement in agriculture, for peaceful conduct, for absence of crime, and for the progress of education and growth of Christianity among them. They are the remnant of the

F

noblest type of the red races in North America. It is not easy to conceive the sacrifice of liberty which their present mode of life involves. They have conformed to it in a manner that justifies the highest expectations of their future achievements in civilized life, and in the cultivation of the arts of peace. The British Government has always kept faith with the Redmen. To the Iroquois they were bound by obligations that would never be forgotten.

It may be asked why we are met here? Why, after the lapse of a century every loyal man's heart beats with the same feeling that animated their ancestors who abandoned their homesteads and all their earthly possessions and made a painful and perilous journey through the wilderness in order to remain under the old flag? The brave loyalist brought with him his honest convictions and his love of constitutional liberty, and his children and his children's children, by their presence here to-day, testify to the endurance and strength of the principles they have inherited, and to their desire to bequeath them unimpaired to those who are to come after them.

An essential difference exists between the political instincts of the people of Canada and those who reside across the borders. Our neighbours have largely extended the bounds of constitutioual liberty, but he (Mr. Plumb) believed that in the end adhesion to the Crown had secured for this Dominion a still larger constitutional freedom than that of the United States in our parliamentary government and direct ministerial responsibility, which involved the immediate appeal to the people, at any moment when the Ministers of the Crown failed to be supported by a majority of the representatives of the people in the House of Commons. Many thoughtful citizens of the Republic clearly saw the advantages of our system, but it could not be adopted there without radical changes, which seem impossible. He hoped that, by God's grace, Canadians might preserve it unchanged, and that

CENTENNIAL CELEBRATION. 91

it would be sacredly cherished by future generations. He believed that it was in the best interests of themselves, and of the world at large that each of the two great peoples who inhabited North America should be permitted to evolve their own separate and several methods without let or hindrance. While Canadians did not intend to be grasping or meddlesome or aggressive, they would never be cringing, or servile or submissive. They intended to maintain their position here, and to defend British institutions on this continent in a manly, straightforward manner. They had the courage of their convictions, and would work out their salvation in their own way, and they desired that their great brotherhood of friends on the other side of the frontier should take the same course, and enjoy the same privilege.

He did not believe in Canadian independence. It was certain to result in annexation, and in neither independence or annexation could he see anything but disaster. We desired to cultivate the most cordial relations with our neighbours, to buy of them, to sell to them, to intermarry with them—he was an example of that, but they wanted to show that they proceeded on parallel lines, which could not meet and coalesce, however closely they might approximate. He scorned those who urged that there would be certain advantages in dollars and cents to be gained by a change in our political allegiance. He believed the sentiment of loyalty in Canadian bosoms could not be brought down to a money standard. There was no sordid taint in the blood of those who served the Crown in two great struggles. They have transmitted that blood to a large portion of the best men and women of this fair Province. Fealty to the monarch is deeply implanted in Canadian hearts, it cannot be weighed, measured or appraised, it is strengthened by a personal love for the Queen, and its foundations are respect for law and order, and its forms are an enduring basis on which our cherished institutions securely rest, and he believed it to be ineradicable.

It was not a principle which was incommensurate with progress and development as its opponents have asserted, and it seemed to harmonize especially with colonization, as might be seen in the vast extent through both hemispheres of a Greater Britain of powerful and prosperous colonies, acknowledging a willing and not a compulsory allegiance to the Throne, adhering to British traditions, and governed by British laws. It is less than three hundred years since the first permanent settlement of white men was made upon this continent. Sir Walter Raleigh, and his half-brother, Sir Humphrey Gilbert, under favour of Queen Elizabeth, fitted out an expedition for America in 1583, which failed disastrously, and Gilbert lost his life by shipwreck on the return voyage. Another expedition of Raleigh's landed at Roanoke, in Virginia, at the end of August, 1584, and had friendly intercourse with the natives. The next year a fleet of seven vessels under command of Raleigh's kinsman, the celebrated Sir Richard Grenville, immortalized in Tennyson's ballad of "The Revenge," settled a small body of colonists at Roanoke. After extreme hardship and suffering, they were taken back to England by Sir Francis Drake in 1586. The same year, fifty settlers were landed by Sir Richard Grenville, and a hundred and fifteen were sent out under Governor White in 1587, all of whom had perished or disappeared when White returned with supplies and recruits in 1590. At the death of Queen Elizabeth, there probably was not an Englishman on this continent. The colony of Jamestown was established three years afterwards in 1606, and the following year Champlain landed on the site of Quebec.

"From small beginnings we date our winnings."

We are celebrating to-day the Centennial Anniversary of the first settlement of the U. E. Loyalists in this Province. There were then, including those hardy pioneers, certainly not more than 20,000 white people within its borders, and in 1790 not more than 25,000, and yet, in 1791, the British Parliament passed the Act separating the Provinces of Upper and Lower Canada, by virtue of which Act Governor Simcoe, in the summer of 1792, ordered an election for the first Parliament of this Province, which met in September of that year, at a point near that on which we are standing, and almost within the sound of the voices of the speakers on this platform. In the eloquent address with which he opened the Session, he said that in consideration of the sacrifices the Loyalists of the Province had made for the Crown, and the evidence they had given of their capacity for self-government, the largest measure of liberty ever granted by the British Parliament to a colony had been given to Upper Canada. He said that the confidence reposed in the colonists had been well earned, and that he was sure that they would never betray the sacred trust.

Among the first acts of the Upper Canadian Parliament was the adoption of the laws of England and the abolition of Slavery. We have been told (said Mr. Plumb) that we are lagging behind our Republican neighbours in the race of development and improvement; but he thought we had reason to be proud of our advancement. He had said that in 1790 the population of Upper Canada did not exceed by the highest estimate 25,000. It was probably far short of that number. That of the State of New York was then 340,120. If the growth of this Province had been on the same ratio of that of the Empire State, which has the greatest sea-port on the continent, we should have had in 1881 a population of but 375,000. The State of New York in 1880 had a population of 5,082,871, or an increase of fifteen fold. This Province had a population in 1881 of 1,923,228, an increase of sixty-four fold.

It was a mistake to suppose that the political organization, under which we have attained this wonderful result, could be compared unfavourably with any which exists. We had a system under which the people, through their representatives, could at any moment compel the Ministry to change their course, to dissolve Parliament, or to resign their offices. The purse-strings being held by a responsible Government, if there was any mismanagement, the elected representative of the people could immediately interfere. All the Cabinet Ministers sat in Parliament, and those in the Commons, after their appointment to office, must go back to the people for re-election and confirmation. The Executive was not a four years tyranny, with a Cabinet that could not be reached except by impeachment. It was a rule that could be changed when it could no longer hold the public confidence, as was exemplified by the dissolution in the autumn of 1873 of the Parliament elected in 1872, it having been claimed by the majority that the Ministry no longer represented public sentiment. The public expenditure is controlled by the Commons. Every item can be fully examined and discussed in Committee of Supply. The estimates for the expenditure are before the Commons in detail from the beginning of the Session, and separate votes are taken on each item. We know nothing of a log-rolling, omnibus supply bill, forced through on the last night of the session when clamour and intimidation burk discussion. Not only has every item to be voted on in committee, but the vote must be afterwards affirmed by the concurrence of the majority, with the Speaker in the Chair.

There was, he said, no proscriptive or exclusive spirit here. Every man was welcome among us no matter of what nationality. There was room for all. The naturalization laws were liberal, the franchise was governed by a trifling property qualification, the main object of which was, through scrutinized registration, to prevent fraud. There was no Elective Judiciary dependent upon popular suffrage. The supremacy of Parliament could only be appealed from to the Throne itself.

It was a matter of pride to him to say that he was an exemplification of the liberality with which the Canadian people treated those of foreign birth who became subservient to the laws. He had been honoured by the people far beyond his deserts in this old borough of Niagara, and now he held from the Queen, one of the highest commissions that could be held by any subject in Canada—a seat for life in the Senate. He had endeavoured faithfully since he entered public life to promote the welfare of his adopted country, and he believed that he would never be found recreant to the trust placed upon him. It might be that there were people in Canada who were endeavouring to sow seeds of dissension between the loyal people and the throne. He said of such, that they could not do it, that while he was willing to discuss most matters with them, that that question was not one which could be entertained, because the hearts of the people were so securely fixed in their allegiance that they did not want any argument on the subject. He trusted that every man and woman before him would never forget that it was their bounden duty to transmit with religious care the noble principles which they inherited from their parents, and to let their children know that there was no uncertain sound in Canada in respect to adhesion to the British Crown. He would conclude by quoting Tennyson's words, which he trusted would sink deep into their hearts :

> Oh, save the one true seed of freedom sown
> Betwixt a people and their ancient throne,
> That sober freedom out of which there springs
> Our loyal passion for our temperate Kings ;
> For, saving that, ye help to save mankind,
> Till public wrong be crumbled into dust,
> And drill the raw world for the march of mind,
> Till crowds at length be sane and crowns be just.

LIEUTENANT-COLONEL GEORGE T. DENISON said :
The arrival of the U. E. Loyalists in this Province one hundred years ago, was an event which has had a lasting effect upon the history of this country, and was, to a

great extent, the cause of our being to-day a portion of the greatest Empire in the world. I need not say here on this historic ground, teeming with recollections of hard fought fights, or to the descendants of those who preserved our liberties in 1812, that to the U. E. Loyalists we owe the fact that we enjoy to-day the true liberty that is to be found under a limited monarchy. Those early settlers who came here one hundred years ago were the very best of the old colonists. They were the law-abiding, God-fearing classes, and this was remarkably shown by the fact that in the early years of this country crime was almost unkown, the settlers being an orderly, peaceable, well-behaved people. They gave a start to this country, the benefits of which we are continually feeling year after year. Ever since the province was established, the fringe of settlement, as it moved slowly into the forest has been almost free from crime, this, strange to say, has continued to this day, and is a remarkable feature of the settlement of the North-West.

How different it has been in the Republic to the south of us—lawlessness and crimes of violence have been rampant for one hundred years back, and life is now more unsafe in the United States than in any civilized or semi-civilized country in the world. It is not the climate that has done this, for in many sections it is very similar to our own. It is not the physical character of the country, for that also is alike. I attribute it entirely to the form of government.

The Republican form of government attracts all those who love license rather than liberty; while those who desire to see liberty given only to do what is right, are much more likely to seek a monarchical form of government. From this reason, while the American Republic has, as one of their own prominent men has well said, been for one hundred years the "cess-pool" of Europe, and has attracted the worst classes from the old world, thanks to our form of government, we have had the best and choicest settlers come to us. I do not pretend to say that immense numbers of estimable men have not gone to the States, but I will say that we have been singularly and fortunately free from getting the bad classes which have had such an evil influence upon the neighbouring country. One of their own writers in the *North American Review*, for this month, one of their own Magazines, laments the want of public honesty in the people and rulers of the United States, and entitles his article "Are We a Nation of Rascals?" It is painful to read the article, and to feel that any English speaking people could have so bad a record. Even in the treatment of the Indians, the contrast between us and our neighbours is as remarkably striking, and the reason is, that there is some honour with us in our treatment of them, while across the border they have been treated by the agents most unfairly, and by all classes most cruelly.

From British Columbia to Cape Breton we, Canadians, can proudly point to one of the largest and finest countries in the world, with as well-behaved and law-abiding a population as can be found anywhere, while south of us, the lawlessness is wide-spread, and the crimes of violence almost without number. Can any one say that the arrival of the U. E. Loyalists here in 1784 did not start this Province well, and that their maintenance of our freedom in 1812 did not preserve a system of government which is a great boon and blessing to us to-day.

Sometimes it is said by strangers and aliens amongst us, that we, Canadians, have no national sentiment, that if we were independent we would have more of it, and it is the fashion to speak loudly of the national spirit of the citizens of the United States. I take issue on this point, and on behalf of our people, I say that the pride of the native Canadian in his country is quite equal to the pride of the Yankee in his, while the willingness to defend it in case of need is far greater in the Canadian.

The strongest national sentiment that has yet been exhibited in the States was shown by the Southern people in their gallant struggle to destroy the Union. The national spirit shown by the Northerners where the bounties rose to about $1800 a man, where patriotism consisted in hiring a man to go and fight while the citizen took a contract to supply the soldiers, as has been well said by their celebrated divine Dr. Talmage, " With rice that was worm eaten, with biscuits that were mouldy, with garments that were shoddy, with meat that was rank, with horses that stumbled in the charge, and with tents that sifted the rain into the faces of the exhausted." The patriotism shown by 3,000 Yankee Militia almost in sight of this spot, in 1812, when they refused to cross at Queenston, to aid their comrades, whom our volunteers shortly afterwards cut to pieces under their eyes, was very different from the patriotism of the Canadians who crossed the river and captured Detroit, or those who fought at Chrysler's farm, or those who drove back Hampton at Chateauguay.

In 1812 every ablebodied man went to the frontier to fight leaving the old men, the boys and the women to till the fields. One might travel a day's journey in this Province during that war without meeting an ablebodied man, as they were all on the frontier. That kind of national sentiment was very different from that of the bountied mercenaries of the Northern armies, or of the three months' men, who left the army of the Potomac in 1861 on the eve of a great battle. What a striking contrast also was this latter incident to the calling out of 10,000 Canadian Militia at the time of the Fenian troubles of 1866. Only sufficient regiments were ordered out to make with their full strength 10,000. In less than eighteen hours after the order was issued the regiments were all at their posts, and the returns showed over 14,000 on parade. The extra 4,000 consisted of volunteers who had served their term and been discharged, but who, on the call of danger put on their old uniforms, rallied around the standards, and fell into the ranks without bounty of any kind, or other obligation save the national sentiment which is the characteristic of our people.

In the Oregon difficulty, in the Trent affair the feeling was admirable. Can we call to mind the conduct of the Nova Scotia Legislature at the time of the Maine boundary difficulty, when the members standing in their places, unanimously passed with three cheers for the Queen, a vote placing at the disposal of the Government every dollar of their revenue, and every ablebodied man in their province to be used in defence of their sister province of New Brunswick that was threatened with attack—can we call to mind the Canadians who came back to Canada from every state in the Union to aid in defending her from the Fenians, without feeling that we have in our people a strong national sentiment?

Canada has never had to call upon her sons to defend her, that they have not cheerfully responded to the call, and there is no doubt that we Canadians have a national sentiment. We have a pride in our country and a confidence in it and in its future. Wanderers and Bohemians, strangers and tramps may, because we are not traitors to our government and our country, say that we have no national sentiment; they may not see, or feel or appreciate the patriotic feeling of the Canadians; but we Canadians know that it is there. The militia force is one proof of it, a finger post to point out to all that we intend to be a free people on this continent, and that our liberties can only be taken from us after a desperate struggle. This loyalty of Canadians to Canada makes them loyal to the Queen, because she is the embodiment of the principles of the government of our country, not because she is the Queen of England, but because she is the Queen of Canada, and they are loyal to our monarchical institutions, because they feel that true patriotism to Canada lies in that direction.

We absolutely govern ourselves, the tie which binds us to England is one in which all the advantages are on our side. There is nothing in it that presses on any of our people, and there is no matter of detail in our system that we have not the power of regulating for ourselves. Unfortunately, however, there are a few who are not satisfied, and who agitate for change for the sake of agitating. This is, and always has been, a difficulty with every form of government in all ages. No form of government could possibly be devised in which there would be no malcontents, no conspirators, no agitators. The grandest poem in our language describes a rebellion against Heaven itself, and in all countries, and in all governments, there have been agitators of the same type. Rome, a republic with the highest national sentiment, had in it the elements of discord in the broken down classes, who rallied around Cataline and formed the famous conspiracy which bears his name; and to-day in most countries the same type of agitators and malcontents abandon useful labour to conspire against lawful authority. In Russia they have the Nihilists, in Germany the Socialists, in France the Communists, in Ireland the Fenians, in England the Dynamiters, in the United States they have all these classes mixed up together, and in addition they have their politicians, while in Canada we have only a few Independence writers, the weakest and most harmless of all these troublesome classes.

These wanderers and Bohemians, with the charming impudence of the three tailors of Tooley Street, speak of themselves as the people of Canada. It is the fashion of men of their type always to talk loudly of the people, as if they were the people. But who are the people? The people of this country are the farmers who own the soil, who have cleared the fields, who till them, and who produce the food that feeds us. The people of Canada are the workers who work in her factories, who carry on her trade, who sail her ships, and spread her commerce,—the artizans who build her cities and work in them. These are the people of Canada, not the few agitators who serve no good purpose, and whose absence would be a relief, if they went back to the neighbouring Republic, from which many of them have drifted in to us. The real Canadians are a unit against change in our Constitution. The farmers do not want it—the Militia, representing all shades of political and religious feeling, are sworn to be faithful and bear true allegiance to Her Majesty, and they will stand by the Constitution to the last. The Roman Catholic church is loyal to the core, for it knows that under our government we have absolute religious freedom. The Orange order owes its existence to a desire to maintain the British Constitution. The English, Irish, and Scotch, who have come here to settle, have come here in preference to the States, because they desired to remain under the old flag, and under the system of government of their fathers. They are true as steel to the Constitution, and are U. E. Loyalists at heart. Both political parties are loyal. There is no class that is not loyal. The vast majority of the newspaper press are loyal to Canada and its institutions, and have no sympathy with the black sheep that hang on the skirts of their profession, any more than the Medical profession have for the empirics and quacks that cling to them, or the lawyers for the pettifoggers who bring discredit upon theirs.

If we were independent to-morrow we would be more dependent upon the United States than we are to-day upon England. Annexation would only be avoided, if at all, by a tremendous struggle and enormous sacrifices, and if annexed, where would our independence be ? Gone for ever ! and we would be governed by the wire-pullers of the factions at Washington, our manufactures sacrificed to the interests of New England, and our own affairs administered by carpet-baggers. The paltry few who argue independence cannot foresee what the result would be, or if they do, having no stake in the country, they do not care. They might ruin us politically and morally and commercially, and then wander off to some other country, and be as well off as they ever were or ever will be.

Why should we dismember the Empire? When the German people have united to make a great State : when the Italians have been consolidated into a powerful kingdom, are the British to divide and weaken? Are the Anglo-Saxons to be the only race to do this? and are we Canadians, without reason or motive, to be the cause? I don't call the United States an Anglo-Saxon community now. Once it was, but since the revolution it has been the dumping ground of Europe, and they are forming a community there entirely different in its characteristics from ours.

I have watched the writings of these independence men, and have at last discovered what their real grievance is, and it is that there are certain people who hold public offices. They do not object to there being public offices, but the real trouble is that they do not hold these offices themselves. Envy and jealousy is at the bottom of all their patriotism. They advocate elective offices. They forget that the people indirectly make the appointments, for they elect representatives who hold office at their will, and who are responsible to them for all they do. They agitate for the election to nearly all public offices by the popular vote as in the States, where the system has produced an office-holding class, where strict integrity is the exception, and where peculation is the rule. These agitators and Bohemians wish to become themselves an office-holding class of this Yankee type. They think that by agitating for a change, by creating anarchy and confusion, they might temporarily come to the top. They know that when the pot is boiling the dregs are forced upwards, but they forget that when the pot stops boiling the dregs go to the bottom. But there is no reason why we should be governed by strangers or tramps, and the people of this country, who have made it what it is, intend to govern it their own way.

The worst feature of this agitation is, that a revolution such as these malcontents ask for, can only be brought about by bloodshed. I cannot call to mind an instance of a revolution being carried out without bloodshed. In fact no system of government recognizes any constitutional method of destroying its fundamental principles. The United States could not establish a despotism under their constitution except by a revolution. The Southern States seceded, not constitutionally, but by conventions of the people in the same way in which their constitution was originally formed, and it was an attempted revolution, and was put down by force of arms. Every attempt from without, or within, in the past to change our system of government has been put down by bloodshed. In fact, the fundamental principle of our government, the Monarchy, cannot be changed constitutionally. The members of Parliament before they can vote, must swear to be faithful to the constitution, and would be foresworn perjurers if they afterward betrayed their country. For this reason I appealed on a former occasion to the good feeling and honesty of the independence agitators, as to whether it was fair or right in them to agitate for a change of government, that can only be brought about by war. And I ask you here again to-day, if it is fair or right for these Bohemians to try to create trouble among a peaceful, happy and contented people, who have no grievances that they cannot easily remedy themselves, when they can so readily find in the neighbouring country the republican institutions they admire? When I say this I say it in a kindly spirit for I would be the last to prevent them writing and talking and advocating their views so long as they do not break out into open treason. Thank God this is a free country, where people can hold what opinions they like and express them freely, so they may go on if they wish and write their little editorials, and air their little theories, and abuse all who disagree with them, it pleases them and hurts no one, and the very freedom that enables them to do this is what makes our institutions so stable and these men so powerless for evil.

It would not be worth while to notice this movement at all, were it not that we are celebrating the centennial of the settlement of this country, on principles diametrically opposed to those advocated now by these few, and under which we have flourished, and increased, and enjoyed so many advantages for one hundred years. I hope that at the next centennial our descendants may have as many causes of congratulation, and as many blessings for which to be thankful as we have, and that the agitators of their day may be as weak and uninfluential, and as powerless as ours are to-day. If so about once every one hundred years will be often enough for our side of the case to be laid down.

WILLIAM KIRBY ESQ., of Niagara, said " Mr. Chairman, Ladies and Gentlemen. Upon an occasion like this the heart as well as the intellect is stirred up with deep emotions. All that is noble, all that is patriotic in us, the pride we have in the loyal and indomitable men who founded Upper Canada, afford a theme that ought to warm the coldest and make the dullest man eloquent in their praise. The United Empire Loyalists of America only need the truth to be told of them, to make them stand out prominently upon the page of history as ranking with the noblest of our race in any land.

I am glad and proud of the fact that celebrations similar to this have already been held in Toronto and the Bay of Quinté, yet we of the Niagara district did not think that those were enough. This spot consecrated by so many honourable memories of the fathers and defenders of our country, is after all the true historical and proper place for the centennial celebration of the settlement of Upper Canada. Here was the principal landing place of the expatriated loyalists, here came the loyal fighting men of the Revolutionary War, and here they planted

CENTENNIAL CELEBRATION. 105

their war torn but glorious flag and said to the waves of revolution : " Come not here ! this is our Canadian home, and our portion of the British Empire for ever ! "

When I look upon the multitude of faces before me, and around me, and recognize, as I do, so many of them as belonging to both of the great political parties which contend for the administration of our goverment; when I see these usually bitter partizans of both sides of politics, laying aside, upon an occasion like this, their party strife and uniting as brothers and true Canadians, to show their common pride in the unity of the Empire, and to pay honour to the memories of the U. E. Loyalists, who have left us this great country as our common heritage—when I see this, I rejoice to know that above all our party noise and confusion, there exists a great firmament where peace reigns, where a common sentiment of Canadian loyalty and patriotism brings us all into accord, and shows that Canadians of all creeds and parties can unite to defend our country in danger ; and maintain, as our forefathers did, the unity of the Empire to which we belong.

This meeting is a proof that, after the lapse of a hundred years, the spirit which animated the U. E. Loyalists is still alive, slumbering perhaps, in quiet leonine strength in the hearts of our people, but ready to wake up as of old, whenever called upon. Superficial onlookers and frivolous scribes may say, that the old spirit is no longer a living principle in us. I say that they who make that assertion know nothing of the U. E. Loyalist stock of this country, and this great loyal meeting is a striking disproof of the base charge.

Who, it may be asked, were those U. E. Loyalists whom we praise so highly, and whose memory we are celebrating to-day ?

I reply, they were that vast number of loyal, law-abiding men, who in the American revolution, formed fully one half of the people of the thirteen colonies, when

G

mainly through the machinations and aid of France, those colonies were led into the great rebellion against the Empire.

They were, if I may use the AMERICAN language, which we all understand very well, the party of *Union* in 1776. as opposed to the party of *Secession* of that time. They were the men who were loyal to the crown, and to the political unity of the English speaking race. They owed a national allegiance as born British subjects to the Crown and Empire, and felt bound by every tie of duty, honour and religion, to resist rebellion, and preserve intact the unity of the Empire to which they belonged. The crime of dividing the English race was none of theirs!

The great civil war which broke out in the United States twenty-three years ago, has to the American mind greatly modified the meaning of the word—loyalty. Instead of being used in a bad and vituperative sense as it had been prior to their own late rebellion, loyalty has since then been discovered to be one of the cardinal virtues, while *rebellion* that was previously looked upon as an honourable thing in itself, has come to be denounced as the blackest of crimes! especially against themselves.

I will read an extract from the letter of a distinguished American General with reference to this loyal celebration of ours. He says:

"I wish I could be there to unite with you in sympathy and feeling, as I do here. Success to the loyal blood! May its memories be ever green, and the recollection of its unparalleled and unrewarded devotion, bravery and sacrifice endure and wax stronger with time! We loyalists lost the game, but we did not in the slightest degree tarnish our record of honour."

I may mention that the general who writes this, is himself a descendant of a distinguished Loyalist family of the old Province of New York,

The declaration of Independence, which passed by a majority of one only, came like a thunder clap upon the people of the colonies. Up to that day, the most unequivocal public expressions of loyalty to the King and Empire had been made, and reiterated by the general Congress as by all the provincial congresses in the colonies. Nay, long after fighting began nothing but a redress of grievances was professed to be demanded. The army which besieged Boston, under Washington, and that which invaded Canada, under Arnold and Montgomery, fought under British colours. It was known that outside of New England a majority of the people were opposed to secession, and that it was necessary to lead them by degrees, and blindfold, as it were, into the pit of revolution —and so it was done.

It is unnecessary for me to discuss, in your presence, the political issues of the revolution. We are all of one mind on that subject. We know that the loyalists were right in the course they pursued, and that for us is enough.

The revolution was not necessary for the redress of such theoretical grievances as formed the subject of differences with the mother country. The Stamp Act, the greatest offence of all, was never put in force, and was promptly repealed in compliance with the general remonstrance against it. The other minor Acts—of no account in themselves, might likewise have been left to be repealed, and the old harmony restored, had not pride and temper on both sides, taken the place of reason and moderation —and rendered a good understanding impossible.

The loyalists of America felt all this, and refused to be hurried into the crime of rebellion; and when the Declaration of Independence was launched upon the country —they denied the truth of the indictments it contained against the King and the people of Great Britain—while the very offensive language in which it was couched, added fuel to their resentment, and perpetuates the bitterness of it to this day.

Their opposition to the revolution was met by the enactment of the most vindictive penal laws against men, whose only offence was a determination to keep their allegiance, and abide by the flag under which they were born. The persons of the loyalists were seized and imprisoned—their property—and in property they were the wealthiest men in the community—was everywhere confiscated—persecutions begat fierce retaliations. Swords were drawn, and the civil war began which devastated America for eight years—and only ended when the powers of France, Spain and Holland intervened, and by their help the thirteen colonies were severed from the Empire.

An able and candid American author has written:—" The loyalists had position and property, the Indians had fertile lands; both were coveted, and both were wrenched from their rightful possessors."

The atrocious penal laws, the proscriptions, the confiscations, and the personal outrages to which aged and respectable loyalists were subjected, even in the presence and with the sanction of some of the highest heads of the rebellion, has left a deep stain upon " the course that was pursued" in establishing the revolution. They added bitterness and animosity to the struggle, for they called forth keen reprisals, and sent into the royal ranks upwards of 25,000 native Americans; and it is a fact that, the continental army, which was largely made up of the foreign element and needy emigrants, had fewer Americans in it than the Royal army. But I need not recount the events of the war.

It is estimated that at the close of the war, a hundred thousand loyalist Americans left the Port of New York alone. The world had not seen such a flight of the best elements of the population of any country, since the exile of the Huguenots from France over a century before. The fugitive loyalists who left their native country were dispersed all over the Empire—many went to Great Bri-

CENTENNIAL CELEBRATION. 109

tain, many to the West Indies, many to the wilds of New Brunswick and Nova Scotia, and thousands came to Canada. Upwards of ten thousand of the best people of New York and Pennsylvania found their way through the wilderness to the very place where we stand, and amid privations, toils and sufferings—the story of which is not yet forgotten—here set up their new homes in the forest and courageously and cheerfully started life anew, and began that career of honour and felicity which is our inheritance in Canada to this day—may it last for ever!

As an instance of the privations endured in this country, which was at that time wholly uncultivated, I will read an original, unpublished letter of the period from General Haldimand to Colonel Claus, Indian Superintendent, at Niagara, in reference to supplies of food needed here for the Indians. General Haldimand writes in May, 1780, "they should consider the trouble, expense and time it takes to transport provisions not only to Niagara but all the way to Detroit and Michilimacinac. Every ounce of provisions, they and we have been living upon for these eighteen months past, was brought from England."

When we reflect upon these words, and consider the length of the ocean voyage to Quebec, and the difficulty and time it required to transport all those provisions in canoes and boats from Quebec to the upper country, all the way to Detroit and Michilimacinac, we may form an idea of the scarcity and suffering that must have prevailed in this wild country, at that time, when the sudden influx of so many people took place.

But Providence had great ends in view, when it settled Canada with men of such heroic strain, and of the purest blood of America.

It has been cast as a reproach upon the U. E. Loyalists, that they were largely the gentry, and not the populace of American society. They formed undoubtedly the best and wealthiest class in the old colonies. But all classes were present among them, judges, lawyers, legislators, clergymen, soldiers, merchants, yeomen and handicraftmen--all filled the ranks of that great emigration. Christian men of all the churches were there, but not one infidel of the type of that arch traitor Tom Paine! He belonged emphatically to the Rebellion! The Loyalists came with their Penates and household gods, their bibles, the sacred communion vessels of their altars, the tables of the ten commandments from the chancels of their churches, these sacred objects they brought with them out of their abandoned temples.

It seemed as if the voice of Christ was heard by them, as he spake to his disciples upon that last day at Jerusalem, "Arise! let us go hence!" And these ten commandments they set up anew in the rude churches which they built to the worship of God in Canada.

The whole congregation of Trinity Church, New York, with their venerable Rector at their head, transported themselves to St. John, New Brunswick, and there set up the old Tables of the Commandments, and the royal arms that had previously adorned their native church in the City of New York. Upon the table beside me, stands one of the grand silver communion flagons and plates given by Queen Anne to the Mohawk Christians in 1711. They were brought here during the revolution, and are still used by the loyal Mohawks of the Bay of Quinté, of whom Chief Hill, a great grandson of the renowned Captain Joseph Brant, sits here in your presence to-day, the last hereditary chief of that great tribe.

There is an immense significance in the fact, Mr. Chairman, and it is worthy of our deep study, that the U. E. Loyalists, leaving all other possessions behind them, brought with them the ten commandments, the Bible, and the sacred vessels of the communion, as the most precious relics of their old homes in the thirteen colonies. What was left to fill the blank of that great religious and loyal exodus American history is now daily recording, and it is a point I need not dwell upon; but discerning men can see the blank places left by the removal of those sacred emblems from that country.

Here came the great body of the adherents of the Church of England, mainly under the lead of that good man, the Rev. Dr. John Stewart, who founded the first Episcopal churches in Upper Canada.

Here came also the pious and zealous John Ashbury, and that godly woman, Barbara Heck, who, after founding Methodism in the City of New York, led a band of loyal Methodists to the Bay of Quinté, and there laid the foundation of the Methodist church in Canada. The old Wesleyans, like their founder, John Wesley, were ever loyal to king and country, and, perhaps, because they were Methodists, were also U. E. Loyalists, when the day of trial came that proved the spirit of men to the uttermost, whether they were faithful, or whether they were untrue, to the sacred precept of Scripture—" Fear God and honour the king."

Here came also a numerous and a gallant band of loyal Roman Catholics, led by their priests, the MacDonalds, from North Carolina and other Southern States, Scottish Highlanders, for the most part, who settled our district of Glengarry, and formed the nucleus of that Highland community, so distinguished for its loyalty and valour in the subsequent history of Upper Canada.

Here, too, somewhat later, came a great number of the peaceful Quakers and Menonists, of Pennsylvania. The fidelity of the Quakers to their lawful government, drew upon them a cruel persecution from the rebels, who stained their record by trying for high treason, and hanging two of the most respectable Quaker gentlemen of Philadelphia, guilty of no offence in the world but loyal adherence to their king and country. This persecution drove some of the Quakers into the army, and the Quaker ancestors of a gentleman present on this platform, were among the hardest fighters in our army during the revolutionary war.

The Quakers bore with characteristic patience the persecution of their enemies, but they flocked into Canada after the peace, to enjoy the protection of English law, and live in allegiance to their native sovereign.

And here, too, came, as I am forcibly reminded by the presence before me of the thirty chiefs of the renowned Six Nations, the successors of a people once the mightiest on this continent. Very different from the Quakers in all respects except in their invincible loyalty, were the native warlike tribes of Central New York, which had been their home and heritage from the earliest times. The Six Nations were largely Christianized and civilized at the outbreak of the revolution. Their villages, castles, cornfields, orchards and pastures abounding in cattle, formed a long line of settlement from the Hudson to the Genessee.

Congress, which so loudly in public denounced the interference of the Indians in the war, had at the very inception of hostilities, sent special commissioners to engage them on their side against the king. A great war belt, with a red axe worked in the middle of it, was presented by the commissioners to the Six Nations, who rejected it with contempt, and instead took up arms to support the king, and under their great chiefs Brant, and John Deseronto, whose descendants are here present to-day, and the distingished Seneca Chief Sakoyenwaraton, "Vanishing Smoke," my friend, Chief Hill, tells me it means, fought bravely throughout the war in maintenance of the old treaties, solemnly made with the king.

Their grand and beautiful country was destroyed and confiscated. The Six Nations were the first who took up the path of exile and settled in Upper Canada—where they form to-day a thriving, loyal, and happy people, proud of the gallant deeds of their fore-fathers, and proud of their loyalty and attachment to the Empire. The great Union Jack, which they have brought with them from the Grand River, has been their rallying flag for almost two hundred years.

Such were the sort of men whose memories we are met to celebrate to-day. A nobler ancestry than the U. E. Loyalists of America no country on earth can boast of. In war they proved themselves to be of the truest mettle. In peace, industrious, law-abiding and honourable—and, it may be recorded, that while during the course of the revolutionary struggle, not a few of the eminent men of, the rebellion drew off and returned to their allegiance. It cannot be recorded, that a single U. E. Loyalist, either for family, for property, or any consideration whatever, went over to the enemy, or returned to them after the war.

The advent of the Pilgrim Fathers at Plymouth, so praised in prose and verse, was a holiday excursion compared with the arrival of the ten thousand expatriated Loyalists who landed at Niagara in 1783-4, a few stone throws only from where we stand. The Pilgrim Fathers, a few in number—came to America leisurely, bringing with them all their goods and the price of all their possessions, at peace and secure under charters, granted by their Sovereign. The U. E. Loyalists, unlike them, came bleeding with the wounds of seven years of war, stripped of every earthly possession, and exiled from their native land. This country was then a savage region of forests and swamps. The trees had to be cut down before a seed could be dropped in the ground, and in fact for two years the brave, suffering exiles had to be fed from the military stores of Fort Niagara, before they were in any condition to support their devoted wives and children.

History, written by party prejudice and blind admiration of mere success as a test of right, has pleased itself by maligning the character and principles of the U. E. Loyalists. But the course they pursued, after their settlement in Canada, was honourable to their humanity, wisdom and generosity. In less than seven years after their arrival in this country they established, with the aid and under the direction of that great statesman and soldier, Governor Simcoe, a Constitution and Goverment for Upper Canada which, they were proud to say, was the very image and transcript of that of Great Britain, and was the model of our Dominion Constitution of to-day.

The first Parliament of this Province met in September, 1792, on the spot now covered by the ruined mounds of Fort George, which we see before us ; and there the first representatives of the people of Upper Canada, few in number, but worthy and capable of sharing in the deliberations of any assembly in the world ; met, and established the old English principles of law, order, and government in this country.

Contrast their acts with that of the Constitutional Congress of the United States, which had established their new republican system of government in that country, only four years before !

The States which had rebelled in the name of Liberty and had declared all men to be free and equal, did, in their new constitution, solemnly sanction the institution of human slavery, and perpetuate it, seemingly, for ever ! While the U. E. Loyalists of Upper Canada, in their first parliament, and on this spot, made sacred by that Act of eternal justice, did without a dissenting voice, and without a claim for compensation, declare slavery to be for ever abolished in this Province ! All honour to the true freemen and their noble governor Simcoe, who won for Canada the glory of being the first country in the world which abolished slavery by an Act of the Legislature !— and they not only set free their slaves, but placed them on a civil and political equality with themselves. We are not a boastful people, or we might justly boast of having taken the lead of all the world in that great act of justice to humanity. So far was Upper Canada in advance of all other people at that time, on this momentous question.

This fact strikes us more forcibly, when we recollect, that England herself did not abolish slavery in her Colonies until 1838, while the United States only did so twenty years ago, and that at the cost of the most frightful and destructive civil war on record; and Spain, another of the liberators of America, has not freed her slaves to this day!

These acts prove better than any words, the noble and generous character of the men who founded this Province. The maintenance of the Imperial connection, of the "Unity of the Empire," as we call it in our Canadian speech, was the moving principle of duty in the hearts of our forefathers. Let it be so in ours also, now and for ever.

If evil days should ever befall us, and we have no right to suppose that, as a people, we shall always be safe from the storms of fate, or the malice of enemies, internal or external, and you Indians will understand me if I say, that, "bad birds are now singing here and there in the trees." I say, if times of trouble and adversity should ever come upon this fair land, we have the noblest example in the deeds and principles of our forefathers, how to meet them. And I have perfect faith in you, brother Canadians, that you, like them, will be found equal to every demand upon your honour and loyalty, in a word your duty.

I am proud, Mr. Chairman, to see so many of the U. E. Loyalist ladies of our district present, and wearing upon their breasts the honoured loyal badges of this Centennial celebration. But, the time never was—and I believe never will be—when, be our men loyal and patriotic as they will, the women of Ontario will not outshine them in ardent love to their Queen and Country! Among them are preserved the honourable traditions of our people, and so long as they teach them to their sons and daughters, Canada will stand in honour for ever, as the right arm of the British Empire.

I will conclude, Mr. Chairman by repeating a few words spoken by me on another occasion:

All honour to the Loyalists! The brave self sacrificing exertions of these men in defence of the unity of the Empire, brought ruin upon themselves in their old homes, but was the making of Canada by settling it with men of such chosen virtue. If, as a Puritan divine once boasted, "England was winnowed of her *choice* grain for the sowing of America." We can truly say that "America was reaped and winnowed afresh at the Revolution, and its very *choicest* men selected by Providence for the peopling of this Dominion! By the loss of these Loyalists the United States were drained of their noblest elements, and suffered a moral loss, which they have never made up for to this day.

Some of the best and wisest men in the United States have brushed aside the covering of prejudice and obloquy cast over the memories of the U. E. Loyalists in popular American history, and boldly express their admiration for the courage and devotion to high principles which actuated them. Truth will have its revenge in justice at last! And I venture to say that in another century America will be more proud of her exiled Loyalists than of the vaunted patriots who banished and despoiled them!

CHIEF HILL of the Mohawks, Bay of Quinté, great grandson of the late Captain Joseph Brant, said: Mr. Chairman, I did not expect to be asked to address an audience like this, but since you have honoured me, I must not shirk the call.

We are here to celebrate the centennial of the one hundredth anniversary of the landing upon Canadian soil of our forefathers, whites and Indians. Red and white fought side by side in the Revolutionary war. The blood of the red man and that of his white brother mixed together to uphold the Loyalists' cause. My ancestors and yours, my white friends, left all their property to come here, where they could hoist the British flag. They sacrificed all to hew out of the Canadian bush new homes.

My great grandfather, the late Captain Joseph Brant, was one of Britain's strongest allies a hundred years ago and in the late American war the white and red blood was again spilled together—some of it on the very ground on which we stand—for the cause of Britain. Now after a hundred years of friendship and many changes, we are still brothers, and I feel happy, as the descendant of one who proved himself a loyal man, to meet so many white Loyalists.

We have been well treated by the British Government, and, should occasion demand, Indians throughout Canada are ready to do as our forefathers did—fight for the dear old flag we love so well.

CHIEF A. G. SMITH said :

Mr. Chairman, Ladies and Gentlemen,—I did not come to make a speech, and consequently am not prepared to do so. But as I have been so honoured as to be called upon to address you, I shall endeavour to do so in a few words. I shall commence by saying that I am very much pleased to see such a large gathering on this very important occasion, and I am also very much gratified in being able to tell you that there is a very large representation of my people, the Six Nation Indians, of Grand River, who are to-day as anxious to be identified with the descendants of the U. E. Loyalists of Canada, as their forefathers were one hundred years ago. And I am gratified in being able to stand before you to-day, to speak to you on behalf of my people, and to remind you that the Six Nation Indians have always been, and are still ready and willing to come to your assistance in every undertaking which is calculated to be for the good or honour of our common country.

It will scarcely be necessary for me to remind you of the historical fact that the Six Nations did not hesitate to leave their beautiful home in the Valley of the Mohawk, in the State of New York; and to sacrifice everything that was dear to them, in order to maintain the honour of the British flag, by fighting side by side with those brave U. E. Loyalists, who counted not their lives dear, so that they might win for their posterity a name, and the many blessings which we, their descendants, enjoy as fruits of the unswerving allegiance of the U. E. Loyalists and the Six Nation Indians to the British Crown. And, although the time may forever have gone by, when the tomahawks of the Six Nations were needed to assist in maintaining the honour and dignity of the British Crown in this Dominion, yet you can not but admit that their assistance and co-operation is still desirable, though in another direction, namely, in doing what they can to aid the loyal and peaceable citizens of this fair Dominion in developing it into a great and prosperous country, and of which I am proud as chief, and one of the many representatives of my people among you to-day, to be able to say they are willing and are endeavouring so to do. And that our relations with the government of the country have always been attended with the happiest results ; and that the government of Canada has in general kept faith with us, and, therefore, we have very few reasons to complain in that respect.

But there is one thing that I must not omit to mention, it is a sad circumstance which has not only grieved me, but one and all of the many of my people, who are among you to-day, when in going about the historic plains of Niagara to visit, as we thought, the different places of interest, we came to Fort Messissauga, and lo! we could scarcely believe our own eyes, but when we came to realize that what we beheld was a melancholy fact, that the old fort was allowed to go to rack and ruin, by the sons of the U. E. Loyalists, we were not only grieved, but we blushed for the descendants of the U. E, Loyalists, and for every true Canadian for allowing the dear old historical landmarks to become a heap of rubbish. Why, the Six Nations would set them an example in that respect. A church, though a frame one, that was built for them a hundred years ago, is to-day in good repair, although they have a good brick one for present use. A set of communion plate that was given by the good Queen Anne, is to-day in a perfect state of preservation; a church bell, Bible and other historical relics equally as old, are almost religiously venerated and taken care of. And we are of opinion that every true and loyal Canadian, and the government itself, should see to it that these historical landmarks be restored, and kept in repair as monuments to the memory of those who were not only willing to undergo hardships, but to die, if necessary, in defending their country.

In conclusion, I desire to say that I am glad that the time seems to have arrived when the Indian is looked upon as being as capable of being educated. and to have his mind cultivated, when his disadvantages are taken into consideration, as any other race of people, and we have undeniable proofs of the same from the fact of our having already quite a number in the different learned professions, as well as many good mechanics and farmers. And, on the whole, the Indians are prospering under the good government in which they live, and I firmly believe, that the day is not far distant, when the Indians will be able to take their stand among the whites on equal footing, when I am quite certain that the white population of the Dominion will be forced by their sense of justice to accord the Indian that right which is their just due, namely, a representation on the floor of the House of Commons by one of their own people, who ought to know what is best for his people better than any one else. And now with these few remarks I beg to be allowed to resume my seat, thanking you, Mr. Chairman, and all for your attention.

JAMES HISCOTT, ESQ., Warden of the County of Lincoln, said :—

Mr. Chairman, Ladies and Gentlemen.—It almost seems presumptious in me saying anything, having heard so many eloquent speakers. But I would not deserve the name of a Canadian, nor would I deserve to represent the County of Lincoln, as its warden, if I did not try to do all honour to the memory of the noble men and women, who sacrificed so much for their country, and who calmly endured hunger, destitution and all the privations of a howling wilderness for the sake of their country. Not only did they give their fortunes and homes, but in many cases their lives, for the love and honour of their country. The memory of these people, we are commemorating to-day, whose last resting place of many is in this and the adjoining county, and whose descendants fought so nobly in the war of 1812, and, had it not been for their bravery, Canada would not be a part of that great Empire, which we all love so well.

MR. WM. HAMILTON MERRITT, was next called upon, and said:—

Here, in this historic town, in the old County of Lincoln, represented so long a time by his grandfather, he would indeed be unworthy of the heritage of the name he bore, did he not testify to the same loyalty still existing in his family, as was manifested by his forefathers in fighting for Canada.

He was confident that this feeling of loyalty to Canada, and therefore at this present, to the Crown, existed as a strong under-current through the whole Dominion. He would mention an instance which took place in a section of the country, where he had resided a great deal during the past few years, as a case in point. It occurred on the Grand River, in the County of Haldimand, near to where the descendants of our brave allies—the Six Nation Indians—come from, and who, to-day, are so well represented at this gathering. At a convention of one of our great parties in 1882, called to nominate a candidate to represent it, when the name of a candidate for nomination, who was not personally well known to many of the delegates, was brought before the convention, one of the leading men in the county rose and said: " Before a nomination could be made unanimous in this convention, they must first know the feelings of the candidate on British Connection." His answer was, that, "If severance from the British Empire took place, and there followed the inevitable annexation to the United States, his inclinations would lead him to sell all that he possessed in this his native land, and leave it for ever." The reply satisfied the convention. This spirit of loyalty as shown there, in Haldimand, Mr. Merritt was confident not only existed strongly in that county, but would be found to be the key-note of the national feelings in every county in Canada.

Being of a younger generation than the previous speakers, he believed he could vouch for by far the largest number of the young men of Canada, when he said the sentiments of loyalty that had been so ably expressed by the Lieutenant-Governor, Col. George T. Denison and Senator Plumb, would sink deep into their hearts and bear fruit of a sterling quality, and that, in spite of the "Bohemian" agitation in the press, the young men of Canada would be found the strongest advocates and warmest supporters of the grand scheme of Federation, and that following in the footsteps of their fathers, they would be found ready, if unfortunately it were ever necessary, to shed their blood for the defence and liberty of their country.

MAYOR GARRETT, of Niagara, I. P. Willson, of Welland, Mr. Kilburn, reeve of Beamsville, Lieut.-Col. Denison, D.A.G., and other gentlemen delivered brief addresses.

Five aged and principal chiefs of the Cayuga and Onondaga tribes, dressed in the ancient costume of the Iroquois, representing the still pagan portion of the Six Nations, then came forward, led by the venerable Captain Buck, head chief of the Onondagas, and Fire keeper of the Confederacy, and performed a ceremonial war dance, semi-religious in its character, expressive of the gladness of the Six Nations in taking part in this U. E. Loyalist Centennial.

H

The proceedings then closed with three hearty cheers for the Queen.

The following extract from "The Hungry Year," a poem by William Kirby of Niagara, was republished in connection with the Centennial.

THE U. E. LOYALISTS.

THE war was over, seven red years of blood
Had scourged the land from mountain top to sea ;
(So long it took to rend the mighty frame
Of England's empire in the western world)
Rebellion won at last, and they who loved
The cause that had lost, and kept their faith
To England's crown, and scorned an alien name,
Passed into exile, leaving all behind
Except their honour, and the conscious pride
Of duty done to country and to king.

Broad lands, ancestral homes, the gathered wealth
Of patient toil and self-denying years,
Were confiscate and lost ; for they had been
The salt and savour of the land ; trained up
In honour, loyalty, and fear of God.
The wine upon the lees, decanted, when
They left their native soil with sword belts drawn
The tighter ; while the women only wept
At thought of old firesides no longer theirs,
At household treasures reft, and all the land
Upset, and ruled by rebels to the king.

Not drooping like poor fugitives they came
In exodus to our Canadian wilds,
But full of heart and hope, with heads erect
And fearless eyes victorious in defeat.
With thousand toils they forced their devious way
Through the great wilderness of silent woods,
That gloomed o'er lake and stream, till higher rose
The northern star above the broad domain
Of half a continent, still theirs to hold,
Defend and keep for ever as their own,
Their own and England's to the end of time.

The virgin forests, carpeted with leaves
Of many autumns fallen, crisp and sear,
Put on their woodland state ; while overhead
Green seas of foliage roared a welcome home
To the proud exiles, who for empire fought
And kept, though losing much, this northern land
A refuge and defence for all who love
The broader freedom of a commonwealth
That wears upon its head a kingly crown.

Our great Canadian woods of mighty trees,
Proud oaks and pines that grew for centuries,
King's gifts upon the exiles were bestowed.
Ten thousand homes were planted ; and each one
With axe, and fire, and mutual help made war
Against the wilderness and smote it down.
Into the opened glades, unlit before
Since forests grew and rivers ran, there leaped
The sun's bright rays, creative light and heat,
Waking to life the buried seeds that slept,
Since time's beginning, in the earth's dark womb.

The tender grass sprang up, no man knew how,
The daisies eyes unclosed, wild strawberries
Lay white as hoar frost on the slopes, and sweet
The violets perfumed the evening air,
The nodding clover grew up everywhere,
The trailing rasp, the trefoil's yellow cup
Sparkled with dew drops, while the humming bees
And birds and butterflies, unseen before,
Found out the sunny spots and came in throngs.

But earth is man's own shadow, say the wise ;
As wisdom's secrets are twofold, and each
Responds to other both in good and ill,
A crescent thought will one day orb to full,
And on the earth reflect true light of Heaven.

But long and arduous were their labours ere
The rugged fields produced enough for all,
For thousands came ere hundreds could be fed ;
The scanty harvests gleaned to their last ear
Sufficed not yet, men hungered for their bread
Before it grew, yet cheerful bore the hard
Coarse fare and russet garb of pioneers,

In these great woods, content to build a home
And commonwealth, where they could live secure,
A life of honour, loyalty and peace.

   * * * * *

* * The world goes rushing by,
The ancient landmarks of a nobler time,
When men bore deep the imprint of the law
Of duty, truth and loyalty unstained.
Amid the quaking of a continent
Torn by the passions of an evil time,
They counted neither cost nor danger, spurned
Defections, treasons, spoils ; but feared God,
Nor shamed of their allegiance to the king.

To keep the empire one in unity
And brotherhood of its imperial race,
For that they nobly fought and all but won,
Where losing was to win a higher fame
In building up our northern land, to be
A vast dominion stretched from sea to sea ;
A land of labour but of sure reward,
A land of corn to feed the world withal,
A land of life's best treasures, plenty, peace,
Content and freedom, both to speak and do,
A land of men to rule, with sober law,
This Christian commonwealth, God's gift, to keep
This part of Britain's empire next the heart,
Loyal as were their fathers, and as free.

APPENDIX.

CONTAINING

A.—A copy of the Order in Council of the 9th November, 1789, ordering a record to be kept of the U. E. Loyalists.

B.—A copy of the old " U. E. List," preserved in the Crown Lands Department at Toronto.

APPENDIX A.

(COPY).

AT THE COUNCIL CHAMBER AT QUEBEC.

Monday, 9th November, 1789.

PRESENT :

His Excellency the RIGHT HONOURABLE LORD DORCHESTER,
The HONOURABLE WILLIAM SMITH, Esquire, Chief Justice.

HUGH FINLAY,	GEORGE POWELL,	
THOS. DUNN,	HENRY CALDWELL,	
EDWD. HARRISON,	WILLIAM GRANT,	Esquires.
JOHN COLLINS,	FRANÇOIS BABY,	
ADAM MABANE,	CHAS. DELANAUDIERE,	
J. G. C. DELERY,	LE. CTE. DUPRE,	

His Lordship intimated to the Council, that it remained a question, upon the late Regulation for the disposition of the Waste Lands of the Crown, whether the Boards constituted for that purpose were authorised to make Locations to the Sons of Loyalists, on their coming to full Age and that it was his wish to put a Marke of Honor upon the families who had adhered to the Unity of the Empire, and joined the Royal Standard in America before the Treaty of Separation in the year 1783.

The Council concurring with his Lordship, it is accordingly Ordered :

That the several Land Boards take course for preserving a Registry of the names of all persons falling under the description afore-

APPENDIX A.

mentioned to the end that their posterity may be discriminated, from future settlers, in the Parish Registers and Rolls of the Militia of their respective Districts, and other Public Remembrancers of the Province, as proper objects, by their persevering in the Fidelity and Conduct so honourable to their ancestors, for distinguished Benefits and Privileges.

And it is also ordered, that the said Land Boards may in every such case provide not only for the *Sons* of those Loyalists, as they arrive to full age, but for their *Daughters* also of that age, or on their Marriage, assigning to each a Lot of Two Hundred Acres, more or less, provided nevertheless that they respectively comply with the general Regulations, and that it shall satisfactorily appear that there has been no Default in the due Cultivation and Improvement of the Lands already assigned to the head of the family of which they are members.

(Signed) J. WILLIAMS, C.C.

APPENDIX B.

Copy of the "Old U. E. List," preserved in the Crown Lands Department at Toronto.

KEY TO ABBREVIATIONS.

S.B.R—Soldier in Butler's Rangers
K.R.R. or R.R.—Is Royl. Regt. N. York.
p. P.—Is p. their Petition.
l.R.—Is Loyal Rangers.
Q.R.—Queen's Rangers.
L.Bd.L.—The Land Board of Lunenburg.
R.L.B.S.—Return Land Board Stormont.
L.B.M.—Land Board Mecklenburg.

L.B.A.—Land Board Adolphustown.
L.B.K.—Land Board of Kingston.
P.L.—Provision List Kingston.
P.L.N.J.—Provision List New Johnstowne.
P.L. 2d.—Provision List Eastern District.
P.L.N.—Provision List Niagara.
B.M.A.—Capt. Barnes' Muster Absentees.

Names.	Residence.	Descendants.
Abbott, Joseph	W. District	Sergeant, disched. from the 26th Regmt., his own Petition in C.O.
Abney, Jonas	Ernest Town	No person of this name on the roll.
Abraham, Christian	Do.	Soldier R.R.N.Y. Called Loyalist P. L. 1786.
Abraham, Daniel	Marysburgh	Discharged Soldier, German Troops. Provision List 1786. (Stamped book.)
Aby or Haby, George	E. District	A Soldier 44th Regt., L.B.L. 200 acres only, how U. E.
Adair, John	H. District	Petition, Soldier Jersey Volunteers.
Adams, Andrew	Edwardsburgh	Soldier p. Petition, K. Rangers.
Adams, Elijah Curtis	E. District	Soldier p. Petition and L.B.L. a Loyalist.
Adams, Erray	Do. (Que. if Ezra)	Soldier p. Petition L.B.L. Came in at the commencement of the War.
Adams, Lt. Gideon	Do. S. G.	Jessup's Corps, L. B. L. Loyal Rangers.
Adams, James	Do.	Soldier K. Rangers, S.G. 200 acres L.B.A., 1794.
Adams, Joel	Do.	Soldier K. Rangers.

APPENDIX B.

Names.	Residence.	Descendants.
Adams, Samuel	E. District	Capt. under Genl. Burgoyne p. Petition.
Adams, Sam. William	Do.	Sergeant p. Petition. Volunteer P., 1789. King's Rangers.
Adcock, John	Marysburgh	British Soldier (P.L. 1786). S. stamped book.
Ainsley, Johannah	H. District	Wife of Sergt. Henry Bougner.
Airhart, Simon	Edwardsburgh	Soldier, Loyal Rangers.
Aker, Lambert	H. District	Que. if Aior? Yes. Butler's Rangers. Had a wife, P.L.N., 1786.
Albertson, Richard	Fredericksburgh	
Albrant, Francis	E. District	R.R.N.Y. Muster Roll, A. Had a wife. P.L.N. 1786.
Albrant, Henry	Do.	R. R. N. Y. Muster Roll. Has a wife and 2 children. P.L. 2d, 1786.
Alexander, Hugh	H. District	In 1782, when a boy.
Algire, Junior, Jacob	E. District	Son of Jacob, Senr.—not U.E. in his own right, p. Petition, 1798.
Algire, Senior, Jacob	Do.	R.R.N.Y., P.L. 2d, 1786. I.F.
Algire, Elisha	New Castle District	O.C. 28th Feb., 1805, ordered to be inscribed on U.E. List.
Algire, Martin	E. District	Soldier, Royal Yorkers, Muster Roll, P.L. 2d, 1786.
Alindelph, Mary	Williamsburgh	
Allan, Western	E. District	Came in after the War, about 1786, M.S. Sherwood.
Allen, John	Marysburgh	} Que. if Sons of Joseph Allen Petition? Yes.
Allen, Jonathan	Do.	
Allen, Joseph	Do.	S.G. apt. Loyalists Captain P.L. 1786.
Allen, Joseph	Cataraqui	No. 1. M.R. No. 4.
Allison, Joseph	Adolphus Town	A private in Col. Delaney's Corps. L.B.M.
Alpin, James	Marysburgh	Sergt. British Regt.
Alt, Nicholas	E. District	R.R.N.Y. Muster Roll, A, a wife. P.L. 2d, 1786.
Aman, John	Do.	Or Amon, John, Soldier, R.R.N.Y. Muster Roll.
Aman, Jacob	Do.	Soldier, R.R.N.Y. Muster Roll, A.
Amey, John Jonas	Ernest Town	With Genl., Burgoyne. Jessups P.L. 1786. L.B.C. M.D.

APPENDIX B. 131

NAMES.	RESIDENCE.	DESCENDANTS.
Amon, Lawrence., ...	E. District	R.R.N.Y., died before the Peace.
Amor, Peter..........	Do.	A Grenadier Royl. Yorkers, J.B. say Philip.
Amor, Philip........	Do.	Royal Regt., New York.
Amsbury, William .. Almsbury	Ernest Town	Soldier, Loyal Rangers, called Loyalist P.L., 1786.
Amy, Nicholas	Do.	Soldier, Loyal Rangers, L. B.M., 1790. 600 ac. (P.L. 1786).
Anderson, Alexander..	Home District........	Niagara, Stamped Book.
Anderson, Alexander..	Discharged Soldier....	Kingston, Soldier 31st Regt. p. Petition. (Stamped Book).
Anderson, Benjamin ..	E. District	Not in the Province J.B. (P.L. 2d, 1786).
Anderson, Cyrus......	Do. expunged	Son of Samuel J.B. (P.L. 2d, 1786).
Anderson, Ebenezer...	Do. expunged	Son of Samuel, R.R.N.York Soldier p. Muster Roll. (P.L. 2d, 1786).
Anderson, Elias.......	Home District........	Inserted by O.C., 8th July, 1806.
Anderson, Elisha.,....	Do. expunged	Son of Samuel, Soldier R.R. N.Y. Ld.Bd.Muster Roll. (P.L. 2d, 1786).
Anderson, George	E. District, expunged	Son of Samuel, J.B. P.L. 2d, 1786.
Anderson, Henry......	E. District	Loyal Rangers. J.F.
Anderson, John.......	Fredericksburgh	Que. If he did not belong to Royal Artillery.
Anderson, Jacob......	E. District	
Anderson, James......	Do. expunged	Son of Samuel and a Soldier R.R.N.Y.,M.Roll. Single man. P.L. 1786.
Anderson, Senior, John	Do.	Son of Benjamin J.B. Discharged British Soldier.
Anderson, Junior, John	Do.	Expunged, Son of Samuel, J.B, (Single man. P.L. 2d, 1786).
Anderson, John;......	Marysburgh	If from Nova Scotia (Soldier BritishRegimentA.Mc.L.)
Anderson, Joseph......	Kingston	Expunged Capt. P.L. 2d, 1786.
Anderson, Joseph ...	E. District, M.C......	Lt. Sir J. Johnson's or R. Yorkers.
Anderson, Peter	Markham	Inserted by O. Council, 2d Dec., 1806.
Anderson, Richard....	E. District	Que. If not Son of Benjamin? Yes. J.B.

APPENDIX B.

NAMES.	RESIDENCE.	DESCENDANTS.
Anderson, Capt. Samuel	E. District	S. G. R. R. N. York. P.L. 2d, 1786.
Anderson, Simon	H. District	S. B. Rangers. (Niagara Stamped Book). S. P.L. N., 1786.
Anderson, Thomas G.	E. District	Expunged, Son of Samuel, J.B. Single man, P.L. 2d, 1786.
Andrews, Benjamin	Elizabeth Town	Joined the Royal Army at Verplank's Point — from himself.
Anderson, Walter	Charlotteville	Order in Council 24th February, 1807. Served in Ward's Block House.
Andrew, William	Marysburgh	British Soldier, P.L., 1786. Stamped Book.
Angle, George	Sophiasburgh and Ameliasburgh	German Soldier, *Engle*.
Angrish, Henry	H. District	S. Genl. Soldier, B. Rangers —a wife and one child. P. L. N., 1786. Niagara Stamped Book.
Angrish, Jacob.,	Do.	Soldier, Butler's Rangers.
Anker, August	H District ⎫ If not Anger, or Aneker.	S,G. B.R. A wife. P.L.N. 1786.
Anker (Ager), Charles	do.	S.G. B.R., Niagara Stamped Book, S.P.L.N. 1786.
Anker, Simon Fredk.	do.	S.G. B.R. A wife & two sons. P.L.N. 1786.
Anker, Junr., Fredk.	do. ⎭	S.G. B.R. S.P.L.N. 1785.
Annable, John	E District	Sergt. R.R. N.Y., Muster Roll E.
Ainslie, Amos	Kingston	At St. Vincent, Gov. Hamilton, 100 (P.L. 1786.) (Stamped Book).
Ansley, Amos	Cataraqui Township	No. 1, M.R. No. 4.
Ainslie, Samuel	Kingston	Sergeant King's Royal Regt. N. York. P.L. 1786.
Appleby, William	Edwardsburgh	An artificer in the King's service 7 years. P. 1794.
Arkenbrack, John	E District	A soldier in Jessup's corps, L. Bd. L.
Armstrong, Senr., Edward	of Elizabethtown	Deceased. Suffered imprisonment in Albany gaol from 1777 to 1783. O.C. 12th May, 1808.
Armstrong, John	E District	Suffered imprisonment in Albany gaol. Loyal Rangers.
Armstrong al Welch, Margaret	Edwardsburg	Came into the Province as Mrs. Ruderbach with her husband.

APPENDIX B. 133

NAMES.	RESIDENCE.	DESCENDANTS.
Armstrong, Junr., ...	E District............	Son of Thomas.
Armstrong, Thomas ...	do. Edwardsburgh	Served under General Burgoyne, J.F.
Arnold, Genl. Benedict		Struck off.
Arnold, Lt. Henry....	Home District	Expunged. M.C.
Arnold, Lt. Richard ..	do.	Son of. M.C.
Ashford, Nathaniel ...		Inserted by O. Council, 6th July, 1798.
Ashley, William	Kingston	Soldier 34th Regt.p.petition. Not U.E. 200 acres. L. B. M., 1791.
Asseltine, John	Ernest Town	Soldier Loyal Rangers, L.B. M. 1790—350. P.L., 1786.
Asseltine, Isaac	do.	L. B. M., 1790—only 200. Loyalist (Stamped Book).
Asseltine, Peter	do.	Soldier Loyal Rangers, L.B. M. 1790—300. P.L. 1786.
Atkinson, William....	Kingston	S.G. Lieut. N. York militia (Stamped Book), P.L.1786.
Atkinson, William....	Cataraqui Township ..	No. M.R. No. 4.
Averall, Robert	E District....	Drummer R.R.N.Y. Muster Roll.
Avery, Joseph........	do.	Fifer Loyal Rangers,or R.R. N.Y., J.F.
Avery, Joseph........	E District............	
Ault, Everhart	do.	Soldier R.R.N.Y., L.B.L., Single, P.L. 2d, 1786.
Ault, Michael	Matilda	R.R.N.Y. M. Roll, A—has a wife and one child, P.L. 2d, 1786.
Austin, Widow Chrisp	E District............	At Montreal, B.M.A., J.F. widow of Dr. Austin.
Ault, John		On original Roll. Soldier R.R.N.Y.
Austin, Joel..........	H District............	Butler's Rangers, S.G.S., P. L. N. 1786. Niagara Stamped Book.
Austin, Solomon......	do.	From North Carolina.
Ackler, William ...... (Eckler).	do.	B.R., Soldier Butler's Rangers—a wife and two children. P.L.N. 1786,Niagara Stamped Book.
Babcock, Benjamin ...	Kingston	A single man, a settler from State N. York, L.B,K. 1792—200. His children in 1804,aged—Rachel,14; David, 12 ; Peter, 10 ; Sarah, 7 ; Jacob, 5 ; John, 3 ; Elizabeth, 1 year ; joined at New York and in Ward's Blockhouse.

APPENDIX B.

Names.	Residence.	Descendants.
Babcock, David	Kingston	Emigrant settler, L. B. K., 1793, from NewYork State —200 acres,Kingston; once served in the Blockhouse; 600 acres.
Babcock, Rachel, widow of Samuel		Who joined the Royal army at New York, order-in-Council 30thJanuary,1808.
Backer, John	Home District	Butler's Ran. (Niagara Stamped Book, S.P.L.N. 1786.
Badderly, Michael	Marysburgh	Discharged British Soldier.
Badgley, now Atkinson, Margt.	M District	If the widow of Samuel or Anthony—late of Kinderbrook—wife of William Atkinson.
Baily, John	E District	Son of Levi J.B.; ship carpenter in the service.
Baily, Levy	do.	A volunteer in Delaney's Regt.; L. Bd. L.
Baker, Senr., Adam	do.	Soldier R.R.N.Y., L. Bd. L. —a wife and 6 children, P. L. 2d, 1786.
Baker, Junr., Adam	do.	Son of Adam, Senr.
Baker, Benjamin	Lancaster	R.R·N.Y.—had a wife and 3 children; P. L. 2d, 1786.
Baker, Conradt	{ E District { Williamsburg	Soldier R.R.N.Y., L.B.L., Muster Roll; had a wife, P.L. 2d, 1786.
Baker, Elisha	Augusta	Has beeen five years in the Province; asks 200 acres.
Baker, Frederick	Ernest Town	Soldier Loyal Rangers, L. B. M., 1790—300, P.L. 1786.
Baker, Jack (Blackman) James	H District	Pioneer B.Rangers (Niagara Stamped Book, S.P.L.N., 1786.
Baker John	E District	Son of Adam, Senr., U.E., (single, P.L. 1786.
Baker, Henry	E District Matilda	Soldier R.R.N.Y., Muster Roll (single, P.L. 2d, 1786, Stamped Book.
Baker, Martin	E District	Son of Adam; a soldier in R.R.N.Y., O.E.
Baker, William	do.	Que., if not son of Adam, Cataraqui, B. M. A., Stamped Book.
Baldwin, Phineas	Landsdown	A settler—did not join before 1783. *R.J. D.G.*
Ball, Senr., Lt. Jacob	H District	Lt. B. Rangers—a wife and four children,P.L.N. 1786, Niagara Stamped Book.

APPENDIX B. 135

NAMES.	RESIDENCE.	DESCENDANTS.
Ball, Jacob	H District	Que., if not son of Peter—a wife and one child, P.L.N. 1786.
Ball, Lt. Peter	do.	Lt. B.R., Niagara Stamped Book—a wife & 2 children, P.L.N. 1786.
Ball, Shadrack	Ernest Town	A soldier Loyal Rangers, L. B.M.,1791, 400 acres—drew land in Charlottenburg, 100 acres — relinquished this land, P.L.N.J., 1786.
Ball, Solomon	do.	P. States M.D.; soldier in Jessup's, also L. B. M. 1790, P.L.N.J. 1786.
Banta, Capt, Weart	H District	His heirs.
Barnhart, Charles	Fredericksbnrg	Soldier R.R.N.Y., L.B.M. 1760. P.L. 1786.
Barnhart, George	E District	Sergeant K.R.R.N.Y., I.F. P.L. 2d, 1786.
Barnhart, John	H District	R.R.N.Y., Muster Roll A, Stamped Book, M.D.
Barnhart, Jacob	E District	⎫ SoldierR.R.N.Y. L.Bd.L. ⎬Sons of George, *J.B.*
Barnhart, Nicholas	do.	⎭ Soldier R.R.N.Y. L. Bd. L.
Barnum, Nathaniel	H District	Dead—a Lieut.
Barnum, Nathan Bunnel	London District	Formerly soldier in 3rd Battalion of Delaney's. O.C. 26th January, 1808.
Barthol, Keepart	H District	B Rangers.
Bartley, Isaiah (Josiah)	Fredericksburgh	Soldier King's R. Regt., N. York—700 acres (Stamped Book), P.L. 1786.
Bartley, Michael Barcley	do.	P.L. 1786 -had drawn 100 acres L.B.A. 1794, grant 200. Soldier R.R.N.Y., G.H. 1784.
Barton, John	Augusta	1789 Land Board Certificate —no description. Son of Thomas.
Barton, Joseph	do.	1789 Land Board Certificate —no description.
Barton, Thomas	E District	Stated U.E. by Land Board of Luneberg. Soldier Loyal Rangers.
Barton, William	Elizabeth Town	1789. No description in Land Board Certificate; a settler —E. Jessup.
Bassey, Jacob	Home District	S. B. Rs.
Bassey, Junr., Robert	do.	B.R.—the senr. a settler.

APPENDIX B.

NAMES.	RESIDENCE.	DESCENDANTS.
Basteder, David	Home District	Nephew to Capt. Tice—how U.E.
Batman, Samuel	E District	Soldier Loyal Rangers, Samuel Beekman, M. Roll.
Bates, William	Niagara District	Sergeant Queen's Rangers—by order-in-Council 2d December, 1806.
Baxter, William	E District	Soldier R.R.N.Y. pr. Muster Roll L. Bd. L. (single), P.L. 2d.
Bayeux, Thomas	H District	Custom House Officer, New York.
Bayman, James	Kingston	p. P. Served three years in Marine Department in 1797—how U.E.
Beach, Serg. John	Johnstown District	
Beach, Samuel	Ernest Town	Loyal Rangers. Order-in-Council, 28th February, 1805.
Beach, Stephen Tod	E District	Son of Sergt. John Beach.
Beardsley, Crannel B.	H District	His Father was never in this Province.
Beasley, Richard	Do	A Loyalist.
Beavins, James Bavins	Ernest Town	L.B.M. 1793, State Loyalist, was shot in Ernest Town. Bounty 200. Soldier Loyal Rangers.
Beebe, Sergt. Edin	H District	N. C. O. B. R. a Sergeant, had a wife P.L.N. 1786, Niagara Stamped Book.
Beebe, Joshua	Do	Deceased.
Beach, John	E District	Son's Petition.
Buck, Bercia	E District	Came to Lower Canada before 1783. Sarah Buck his widow.
Beack, George	Do	See George Buck.
Bedford, Jonathan, sr.	New Castle	Inserted by O.C. 24th Aug., 1802, Engineer Dept.
Bedford, Edward	Marysburgh	Discharged British soldier, from 53rd Regt. (Stamped Book) p. Sergt. McIntosh's certificate.
Begraft, Benjamin Beacraft	H District	S. G. Corpl. Becraft, Indian Dept. single, P.L.N, 1786, Niagara stamped book.
Behn, John	Fredericksburgh	Soldier R.R.N.Y. P.L.1786.
Bell, Derick	H District	S. G. No. 2, Soldier Butler's Rangers, O.C. 13th Oct., 1796, S., P.L.N., 1786.

APPENDIX B. 137

NAMES.	RESIDENCE.	DESCENDANTS.
Bell, Duncan..........	Fredericksburgh.....	S.G. Sergeant King's Rangers, P.L. 1786.
Bell, Thomas.........	Do	1785, Gov. Hamilton, 100, Loyalist Soldier, R.R.N. Y., P.L. 1786.
Bell, William	Kingston...............	Treasury Loyalist.
Bell, William	Fredericksburgh	Sergt. King's Rangers, R. Roll (Stamped Book) P.L. 1786.
Bell, William	Thurlow...............	Sergt. 31st Regt. R.
Belton, George........	E District............	Geo. Boulton, joined in 1777 O. E.
Bender, Dennis.......	Do	
Bender, George........	E District............	Soldier R. Regt. N. York, Muster Roll A.
Painter, J. F..........		
Bender, Philip........	Home District........	B. R., a wife and four children, P. L. N. 1786, Niagara Stamped Book.
Bender, Tunis	E District............	Son of George, States p. Petition, in 1798, to be of age.
Benedict, John.........	Do Matilda	R.R.N.Y., Muster Roll (A) single, P.L. 2d, 1786.
Benedict, Joseph.......	Do G.G...............	Corpl. R. R. N. Y., Muster Roll, P.L. 2d, 1786, a wife and two children.
Benegar, John......... Benninger.	Adolphustown	Issuer of Provisions and afterwards clerk in Commissary Dept. L. B. M., 1791, 200, and L. B. A., 1794, 300 acres more.
Bennet, Corporal......	E District............	Soldier Loyal Rangers.
Bennet, if Charls, Jas..	H District............	S. G. List 2, Corpl. Indian Dept., one of this name, H. D. states to have come here in 1791.
Benson, Albert	Adolphus Town	Loyalist, 1786, P. L. from New York, Mc. L.
Benson, Cornelius	Fredericksburgh	Son of Mathew.
Benson, Garret	Adolphus Town	Loyalist, L.B.M. 1790, and P.L. 1786, from New York
Benson, Mathew......	Fredericksburgh	U. E. Soldier, Orange Rangers, L. B. M. and P. L., 1786. Bounty by his heirs, 200 L.B.M., 1791.
Benth, John..........	Marysburgh	Discharged German soldier, p. Provision List, 1786.
Berdan, Albert	H District............	Sergeant 2nd Batln., New Jersey Volunteers.

I

APPENDIX B.

NAMES.	RESIDENCE.	DESCENDANTS.
Berkley, Averhart....	Williamsburgh........	Soldier Butler's Rangers.
Berrard, Alexander .. Bernard............	E District............	Soldier Loyal Rangers.
Bethune, Angus.......	Do	Dead. J.B. R.R.N.Y., M. Roll, P.L.N.J., 1786.
Bethune, Revd. John...	Do	S. G. Chaplain, 84th Regt.
Betron, David........	H District............	States the loss of property for his loyalty. In 1795 came with a wife and 9 children. John Silverthorn says that he drove a continental waggon; no property.
Bettersworth, James..	E District.......... ..	Was taken prisoner by the Indians and afterwards served in R.R.N.Y.
Beygar, Christopher...	E District............	Que, If not Biringer who came in 1737. P. states no service.
Bibby, Richard.......	Marysburgh	Discharged British Soldier. Que. what Brit. Regt. 29th per Sergeant McIntosh's Certificate.
Binker, William...... Bineker.	Do	Discharged Brit. Sol. Que. what British Regt. 53rd Regt. L.B.M. 1791, 350, and P.L. 1786 (Stamped Book), a wife.
Birch, Jacob..........	Fredericksburgh	R. R. N. Y., A. McL. (Stamped Book), S. P. L, 1786.
Bird, Henry..........	Marysburgh	Discharged Brit. Sol. Que. what Regt. 29th Regt. per Land Board Certificate, 450 L.B.M., 1791, and Provision List, 1786.
Boid, James.....	E District............	Son of Thomas.
Boid, Senr, Thomas...	Do Edwardsburgh.....	Served in Quarter Master Dept.
Boid, Junr, Thomas ..	Do	Son of Thomas Boyd, senr.
Birdsall, Jeremiah....	Elizabeth Town	Emigrant from U.S., L.B.L. 1790.
Birdsall, Samuel......	Of Stamford..........	Died in 1789, O. C. 4th May, 1802. Recd. from C.O.
Bishop, John.........	E District Matilda....	R. R. N. Y. Muster Roll— gone into the States, B. M.A.
Bissle, David.	Augusta..............	
Bissle, Joseph	Do	1789, Resident three years— drawn 100 acres.

APPENDIX B.

NAMES.	RESIDENCE.	DESCENDANTS.
Bistedo, Jacob........	Kingston.............	Incorporated Loyalists. One son, P.L., 1786.
Black, Jonathan......	Augusta..............	p P. Sergeant in Col. Brevington's Regiment.
Blackburn, John......	Chatham..............	O.C. 5th Jan., 1808. Soldier in Capt. Suman's Compy., Maryland.
Blakeley, James......	Marysburgh and Sophiasburgh.......	M. C. Commissary, O. C., 30th August, 1797 (P. L. 1786).
Blakeley al Flynn, Margt..............	E District, Lancaster..	Had three children, P.L. 2d, 1786.
Blacher, John........	Marysburgh and Sophiasburgh.......	Soldier Loyal Rangers. L.B. M., 1790, 300, King's Rangers, P.L., 1786.
Blanchard, William...	Marysburgh..........	44th Regt., Genl. Haldimand, 100 and P.L., 1786. (Stamped Book).
Bland, William.......	E District............	Warranted artificer from the Tower, not U. E., had a wife and one child, P. L. 2d, 1786.
Bogart, Abraham......	Adolphustown........	Loyalist L.B.M., 1793, 300, Loyalist from New York, McL., P.L., 1786.
Bogart, Christopher ..		O.C., 16th June, 1807.
Bogart, Gilbert or Gyspert...........	Do	Soldier Loyal Refugees, L. B.M., 1789, 450 in all. P. L. 1786.
Boice, Senior, John....	H District............	Soldier B. R., p. P. a wife and four children, P. L. 2d, 1786. Soldier R.R.N.Y. Muster Roll.
Boice, Junior, John...	Do	Son of John, senr.
Bond, George	York	O. C. 7th March, 1808. Served as Captain in Col. Richd. King's Regiment., South Carolina.
Bonistal, Jacob........	E District............	Soldier Loyal Rangers.
Bolton, Richard.......	Edwardsburg..........	On original Roll.
Booth, Abner.........	E District, late of Elizabeth Town	1789. P. States as settler. A settler, R.J., D.G.
Born, John, Senr......	Home District........	On original Roll.
Booth, Benjamin	Ernest Town	
Born, John, Junr.....	Home District........	On original Roll.
Booth, Bethea	E District............	
Booth, Charles........	Do	Son of John Booth, a Pensioner, Ld. Bd. L.
Booth, John..........	Augusta..............	Son of John Booth, senr.

APPENDIX B.

Names.	Residence.	Descendants.
Booth, Senior, John...	E District............	U. E. Pensioner during the war.
Booth, Joshua........	Ernest Town	S. G. Sergeant and for his father who died in New York (P.L. 1786.)
Booth, Isaac..........	E District............	Son of John Booth; a pensioner, Ld. Bd. L.
Booth, Phabe	Do	Now Campbell, daughter of John Booth, a pensioner, L.B.L.
Booth, Samuel........	Do Elizabethtown.....	Son of John Booth, a pensioner, L. Bd. L.
Booth, Vincent........	Do	Son of John Booth, p. Petition J.J, a pensioner.
Booth, Zeaks	E District...........	Joined the Royal Standard at New York in 1776, and was in the King's service, O.E.
Borman, Sigismund ..	Marysburgh	Dischd. Soldier German troops p. Provision List 1786.
Boss, Elizabeth	H District............	A single woman—not entitled.
Bostwick, Joshua	E District, Augusta ⎫	Employed in the Lumber Service for Government.
Bostwick, Joshua	Augusta............ ⎭	
Bottom, Ensn. Elijah..	E District............	S.G.–Jessups–Ensign Loyal Rangers, B.M.A.
Bottom, Richard......	do.	
Bouchette, Commodore	M District............	Expunged by order of C. Not U.E.
Bough, John..........	E District............	(if Bouks) a soldier R. R. N. Y.
Bough,Senr., Frederick	do.	R.R. N. York, Muster Roll.
Bough,Junr.,Frederick	do.	R.R.N.Y. Muster Roll (A). Single. P. L. 2d, 1786.
Bouk, Adam..........	do.	R.R.N.Y. Muster Roll—P. L. 2d, 1786—had a wife & four children.
Bouk, Senr., Christian	do.	Soldier R.R.N.Y. Muster Roll—P.L. 2d, 1786.
Bouk, Frederick.....	Williamsburgh........	Soldier K. R. Regt. N. Y. L.Bd.L. 200, P.L.2d,1786. R.R.N.Y. M. Roll.
Bowen, Abraham	Fredericksburgh	Son of William Bowen of R.R.N.Y.
Bowen, Cornelius	H District............	Soldier Butler's Rangers, S. Genl. A wife & four children, P. L. N. 1786; Niagara Stamped Book.

APPENDIX B. 141

Names.	Residence.	Descendants.
Bowen, Henry	Richmond	L.B.M. 1790—550. Loyalist from N.Y. Provision list 1786—a wife.
Bowen, John	Fredericksburgh	Son of William Bowen of R.R.N.Y.
Bowen, Luke	E District, Matilda	Soldier King's Royal Regt. N. York, Muster Roll.
Bowen, Corporal Peter Bown	H District	⎫ B.M.A.
Bowen, Peter Bower	Fredericksburgh	⎬ A Corporal Butler's Rangers, L.B.M. 1790.
Bowen, Peter	do.	⎭ Son of Wm. Bowen of R.R. N.Y.
Bowen, Victor	do.	Son of Wm. Bowen of Fredericksburgh. L.B.M. 1790. 200.
Bowen, William	H District	B. Rangers. A soldier.
Bowen, William R.	Richmond	Lieut. Indian Department, L.B.M. 1791.
Bowen, William	Fredericksburgh	Soldier Royal Yorkers. L. B. M. 1790—650. P. L. 1786, Muster Roll, A.
Bower, Adam	Ernest Town	⎫ (Stamped Book).
		⎬ Same person--soldier in R.R. N.Y., P.L. 1786—has land
Bower, Adam	Fredericksburgh	⎭ in Matilda, N.M.L.
Bower, Gaspar	do. (Kaspar)	Corporal R.R. N.Y.—P. L. 1786. Stamped Book.
Bower, William Bowen	Kingston	Son of William Bowen of R.R.N.Y.
Boulsby, Richard	H District	Bucks County Volunteers.
Boulsby, Thomas	do.	Volunteer in Capt. Thomas's Company--P.
Bowman, Abraham	do.	Drummer Royal Regiment New York—Muster Roll —A.
Bowman, Senior, George Adam	do.	Niagara Stamped Book—a wife & 7 children—P.L.N. 1786.
Bowman, Junior, Adam	do.	Que., Butler's Rangers, Niagara Stamped Book—S. P.L.N. 1786.
Bowman, Henry	do.	Butler's Rangers, S.G. O.C. 13th Oct., 1796. Niagara Stamped Book.
Bowman, Jacob	do.	B. Rangers—a wife and five children, P.L.N.1786. Niagara Stamped Book.
Bowman, Peter	H District	B. Rangers, S. P.L.N. 1786 (Niagara Stamped Book).

142   APPENDIX B.

NAMES.	RESIDENCE.	DESCENDANTS.
Boyce, Andrew	Ernest Town	R.R.N.Y. Muster Roll.
Boyce, John	E District, Matilda	R.R.N.Y.—had a wife and 4 children, P.L. 2d, 1786. Joseph Griffin says in Albany Gaol; afterwards enlisted with the Rebels; deserted in two days; for 7 years lived after on Connecticut River.
de Boyce, Jehdda	Elizabeth Town	Was a soldier in the Contitinental service. Not U.E. O.E.
Boyce, Stephen	Ernest Town	Soldier in Jessup's Corps, p. M. (P.L. 1786).
Brackenridge, David	E District	S. G. Ensign—Rogers—say Loyal Rangers, L.B.L.
Brackenridge, James	do.	S.G. Captain, Rogers, say Loyal Rangers, L.B.L.
Brackenridge, Francis	H District	Joined Genl. Burgoyne; was taken prisoner; came to Canada in 1786; drew 200 acres, and returned immediately to the States. Information of Col. James Brackenridge.
Bradshaw, Asal	Fredericksburgh	S.G. King's Rangers, a soldier, L.B.M. 1790. P.L. 1786.
Bradshaw, David	do.	Engineer Department artificer. Son of Jas. Bradshaw, Senr. Restored to U.E. List O.C. 14th January, 1808, p. Certificate P.L. 1786.
Bradshaw, John	E District, Oynaburgh	Corporal R.R.N.Y. M.Roll, P.L. 2d, 1786.
Bradshaw,Senr., James	Fredericksburgh	Soldier Delaney's Brigade, L. B. M. 1790—300 P. S. 1786, K. R.'s, 1784, by Genl. Haldimands—one of this name Lieut. unin corpd, Loyalists.
Bradshaw,Junr.,James	M District. Que..	King's Rangers,son of James Bradshaw,Senr. P.L.1785.
Bradshaw,Junr.,James	Fredericksburgh.Que	Same.
Bradt, Capt. Andrew	H District	B. Rangers. A wife & one child, P. L. N. 1786. Niagara Stamped Book.

APPENDIX B. 143

NAMES.	RESIDENCE.	DESCENDANTS.
Bradt, Arent	H District	Soldier R.R.N.Y., M. Roll, Niagara Stamped Book. A wife and five children. P.L.N. 1786.
Bradt, Lt. John	do.	2000 B. Rangers. Niagara Stamped Book.
Bradt, John	do.	Sergt. B. Rangers S.G.
Bradt, Minar	do.	Butler's Rangers (P.L.1786).
Brannan, William	E District	Soldier 84th, p. P (P.L. 2d, 1786).
Brant, Capt. Joseph	Home District	By order-in-Council, 9th July, 1806.
Brant, Mary	Kingston	A principal Indian woman,
Brant, Henry	Fredericksburgh	Soldier 34th Regt.p.P.(R.R. N.Y., P.L. 1786).
Brant, Capt. Joseph	Home District	By order-in-Council of 1806.
Brass, David	Kingston	M.C. Lt. B.R. p. P. P.L. 1786.
Bready, James	do.	Incorporated Loyalist N.Y. P.L.1786 (Stamped Book).
Bready, Luke	E District	Soldier R. R. N. Y. J. W. P.L. 2d, 1786.
Brewer, Aaron	Kingston	Associated Loyalist. (P.L. 1786).
Brewer, Lazarus	do.	No description. Ld. Bd. Certificate of 1794. Emigrant settler from Monmouth, N.Jersey. L.B.K. 1794. 200.
Brewort. Elias —vort	H District	A settler in 1787.
Bridge, William	Marysburgh	Corpl. 53d Regt., Genl. Haldimand 1784—100 (P. L. 1786, Stamped Book). A wife & six children.
Briscoe, Isaac	Ernest Town	S.G. Sergeant K.Rangers or Loyal Rangers (P.L.1786).
Briscoe, Nathan	do.	Restored O.C. 15th Decr., 1807—son of Isaac—200 acres—L.B.M. 1791 (soldier in Jessup's), P. L. 1786.
Brooks, John	Sophiasburgh & Ameliasburgh	
Browce, George	E District	Royal Yorkers, L. Bd. L.
Brown, Abraham	Augusta	Soldier Loyal Rangers—200 acres.
Brouse, Joseph	Matilda	R.R.N.Y.
Brouse, Peter	E District	R.R.N.Y.

APPENDIX B.

Names.	Residence.	Descendants.
Brouse, Peter	E District	Soldier R.R.N.Y. Muster Roll.
Brown, Edward	Augusta	Son of Abraham.
Brown, Ezekiah	E District Yonge	Joined Royal Standard in 1777—had a warrant to raise a company—affidavit of J. Scovell, 1808.
Brown, John	H District	Soldier Butler's Rangers, L. B. Nassau 1794, and one of same name in B.R.—a wife & 5 children P.L.N. 1786, Niagara Stamped Book.
Brown, John	Kingston	Discharged soldier.
Brown, James	H District	Sergeant in Delaney's.
Brown, James	E District	If not son of Nathaniel, to Eliz. Town (Single). P. L. 1786.
Brown, Jesse	E District	
Brown, Senr., Jesse	do	Soldier Loyal Rangers.
Brown, Junr., Jesse	do	Soldier Loyal Rangers.
Brown, Joseph	H District	B. Rangers, S. G. (Niagara Stamped Book) Stamped Book, M.D.
Brown, Nathan	Augusta	Soldier Loyal Rangers, one in Jessup's.
Brown, Nathaniel	E District	Soldier from Vermont, L.B. G., reserved, 1793, O.C., 28th April, 1807, reinstated, one belonged to Jessups, B.M.A.
Brown, Samuel	do	Had a wife and one child, P.L. 2d, 1786.
Brown, Thomas	do	Soldier Loyal Rangers, T.F.
Brown, William	H District of Stamford	Soldier 10th Regiment. A soldier Butler's Rangers, a wife and two children, P. L. N., 1786, Niagara Stamped Book.
Bruce, Alexander	E District	A soldier, Glengarry, J.B., P.L. 2d, 1786.
Bruce, David	do	Son of Alexander, J.B.
Bruce, Margaret	do	Widow of Alexander, J.B.
Bruce, Junior, Margt	do	How. Daughter of late Alexander, J.B.
Bruce, Sally	do	How. Daughter of late Alexander, J.B.
Bruce, William	do Cornwall	Son of a soldier, 200 acres, L.Bd.L.

APPENDIX B. 145

NAMES.	RESIDENCE.	DESCENDANTS.
Broundage, John.....	E District	Soldier in Delaney's Regt. of Refugees, L.B.L., his widow Mary.
Broundage, James....	H District............	Firm Loyalist, joined the troops in 1777.
Brunner, Peter.......	Adolphus Town.......	Que. if of Williamsburg, son of Peter Bruner, a soldier R.R.N.Y.
Brounson, Sr., Samuel.	Fredericksburg	Soldier King's Rangers, p. Regt. Roll, Corpl., p. L. B.M., 1790, 600.
Brounson, Samuel J.S.	do	King's Rangers. K. Rangers, P.L., 1786.
Bryan, John..........	E District............	S.G. Revd. Jessups Corps. E. J., Stamped Book- One of this name a British soldier, P.L., 1786.
Buck, Mechitable.....	do	Her husband was a soldier in the Loyal Rangers and died at Sorell in 1791. Samuel, reinstated on the U. E. list, order in Council, 7th March, 1807.
Buck, Berecu.	Elizabeth Town	On original Roll, Sarah his widow.
Buck, Jonathan.......	H District.............	Original Roll, John Buck.
Buck, George	Kingston.............	O.C., 7th April, 1807. Employed in assisting and directing persons on secret service.
Buck, Philip..........	do	Soldier B. R., p. P. Frederick Buck, his son, p. affidavit of P. Terry, 24th Aug., 1806. A wife and seven children, P. L. N., 1785, (Niagara Stamped Book.
Buck, George	Elizabeth Town.......	On original Roll.
Buckner, Sergt. Henry	do	p. P. Sergeant in Delaney's Brigade, 550 and 6.
Buckner, Henry......	do	Joined the Royal Standard at New York, R.C.
Buckner, Mathias	H District............	States to have joined the Royal Army in the Jerseys in 1777. Came to this country with his family in 1795.
Bemsley, Buel........	E District............	Was in before 1789. King's Rangers, J.F.

Names.	Residence.	Descendants.
Buel, Jonathan	E District	Son of Timothy.
Buel, Samuel	do	Son of Timothy.
Buel, Timothy	do	Joined the Royal Standard before the Treaty of Separation, was in during the war.
Buell, William	do	Ensign Loyal Rangers, by order in Council, 2d Dec., 1806.
Buckner, Senr., John	H District	Joined the Royal Standard in 1779 at New York.
Bull, Margaret	Midland	Widow of Aaron Bull, Soldier Loyal Rangers, by Order in Council, 19th November, 1807.
Bull, Berar	M District	Que. If Bryer Bull who came from Sorel in 1795 or 6. His father did not come into this Province, but died at Sorel.
Bulson, Cornelius	Williamsburgh	Dead, J.B. A drummer R. R.N.Y., M;R.M.A. (P.L. 2nd, 1786.
Bungar, Conrad	Marysburgh	Soldier German Troops, U. E. list.
Bunker, Bethuel	E District	Soldier R. R. N. Y. Muster Roll. B.MA.
Bunker, John	do	R.R.N.Y. Muster Roll.
Bunker, Henry	Marysburgh	
Burch, Esq., John	H District	Loyalist. Niagara Stamped Book.
Burch, Nathan	London	By order in Council, 2d December, 1806.
Burch, Mrs. Martha	H District	Wife to John Burch.
Burges, Dennis	E District	If not one of a Stevens settlers, he is a settler.
Burley, Freeman	Ernest Town	M. C., King's Loyal Rangers, L. B. M. in Ld. Bd. Certificate (P.L., 1786.)
Burley, John	do	} Stepson of Mathias Rose, L.
Burley, John	do	} B.M., 1790.
Burnet, John	Kingston	Loyalist from New York, son of Thomas, P.L., 1786
Burns, James	H District	S.G., soldier, p P. in Indian Dept., (S., P.L.N., 1786.
Burrit, Adoniram	Augusta	Joined the army under Gen. Rurgoyne. J. F. order in Council, 11th March,1807.
Burnet, Mathew	Kingston	Loyalist from New York. Son of Thomas, P.L. 1786

APPENDIX B. 147

NAMES.	RESIDENCE.	DESCENDANTS.
Burnet, Thomas......	Kingston	Incorporated Loyalist, P.L. 1786.
Burrit, Daniel........	Augusta..............	Land Board Certificate of 1792, not stated U. E., only a settler, L.B. 1790, Loyalist from Vermont, 4 article. Restored O. C., 9th March, 1808.
Burrit, Stephen	E District............	S.G., drew land as Corporal. Petition states Sergeant, 1799, 200 to Corpl. N.R.K. Rangers.
Burtch, Charles	H District............	Delaney's Corps of Refugees
Burtch, Edse.........	do Grand River	12th July, 1800. Lot on Dundas street, p. M.
Busby, Thomas	E District............	Never was in the Province.
Bush, Charles........	Osnabruck............	J.F., says son of a Loyalist, who?
Bush, Julius..........	M District............	
Bush, Henry	do	Soldier R.R.N.Y., L. Bd. L., O.C., 20th July, 1797. son of, J.F.
Butler, Lt. Andrew ..	H District............	B. Rangers, Niagara Stamped Book.
Butler, Elias	E District............	
Butler, Senr., Freelove	Elizabeth Town	Soldier in Jessups, p. son's Petition Truelove.
Butler, Junr., Freelove	Augusta..............	Son of Freelove, Senior, should not be on U.E. list
Butler, Lt.-Col. John..	H District............	B. Rangers.
Butler, James	Elizabeth Town	Soldier in the last French war from 1755 to 60. Where from ?
Butler, Philip.........	H District............	
Butler, Lt. Thomas....	do	B. Rangers. Niagara Stamped Book.
Byrnes, John	Marysburgh	Soldier 47th Regt. P.
Byrnes, Esq., William.	Charlottenburgh......	S.G., Capt. R.R.N.Y.
Buttersworth, James..	Cornwall	On original Roll. See Butterworth, James.
Cadman, Alpheus	Fredericksburgh	Son of William, 200 acres. L.B.M., 1790.
Cadman, Asa..........	do	Son of William Cadman
Cadman, Senr., John..	E District............	Soldier R.R.N.Y., Muster Roll, P.L. 2d, 1786.
	Osnabruck.	
Cadman, Junr., John.	do	R. R. N. Y. Muster Roll, young man, P.L. 2, 1786.
Cadman, William	Fredericksburg....	Soldier K. R. Regiment. N.Y., L.B.M., 1790., 700 (Stamped Book) P.L.1786.

148   APPENDIX B.

NAMES.	RESIDENCE.	DESCENDANTS.
Cain, Barnabas...........	H District............	Sergeant Indian Department, S.G.
Cain, John	do	John Cain, senr., a soldier Butler's Rangers, O.C., 21 July, 1796.
Cain, John	E District............ Charlottenburgh......	1789, P. States, no service, only a wish to emigrate from U.S. B.M.A.
Cain, Josiah..........	Fredericksburgh	P. within the British lines in 1779.
Cain, Isaiah...........	Yonge................	A settler, R.J.D.G.
Calder, William	E. D................	Soldier R.R. N.Y. Muster Roll.
Caldwell, John	Home District, Charlottenburgh	From Nova Scotia in 1796.
Caldwell, John	E District	Came in 1786. Soldier R.R. N.Y. Muster Roll—P.L. N.J. 1786.
Campbell, Alexr......	Adolphus Town	Loyalist, Govr. Hamilton's Certificate. P.—850 acres. L.B.M. 1790—P.L. 1786.
Campbell, Esq., Alexr.	E District	Lieutenant Loyal Rangers.
Campbell, Alexr......	do. of Johnstown	Had a wife and four children P.L. 2d, 1786.
Campbell, Junr., Alexr.	do.	Son of a Soldier—250, Ld. Bd.L.
Campbell, Alexander..	do. Lancaster..	
Campbell, Allan	Elizabeth Town	Soldier Loyal Rangers—J.F. P.L. 2d, 1786.
Campbell, Allan......	E District, Lancaster	Son to Moses Campbell, single. P.L. 2d, 1786—who was Store Keeper to Indian Department and joined in 1777, N.M.L.
Campbell, Allan......	do.	
Campbell, Ami...........	do.	
Campbell, Archibald..	Adolphus Town	P. only says Loyalist. L. B.M. 1793. 300. P.L. 1786—Son of Alexander Campbell.
Campbell, Daniel......	E District	Sergeant Roxboro' and Williamsburg, R. R. N.Y. Muster Roll
Campbell, Senr., ... Daniel	do. Charlottenburg	Soldier R. R. N.Y. Muster Roll — a wife and child, P.L.N.J. 1786 and P.L. 2d, 1786.
Campbell, Junr., ... Daniel	do.	R.R.N.Y.

APPENDIX B. 149

NAMES.	RESIDENCE.	DESCENDANTS.
Campbell, Duncan	E District.............	One of this name asks land as a settler from N. Y. State. L.B.L. 1793, and one joined the Standard under Genl. Burgoyne in 1777, O.E.
Campbell,. Widow .... Elizabeth	do. Lancaster..	Widow of the late Moses Campbell Soldier. Restored to U. E. by Order in Council, 2d June, 1808.
Campbell, Sergt. George	H District	⎫
Campbell, George	E District	⎬ S.G.K. Rangers.
Campbell, George	do.	⎭
Campbell, Hugh......	Kingston	Corpl. late 38th Regt., p. P.
Campbell, John Law..	Sophias and Ameliasburgh	His name is John Law, came in as a youth. P L. 1786.
Campbell, James	H District	From Nova Scotia, served in Refugee Corps.
Campbell, James	E District, Augusta ..	Lieutenant Loyal Rangers— L.B.L (*Ensign.*)
Campbell, James	do. Osnabruck	R.R.N.Y.—Mr. Crysler.
Campbell, Oliver......	Adolphus Town	Soldier Associated Loyalists three sons John, William and Stephen. Land in Cramahe.
Campbell, Richard....	Marysburgh	(Stamped Book). A Sergeant in British Regt., 84th, Gov. Hamilton's Certe. 200—a wife and 2 children and P.L. 1786.
Campbell, Sergt. .... Robert	H District.............	B. Rangers, P.—Had a wife and two children, P.L.N. 1786. Niagara Stamped Book.
Campbell, William....	Adolphus Town	Sergeant New York Volunteers. L.B.M. 1792—400.
Campbell, William......	E District, Elizabeth Town	A Settler—Came in 1788. L.B.L. 1790.
Cameron, Alexr.......	do. Lancaster	R. R. N. Y. M. Roll. R.R. N.Y. P.L. 2d, 1786.
Cameron, Senr., Alexr.	do. Cornwall	R.R.N.Y. M. Roll—Had a wife and four children, P.L.N.J. 1786.
Cameron, Junr., Alexr.	do.	Soldier R. R. N. Y.—Son of John Cameron, R.R.N.Y. Single man, P.L. 2d, 1786.
Cameron, Alexander...	Charlottenburg	On Original Roll.
Cameron, Allan.......	E District.............	R.R.N.Y.
Cameron, Angus......	do. Charlottenburg	Soldier R. Regt., N. Y.— (P.L. N.J. 1786).

150   APPENDIX B.

NAMES.	RESIDENCE.	DESCENDANTS.
Cameron, Archd......	E District............	Soldier R.R.N.Y. Ld. Bd. (P.L.N.J. 1786).
Cameron, Daniel .... Donald	do.	S.G. Soldier K. Rangers— Ld. Bd. L. A wife, one child—P. L. N. J. 1786. One son of Wm. Buy Cameron.
Cameron, Donald	E District, Charlottenburg	84th Regt., S.G. One on Niagara Stamped Book.
Cameron, Donald	do. 15.5 Con. Cornwall	Son of a Soldier, Ld Bd. L. of John Cameron, R. R. N.Y.
Cameron, Duncan	do. Edwardsburg	Jessup's Corps—R.J.D.G.
Cameron, Duncan	do. Lancaster ..	
Cameron, Duncan	do. do. ...	Son of
Cameron, Senr., Hugh	do. Cornwall ..	R.R.N.Y. P.L.N.J. 1786.
Cameron, Junr., Hugh	do. do. ...	Son of John Cameron of R.R.N.Y.
Cameron, Hugh.......	Charlottenburgh	R. R. N. Y. Muster Roll. P.L. 2d, 1786.
Cameron, John	E District, Charlottenburg	States Service as a Subaltern under General Burgoyne and afterwards as a Millwright and Master Carpenter in the P. Works, L.B.L. - Came in early in the War. Mr. McD.
Cameron, John	do. Lancaster ..	I. Battn. R.R.N.Y. Muster Roll, P. L. N. J. 1786.— One a Soldier 54th Regt.
Cameron, Senr., John	do. Cornwall ..	Soldier R.R.N.Y. M. Roll. Ld.Bd. (a wife and 3 children. P.L. 2d, 1786.
Cameron, Junr., John	do. Charlottenburg	Son of John Cameron of R.R.N.Y.
Cameron, Junr., John	do. Lancaster..	Son of Alexr. Cameron of Indian Dept.
Cameron, Junr., John	do. Cornwall ..	Son of John Cameron of Royl. R.N.Y.
Cameron, William Buy	do. Charlottenburg	1st Battn. R.R.N.Y. N. McL.—P.L.N.J. 1786.
Cameron, William	do. Cornwall ..	Soldier 84th Regt. Ld. Bd. L.—P.L. 2d, 1786.
Cameron, John	Kingston	Son of EnsignDuncan Cameron, R.Y.
Canon, John	do.	By Order in Council, 23rd Novr., 1802.
Carll, } John ...... Carroll, }	H District	Soldier Butler's Rangers. S. P.L.N., 1786.

APPENDIX B. 151

NAMES.	RESIDENCE.	DESCENDANTS.
Carll, Jonas	H District	Served under Col. James Delaney, P.
Carey, Bernard	do.	19th December, 1806. Resided in Virginia and joined Royal Standard at York Town.
Carley, Barthow	E District, Augusta	Soldier Loyal Rangers. Jessup's Corps. E.J.
Carley, Abraham	New Castle Dist.	Served in Cap.Saml. Adam's Company. Order in Council, 30th June, 1807.
Carman, George	E District, Matilda	1st Bat. R.R.N.Y.
Carman, Jacob	do. do	Son of Michael Carman, U.E., Ld.Bd.L. 200.
Carman, Senr., Michael	do. do.	Soldier Royal Yorkers, R.R. N.Y. M. Roll.—A wife and 5 children. P.L. 2d, 1786.
Carman, Junr., Michael	do. do.	Son of Michael Carman, Senr., U.E. 200. Ld.Bd. L.—(has a wife P.L. 2d, 1786.
Carnahan, Joseph	M District	Had drawn 200 acres, L.B. A. 1794; grant 200 more P.L. 1786—Genl. Haldimand Certe. 100. Loyalist from New York. A.Mc.L.
Carns, Christian	E District, Matilda	Son of Jacob Carns.
Carns, Senr., Jacob	do.	Soldier Royal Yorkers. P— has a wife and 2 children. P.L. 2d, 1786.
Carpenter, John	W District	Served at Miamis during Waynes' aggression —belonged to the Royal Navy.
Carpenter, Peter	E District, Cornwall	A Soldier Loyal Rangers— J.B. P.L.N.J. 1786.
Carr, Senr., Daniel	Ernest Town	Volunteer Loyal Rangers— 500 acres. L.B.M. 1790; family land included.
Carr, Junr., Daniel	do.	Son of Daniel Senr.
Carr, Norrice Kerr	Adolphus Town	Served in the Engineers' Department—was at York Town.
Carrigan, Peter	E District	Sergeant Loyal Rangers— J.F.
Carr, William	do. Cornwall	R.R.N.Y. Muster Roll. P. L. 2d, 1786.
Carrscallon, Edward	Fredericksburgh, M.C.	Lieut. (Stamped Book) R.R. N.Y. P.L. 1786.

APPENDIX B.

NAMES.	RESIDENCE.	DESCENDANTS.
Carscallon, George....	Fredericksburgh, M.C.	P. States Soldier, Royl. Yorkers — L. B. M. 1790 R.R.N.Y. P.L. 1786.
Carscallin, John	do.	Sergt. K. R. Regt., N. Y. (Genl. Haldimand 100). Stamped Book. O.C. 18th Novr., 1797. P.L. 1786.
Carscallon, James.....	do.	500. Sergt. M.C. K.R. Regt. N.Y. O.C. 18th Novr., 1797, P.L. 1786 –1784 G. Haldimand, 100.
Carscallen, Luke......	do.	M.C. Sergeant R. R. N. Y. Genl. Haldimand 200. (Stamped Book). P. L. 1786.
Carson, William	Marysburgh.........	Sergeant 29th Regt. P. Provision list (Stamped Book).
Carter Thadeus	Augusta.............	Emigrant from Connecticut, L.B.L., about 1793.
Cartwright, Senr.,.... Richard	Kingston	Joined the Royal Standard before 1783.
Cartwright. Junr.,.... Richard	do.	Son of Richard, Senr.
Carty, Thomas........	H District............	200 acres N.R. –his father stated killed at Eutaw Springs.
Case, Josiah.......... Cass	E District............ Grand River	R.R.N.Y. Muster Roll–his sons, Joseph P. Cass, Elihu, Daniel.
Case, Joseph Pomroy..	E District............	Drummer R.R.N.Y. See order - in - Council 17th March, 1807.
Case, Peter	do.	R.R.N.Y. Muster Roll, P.
Chase, Walter, Senr...	do.	A Loyalist in New York; went to New Brunswick in 1803, p. Jno. Williams' certificate in 1805 (Stamped Book) Loyalist P.L. 1786. Order - in - Council 11th March, 1807, misnomer rectified — his sons, Walter and John Chase.
Casey, William	Adolphus Town	William Casey was a master carpenter in Qr. Mr. Genl. Depart. at Yorktown—500 L.B.M. 1790. Came in 1786—P.L. 1786 & L.B.M. 1793, 200. Says no land drawn before—L.B.A.1790 —200. Says only 200 before.

APPENDIX B. 153

NAMES.	RESIDENCE.	DESCENDANTS.
Cashin, John	E District............	Soldier in 84th Regt., Ld.
Cason	Charlottenburgh	Bd. P.L. 2d, 1786.
Cash, Josiah..........	M District............	
Cassady. Daniel	H District............	Soldier in B. R. p. P. Niagara Stamped Book—S. P.L.N. 1786.
Cassleman, Conradt ..	E District............ Williamsburgh	Soldier in R. Regt. N. York —300 Muster Roll (single) P. L. 2d, 1786. Son of Suffrenus.
Cassleman, Henry	do., Williamsburgh..	Drummer R.R. N.Y. M. Roll—single, P.L.2d,1786.
Cassleman, John......	H District, M. C.	Soldier B.R.—P. O.C. 18th Novr., 1797, Niagara Stamped Book—a wife & one child—P.L.N. 1786,
Cassleman, Richard ..	Williamsburgh........	R.R.N.Y. Muster Roll. A. Had wife & child. P. L. 2d, 1786.
Cassleman, Suffrenus..	E District, Matilda ..	R.R.N.Y. Muster Roll—one child—P.L. 2d, 1786.
Cassleman, Junr., ... Suffrenus	do.	Son of Suffrenus, Senr., 200.
Cassleman, William ..		See order - in - Council 17th March, 1807. Soldier R.R. N.Y.
Cassleman, Thomas ..	do., Williamsburgh	Drummer R.R.N.Y., Muster Roll. Single—P. L. 2d, 1786.
Cassleman, Warner .. Verner	Williamsburgh........	R.R.N.Y. Muster Roll—a wife & two children. P.L. 2d, 1786.
Castles, John	Lancaster	Single. P.L. 2d, 1786.
Caswell, Lemuel	E District............	S.G. Sergt. King's Rangers. A. McL.
Cesar, blackman, John	H District............	
Chambers, Sergt. .... Abijah	do.	Jersey volunteer.
Chambers, James	E do.	Soldier Loyal Rangers. J.F.
Chambers, James	do.	Son of James.
Chavasey, James ...	Marysburgh	Discharged British soldier, 84th Regt.
Chester, John	E District............	Soldier Loyal Rangers. P.
Chew, W. Johnson....	H District............	Ensn. Orange Rangers.
Chietsey, Baria	{ E Dictrict.......... { Elizabeth Town	
Chisholm, Senr., Alexr.	E District,Lancaster..	R.R.N.Y. Muster Roll—P. L. N. J. 1786.
Chisholm, Alexander..	do. do. ..	

J

APPENDIX B.

NAMES.	RESIDENCE.	DESCENDANTS.
Chisholm, Alexander..	Thurlow, M.C...........	At the siege of Quebec in 1775, commanded a compy. of Loyalists—dischd. B.S.
Chisholm, Allan	E District, Lancaster..	Drummer R.R.N.Y. (Mr. McDougal), P. L. N. J. 1786.
Chisholm, Archibald..	Thurlow..............	Sergeant 71 Regt. p. P. British soldier, P.L. 1786. S.
Chisholm, Donald	E District............ Charlottenburgh	R.R.N.Y. P.L.N.J. 1786.
Chisholm, Duncan	E District............ Lancaster	Corpl. R.R.N.Y. (Son of Donald.) P.L.N.J. 1786. p. Revd. Alex.McDonell's cert.
Chisholm, George	H District............	P. states a carpenter in Genl. Burgoyne's army.
Chisholm, Hugh	E District, Lancaster..	R.R.N.Y. (son of Donald), P.L.N.J. 1786.
Chisholm, John	H District............	Indian Department S.G.— had a wife, P.L.N. 1786. Niagara Stamped Book.
Chisholm, John	Cornwall	Soldier Loyal Rangers (W. Fraser), P.L. 2d, 1786.
Chisholm, Lewis.......	E District Lancaster..	Son to a soldier—200 acres— L. Bd. Lu. (of Donald).
Chisholm, William....	do. Charlottenburg	Soldier K. R. Regt. N.Y. Muster Roll P. L. N. J. 1786.
Chridmoger, John .... if Christopher	Ernest Town..........	B.S. discharged British soldier. P.L. 1786.
Christie, Abijah	E District............	Son of John, Senr. J.B. a soldier R.R.N.Y., L. Bd. (Stamped Book.) P. L. 1786.
Christie, Senr., John..	do.	Soldier Royl. Yorkers—Muster Roll, P.L. 2d., 1786.
Christie, Junr., John..	do.	Son of John, Senr., J. B. Rept., L.B. Stormont.
Chrysler, Lt. Adam ..	H District............	Indian Department S.G.— had a wife and 3 children, P. L. N. 1786. Niagara Stamped Book.
Chryster, Peter	do.	Soldier B.R, p. P.
Church,Jonathan Mills	Elizabeth Town	P. states service as a non com. No corps mentioned. A sergeant R.R.N.Y. P. P.L. 1786.
Church, Oliver........	Fredericksburgh	S.G. Lieut. R. R. N. Y. Stamped Book. P.L.1786.

APPENDIX B. 155

NAMES.	RESIDENCE.	DESCENDANTS.
Church, Junr., Oliver	Fredericksburgh	Volunteer—400 acres — and son of Lt. O. Church, R. R. N.Y., P.L. 1786.
Church, William......	Yonge...............	Soldier in Fanning's Regt. L.B.L. 1792.
Chancey, Michael .... or Clancey	Marysburgh	British Soldier, P.L.1786. S. Stamped Book.
Clandelling, Abraham.	H District............	nnyng Son of James Rangers S.—P.L.N. 1786. Niagara Stamped Book.
Clandenning, John....	do.	Restored to U.E. 26th Jan., 1808. Jersey Volunteers.
Clandenning, Senr., .. James	do.	Soldier B. Rangers. Had a wife and three sons. P. L. N. 1786.
Clandenning, Walter..	do.	Son of James. Soldier B. Rangers, S.G. Niagara Stamped Book.
Clapwood, Ernest .... Claproadt	Marysburgh	Soldier German troops, C. Book and Provision List 1786.
Clarke, Alexander	H District............	S.G. McAlpine's corps.
Clark, Alexr.	Fredericksburgh	S.G. Sergeant R. Yorkers, P.L.B.M. 1790, 550, P.L. 1786. Stamped Book.
Clark, Henry	Ernest Town	Soldier Loyal Rangers.
Clark, Hugh	Fredericksburgh	P. a seaman from the States in 1796.
Clark, Joseph	Adolphus Town	p. P. Employed on Secret Service. Joined 1776.
Clark, Mathew	Ernest Town	Son of Robert. L.B.M.1792.
Clark, Robert	do	Served in Jessup's corps. P. L. 1786.
Clark, William	Adolphus Town	Soldier Associated Loyalists. L.B.M. 1790. P.L. 1786.
Classen, Caleb........	E District Augusta ..	A sergeant Loyal Rangers.
Claus, Col. Daniel	H District............	
Claws, Capt. William..	Niagara District......	By order-in-Council 16th April, 1798.
Claus, Gasper John ..	Marysburgh	John Gasper Clawse, a soldier of Brunswick troops. L.B.M. 1791—300—P. L. 1786.
Clement, Lt. John....	H District............	Indian Department S.G.— had a wife, 3 children & 2 servants. P.L.N. 1786.
Clement, John........	Ernest Town	
Clement, James	H District............	Issuing Commissary Indian Dept. S. G. Niagara Stamped Book.

APPENDIX B.

Names.	Residence.	Descendants.
Clement, Lt. Joseph..	H District............	Indian Department,Niagara Stamped Book.
Clement, Sergt. Joseph	H District............	Had a wife, one child and 2 servants, P. L. N. 1786.
Clement, Senr., Lewis.	do	
Clinch, Lt. Ralph.....	do	S.G.R. R. N. York, Niagara Stamped Book.
Clinch, Benjamin N...	do	How? resident in the United States, 2000 acres granted him in Mechlinburgh.
Clerk, Francis.........	E District............	Sergeant R. R. N. Y.Muster Roll, P. L. N. J. 1786.
Clerk, James	do Charlottenburgh	Corporal R. R. Regt. N. Y. Muster Roll.
Clew, William........ or Clough.	do	A Corporal in Jessup's.
Cline, George.........	do	Son of Michael J. B.
Cline, John...........	do	do do
Cline, Adam.........		See Order-in-Conncil 17th March 1807, Soldier R. R. N. Y.
Cloady, Henry........ Cludy.	Marysburgh	Soldier 53rd Regt. Genl. Haldimand's, 1784(Stamped Book).
Clous, Corpr. John....	H District............	B. Rangers, p. P.L. P. S. N. 1786.
Clow, Henry..........	E District............	Thomas Sherwood,Esq., certifies that H.Clow left this Province in 1789. 1794 served as Sergeant R. McLean's P.
Cluny, James........	do late of Augusta	A drummer in Jessups Corps R. J. D. G.
Clyne, Michael .... Cline.	do	Gunsmith from Mohawk River, supposed R. R. N. Y., P. L. 2d, 1786.
Cockle, George, Junr..	of Niagara............	Restored O. C. 18th March, 1808.
Cork, John	Ernest Town	
Cockle, John..........	Niagara	O. C. 17 March, 1808. Soldier Butler's Rangers.
Coffin, William	Kingston	Lieut. R. R. N. Y., P. L. 1786. N. I.
Coffin, Commy. James.	H district.............	Son of resident in Quebec.
Coghill, Senr., George.	do	Deceased; soldier Butler's Rangers,L.B.Nassau 1794.
Coghill, Junr., George.	do	Son of George Coghill, Snr.

APPENDIX B. 157

NAMES.	RESIDENCE.	DESCENDANTS.
Coghill, Peter..........	H District............	Came in when a boy, son of George—Mr. Clinch's information.
Coghill, (above) John..	do	Nov. 1st 1804, discovered on the original roll, a soldier Butler's Rangers, himself.
Coll, Adam...........	E Dist.,ElizabethTown	Late of Jessups' Corps, R.J. D. G.
Coll, Bernard............. Barnat.	Sophias & Ameliasb'g..	Son of Daniel, U. E., L. B. A. 1793. 200 P. L. 1786.
Coll, Daniel	Adolphus Town.......	Soldier Orange Rangers, L. B. M., P. L. 1786.
Cole, John............	H District............	
Cole, Peter	Sophias & Ameliasb'g..	States Loyalist, P.from New York, A. McL.
Cole, Simon J.........	do do ..	Soldier in Corps not stated in P. Loyalist from New York P.L. 1786. A. McL.
Cole, John............	E District, Augusta...	Loyal Ranger.
Colder	do Lancaster...	Inserted Calder, Wm.
Colhier, William......	Ernest Town	
Colins, Alexander.....	H District............	P.States a soldier, 100,Corps mentioned, New York volunteers.
Collard, John.........	do	Was a guide to the army at N. York & C. P.
Collier, Peter	Marysburgh	Sergt. 29th Regt. L. B. M. 1792—in all 600 and Govr. Hamilton(Stamped Book).
Collins, John	H District...	Soldier 71st Regt. P.
Collison, John........	Matilda	Drummer R.R.N.Y. Muster Roll I.—has a wife P. L. 2d 1786.
Colrake, Peter........	H District	Que.? if not Peter Colrick expunged — Volunteer I. Department S. P. L. N. 1785. Niagara Stamped Book.
Coltman, John........	H District, M. C......	Soldier King's R.R.N. York Muster Roll A.
Comber, Jacob........	Ernest Town	Loyal Rangers, A. McL.
Comber, Paul......... Comer.	do	Soldier O. C. L.B.M., 1790. (P. L. 1786).
Comber, Thomas	do	Que.? if not Comar, soldier Loyal Rangers, P. (P. L. 1786.
Concklin, John	do	Had drawn 100 acres. L. B. A. 1794. 200. A soldier, A. McL.

APPENDIX B.

NAMES.	RESIDENCE.	DESCENDANTS.
Conklin, Joseph....		Loyal Rangers, A. McL. P. L. 1786.
Conklin, Robert......	H District............	Soldier in B. Rangers. P.
Conlon, Michael......	Kingston...............	Soldier 84th L. B. M. 1791. (Stamped Book).P.L.1786. Loyalist, A. McL.
Cook, George.........	E District, Williamsb'g	Son of John Cook. J.C.
Cook, Michael........	Edwardsburgh........	84th Regt.
Cook, Michael........	E District, Williamsb'g	Served in the Commissary Department. P. 1793. L. B. L. 300 acres.
Cook, Thomas........	Kingston...............	Que.: how U.E.? discharged soldier (British). 34 Regt. P. L. 1786.
Cook, John............	E District, Osnabruck.	From South Carolina Order-in-Council 17th Feb. 1807.
Cook, William........	Ernest Town..........	Soldier in 65 Regt. Warrant Officer R. Artily. L.B.W. Dist. Son of John Cook.
Coon, Sergt. John......	H District...	B. Rangers, had wife and 6 children. P. L. N. 1786, Niagara Stamped Book.
Connor, John.........	Midland	By Order-in-Council 13th January 1807.
Coons, Conradt.......	E District, Williamsb'g	R. R. N. Y. Muster Roll A.
Coons, Gasper........	do Matilda....	R. R. N. Y. Muster Roll, A. a wife and one child, P.L. 2d 1786.
Coons, John..........	do Osnabruck..	Original settler, soldier R.R. N. Y. Muster Roll, A. (Single, P. L. 2d 1786.
Cooper, James........	Home District........	Nov.1, 1804, on original Roll.
Coons, Jacob.........	E District, Williamsb'g	Soldier R. R. N. Y. Muster Roll, P. 1794 (Stamped Book), a wife, P. L. 1786.
Cooper, Thomas...... .	Home District........	Nov.1, 1804, on original Roll.
Corban, Daniel.......	Ernest Town..........	A settler from State of New York, L. B. L.
Corbin, Nathaniel.....	E District............	Soldier Loyal Rangers.
Corbman, Jacob	Sophias & Ameliasb'g..	Sergeant K. Regt. N. Y. P. had drawn 200 L. B. A.; 1794, 200 (Stamped Book).
Cornelius, John.......	Fredericksburgh	Soldier R. R. N. Y. L.B.M. 1790, 100 acres and sold, 1793, 200 Bounty, P. L. 1786 (Stamped Book).
Cornel, Albert........	Adolphustown..........	Loyalist P. L. 1786, from New York, A. McL.
Cornell, Joseph.......	do	Son of Albert Cornell.

APPENDIX B.   159

NAMES.	RESIDENCE.	DESCENDANTS.
Cornwall, Senr., John.	Malden.................	His son, U. E. soldier Butler's Rangers, U. list 1789.
Corns, Cors............ Castle.	H District............	Niagara Stamped Book, S. P. L. N. 1786.
Corby, George........	do	Soldier, M. C. in K. R. R. N. York O. C. 25th April, 1797.
Corway, James.......	Ernest Town..........	
Cottier, Senr., James..	Fredericksburgh........	M. C. 450 acres R. R. N. Y. a soldier L.B.M. 1791 and P.L., says R.R.N.Y.1786.
Cottier, Junr., James..	do	Son of James Senr. L. B. A. 1794, 200.
Cottier, Richard....... Cotta.	do	S. G. Sergt. Ameliasburgh, a Sergeant R. R. N. Y., L. B. M. 1790, 200 (Stamped Book) P.L. 1786, L.B.A. 1794, 200 acres to the heirs of R. Cotter.
Covil, John...........	E District, Augusta...	Son of Simon.
Conville, Simeon......	do ...	S. G. Capt. Jessups.
Cough, John..........	do Osnabruck...	R. R. N. Y. Muster Roll A.
Countryman, Conradt.	E District............	Son of Jacob Senr. J. B
Countryman, Sr.,Jacob	do	Soldier R. R. N. Y. Muster Roll A. Govr. Hamilton's Certe. P. L. 2d 1786.
Countryman,Jr., Jacob	do	Son of Jacob Senr. J.B.
Cox, Samuel....	H District, M.C........	An Artificer P. B. Rangers. J. S. a wife P. L. N. 1786. Niagara Stamped Book.
Crammer, Frederick... Cromner.	Marysburgh..........	Soldier 53rd Regt. L. B. M. 1791 300 (P. L. 1786) S.
Crane, Elisha........ Elijah.	do	Soldier 44th Regt. L. B. M. 20th April, 1791, 300 (P.L. 1786) Stamped Book.
Cranty, Michael	H District............	Niagara Stamped Book.
Crawford, John	do.	Sergeant last war p. P. does not state the corps—Treasury Loyalist—one of this name a soldier R.R.N.Y. Muster Roll, in Col. Em ricks—lost an arm.
Crawford, James......	do.	
Crawford, David......	Pickering	Order-in-Council 13th May, 1807. Soldier Loyal American Regiment.
Crawford, William....	Fredericksburgh	Ensign in Sir John's R.R. N.Y. P.L. 1786.

APPENDIX B.

NAMES.	RESIDENCE.	DESCENDANTS.
Crippon, Darius	E District, bastard	1793. P. late from N. York State—wishes to become a subject and settler.
Critus, George } Crytes	do. Cornwall	R.R.N.Y. Muster Roll.
Crane, John } James	do.	
Cross, Henry	do.	Soldier King's Rangers. p. Regl. Roll.
Crouder, Anthony	do.	Soldier R.R.N.Y. L. Bd. L. P.L.N.J. 1786.
Crouder, John	do., Charlottenburgh	R.R.N.Y. McDougal.
Crouder, John	Osnabruck	Soldier R.R.N.Y. L.B.L. 1790. P.L. 2d, 1786.
Crouder, James	E District	Loyalist. P.L. 2d, 1786.
Crouder, Isaac	do. Osnabruck	Soldier R. Regt. N. York. P.L. 2d, 1786.
Crouder, Senr., William	do.	Land Board Certificate states U. E. P. L. N. J. 1786.
Crouder, Junr., William	do.	(P.L.N.J. 1786.)
Crouder, 3rd, William	do.	R.R.N.Y.
Crouse, John	do. Matilda	R.R.N.Y. Muster Roll.
Cruikshank, Widow	do.	Cedars.
Crumb, Benoni	H District	Que., if the same as Benjamin. B.R. S.G. S. P.L. N. 1786.
Crumb, William	do.	p. P. a volunteer in the Indian Department.
Crumb, William	do.	O.C. 13th Oct., 1796—volunteer Indian Department. S. P.L.N. 1786.
Cryderman, Widow C.	E District, Cornwall	P.L. 2d, 1786.
Cryderman, Hermanns Crithuman	E District	A soldier R.R.N.Y. J. T. P.L. 2d, 1786.
Cryderman, John	do.	Sons of Widow Cryderman. J.B. Late from the U. States, 1790, 200 acres— emigt.—P.L.2d,1786. One of this name a corporal. Soldier R.R.N.Y. Muster Roll. P.L. 2d, 1786.
Cryderman, Joseph	do.	
Cryderman, Michael Cruderman	Marysburgh	R.R. N.Yk. Michl. Cryderman E.D. Soldier Muster Roll. A. (Provision list 1786. British Regt.)
Chrysler, John Chrysdall	Thurlow	Soldier Loyal Rangers. L. B. M. 1790.
Chrysler, Geronomus	E District	Order-in-Council 21st February, 1807. R.R.N.Y.

APPENDIX B. 161

NAMES.	RESIDENCE.	DESCENDANTS.
Chrysler,Senr., John..	E District, Matilda ..	Soldier R.R.N.Y.
Chrysler,Junr., John..	do.	See order - in - Council 21st Feby., 1807. Drummer Butler's Rangers. A wife. P.L. 2d, 1786.
Crysler, William......	....	See order-in-Council 17th March, 1807. Soldier Butler's Rangers.
Chrysler, Philip	E District, Cornwall ..	Soldier R.R.N.Y.—had a wife and 5 children. P.L. 2d, 1786.
Culbert, Donald	Charlottenburgh	Soldier K. R. Regt. N. Y. P.L.N.J. 1786.
Culver, Timothy......	H District............	On Staten Island.
Cumming, William....	E District............	Soldier 84th Regt. R.L.B.S. M. & E. D.— Stamped Book — Niagara Stamped Book.
Cummings, John......	Marysburgh	Soldier 84th Regt. p. P. 300 —L.B.M. 1791 (P.L. 1786) P.L. 2d, 1786 S. Stamped Book.
Cummings, Mrs Jane..	H District............	Wife of Thomas Cummings. Stated daught. of a Loyalist.
Cummings, Thomas ..	do.	B.Rangers. Niagara Stamped Book. P.L.N. 1786.
Cuniff, John.......... Canniff	Adolphus Town	Was within the British lines at New York in 1782. P. Dorland's afft.
Cuniff, James	do.	P. states only Loyalist, and not to have had any land in 1797.
Curry, Ephraim	E District............	A sergeant Loyal Rangers.
Curry, George........	E District, Lancaster..	Son to a soldier. L. Bd. L. 200.
Curry, John	do. do. ..	Soldier King's Rangers, p. Regt. Roll.
Curry, James	do.	P. states late of 31st Regt.— his family not in before 1798. One of King's Rangers. N.M.L.
Curry, James	do. Lancaster ..	Soldier Royal Yorkers. Had a wife and three children. P.L. 2d, 1786.
Curry, alias Picard, M.	do. do. ..	Widow of James Curry, a soldier King's Rangers. (Lt. Col. Green. August, 1804.)

APPENDIX B.

NAMES.	RESIDENCE.	DESCENDANTS.
Dacksteder, George Adam	Niagara District	By order - in - Council 4th February, 1807.
Dacksteder, Lt. John	H District	S. G. Indian Department. Niagara Stamped Book. S. P.L.N. 1786.
Dacksteder, Junr., Corl. John	do.	S. G. Indian Department. Niagara Stamped Book.
Dagherty, Anthony	do.	Bore arms at Hillsborroughs under Lord Cornwallis.
Dalhunty, John Dalyhunlough	Marysburgh	British soldier. P.L. 1786. S.
Dalson, Isaac	W District	S.G. U.E. Loyalist at Fort Stanwix.
Dalson, Matthew		S.G. Loyalist. Petition states a volunteer in Butler's Rangers. Q.
Daly Peter	Ernest Town	Soldier in Jessup's corps.
Damderf, John	Marysburgh	Soldier German troops. Provision List 1786.
Danby, Chris.	Kingston	Not U.E. Treasury Loyalist *Ann* not U.E. Stamped Book.
Dap, Peter	Marysburgh	
Darby, John	H District	Soldier in the war of 1763 S. P.L.N. 1786.
Dauson, John	E District	
Davey, Henry	Ernest Town	Soldier R.R.N.Y. L.B.M. 1789.
Davey, John	Ernest Town	Soldier R.R.N.Y. Muster Roll (P.L. 1786).
Davey, Michael	do.	States residence since 1784.
Davey, Peter	do.	1790. L. B. M. 500 acres. Gov. Hamilton's certificate states Loyalist. Two deeds issued. 500. P.L. 1786.
David, Henry	Marysburgh	Soldier German troops. C, Book & Provision List of 1786.
Davies, Peter	E District	Soldier Royal Yorkers— Muster Roll.
Davies, Richard	do.	Soldier 29th Regt. One R.R. N.Y. A drummer, Muster Roll.
Davies, William	Elizabeth Town	States having bore arms on Long Island & in N. York.
Davis, Benjamin	H District	M.C. Sergt. B. Rangers, O. C. 24th Jany., 1797.
Davis, Isaac	do.	Engineer Department. Que., Was he resident in the States before the war?

APPENDIX B. 163

NAMES.	RESIDENCE.	DESCENDANTS.
Davis, Henry	Adolphus Town	29th Regt. A sergeant. Gov. Hamilton, 1785, says soldier. 100. P. L. 1786. Stamped Book.
Davis, Thadeus	Willoughby	Joined at NewYork in 1781. O.C. 22d February, 1808.
Davis, Thomas	H District	From North Carolina. Not on original Roll.
Davis, William	do.	From North Carolina—his sons, Jonathan, Asahel.
Davis, Walter	E District	Reinstated by O. C. 18th February, 1806.
Dawson, James	Kingston	Sergeant N.York Militia P.
Day, Barnabas	do,	(Stamped Book). Incorporated Loyalist from N. York. Called Loyalist. P. L. 1785. A.M.L.
Dayton, Nathan Mathew	Leeds	States services in Genl. Delaney's Brigade as sergeant. Is desired to appear in person. Joel Stone certifies loyalty.
Dean, Aaron	H District	Buck County Volunteers, was a Guide.
Dean, Josiah	Sophias and Amelasburgh.	
Dean, Samuel	do do	Lieut.-General Haldimand. Certificate P. L. 1786, Loyalist from New York.
Decker, Thomas Dyker	H District	S.G. Dyke, Br.'s Rangers, a soldier.
Decon, Jacob	do	Came in 1790, was a soldier, Jersey Volunteers, I. S., restored to U.E. List, 4th May, 1804.
Dederick, Michael	Kingston	Stamped Book, Soldier Associated Loyalists, L. B. M., 1791, 300, P.L. 1786.
Defoe, Abraham	Fredericksburgh	Corporal King's Rangers, p. Regt. Roll, L.B.M. 1790, 550, L.B.M. 1792, 100, in right of his late brother Jacob.
Defoe, Daniel	Fredericksburgh	Soldier King's Rangers, L. B.M. 1790, 200, P.L. 1786
Defoe, John	do	Soldier King's Rangers, p. Regt. Roll, L.B.M. 1790, 400.

APPENDIX B.

NAMES.	RESIDENCE.	DESCENDANTS.
Deforest, Abraham ..	H District............	Son of Mary Defriest, one Abraham, a soldier in B. R. Niagara Stamped Book, B. M. A., R. R. N. Y., a wife and one child, P.L,N., 1786.
Deforest, Rebecca	Leeds	On the 8th December, 1791, Rebecca McLean alias Deforest was refused land, her father Simon Deforest not having joined the Royal Standard, L.B.L.
Defriest, Mary	Of Niagara	Deceased, O.C., 18th March, 1808.
Dell, Henry..........	H District............	States soldier New Jersey Volunteers- Discharge required.
DeMills, Isaac........	Sophias and Ameliasburgh.	States service in the Naval Department at New York.
DeMills, Anthony	New Castle	By order in Council, 3rd March, 1806.
DeMorest, James	Fredericksburgh	Sergeant Orange Rangers.
Denault, Joachim	E District...........	Volunteer, 84th Regt.
Denhart, James	Marysburg	Soldier German Troops, p. Provision List.
Dennis, William......	Marysburg	Stamped Book.
Dennis, John	H District............	Employed in the King's yard during the war as shipwright.
Deniston, Robert	do	S. G. Gov, Hamilton's Volunteers to Fort Vinecens, L.B.W.D.
Denowe, Joiaham	E District............	Indian Department.
Denych, Andrew	Kingston	Soldier New Jersey Volunteers.
Depew, Charles	H District............	Soldier Butler's Rangers, a wife and one child, P. L. N. 1786.
Depew, Senr., John ..	do	S. G., Loyalist, Lieut. Indian Dept., S.G., a wife and four children, P.L.N. 1786, Niagara Stamped Book.
Depew, Junr., John ..	do	S. G., Loyalist, Niagara Stamped Book, S. P.L.N. 1786.
Depew, William......	do	S.G., Loyalist, Son of Lt. John Depew, Niagara Stamped Book, S. P.L.N. 1786.

APPENDIX B. 165

NAMES.	RESIDENCE.	DESCENDANTS.
Dell, Senr., Barsnet ..	H District............	1788, came into the Province, no active service stated, his sons, William Henry, Barsnet, Barrie, Nathaniel.
Derheart, John	E District............	Soldier Loyal Rangers.
Derry, London.......	Edwardsburgh........	Butler's Rangers (single P. L. 2d, 1786).
Detlor, George........	Fredericksburgh......	Son of Valentine Detlor—dead.
Detlor, John	do	Stamped Book, when a boy drew 100 acres. L.B.M. 1791—100 acres more R. R.N.Y. B.M.A..
Detlor, Jacob	Fredericksburgh	M.C. Sergeant King's R. Regt., N. York, O.C. 12th July, 1797 — 1784 Genl. Haldimand's, 100 sold to Cyrenus Parks.. Stamped Book.
Detlor, Peter	do	M.C. Corporal S.B.M. 29th, 400—Says Sergt. R.R.N. Y., 25th July, 1796. P.L. 1786.
Detlor, Samuel	do	M.C. Soldier Royl.Yorkers. Only 100, as he is still a young man, and resides with his father. 1790, L. B. M. 1791. Bounty 200, L.B.M.
Detlor, Valentine.....	do	Soldier K. R. Regt., New York, 1784. Genl. Haldimand. 100. P. L. 1786. Sold to Cyrenus Parks.
Devoe, Conradt	E District............	R.R.N.Y. Muster Roll. A. P.L. 2d, 1786.
Dewit, Gaston........	do	Soldier R.R.N.Y. P.L. 2d, 1786.
Dewit, John..........	do	A drummer R.R.N.Y. Ld. Bd. P.L. 2d, 1786.
Diamond, John	Ernest Town	Son of Jacob, Senr., P.1794. Say Loyalist, and to have drawn 100. King's Rangers. P.L. 1786.
Diamond, John, Senr..	Fredericksburgh	Soldier King's Rangers. P. L.1786. L.B.M. 1791. 350.
Diamond, Jacob......	do	Soldier King's Rangers. L. B.M. 1790. 500. P.L.1786.
Diamond, Junr., Jacob	do	Son of King's Rangers. P.L. 1786.

APPENDIX B.

Names.	Residence.	Descendants.
Dick, John............	Marysburg	Discharged Brit. soldier. P. L.1786. 34th Regt. Stamped Book.
Dickson, Francis......	Ernest Town..........	84th Regt. soldier (Stamped Book.) (P.L. 1786.)
Dicky, William	Charlottenburgh......	Soldier R. R. N. Y. Muster Roll. P.L.N.J. 1786.
Dies, John	Fredericksburgh......	Son of Mathew Dies, Senr.
Dies, Senr., Mathew..	do	Quarter Master R.R.N.Y. Stamped Book. P.L.1786.
Dies, Junr., Mathew..	do	Son of Mathew Dies, Senr.
Dingman, Garret	do	Stamped Book R. R. N. Y. Muster Roll. R. R. N. Y. P.L. 1786. Had drawn 100 acres, L.B.A. 1794. Grant 200.
Dingman, Richard....	Osnabruck............	R.R.N.Y. Muster Roll. Has a wife and 5 children. P. L. 2d, 1786.
Dingwell, John	E District, Glengarry.	Soldier R. R. N. Y. Muster Roll. P.L.N.J. 1786.
Dingwell, James......	do	Soldier Royal Regt.N.York. MusterRoll P.L.N.J.1786.
Disman, Timothy	W District	Soldier 84th Regt.
Disson, John	E District...........	
Dixon, John..........	do	Soldier Royal Yorkers. P.L. 2d, 1786.
Dixon, Senr., Robert..	do	With General Burgoyne.
Dixon, Junr., Robert..	do	
Dixon, William	Lancaster	With General Burgoyne.
Doan, Joseph	H District............	States to have joined Royal Standard prior to 1783; came to the Province 1787; was wounded in the face. A. Burwell.
Dockstader, Lt. Frederick	do	Indian Department. S.G.
Docksteder, Jr., John.	do	Son of John. S. P.L.N.1786.
Donahon, John........	M District............	States to have served in the Royal Artillery, and afterwards on Lake Ontario as a mariner.
Donawan, Florence ...	Fredericksburgh......	Soldier Royal Regt.N.York. Muster Roll. J. P.L.1786.
Dunavan.		
Dopp, Peter..........	Montague	R.R.N.Y. Muster Roll.A.S.
Dorin, David.........	E District............	Son of John Dorin. Single. P.L.2d,1786. L.B.A.1794 had drawn 90 as. Grant 200 more.
Dorin, John..........	Matilda	Settler — N. McL., Esq.— Mr. Paterson.

APPENDIX B. 167

NAMES.	RESIDENCE.	DESCENDANTS.
Dorin, Jacob........ Dorn	E District............	Soldier R.R.N.Y. M. Roll. Has a wife and one child. P.L. 2d, 1786.
Dorin, Jeremiah......	E District............	Soldier R.R.N.Y. Muster Roll, single. P.L. 2d, 1786.
Dorland, Philip......	Adolphus Town	S.G. Lieut.Cuylers Loyalist. P.L. 1786.
Dorland, Thomas	do.	Sergeant. Served in Associated Loyalists. L. Bill 1790—600. P.L. 1786.
Dorn, Peter	E District............	Soldier R.R.N.Y. Muster Roll.
Dougall, William	M District............	Only came to the Province about 1794. States being on survey on the coast of N. Scotia. Resided in Nova Scotia before the rebellion. J. W. Myer's letter.
Dougharty, James	E District............	Soldier R.R.N.Y.
Dowlar, Robert	W District	S.G. U.E.
Downley, Cornelius .. Downey	Marysburgh	Soldier 84th Regt. Stamped Book. B.M.A.
Doyle, Benjamin......	H District............	Soldier Butler's Rangers. A wife & two children. P. L. N. 1786. Niagara Stamped Book.
Doyle, Sarah	....	By order-in-Council 30th June, 1792.
Dorder, Martin	Marysburgh ,.........	Soldier German troops. p. Petition 1797, soldier L. B. M. 1793, 300, and Provision List of 1786.
Drummond, Esq., Per.	E District............	Captn. Jessup's.
Ducklin, Stephen .... or Duchin	Elizabeth Town	Employed on Secret Service. Had a wife & 4 children. P.L. 2d, 1786.
Dugan, Cornelius	H District............	Soldier New Jersey Volunteers.
Dulmadge, David	Marysburgh	Soldier in Jessup's, L.B.M., say N.C.O.1791. 650 acres. P.L. 1786.
Dulmage, John	Edwardsburg	Found on original Roll 5th November, 1804. Lieut. Loyal Rangers.
Dulmage, Elias	E District............	Son of Lt. John Dulmage.
Dulmage, Philip......	do.	Son of Lt. John Dulmage. Soldier Loyal Rangers. P. 1789.

NAMES.	RESIDENCE.	DESCENDANTS.
{ De Mill or { Dumel, Anthony....	Kingston	Restored to U.E.3rd March, 1806. Loyalist from New York, A.M.L.
Dunbar, Alexander....	M District............	Artificer during the war. Joined in 1776.
Duncan, John	Kingston	Dischd. fifer.
Duncan, John	do.	Discharged artificer.
Duncan, Esq.,' Richard	Williamsburgh........	S.G. Captain R.R.N.Y. A wife. P.L. 2d, 1786.
Dunham, Daniel......	E District............	M.C. Lands as a sergeant, in Jessup's O.C. 8th Nov., 1797, 1st April, 1793, 200 acres for his daughter Ann, deceased. Ld.Bd.Grenvill.
Dunham, John	do.	R.R.N.Y.
Dunham, James	do.	R.R.N.Y.
Dunn, John	Lancaster	Joined Sir John Johnson in 1776. Volunteer I. Dept. L.B.L.
Dunn, Junr., John....	E District............	Son of John.
Dunn, James	do.	Son of a soldier. L.B.L.1790.
Dunn, Terence........	Kingston	(Stamped Book). Discharged artificer. Loyalist.A.M.L. (P.L. 1786.)
Durolemey, James.... Gerolomey	Marysburgh	
Duylea, Joseph.......	Adolphus Town	Son of Peter Dulay.
Dulay, Peter..........	do.	P. L. 1786. Loyalist from New York. A.M.L.
Duylea, Junr., Peter..	do.	P.L.1786.Loyalist from New York. (A.McL. Suspended, only a boy ; so says Capt. Rattan.)
Duylea, Samuel	do.	Son of Peter Dulay.
Duynes, Martin ...... or Dyhnars	M District, Fredericksburgh	German soldier p. Petition. Stamped Book.
Dugenberry, John .... Dusenberry	Ernest Town..........	Ensign Loyal Rangers. (P. L. 1786.)
Dyer, Barret, Capt. ..	Marys & Sophiasburghs	A captain, Cuyler's S. G. (Stamped Book.) P. L. 1786.
Dyer, Silas	do.	Son of Captain Barret Dyer.
Dyer, Martin	do.	
Eaman,or Aman,Jacob	Osnabruck	O.C. 7th March, 1808. Restored soldier R.R.N.Y.
Earhart, Adam	Fredericksburgh	Soldier Loyal Rangers A. McL. Single. P.L. 1786.
Earhart, John	E District............	Soldier Loyal Rangers. J.F.

APPENDIX B. 169

NAMES.	RESIDENCE.	DESCENDANTS.
Eastman, Benjamin ..	....	Soldier L. Rangers.
Eastman, Nadab......	E District............	Soldier Loy. Rangers, p. Regt. Roll (Jessup's) L.B. C.L. says *King's Rangers*.
Easton, Joseph	Elizabeth Town	This man protested against by Capt. Fraser from being put on U.E. List.
Edgar, John..........	Kingston	(Stamped Book.) A sergeant in Col. Connor's Corps. One of this name was wounded in defence of the Block-house. A wife and child. P.L. 1786.
Edge, Widow Mary ..	E District............	of Samuel Edge, a volunteer at the battle of the Cross or Barn, 1775. One child. P.L. 2d, 1786.
Edwards, James......	Marysburgh..........	Soldier 84th Regt. L.B.M. 1793, 300 (Stamped Book.) In America before the war —listed in 1777. Dond. McIntosh.
Eldam, Lawrence	Kingston	German soldier.
Elderbeck, Emanuel ..	do.	(Ellerbeck). Stamped Book. Land as a subaltern — Lieut. of Militia at New York. P.L. 1786.
Elliot, David	Elizabeth Town	From Duchess County. Settled April, 1785, Provision List N.J., Sivagache, 1785. Joined the Queen's Rangers under Col. Robt. Rogers at New York.
Elliott, Jacob, Senr. ..	do.	O.C. 7th April, 1807. Sergt. Capt. Barnes Hatfield's company, under Col. Delaney.
Elliot, Jacob	do.	Son of John Elliott, deceased. Asks land as a settler, 1791. L. Bd. L. From Duchess County. Settled in April, 1785.
Elliot, Esq., Mathew..	Malden	Captain Indian Department. P.L.D. 1786.
Elliot, Thomas	Elizabeth Town	— Campbell, Esq., J.P., certifies loyalty & first settlement.
Ellis, Andrew	Marysburgh..........	Discharged British soldier, 34th Regt. & P.L. 1786, p. Serg. McIntosh.

K

APPENDIX B.

NAMES.	RESIDENCE.	DESCENDANTS.
Elsworth, Francis	H District............	Soldier Butler's Rangers. A wife. P. L. N. 1786. Niagara Stamped Book.
Emberry, Samuel	Augusta.............	Step-son of John Lawrence.
Embrie Andrew ...... Embury	Fredericksburgh	Stamped Book. Sergeant King's R. Regt. New York. L.B.M. 1790—500; 1784, G. Haldimand, 200—his wife and daur. of William Bell, Senr., not U.E. P.L. 1786.
Embrie, David........	Marysburgh	A settler. N.P.
Embrie, Junr., David	Fredericksburgh	R.R,N.Y. P.L. 1786.
Embrie, John .... Embury	do.	Sergt. K. R. Regt. N.York. P. Lands as a magistrate. L.B.M. 1791. 600 acres— P.L.1786.(Stamped Book).
Emerson, John	E District, Cornwall ..	States a variety of services, and to have joined at Boston—500 acres.
Emery, John	do.	Emigrant U.S. L. Bd. Stormont, 1790.
Emery, Thomas	do.	R.R.N.Y. Mr. McDougal.
Emery, Senr., William	do.	Emigrant from U.S. 1790— L,Bd.L. P.L.N.J. 1786.
Emery, Junr., William	E District............	Emigrant from U.S. 1790. L. Bd. L.
Emmet, Stephen......	H District............	No service stated. (Niagara Stamped Book.) S. P.L. N. 1786.
Emons, John	Midland.............	Was a soldier in Prince of Wales' Regiment, by order-in-Council 19th November, 1807.
Empey, Adam........	Osnabruck...........	Corporl. R.R.N.Y. Muster Roll. A wife & four children. P.L. 2d, 1786. Died at the Cedars.
Empey, Junr., Adam .	E District............	R.R.N.Y. Muster Roll. P. L. 2d, 1786.
Empey, Chrirtr.	do.	Soldier R.R.N.Y. Muster Roll.
Empey, Henry	do.	Son of Philip Empey, Senr.
Empey, Senr., John ..	Osnabruck...........	Corpl. R. R. N. Y. Muster Roll—R. R. N. Y.— P.L. 2d, 1786. Son of Philip.
Empey, Junr., John ..	E District............	S.G. Corporal R. R. N. Y. Muster Roll. A son of Philip, Senr. J.B. (P.L. 2d, 1786.)

APPENDIX B. 171

NAMES.	RESIDENCE.	DESCENDANTS.
Empey, Jacob	E District............	Son of Philip, Senr. Soldier R.R.N.Y. Muster Roll.
Empey, Peter	do.	Son of Philip, Senr. A soldier R.R.N.Y., supposed. P.L. 2d, 1786.
Empey, Senr., Philip..	do.	Soldier R.R.N.Y. M. Roll. P.L. 2d, 1786.
Empey, Junr., Philip..	do.	R.R.N.Y. Muster Roll. A. Son of Philip, Senr. J.B. P.L. 2d, 1786.
Empey, Richard......	do.	Son of William, Senr. B. M. A. P.L. 2d, 1786.
Empey, William......	do.	.
Empey, Senr., William	do., Cornwall ..	Soldier Royal Yorkers. Muster Roll. P.L. 2d, 1786. Son of Philip Empey, Senr.
Empey, Junr., William	do.	Son of William, Senr. J.B.
English, Andrew......	H District............	Dead. B. Rangers.
England, William	Eastern do.	Was a sergeant Loyal Rangers—by order-in-Council 19th November, 1807.
Egell, Gasper .... Etsell	Marysburgh	Que., if not a German soldier.
Evans, Bolton	M District............	P. 1794 states Loyalist, and to have drawn 100 as. Genl. Haldimand. 1784, 100. Soldier. P.L. 1786. Soldier R.R.N.Y. L.B.M. 1794, 200.
Evans, Henry	Fredericksburgh	
Elveston, Edward	E District............	Soldier Loyal Rangers.
Everitt, Lt. Peter	do.	S.G. R.R.N.Y.
Everitt, John	Kingston	M.C. Captain from New York. S. G. Associated Loyalist. (Stamped Book.) A wife and two children. P.L. 1786.
Everitts, Sealvanus ...	E District............	
Everson, John........	Williamsburgh	Soldier Royal Regiment, New York. See Hannah Reynor's petition, 3rd March, 1807.
Everts, Oliver	E District............	300 acres. Inspector of Engineer's accounts, and storekeeper Q.M.G. Depart.
Everts, Roswell	do.	P. 1790 states Loyalist.
Everton, John........	H District............	No service stated. Came in with his family in 1788.

APPENDIX B.

Names.	Residence.	Descendants.
Evringham, James....	H District............	Niagara Stamped Book. Soldier Jersey Volunteers, by his widow Catherine. P.L. N. 1786.
Estman, Benjamin ...	E District............	Soldier in Jessup's corps, p. affidavit of Alex. Cameron, p. March, 1803.
Eyres, Ephraim	....	Deceased. Came in in 1782. O.C, 8th Febry., 1808.
Farchild, Corpl....... Benjamin	H District............	R.R.N,Y. A.McL. (Stamped Book.) M.D.
Fairchild, Benjamin,.. Senr.	do.	Deceased. Inserted by order-in-Council 18th June,1807.
Fairfield, Benjamin ..	Ernest Town	Son of William Fairfield, Senr.
Fairchild, Eleazer	Yonge	Ensign King's A Regiment; p. petition.
Fairchild, Peter	Townsend	O.C. 10th May, 1808. Joined the Royal Standard in 1777
Fairfield, Jonathan ...	Ernest Town	Son of William, Senr.
Fairfield, Stephen	do.	Son of William, Senr. P.L. 1786.
Fairfield, William	do.	Son of William, Senr.
Fairfield, Archibald ..	Kingston	Loyalist. L.B.M. 1791. Collins' 200. (Loyal Rangers.) P.L. 1786. A. McL.
Fairfield, William,.... Senr.	Ernest Town	U.E. Loyalist. A pensioner during the war. P.L. 1786.
Fairman, Senr., John	Thurlow.............	A U.E. Loyalist, p. Mr.Collins' certificate. Has got his deed for 590 acres. L. B. M. 1790. A sergeant Loyal Rangers—600 in all --or K.Rs. P.L. 1786.
Falconer, James	Adolphustown	From Virginia. Served on board His Majesty's fleet. O.C. 22d Feby., 1808.
Falkner, Joseph	E District............	Son of William. J.B. Ld. Bd. L.
Falkner, Senr., Ralph	do.	Family, four. P.L. 2d, 1786.
Falkner, Ralph, Junr.	Lancaster	Son of Ralph Falkner, Senr.
Falkner,Esqr.,William	do.	Had a wife and 4 children. P.L. 2d, 1786.
Farlinger, Senr., John	E District............	Soldier R.R.N.Y. J.F.
Farlinger, Junr., John	do. .... }	Son to a soldier. L. Bd. L. 200.
Farlinger, Nicholas ...	do. .... }	Sons of John, Senr. J.B.
Farrand, Esqr., Jacob	do.	S.G. Lieut. R.R.N.Y. (P.L. 2d, 1786.)

APPENDIX B. 173

NAMES.	RESIDENCE.	DESCENDANTS.
Farrington, Robert....	Marysburgh	Stamped Book. Soldier Royal R. N.Y. L.B.M. 1791. 400. (British regiment, P. L. 1786. Muster Roll. A wife.
Farrington, Samuel ..	do.	M.C.Soldier 84th Regt.(P.L. 1786). British soldier. S. (Stamped Book.)
Farrington, Stephen ..	do.	M.C. 300 acs. Soldier Royal Yorkers. Muster Roll. O.C. 30th August,1797. A British soldier. P.L. 1786. 2 children (Stamped Book.)
Feader, Lucis .... Lucas	E District............	Soldier R.R.N.Y. Muster Roll.
Fearman, John	Marysburgh	Son of John Fairman, Senr., Thurlow.
Feero, Peter..........	H District............	M.C. Soldier Butler's Rangers. A wife & one child. P. L. N. 1786. Niagara Stamped Book.
Fell, Frederick	Augusta....	A settler after the war. J.F.
Fennel, Jacob	E District............	
Fennel, John	....	Found on Original Roll, 5th Nov., 1804. Soldier R. R. N. Y.
Ferbust, Nicholas	H District...	
Ferguson, Aaron......	Fredericksburgh	Que., if not King's Rangers, as a P.L. 1786.
Ferguson, Alexr.	E District............	R.R.N.Y.
Ferguson, Alexr.	Edwardsburgh........	
Ferguson, Senr., Alexr.	E District............	Soldier Royal Regt. New York. Muster Roll. P.L. 1786.
Ferguson,Junr., Alexr.	do.	Son to a soldier. 200 acres. L. Bd. L.
Ferguson, Farrington..	Marys & Sophiasburgh	P. King's Rangers. P. Loyalist, 200. Genl. Haldimand,1784,100. P.L. 1786.
Ferguson, John	Kingston	(A Commissary & L.B.M. 1790.) One of this name not privileged. 100 acres.
Ferguson, Israel	Thurlow	S.G. Lieut. King's Rangers. P.L. 1786.
Ferguson, Jacob......	Fredericksburgh	Soldier King's Rangers. L. B. M. 1790. P.L. 1786.
Ferguson, Peter	E District............	Only came into the Province in 1793. Soldier R.R.N.Y. Muster Roll. N.B. P. L. N.J. 1786. Restored 19th April, 1808.

NAMES.	RESIDENCE.	DESCENDANTS.
Ferguson, Richard, Senr.	Marys & Sophiasburgh	A pensioner L.B.M. 1791. 550 acres. P.L. 1786.
Ferguson, Junr., Richard	do. do.	M. C. Volunteer p. Regl. Roll.
Ferguson, Rozel	do. do.	Son of Richard Ferguson, U.E. Ld. Board certificate 1794. 200.
Ferguson, William	E District	Soldier R.R.N Y. J.F. P.L. 2d, 1786.
Ferguson, William	do.	Son of Alexander Ferguson.
Ferrier, John	Kingston	Master shipwright in King's yard at Quebec, St. John & C.
Ferris, John	do.	A volunteer from NewYork. A wife. P.L. 1786.
Ferris, Joshua	H District	Colonel Delaney's Refugees. Had received several wounds.
Fetterly, Peter	Williamsburgh	Original Roll. Soldier R. R. N. Y.
Fields, George	do.	Soldier Butler's Rangers--- deceased.
Fields, Gilbert	do.	Butler's Rangers. A wife & child. P.L. 1786. Niagara Stamped Book.
Fields, Mrs Rebecca, for Mrs. Johnston	Williamsburgh	
Fike, Daniel		See order-in-Council, March, 1807. Soldier R.R.N.Y.
File, John	Williamsburgh	Corporal Royal Yorkers. O. C. 13th Oct., 1796.
Files, John	do	M.C. Corporal Royal Regt. N.Y.
Finch, James	Kitley	Settled with his family in 1795; was settled in Nova Scotia before the war; originally settled in Nova Scotia; an Irishman; his own story. N.P.
Finkle, George	Fredericksburgh	Stamped Book. Soldier R. R. N.Y. 650 acres Ld. B. M. 1791. (P.L. 1786.)
Finkle, Henry	Ernest Town	M.C. Corporal in Jessup's. (P.L. 1786.)
Finkle, John	Fredericksburgh	} Sons of George Finkle of R.R.N.Y.
Finkle, Jacob	do	
Fields, Daniel	W District	Sergt. B. R., and a magistrate. 1,200.

APPENDIX B. 175

NAMES.	RESIDENCE.	DESCENDANTS.
Fields, Nathan	W District	Soldier Bro. R. & N. Co. S. G. (Niagara Stamped Book.) S. P.L.N. 1786.
Finney, George	E District	Son of Peter Finney.
Finney, Peter	do	Soldier Royal Regt. N. York. Muster Roll. P. L. N. J. 1786.
Fisher, Alexr	Adolphus Town	An assistant Commissary at Carleton Island. L.B.M. 1790—700.
Fisher Daniel	M District	A discharged seaman (200).
Fisher, Frederick	Marysburgh	Soldier — Regt.—not U.E. (P. L. 1786.) (Stamped Book.) p. Sergt. McIntosh's certificate.
Fisher, John	M District	Came into Canada at commencement of the war. R.R.N.Y. M. Roll.
Fisher, George	H District	Soldier Jersey volunteers.
Fisher, Widow Mary	Adolphus Town	Her husband, John, came in at commencement of the war. L.B.M. 1792. 200 as.
Fitchet, James	Fredericksburgh	P. King's Roy. R. N. Y. L. B. S. & G. 200 E.D. P.L. 1786.
Fitchet, Richard	do	(*Fitchell*). Soldier 84th. Genl. Haldimand. 100. P.L.1786.
Fitchet, Joseph	E District	Soldier R.R. N.Y. Muster Roll. P.L. 2d, 1786.
Fitz, Titus	Kingston	Blacksmith Qr.Mr.General's Department.
Fitzgerald	Adolphus Town	Loyalist, P. L. 1786, from New York. A.McL. One a soldier Loyal Rangers.
Fitzpatrick, Peter	E District	Ld. Bd. in Royal Yorkers. J. B. This man deserted from R. Canadian volunteers. P.L. 2d, 1786.
Fitzpatrick, William	do	Son of Peter. J. B.
Flack, Archd	H District	With Genl. Burgoyne in McAlpin's corps, &c.
Flaack, Richard	Newark	O.C. 1st August, 1797.
Flynn, John	E District	Soldier 84th Regt., approved list.
Force, Philip	H District	His father was a soldier, and went to New Brunswick. Philip did not join the Royal Standard; remained with his mother. Petition O.C. 20th August, 1795.

APPENDIX B.

NAMES.	RESIDENCE.	DESCENDANTS.
Forner, John	Marysburgh	P. 1794. States Loyalist, and to have drawn 100. Soldier 53rd Regt. Donald McIntosh affidavit. (Stamped Book.)
Forrest, Laurania, formerly Mrs. Morden	H District	Widow of Mathew Forrest, R.R.N.Y.
Forsyth, George	do	Loyalist U.E., from Schenectady.
Forsyth, James	do	Niagara Stamped Book. Had a wife and four children. P.L. 1786.
Forsyth, James	E District	Non-com. offir. King's R. R. N.Y. A corporal. (P.L. 2d, 1786.)
Fortune, Joseph	do	Son of William, I.B.
Fortune, William	do	S.G. Capt. from Southeward; Capt. of Guides, South Carolina.
Forbish, Nicholas	Home District	1st Novr., 1804, on Original Roll.
Foster, Edward	do Eastern	Soldier R.R.N.Y. Ld. Bd. L. & Muster Roll. A wife, 2 children. P.L. 2d, 1786.
Foster, John	do	R.R.N.Y. P.L. 1786. Muster Roll.
Foster, Moses	Fredericksburgh	R. R. N. Y. P. L. 1786. (Stamped Book.)
Fountain, Richard	E District	Had a wife. P.L. 2d, 1786.
Fowler, John	H District	A volunteer in the war; resided seven years in New Brunswick.
Fox, Frederick	Sophias & Ameliasburgh	1786 Provision List says Loyalist N.Y. (3 children.) Soldier R.R.N.Y. Muster Roll.
Fox, William	do	Soldier, Associated Loyalist.
Fralick, Adam, Esq	Matilda	O.C. 21st July, 1807. Captain of Militia during the American War.
Francis, Mrs. Catherine	H District	Que., wife of John Francis, late 34th Regt.
Francis, Qr.-Mr. Wm.	do	King's American Dragoons.
Franklin, Senr., Joseph	Kingston	At Carleton Island, 1782, from Lake George. Called Loyalist. P.L. 1786.
Franklin, Junr., Joseph	do	Son of Joseph.
Franks William	E District	R.R.N.Y. Muster Roll (single. P.L. 2d, 1786.

APPENDIX B. 177

NAMES.	RESIDENCE.	DESCENDANTS.
Fraser, Angus	E District	Son of widow Isabella. J.B.
Fraser, Senr., Daniel	Ernest Town	A magistrate, 1,200. Served during the war; an artificer; in all 700, L. B. M. 1791, includes for family (wife, 4 children), P. L. 1786.
Fraser, Junr., Daniel	do	Son of Daniel,Senr. L.B.A. 1794. 200.
Fraser, David	do	
Fraser, Donald	E District	Soldier 84th Regt. P.L. 2d, 1786.
Fraser, Hugh	do	M.C. 600 as. Foreman Engr. Depart. *I.* O.C.22nd June, 1797.
Fraser, John	Ernest Town	Son of Daniel. Joined at Saratoga; afterwards discharged from 53rd Regt.; was a non-commd. officer; had drawn 140 acres. L. B.A. 1794. 200.
Fraser, John	E District	R.R.N.Y. M. Roll. States to have been employed on secret service (P.L.N.J. 1786.) Jenny Mills his daughter.
Fraser, John	do Edwardsburgh	Soldier 42d Regt.
Fraser, Widow Isabell	do	Widow to Simon Fraser, U.E. N. McL. March, 1793. His son, William, states that he was Secretary to the Indian Dept.
Fraser, Jeremiah	do	M.C. Soldier in Jessup's Loyal Rangers. O.C. 12th June, 1798.
Fraser, Kenneth	Ernest Town	Soldier Loyal Rangers—by his widow, Elizabeth Fraser, 350 acres. L. B. M. 1791. P.L. 1786.
Fraser, al. McNeal, Mary	E District, Lancaster	
Fraser,Captain Thomas	Edwardsburgh	Captain Jessup's.
Fraser, Thomas	E District	Soldier in Jessup's. L.B.L. 1793.
Fraser, Thomas	Ernest Town	Soldier Loyal Rangers. L. B.M. 1791. 200. P.L.1786.
Fraser, Thomas	Edwardsburgh	Son of Capt. William. J.B.
Fraser, Thomas	E District	A volunteer in Jessup's. P. 1793.

APPENDIX B.

NAMES.	RESIDENCE.	DESCENDANTS.
Fraser, Thomas	E District............	Son of Kenneth.
Fraser, William	Fredericksburgh	Adjutant R.R. N.Y. P.L. 1786. Stamped Book.
Fraser, Capt. William	E District............	S. G. Jessup's Loyal Rangers.
Fraser, Senr., William	do	Father of Capts. William and Thomas. P.L. 2d, 1786.
Fraser, Junr., William	do	Son of Capt. Thomas.
Fraser, William	do	Volunteer in Jessup's. P. 1793.
Fraser, William	do of Roxborough	A corporal S. G. Soldier Loyal Rangers.
Fraser, William	do	Soldier in Jessup's.
Fraser, Lt. William ..	do	Son of Widow Isabell; resides at Cotteaux de Lac. J.B. Lt. R. Regt. New York—Stamped Book.
Fratts, Henry	E District............	(O.C. 7th April, 1807), R.R. N.Y. Muster Roll, Single —P.L. 2d, 1786.
Frederick, Barnet	do	Soldier R.R. N.Y. Muster Roll. Has a wife. P.L. 2d, 1786.
Frederick, Conrod	M District............	Joined the army at New York in 1777; was taken prisoner when recruiting for Colonel Buskirk's corps. A sergt. Jersey Vols.—200 acres. Came in 1788. Has a son, Martin.
Frederick, John	Thurlow.............	Came into the Province in 1786.
Frederick, Peter......	Fredericksburgh	Sergt. Orange Rangers.
Freelick, Peter	Ernest Town	Restored O.C.12th July,1808. Soldier Delaney's Corps.
Freel, John	Niagara District	By order-in-Council 22d July, 1806.
Freeman, Thomas	Ernest Town	Soldier Loyal Rangers. L. B.L.
Freke, Everhart	Marysburgh	German soldier. G Book & Provision List 1786.
Frelick, Corpl. Benjn.	H District............	M.C. Butler's Rangers—N. C.O. S.G. A wife & 4 children. P.L.N. 1786. Niagara Stamped Book.
Frelick, John	do	M.C. Stamford, soldier B.R. (Niagara Stamped Book.) O.C. 17th Novr., 1797. S. P.L.N. 1786. Has a son, Benjamin. P. Clinch's affidavit, 1807.

APPENDIX B.

NAMES.	RESIDENCE.	DESCENDANTS.
Freligh, Martin	M District	Employed in secret service.
Freeman, John	H District	Volunteer Sir John Johnson's, and soldier B. R., and one of Jessup's. L.B.L.
French, Albert	E District	Son of Jeremiah. J.B. 600.
French, Benjn	do	Son of Jeremiah. 600.
French, Lt. Gersham	Cornwall	S.G. Jessup's. Resides at Cotteaux on lake. J.B.
French, Henry	E District	Loyal Rangers. Joined in 1777. A corporal in Capt. Drummond's company. L. B.L. (Jessup's).
Freen, Peter	Elizabeth Town	On original Roll. Yonge. Common settler.
French, Henry	E District	Son of Jeremiah French.
French, Esq., Jeremiah	do	Lieut. R.R.N.Y. P.L. 2d, 1786.
Frees, John	do	Inserted by order-in-Council 29th January, 1808 ; taken prisoner in 1777 ; confined till 1783.
Frey, Capt. Bernard	H District	Butler's Rangers--a wife and 3 children. P.L.N. 1786. Niagara Stamped Book.
Frey, Ensn. Philip	do	8th Regt.
{ Friermut, John Adam { Freerniouth	Ernest Town	Came from East Florida-- known by Cap. Lithbridge. L.B.M. 1792. 200, and recommended for an addition.
{ Frill, Peter { Friell	Marysburgh	L. B. A. 1794. States the step-son of John Green, and granted 200 acres.
Froom, David	E District	Son of James Froom.
Froom, Senr., James	do	Soldier King's Royal Regt. N.Y., or corporal.
Froom, Junr., James	do	Soldier King's Loyal Rangers.
Frost, Edmund	H District	Corporal in McAlpin and Jessup's.
{ Fryke, John { Fyke	E District	Son of Francis Fyke. J. B.
Frymire, Nicholas	do	R.R.N.Y. Muster Roll A. Had a wife and 2 children. P.L. 2d, 1786.
Frymire, Philip	do	Soldier Royal Yorkers. L. B. L. Muster Roll. A. (P.L. 2d, 1786.)
Fulford, Abel	do	

180 APPENDIX B.

NAMES.	RESIDENCE.	DESCENDANTS.
Fulford, Senr., Jonathan	E District	Soldier King's Rangers, p. Regl. Roll.
Fulford, Junr., Jonathan	do	Son of Jonathan—1789—P. 200.
Fullarton, James	do	M.C. Royal Rangers.
Fulton, Ct. James	H District	Capt. King's American Dragoons.
Furnier, Chrisn	Kingston	Que., Furnyea—Sir J. J. Corps.
Fykes, Peter	Fredericksburgh	Soldier in K. R. Regt. N.Y. L.B.M. 1792. 500 Genl. Haldimand 100. P.L.1786. (Stamped Book.)
Frederick, Lodwick	Marysburgh	(From L.) Soldier R.R.N.Y. Muster Roll.
Goffield, Nat A	Marysburgh & Sophiasburgh	Soldier Loyal Rangers.
Gahagan, Oliver	H District	Soldier Butler's Rangers. S. G. (A wife and one child.) P. L. N. 1786. Niagara Stamped Book.
Galbraith, John	E District	A soldier in Jessup's. P.
Gale, James	Kingston	Loyalist from New York. A. McL. Stamped Book.
Gallagher, Hugh	Marysburgh	Discharged British soldier. Had drawn 100 as. at L. B. A., 1794. 200 and P.L. 1786. A wife, P.L.N,1786. Stamped Book.
Gallinger, Christian	E District	Soldier R.R.N.Y. Muster Roll. P.L.2d, 1786.
Gallinger, Christopher		L. B.
Gallinger, George	E District	Soldier R.R.N.Y. P.L. 2d, 1786.
Gallinger, Henry	do	R.R.N.Y. Muster Roll. P.L. 2d, 1786.
Gallinger, Senr., Michael	do	R.R.N.Y. Muster Roll. P. L. 2d, 1786.
Gallinger, Junr., Michael	do	Son of Michael, Senr. (P.L. 2d, 1786.)
Galloway, George	Kingston	S.G. Lieut. Associated Loyalists. L. B. M. 1791. Stamped Book. P.L. 1786.
Gamble, William		
Gants, Chrisn	Marysburgh	German soldier—C Book and Provision List 1786.
Gardiner, John	E District	Soldier R.R. N.Y. Muster Roll. P.L. 2d, 1786. S.B. S.G.

(Sons of Michael.) — bracketed beside Gallinger, Christian / Christopher / George / Henry / Senr. Michael / Junr. Michael

APPENDIX B. 181

NAMES.	RESIDENCE.	DESCENDANTS.
Gardiner, George	E District, Yonge	Served with Genl. Burgoyne, J.F.
{ Gardner, John...... { Garner	H District of Crowland	B.R. a soldier. S.G. Niagara Stamped Book—S. P. L. N. 1786.
Garlock, Henry	E District............	R.R.N.Y. J.F. Had a wife & one child. P.L. 2d,1786.
{ Garlock, John...... { Garlough	Ernest Town	Corpl. Loyal Rangers. L.B. M.1790—400 as.—A.McL. (P.L. 1786.)
Garlough, Jacob.....	E District............	R.R. N.Y. Muster Roll—a wife and child. P.L. 2d, 1786.
Garlough, Senr., Peter	do	R.R.N.Y. Muster Roll—a wife—P.L. 2d, 1786.
Garlough, Junr., Peter	do	Son of Peter (single), P. L. 2d, 1786.
Garner, William......	H District............	(Niagara Stamped Book)— had a wife, P.L.N. 1786.
Gay, Edward	E District............	R.R.N.Y. Muster Roll.
German, Chrisn.......	Adolphus Town	M.C. Soldier Loyal Rangers —a boy—100—junr. son of John ; no bounty 1790. Ld. Bd. certe. P.L. 1786. Gov. Hamilton, 150. Senr. brother of John.
German, John........	do	Corporal in Jessup's Corps, L.B.M. Say soldier, 1790, 350.
German, Jacob	do	Drummer Loyal Rangers—a boy, 100, 1790. No bounty 1790.
Gerolomey, James	Ernest Town	Soldier Jessup's, A. McL. P.L. 1786.
George, John	do	(Stamped Book) Butler's Rangers, 84th Regt., a soldier P.L.N. 1786. One of the name a British soldier, P.L.N. 1786—a wife.
Georgen, Christoph...	Kingston	Stamped Book. Petition states sergeant 84th Regt. L. B. M. 1790- -400—(P.L. 1786.)
Geoberg, William	Marysburgh	Soldier German troops.
Gibbons, Mary		
{ Gibson, John ...... { Gipson	E District.....	Soldier King's Rangers—L. Bd.L. P.L. K. Rangers, 1789.

APPENDIX B.

NAMES.	RESIDENCE.	DESCENDANTS.
Gibson, Mathew	W District	Soldier R. R. N.Y. Muster Roll (single man)—P. L. 2d, 1786.
Gichland, Henry	Ernest Town.	
Gilbert, Josiah	H District	Corpl. King's American Regt., or Fanning's.
Gilchrist, Archid.	E District	Emigrant settler. L. B. L. 1790.
Gilchrist, Neal	Ernest Town	Son of Peter Gilchrist.
Gilchrist, Peter	do	M.C. 300—a soldier in Jessup's Corps, L.B.L. (in all 500), L.B.M. 1790. O.C. 21st August, 1797, (P. L. 1786).
Gilchrist, William	do	Son of Peter Gilchrist.
Gilmore, Benjamin	H District	Jersey Volunteers.
Girty, James	Malden	Partisan all the war. U. list 1789.
Girty, Simon	do	Do., do.
Glassford, John	E District, Augusta	Joined at Niagara in 1779, and died in 1792; his son's affidavit 1805; has a wife and 4 children. P. L. 2d, 1786.
Glassford, William		Son of John, p. P. S. Sherwood's certificate, 1807.
Glassford, John	Matilda	Soldier R.R.N.Y. Muster Roll A.
Glassford, Lyttle	E District	Served under Capt. Brant in 1778; went to Quebec in 1780; O. E., resided in Lower and Upper Canada since 1798. I. Cronders.
Glassford, Paul	do	Son of John. Said to be U. E. R.J. D.G.
Glassford, Paul	do	Son of Robert.
Glassford, Robert	do	Soldier R.R.N.Y. M. Roll. A. Single. P.L. 2d, 1786.
Glover, Jacob	H District	Sergeant under the command of Lord Rawdon.
Goheen, Thomas	Newcastle	Was within the British lines before 1783—by order-in-Council 24th November, 1807.
Goldsmith, Thomas	Marys & Sophiasburgh	Loyalist from New York. A. M. L. Loyalist P.L. 1786.
Goes, Lawrence		By order-in-Council 19th January, 1802.

APPENDIX B. 183

NAMES.	RESIDENCE.	DESCENDANTS.
Goose, Frederick......	Cornwall	Supposed R.R. N.Y. P.L. 2d, 1786.
Gooseberry, Thomas ..	E District............	Soldier in Loyal Rangers, L.B.L. 1793.
Gordon, John	W District	Loyalists' List — Loyalists U.D. 1789.
Gordon, Robert	Charlottenburgh	R.R.N.Y. Muster Roll—P. L.N.J. 1786; another R. Gordon was ensign in militia before the war. L. B. L. 200.
Gordonier, Henry	Ernest Town	Soldier Loyal Rangers. A. M. L. (P.L. 1786.)
Gordonier, Jacob	do	Soldier Loyal Rangers. A. M.L. P.L. 1786.
Gorman, Rebecca	E District, Elizabeth Town.	
Gosley, Mathew	Yonge	Sergeant Prince of Wales' Regt.
Gould, John..........	H District....	Soldier B. Rangers. S. G. S. P.L.N. 1786.
Graham, William	Home District	Capt. Lieut. Lord Charles Montague's Regt. Order-in-Council 30th June,1807.
Graham, John........	E District............	Son of a soldier—200, Ld. Bd. L. One a wife and 2 children. P.L. 1786.
Graham, Isabella, ... alias McDonell	do Lancaster ..	
Graham, Murdoch	do	Son of Thomas. U.E. L. B. L. 1790. (P.L.N.J. 1786.)
Graham, Oliver	do	Soldier King's Rangers, p. R. Roll.
Graham, Robert	Kingston	S. G. Sergeant. Loyalist from New York. A.M.L. (Stamped Book.)
Graham, Thomas	E District............	R.R.N.Y. Had a wife and 4 children. P.L. 2d, 1786.
Graham, William	do	Sergeant 84th Regt.
Grant, Alex..........	do of Edwardsburgh	Gone to Scotland. Soldier 84th Regt., P. L.B.L. P. L.N.J. 1786.
Grant, Alexander	do, Charlottenburgh	Son of a soldier. Ld. Bd. L. (Young man), P. L. 2d, 1786. Duncan Murchison says that he died in 1777. Isabell Martin his daughter.
Grant, Alexd.........	do do ..	Had a wife and 2 children— P.L. 2d, 1786.

APPENDIX B.

NAMES.	RESIDENCE.	DESCENDANTS.
Grant, Alexd........	E District, Charlottenburgh	A wife and child—P. L. N. 1786.
Grant, Alexd........	Charlottenburgh	R.R.N.Y. Muster Roll.
Grant, Allan	E Dist.,Elizabeth T'wn	Sergt. 84th Regt. U.E. J.F. P.L.N.J. 1786.
Grant, Allan	do	
Grant, Allan	do	
Grant, Angus	do	.. R.R.N.Y. Muster Roll. N. B. P.L.N.J. 1786.
Grant, Archd.	do	.. R.R.N.Y. M.Roll. (A British soldier of this name on P.L. 1786 Kingston), one P.L.N.J. 1786. S.
Grant, Donald.......	Marysburgh	British soldier, A. M. L. (Stamped Book),P.L.N.J. 1786.
Grant, Senr., Donald.. (Croskey)	E Dist.,Charlottenb'gh	Soldier R.R.N.Y. Muster Roll. P.L.N.J. 1786.
Grant, Junr., Donald..	do do	.. Soldier R. R. N. Y. Muster Roll.
Grant, Duncan	E District............	Soldier R. Regt. N. York— P. P.L.N.J. 1786.
Grant, Duncan	do	Son of Peter Grant, R. R. N.Y. Son to a soldier, Ld. B. L.
Grant, Duncan	do	Son to a soldier, L. Bd. L.
Grant, Duncan	do	P.L.N.Y. 1786.
Grant, Duncan	do of NewJohnston	Was at St. John's in Lower Canada in 1782. P.L.N.J. 1786—Reuben Sherwood's certificate.
Grant, Duncan	do	One of 76th Regt.—joined in 1778.
Grant, Finlay	do	R.R.N.Y. Muster Roll—P. L. N. J. 1786.
Grant, John.........	Kingston, Pittsburgh..	A Loyalist—volunteer in King's Rangers, p.petition 1808.
Grant, John..........	Marysburgh	One a soldier in 84th Regt. J.F.
Grant, John..	E District............	One of this name drew land in E.D. as son of a soldier, 1789.
Grant, John.........	do	R.R.N.Y. Muster Roll—P. L. N. J. 1786. Another P.L.N.J. 1786.
Grant, John.........	Lancaster	B.M.A.
Grant, James	Marysburgh	Sergt. 84th Regt. L. B. M. 1790, 400, and P.L. 1786 S. Stamped Book.

APPENDIX B. 185

NAMES.	RESIDENCE.	DESCENDANTS.
Grant, James	E District	(P.L.N.J. 1786.) Recruited men; suffered loss of property, and imprisonment; bore arms as an ensign for two years, on Majr. McAlpin's Muster Rolls; 2000.
Grant, John	do	
Grant, Senr., Lewis	do	
Grant, Junr., Lewis	do	Son of a soldier—200 acres, Ld. Bd. L. Son of Finlay Grant.
Grant, Peter	do	Soldier 84th Regt.—L.B.L. One a subject and settler from L. C.
Grant, Peter	do	Son of a soldier—200 acres, Ld. Bd. L. One P.L.N.J. 1786.
Grant, Peter	Charlottenburgh	R.R.N.Y. Muster Roll—P. L.N.J. 1786.
Grant, William	E District	R. R. N. Y. Muster Roll— (single) P.L.2d, 1786—one Loyal Rangers.
Grant, Wm.	Lancaster	Soldier 84th Regt.
Grass, Daniel	M District	Son of Michael Grass.
Grass, Eve, now Wartman	do	Daught. of ditto.
Grass, John	do	Son of ditto.
Grass, Lewis	Kingston.	
Grass, Mary		Daught. of Michael Grass.
Grass, Michael	Kingston	S.G. Capt. N.York Militia. Stamped Book, P.L. 1786.
Grass, Peter	do	Son of Michael Grass.
Grass, Peter	M District.	
Gray, John	E District	Sergt.84th Regt.,from South Carolina—wife & two children, 1787; Collins, 200; P.L. 1786.
Gray, James	Yonge	Loyal Rangers—by order-in-Council 2d December,1806.
Gray, Col. James	do	S.G. Major R.R.N.Y.
Gray, Alexander	Yonge Street	Soldier Jersey Volunteers— by order-in-Council 13th Oct. 1807.
Green, Benjamin	H District	Soldier King's Rangers, p. R. Roll.
Green, John	Flamborough West	O. C. 29th March, 1808— joined the Royal Standard in New Jersey in the year 1776.

L

APPENDIX B.

NAMES.	RESIDENCE.	DESCENDANTS.
Green, John..........	Marysburgh	Soldier Loyal Rangers, L.B. M. P.L. 1786.
Green, William.......	Marysburgh	Stamped Book, Soldier Queen's Rangers, L. B. M. P.L. 1786, wounded at the battle of Brandywine, invalided and discharged at his own request—afterwards in secret service.
Greenop, Britain...... *alias* Gulep.	Kingston	84th Regt. a soldier U. E. Stamped Book P. L. 1786.
Grey, John...........	"	Soldier 42d Regt. Ld. Bd. Cert. an Artificer this one A. M. L. M. C. O. C. 25th July, 1797.
Griffiths, John........	M. District	New Jersey Loyalist. Myrtle.
Griffin, Joseph........	E. District	Was a soldier in Jessup's—is resident in Montreal, R.J. D. G.
Griffin, Isaac	"	
Griffiths, William.....	Adolphustown	Joined at New York, 1782.
Grigg, John	H. District	Loyalist express in the war. S. G.
Grooms, Elijah	Kingston	Soldier New Jersey Volunteers, L.B.M. 1791, P. L. 1786.
Grooms, Joseph	do	Sergt. Incorporated Loyalist N. Y. Stamped Book.
Grout, Ferdinand.....	Marys & Sophiasburghs	
Gunn, David.........	Lancaster.............	Early, was at the conquest of Canada in 78th Regt. had a wife and two children, P.L. 2d 1786. Joined Royal Standard in 1776, served in Capt. Herchmer's Company till 1778—his own affidavit.
Hagerman, John......	Elizabeth Town.......	Not privileged — Solicitor-General's information in 1802. A common settler in 1785. F. Smith and J. Fraser.
Hagard, Peter	E. District	
Haggart, John........	Charlottenburgh	Employed as an Artificer— L. B. Lunenburg.
Hagerman, Sergt. Arnold...............	H. District.	B. Rangers S.P.L. N., 1786, not U. E., had previously been a German Soldier. Niagara Stamped Book.

APPENDIX B.

NAMES.	RESIDENCE.	DESCENDANTS.
Hagerman, Tunis.....	Ernest Town	Soldier Loyal Rangers L. B. M., 1790.
Hagerman, Nicholas ..	Adolphus Town.......	Gen. Haldimand 200 and P. L. 1786, Loyalist, A.M.L.
Haggerty, Hugh......	H. District	Jersey Volunteers.
Hainer, Albert........	do	M. C. soldier B. Rangers S. G. O. C. 11th March 1797, Niagara Stamped Book.
Hainer, John	H. District	Soldier Butler's Rangers, had a wife and four children, P. L. N.. 1786. Niagara Stamped Book.
Hainer, Richard	do	Soldier B. Rangers, S.G. had a wife and 2 children, P.L. N. 1786, Niagara Stpd.Bk
Haines, Senr., Joseph.	do	Butler's Rangers, U. E. P.
Haines, Nathaniel	do	Soldier B. Rangers, S. G. L. B. Nassau 1794, a wife P. L. N. 1786, Niag. Stpd.Bk.
Haines, Christopher...	E. Dist. Williamsburg.	Soldier R. R. N. Y., Muster Roll A.single, P.L.2d 1786.
Hains, John..........	do do	Emigrant 1790, L. B. L. his brother Michael, a Sergt. Niagara Stamped Book.
Hains, Joseph	do do	Soldier R.R.N.Y., had a son named John, p. affidavit of Mr. John Chrysler.
Haines, Michael......	do do	Sergt. R. R. N. Y., L. B. L. and Muster Roll, had a wife P.L. 2d 1786.
Haley, Abijah........	do do	
Hall, Richard.........	Kingston	S.G. Sergt. Loyalist from N York Stpd. Bk. P.L. 1786
Hall, Samuel	W. District	S. G. Queen's Rangers L. Loyalists U. D.
Halley, Abijah	E. District	See Hawley, Abijah.
Hollowell, Benjamin..	H. District	
Halister, Elisha.......	E. District	of Cornwall, lately of age.
Hamblin, David	do Augusta ...	Son of Silas.
Hamblin, Silas........	do	Sol. in Maj. Jessup's L.B.L. Muster Roll.
Hamblyn, David......	do Elizabeth T.	Son of Silas.
Hamblyn, Francis.....	do do	
Hamilton, Andrew....	W. District...........	Butler's Rangers, a Corporal 2 U. E. List. 1789.
Hamilton, Thomas....	York	by Order-in-Council, 13th Jan. 1807.
Hansen, Lt. Richard..	do	B. Rangers, Niag. Stpd. Bk.
Hancock, John.......	Marysburgh	Discharged British Soldier, Stamped Book.

APPENDIX B.

Names.	Residence.	Descendants.
Hans, Edward	Litley	
Handshaw alias Moody, M.	H. District	Secret service.
Hard, James	E. District	Soldier Loyal Rangers.
Hard, Phili	do	do do
Hardison, Benjamin	H. District	8th Regt. not U. E.
Hardy, John, Sergt	do	84th Regt.
Hare, Barny	E. District	Son of Ensign John Hare, Ld. Bd. L.
Hare, Henry	do Lancaster	Lieut. Indian Department.
Hare, John, Senr	H. District	Deceased Capt. Indian Dept. Niagara Stamped Book.
Hare, Lt. John, Junr	do	Capt. Indian Department S.P.L.N. 1786.
Hare, John	E. District	Soldier Butler's Rangers Ld. Bd. L.
Hare, John	Osnabruck	
Hare, James	Lancaster	Ensign Indian Dept. Ld.Bd. L. a wife and six children P. L. 2d 1786.
Hare, Capt. Peter	Home District	Indian Dept. 2 children, P. L.N. 1786, Niag. Stpd. Bk.
Hare, Peter	do	Deceased, Volunteer Indian Department, S. P. L. N. 1786, Niagara Stpd. Book.
Hare, Wm	do	Volunteer Indian Dept. a wife and 2 children, P. L. N. 1786, Niag. Stpd. Bk.
Hare, Wm	E. District	Late Emigrant from U. S. Ld. Bd. L.
Haret, Edward	W. District	
Harley, James	Kingston	Discharged Artificer Loyalist New York, A. McL. single, P.L. 1786.
Harlowe, William	Fredericksburg	M.C. German Royal Artil'ry
Harn, James	Ernest Town	
Harns, Gilbert Harris.	Fredericksburg	M.C. Soldier King's Rangers Ld. Bd. Certificate, 1784, G. Haldimand 100 ditto 100, a wife, P.L. 1786.
Harns, Gilbert	do	King's Rangers, A. McL.
Harns, Isaiah Josiah.	do	Soldier Kings Rangers, p. R. Roll, Josiah, P.L.1786.
Harns, Johnston	Fredericksburgh	Soldier King's Rangers, p. R. Roll, 1784, G. Haldimand 100 sold.
Harns, Thomas		On Original Roll 1st Nov. 1804.
Harper, Wm	W. District	Butler's Rangers, L.I.U.D.

APPENDIX B. 189

NAMES.	RESIDENCE.	DESCENDANTS.
Harple, George....... Harper.	Kingston.............	Harper his name, L.B.Mecklenburgh 1791, 200 acres, a Loyalist (P. L. 1786), Incorporated Loyalist Stpd. Book.
Harris, Batties........	M. District...........	
Harris, David.........	Ernest Town	Was not in the service, did not come to this country till after the Peace, Emigrant Settler, 200 acres L.B.M., 1790.
Harris, Henry.........	H. District............	Soldier B. Rangers, S.G.S. P.L.N., 1786.
Harris, John...........	do	Soldier B.R. S.G. S.P.L.N. 1786.
Harris, Joseph........	M. District...........	Son of Minard Harris.
Harris, Minard........	do	Served in Colonel Hurlyhoy's Corps, joined 1777.
Harris, Peter..........	do	Son of Mindart Harris,dead.
Harris, Thomas.......	H. District...........	Incorporated Loyalist.
Harrison, Thomas.....	Marysburgh..........	Soldier British Regiment, A. McL. Painter, Stpd. Bk.
Harrison, Senr., Wm..	Marysburg	Sergt. 53rd Regt., not U. E. (P.L. 1786).
Harrison, Junr., Wm..	do.	Son of ditto, not U. E. 200 acres, 1793, L.B.M.
Harson, Felix	Fredericksburgh	A soldier in Jersey Volunteers.
Hart, Barny..........	E District............	R.R.N.Y. Muster Roll, P. L. 2d, 1786.
Hartle, Adam	do.	Soldier R. R. N. Y. Muster Roll, P. L. 2d, 1786.
Hartle, Christian	do.	Son of a Loyalist. J. F.
Hartle, Senr., John ..	do.	Soldier R.R.N.Y. J.F. Muster Roll. P.L. 2d, 1786.
Hartle, John	do.	Son of ...., P.L. 2d, 1786.
Hartman, David......	Ernest Town	Soldier Loyal Rangers, called Loyalist, P.L., 1786.
Hartman, Jacob......	do.	Son of David.
Hartman, Ludswick ..	do.	Son of David Hartman.
Hartman, Philip......	do.	Son of David.
Hartman, Wm.	Marysburgh...........	
Haskins, Abel.........	Johnstown District ..	By Order in Council, 26th May, 1801.
Haskins, David	Augusta..............	1792 Petition, has resided several years and is come of age. L.B.L., son of Abel.

APPENDIX B.

Names.	Residence.	Descendants.
Haskins, Nicholas	E District	Son of Abel.
Hatler, Thomas	do.	Late of Cornwall, deceased, O.C. 28th April, 1807. Soldier R.R.N.Y.
Havens, George	Ernest Town	Came in during the War with his family—several sons in Jessup's.
Havens, John	do.	M. C. Soldier in Jessup's Loyal Rangers. Mr. Cotlin's Certificate.
Havens, Robert	do.	Emigrant from the States—wishes to become a settler. L.B.M. 1793. 200.
Haverland, Andrew	H District	B. Rangers by Order in Council, 21st June, 1806.
Haverland, Junr., Hermn.	H District	Son of Andrew Haverland.
Haviland, John	Adolphustown	By Order in Council, 30th January, 1808, Engineers' Department and Incorporated Loyalists.
Haver, Daniel	H District	
Hawley, Abijah	Augusta	On Original Roll.
Hawley, Davis	Ernest Town	Son of ——— Soldier, King's Rangers, p. R. Roll (P.L. 1786).
Hawley, Ichabod	do.	Soldier N. C. O. Loyal Rangers, L. B.M. (P. L. 1786).
Hawley, Jeptha	do. M.C.	Lieut. of Batteaux. L.B.M. 1789—L.Bd. Certe. and Quebec plain, P.L. 1786.
Hawley, Martin	do.	Son of Jeptha, a soldier Loyal Rangers. L.B.M. P.L. 1786.
Hawley, Rupell	do.	Son of Jeptha, L.B.A. 1793. 200 acs.
Hawley, Sheldon	do.	Son of Jeptha, a Loyalist, in all 350 acres.L.B.M., 1789.
Hawley, Zadock	Fredericksburgh	Soldier Loyal Rangers. A. M.L.
Hawn, Christian	E District	R.R.N.Y. Muster Roll A.
Hawn, Henry	do.	R.R.N.Y. Muster Roll.
Hawn, Hermanus	do.	Soldier R.R.N.Y. L.Bd. H. Grenville. Son of Henry Hawn, P.L. 2d, 1786.
Hawn, John	Cornwall	On Original Roll.
Hawn, Jacob	E District	R.R.N.Y. Muster Roll A.
Hayslip, Corpl. James.	H District	B. Rangers, S.G. Niagara Stamped Book.

APPENDIX B.

NAMES.	RESIDENCE.	DESCENDANTS.
Hazen, Sergt. Daniel...	H District............	Jersey Volunteers, Barlow's Regt., S.G.
Hiald, Nathaniel.....	Marysburgh..........	Corporal 29th Regt. L.B.M. 1791–650 acres and P.L. 1786.
Heck, Paul	E District............	S. G. Corporal with Burgoyne.
Hedler, Adam	Fredericksburgh......	R.R.N.Y. P.L. 1786 and A.Mc.L. Stamped Book.
Heford, John	Marysburgh	Discharged British Soldier.
Hehn, John	....	....
Hek, Gotlep..........	Marysburgh..........	Soldier in the GermanTroops O. U. E. List.
Helmer, John	E District, Cornwall..	R.R.N.Y. Muster Roll A. 24 years.
Helmer, John	Williamsburgh........	A Soldier R.R.N.Y. L.Bd. L. 1791 and Muster R:ll. 21 years—A. and Hilırer John, R.R.N.Y. Muster Roll, 18 years A.
Hendershot, Peter	H District.............	Soldier Jersey Volunteers.
Henderson, Cateb.....	do.	A Sergeant Loyal Rangers, L.B.L.
Henderson, David	Elizabeth Town	Order in Council 2nd December, 1806, replaced on the U. E. List.
Henn, Michael	Home District	Found 1st Nov., 1804, to be on the Original Roll. Soldier Butler's Rangers.
Henry, James	H District............	B. Rangers, S. G. — had a wife, P.L.N. 1786, Niagara Stamped Book.
Herchimer, Catharine. now Markland	M District	⎫
Herchimer, Mary, ... now Hamilton.	do.	⎬ Daughters and Sons of Capt. Jost Herkemer.
Herchmer, Jane, now . Anderson.	do.	
Herchmer, Jacob	Kingston	
Herchmer, Joseph	do.	
Herchmer, Lawrence..	do.	⎭
Herchmer, Lieu. .... George.	Home.................	Deceased—P.L. 1786.
Herchmer, Nicholas .	Kingston	Son of Capt. Jost Herkeme of Batteaux.
Herman, Valentine ..	Augusta..............	Original Roll, Soldier Loyal Rangers.
Heron, Andrew .... Herring.	Fredericksburgh......	Soldier R.R.N.Y. Stamped Book. P.L. 1786.

APPENDIX B.

NAMES.	RESIDENCE.	DESCENDANTS.
Hervey, Philip	H District	
Hesse, Andrew	Marysburgh	Soldier 34th Regt. L.B.M. 1790 and P.L. 1786.
Hesse, Jacob	Ernest Town	M.C. Soldier in Jessup's A. Mc.L. P.L. 1786.
Hewit, Jacob	Yonge	Late from the State of New York, desires to become a subject and settler. 200 as. L. B L., 9th April, 1783. No privilege.
Hewston, Joshua	H District	Killed when on secret service near Gosham.
Hick, John	E District	Soldier King's Rangers— P.L. 1786.
Hick, Samuel	do.	Son of Paul Hicks, p. Land Board Certificate in C. Office.
Hicks, Benjamin	Marysburgh	M.C. Soldier Butler's Rangers. Stamped Book. O.C. 30th Augt., 1797.
Hicks, Daniel	do.	His Father died in New York—Son of the late Edward who served in Butler's Rangers —L. B. M. 1793. 200.
Hicks, David	do.	His Father died in New York—Son of the late Edward who served in Butler's Rangers. L. B, M. 1793. 200.
Hicks, Edward	do.	Died at New York in 1779. Affidavit of Parskel Terry, 7th March, 1807 — Mary Cryderman, his daughter. Soldier Butler's Rangers, L.B.M. (Stamped Book) British Soldier, P.L. 1786, S. A.McL.
Hicks, Joseph	do.	Son of Edward who died in New York, L.B.L. 1791. Emigrant N. Y. S.—300. L. B. M. 1790. British Soldier, P. L. 1786—S. A.McL.
Hicks, Joshua	do.	His Father died in New York—Brother to Edward and Son of Edward.
Hicks, Lewis	Ernest Town	Loyal Rangers A.McL.— Called Loyalist 1786.

APPENDIX B. 193

NAMES.	RESIDENCE.	DESCENDANTS.
Hickey, John	E District	Soldier R.R.N.Y. L. B. L. and Muster Roll.
Higgins, Samuel	Marysburgh	British Soldier, A. Mc L. 53rd Regt. (Weaver Stamped Book).
Hill, Corney	H District	A Settler.
Hill, Senr., John	do.	This one a Loyal Quaker, one a Soldier King's Rangers, p. R. Roll.
Hill, Junr., John	do.	Son of John Hill, Senr., the Junr. served in N.Y. Militia.
Hill, Nazareth	Kingston	Served as Guide to the Army.
Hill, Solomon	M District	N. C. O. Corporal Loyal American Regt.
Hill, Thomas	H District	Loyalist from Nova Scotia.
Hill, Wm.	Marysburgh	Soldier British Regiment. A.McL. (Stamped Book)
Hilts, Joseph	H District	Came in with his grandfather, Joseph Petry.
Hilton, Sergt. B. Wm.	do	King American Dragoons.
Hitchcock, Miles	do	A drayman in New York during the war.
Hitchler, Six	E District	Soldier Loyal Rangers.
Hodge, Timothy	do	Soldier Loyal Rangers, L.B. L.
Hodogan, Peter	do	Hogodoom, soldier, Loyal Rangers.
Hodgekinson, Wm	H District	B. Rangers, Niagara stamped book.
Hodgkinson, John	do	B. Rangers.
Hoff, Henry	do	Indian Department S.G.— one woman, P.L.N., 1786.
Hoff, John	do	Indian Department, S. G., Niagara stamped book.
Hoffman, David	Ernest Town	A soldier in Jessup's (P. L., 1786).
Hoffman, Elias	Fredericksburgh	Had not been in the service of Government, I. O. C. Came in after the peace, emigrant settler, 100 acres only L.B.M., 1790.
Hoffman, Jacob Haufman	Ernest Town	German soldier—C. Book.
Hoffman, Jacob	do	Soldier R.R.N.Y. L.B.M., 1790 (Stamped Book), P.L. 1786.
Hoffman, Ludowick	Marysburgh	British soldier, P.L., 1786, A.Mc.L. S.

APPENDIX B.

Names.	Residence.	Descendants.
Hoffman, Philip	Fredericksburgh	Soldier R. R. N. Y., P. L., 1786.
Hofftail, Isaac	E District	If Hockdel, a soldier Loyal Rangers.
Hogan, David	Marysburgh	M.C. soldier 34th Regt., L. B.M., 1792, 300 P.L.,1786 (Stamped Book).
Hogan, Major Wm	Cornwall	S.G. in war of 1759-69. P.L. N.J., 1786.
Hoghtelling, James	H District	Soldier Butler's Rangers O. C. 21st July, 1796.
Hogle, Bostian	Ernest Town	His father, Captain Hogle was killed at Berrington, L.B.M., 1790.
Hoffman, Joseph	do	Received compensation for losses—Jessup's.
Hogle, Francis	do	Son of Capt. Francis Hogle (Stamped Book), Francis his son 200as. L. B. M., 1790.
Hogle, James	do	Loyal Rangers—his father, Captain Hogle killed at Berrington, L.B.M., 1790.
Hollingshead, Anthony	H District	W.E. from N. Brunswick.
Holmes, Asa	do	Lives in Yonge. A. Homes, of Niagara. Joined Genl. Burgoyne. A settler, one of this name a Loyalist, list 1789.
Holmes, John	Kingston	Loyalist from New York (P.L., 1786).
Hoople, Henry. Hupole.	E District, Osnabruck.	R. R. N. Y. Muster Roll, young man P.L. 2d,1786.
Hoople, John	do do	Soldier R. R. N. Y. Muster Roll, P.L. 2nd., 1786.
Hopkins, Senr., Silas	H District	It was said he accepted of a pardon from Genl. Washington. I. S. Niagara Stamped Book.
Hopper, Abraham	E District	Soldier R. R. N. Y. Muster Roll (Single P. L. 2d., 1786).
Horton, Isaac	H District	Pilot to New York army, S. G.
Hoskins, Leda	E District	Elizabeth Town.
Hosteder, Herman	H District	Served in Bucks County Volunteers and Engineer Department.
Hovenden, Moore W.	M District	S.G. Lieut. of Horse, Tarlton's Legion, P.L., 1786.

APPENDIX B. 195

NAMES.	RESIDENCE.	DESCENDANTS.
Hover, Caspar........	Adolphustown........	Loyalist P.L., 1786.
Hover, Henry........	do	Soldier Butler's Rangers, son of Casper L.B.M., 1790. 300. Provision list, 1786, p. Discharge.
Hover, Jacob........	do	(Stamped Book), son of Caspar L.B.M., 1790,100. No bounty land, 1786, P. list.
Hough, Barnabas....	Ernest Town........	Genl. Haldimand,300. Loyal Rangers, P.L. King's Rangers, 1786.
Hough, Broner......	do	Soldier King's Rangers, p. R. Roll (S.P.L., 1786.
Hough, Elijah........	do	
Hough, John........	Fredericksburgh........	Soldier R.R.N.Y., L.B.M., 1790—300, including family P. L., 1786, Stamped Book.
Hough, Isaac........	Ernest Town..........	Son of Barnabas, only of age.
Hough, Samuel......	do	Son of do.
House, Frederick....	H District............	B.R.
House, George........	do	S.G.B. Rangers, a soldier, a wife and 5 children, P. L. N., 1786, Niagara Stamped Book.
House, Hermanns....	H District............	Soldier R.Rangers S.G—had a wife and five children, P.L.N., 1786. Niagara Stamped Book.
House, James........	do	A soldier Butler's Rangers, See O.C. 14th July, 1796.
House, John..........	do	S.G., B.R., N.C.O., R.R.N.Y., P.L., 1786, a wife and three children, P. L. N., 1786 (Niagara Stamped Book).
House, Joseph........	do	Son of Hermanus House.
House, Philip........	do	Soldier B. Rangers S.G.S., P.L.N., 1786.
House, Daniel.........	do	Found 1st November, 1804, to be on the original Roll, Butler's Rangers(R Nelles)
Howard, Edward....	Ernest Town........	R.R.N.Y., son of Lt. John, B.M.A.
Howard, John........	E District............	O.C., 10th Feb'y 1808, had been employed in Public Works, L.Bd.L.
Howard, Senr., John...	Ernest Town...........	Lieut. R.R.N.Y. (Stamped Book), P.L, 1786.

APPENDIX B.

NAMES.	RESIDENCE.	DESCENDANTS.
Howard, Junr., John..	do	Soldier 65th Regt., L.B.M. Son of Lt. John, P.L., 1786.
Howard Mathew	E District	Ensign in Genl. Burgoyne's Campaign.
Howard, Peter	do	Son of Mathew Howard, L. Bd.L.
Howard, Dier	do	Employed in Public Works in 1782, L.Bd.L.
Howard, Stephen	do	Son of Mathew, employed in the King's works, L.B.L.
Howard, Stephen	Elizabethtown	Same person O.C 10th Feb., 1803.
Howard, Thomas	Ernest Town	Son of Lt. John, R.R.N.Y. A.Mc.L. B.M.A.
Howard, William	E District, Elizabeth Town	Stamped Book.
Howe, Wm	Kingston	State Loyalist, L.B.M.,1791 —from New York (P.L. 1786, Stamped Book).
Howell, John	Sophias&Ameliasburgh	M.C., Sergeant-Major R.R. N.Y., L.B.M., 1791—650 acres, Stamped Book.
Howell, Warren	Fredericksburg	R.R.N.Y., A.Mc.L.
Howey, Robert	H District	New Jersey Volunteers.
Hubert, Thomas	Kitley	1793—late from the State of Vermont, L.B. Grenville.
Hudson, G. J	Marysburg	(Labourer Stamped Book), B.M.A.
Huen, John	E District	
Huffman, Christopher.	H District	Sergeant Jersey Volunteers, p. discharge.
Huffman, Christr	do	Que : If son of John Senr.
Huffman, Jacob Haufmun	do	Soldier German Troops, p. Provision list, 1786.
Huffman, Jno. Nicholas, Junr	do	Loyal Rangers (Niagara Stamped Book),S. P.L.N. 1786, the Senr. not privileged, only one daughter, named Marg.
Hughes, Reuben	Marysburgh	Sergt, S.G. and Govr. Hamilton, 100 (British Regt., P.L. 1786), a wife & child (Stamped Book).
Hughes, James	do	Loyal American Regt., informed by J. Crawford.
Huff, Asa	Fredericksburgh	Soldier Loyal Rangers, called Loyalist, P.L. 1786.

APPENDIX B. 197

Names.	Residence.	Descendants.
Huff, Paul............	Adolphus Town	Lieutenant Loyalist, P.L. 1786, from N. York, A. Mc. L.
Huff, Senr., Solomon..	do	A Settler in 1788, P.
Huffnail, Andrew	Fredericksburgh	Drummer Loyal Rangers, L.B.M. 1791.
Huffnigle		
Huffnail, Jeptha......	Adolphus Town	Soldier Royal Yorkers, Jobet
Humphrey, James	E District............	Soldier Loyal Rangers.
Humberstone, Samuel.	District Johnstown....	By order in Council, 13th Oct., 1807, Lieut. Associated Loyalists.
Hunt, Edward........	H District............	M.C. Soldier Col. Church's Connecticut Volunteers, O.C. 18th April, 1797.
Hunter, David.........	E District............	S.G. Lands as CorporalL.B. L. 1791, Artificer & Loyal Ranger.
Hunter, David, Junr..	do	Son of David.
Hunter, John	H District............	A soldier R. Hamilton.
Huntsinger, John	do	M.C. Soldier Royal Yorkers, Muster Roll A. O.C., 28th March, 1807. Niagara Stamped Book.
Hurlbert, Moses......	E. District............	Soldier King's Rangers. P. L. Roll.
Hurley, John	Mary's & Sophiasburgh	(Stamped Book), P. L. 2d, 1786.
Husley, John	Marysburgh	Discharged B. Soldier.
Huson, Nathaniel	H. District............	Son of Lieut. Huston, of Col. Robinson's corps.
Hutchinson, Asa	Yonge......	Joined Royal Standard in Rhode Island.
Hurd, Jehiel.........	Augusta......	Sergeant R.R.N.Y.,L.B.L., 1790. G. Haldimand, 1784, 100. Stamped Book.
Huson, Caleb	....	By Order in Council 5th July, 1798.
Huych, John	Adolphus Town	Loyalist P.L., 1786. Lieut. by L.B.D. A. McL.
Hyndmann, Samuel..	H. District	
Henn, Michael........	....	Butler's Rangers. O.C. 11th March, 1797.
Imendol, Christian.... Christopher.	Marysburgh	Soldier German Troops, p. Provision list, 1786 (Stp'd Book).
Inglehart, Bernard.... or Barnhart.	do	A Soldier German Troops, p. Provision list, 1786.
Irish, Peter..........	M. District	
Jackson, Jethro	of Richmond....	Order in Council 24th Feb., 1807.

APPENDIX B.

NAMES.	RESIDENCE.	DESCENDANTS.
Jackson, David	Ernest Town	Pt. in Jessup's corps. L.B. P.L., 1786.
Jackson, Henry	E. District	Volunteer Loyal Rangers, L.B.L.
Jackson, James	Ernest Town	One James. A soldier in Butler's Rangers. A wife. P.L. 1786. Niagara Stp'd Book. Do. A. McL.
Jackson, James	E. District, Augusta	Loyal Rangers, A. McL. P. L., 1786.
Jackson, Peter	do do	
Jackson, Thomas	do	A Soldier Loyal Rangers. Drew 100 acres in M.D. L.B.M. 1790. P.L. 1786.
Jacocks, David Jacobs.	E. District	Soldier R.R.N.Y. A wife and daughter. P. L. 2d, 1786. Muster Roll A.
Jacocks, David	do	Same.
Jarvis, Esq., William	H. District	M. C. Queen's Rangers Cornet.
Jessup, Esq., Edward.	Augusta	M. C. Major Commandant.
Jessup, Edward	E. District	S. G. Lieutenant Jessup's, son of Edwd. Jessup, Sen.
Jessup, Henry	do	
Jessup, Joseph, Capt.	do	Captain Jessup.
Jemmison, Wm.	W. District	
Johns, Lieut. Solomon.	H. District	S. G. Lieut. L. Rangers.
Johnston, Adam	E. District, Cornwall	Joined the Royal Standard at Saratoga in 1777. J. Anderson,'s certificate. P. L. 2d, 1786.
Johnson, Lieut. Brant.	H. District	Indian Dept., S.G. Niagara Stamped Book.
Johnson, Coonrad	do	Private Indian Dept., Butler's Rangers P. Single. P. L. N. 2d, 1786.
Johnson, Frederick	Yonge	A common settler in 1785. O.E.
Johnson, George	E. District, Cornwall	R. R. N. Y. Muster Roll. Corporal. P.L. 2d, 1786.
Johnson, George	do Matilda	Soldier R. R. N. Y. Muster Roll A.
Johnson, Sir John	H. District	Colonel or Lieut. - Colonel Commandant.
Johnson, James	E. District, Cornwall	A Corporal R.R.N.Y.L.Bd. G. & S., M. Roll. P. L. 2d, 1786.
Johnson, Laurence	H. District	Served in Col. Robinson's Regiment.

APPENDIX B. 199

NAMES.	RESIDENCE.	DESCENDANTS.
Johnson, Robert......	E. District, Cornwall...	
Johnson, Lieut. Wm..	H. District	Indian Department, S.G.
Johnston, Andrew	Ernest Town..........	Son of Sergt. James Johnson.
Johnston, Daniel......	do	Son of Sergt. James Johnson, of Ernest Town. L.B.M.
Johnston, Mrs. Elizab'h	H. District............	Widow of Capt. John Johnston of Indian Dept.
Johnston, Elizabeth ..	Kingston	Daughter of Mary Brant.
Johnston, George	do	Son of Mary Brant.
Johnston, Henry......	M. District *..........	Farmer. Stamped Book.
Johnston, Capt. John..	H. District	Indian Department, S.G. Niagara Stamped Book.
Johnston, John	H. District	One of this name, a soldier in R.R.N.Y. and got land in E.D. One a settler of 1787, of Stamford.
Johnston, John	do of Bertie..	Joined in 1777, Esopus. Had a wife and 4 servants. P. L.N. 1786.
Johnston, James......	Ernest Town	O.C. 24th February, 1807— restored — and Johnston, James, Fredericksburgh, O.C. 14th February, 1807 —suspended. This one, a soldier in Jessup's. Fredericksburgh, James, P.L. 1786, if from Ireland.
Johnston, Jonas	H. District	B. Rangers, S.
Johnston, Margaret ...	Kingston	Daughter of Mary Brant.
Johnston, Magdalene..	do	Daughter of Mary Brant.
Johnston, Ralph	H. District	Niagara Stamped Book. Single. P.L.N. 1786.
Johnston, Lt. Wm....	M. District	Son of Sir John (natural).
Johnston, Wm.........	Ernest Town	Captain Indian Department. P.L. 1786.
Johnston, Wm........	M. District	One a soldier from Loyal Rangers from Yorkshire, N.P.
Jones, Daniel	E. District............	1784, G. Haldimand, unincorporated Loyalist, 100.
Jones, David..........	do	One a Lieutenant in Loyal Rangers, 1793, wishes to become a settler. Lately from New York State. L. B.M. 200.
Jones, Ebenezer	H. District	Sergt. in Orange Rangers, S.G.

Names.	Residence.	Descendants.
Jones, Esq., Ephraim.	E. District	S. G. Commissary.
Jones, Esq., John	do	S. G. Captain Jessup's.
Jones, James	H. District	Soldier B. Rangers, S. G. Had a wife and 6 children. P.L.N. 1786.
Jones, Mrs. Jane	do	Who was she?
Jones, Senr., Mary	do	
Jones, Richard	do Augusta	Son of Daniel Jones, R. I. D. G.
Jones, Sarah		
Jones, Solomon	E. District	Surgeon's mate, Loyal Rangers.
Jones, Thomas Irish.	do	Soldier Loyal Rangers. L.B: 1793. One R.R.N.Y., M. Roll. One emigrant from the States. L.B.M. 1793. 200.
Judson, Silas	Elizabeth Town	L. B. L., 1790. Satisfied of his good character as a Loyalist, Connecticut. On the 12th April, 1805, Mr. Silas Judson was at this office and said that he was not within the British lines' resident before the Treaty of Peace in 1783. Came to Canada in 1790. His land was not confiscated.
Julian, John	W. District	
Keaning, John	Marysburgh	Soldier German Troops.
Keefer, Senr., George	H. District	Deceased. Jersey volunteers.
Kelhnam, John or Killman.	do	If Killman. Single. P. L. 2d, 1786.
Keller Charles Koeller.	Fredericksburg	Royal Yorkers L.B.M.1791. His name *Koeller*. 350 acres, A. McL. P.L.1786. Stamped Book.
Keller, Frederick	do	Soldier King's Rangers, P. R. Roll. Stamped Book.
Keller, John		Soldier R. R. N. York, p. Stamped Book.
Keeler, James	Augusta	Soldier Jersey volunteers, p. Affidavit 14th Jany, 1805.
Keller, Philip Martin.	Marysburgh	German soldier. Collins' Book and Provision list, 1786. A. McL. L.B.M. 1793. 300 acres.
Kelly, Patrick	do	Soldier 84th Regiment. L. B. M. 1790, 300 (& P. L. 1786) S.

APPENDIX B. 201

NAMES.	RESIDENCE.	DESCENDANTS.
Kelsey, James........ or Celsiy.	E. District, Augusta..	Soldier in Jessup's corps. L. B. L.
Kelsey, Wm.......... or Celsey.	do do	Son of Jas. Kelsie. L.B.L.
Kelsie, James	do Elizab'h Town	
Kemp, Senr., John, ..	Fredericksburg	Soldier L.B.M. 1790. 300 & L.B.M. 1793, 200. King's Rangers, P. L. 1786. A. McL.
Kemp, Junr., John ...	do	Son of John Kemp, Senr. P. L. 1786. King's Rangers.
Kemp, James	Fredericksburgh	Soldier in King's Rangers,p. R. Roll, L.B.M. 1793, 300. A. McL.
Kemp Joseph	do	Soldier King's Rangers, p. R Roll, L.B.M. 1793, 300.
Kemp, Mathew	H District............	
Kenard, John	Marysburgh..........	Discharged British soldier.
Kenedy, Alexander ...	E District............	Corpl. his sons Allan 200, Alexander 200, R.R.N.Y. Muster Roll, P. L. N. J. 1786.
Kenny, James........	H District............	Soldier 84th Regt. drew 200 as. in 1793, p. L. B. Adolphustown.
Kintner, George......	E District	Soldier R. R. N. Y. has wife and five children, P.L. 2d, 1786.
Kern, Mattice .... Mathew	H District............	Soldier Butler's Rangers, P. S. P. L N. 1786.
Kesler, Michael.......	Marysburgh	German soldier, C. Book & Provision list, 1786, A. McL.
Kessler, Stephen......	W District	
Kief, Imamiel	Marysburgh	
Kilburn, Benjamin ...	E District	Did not join the Royal Standard, but suffered imprisonment and loss of property,p. 1793, *not privileged.*
Killen, Daniel	Marys & Sophiasburgh	
Kimmerly, Andrew ...	Richmond	Soldier R.N.N.Y., L.B.M., 1790, 100 and bounty 200, P. L. 1786, A. McL.
King, Constant	E. District, Edwardsburgh........	A soldier in Jessup's Corps, R. J. D. G.
King, Ebenezer	do Elizabeth Town	Soldier Loyal Rangers.
Kirby, Elizabeth......	M District............	Not privileged.

M

APPENDIX B.

NAMES.	RESIDENCE.	DESCENDANTS.
Kitcheson, Willliam Keitcherson	Fredericksburgh	Dragoon in Tarlton's Legion, L. B. M. 1789, 450.
Kilman, Jacob	H District	B. R. a wife and five children, P. L. N. 1786, has a son named Jacob, Christian James, Niagara Stamped Book.
Kilman, John	do	Found 1st Nov. 1804, on or ignal Roll.
Kittle, senr., Jeremiah	do	Soldier Butler's Rangers.
Knapp, Benjamin	W District	Soldier in Butler's Rangers, A list 1789.
Knapp, Joseph	E District	S. G. lands as sergeant, L.B. L., U. E. Loyal Rangers.
Knoppin, Trueman	Sophias & Ameliasb'gh	Son of John Knappin, not on U. E. See John Nopping, on U. E.
Knight, Benjamin	E District	Above Leeds, M.D., R.J.D. G.
Knight, John	do Cornwall	R. R. N.Y. Muster Roll, A.
Knight, James	do do	Corpl. R. R. N. Y., Muster Roll I, B. M. A.
Knight, Mahalon	Kingston	A settler in 1784 (a Taylor Stamped Book), Loyalist P. L., 1786. A. McL.
Koughnet, William	Fredericksburg	Soldier, Royal Yorkers, p. P.(Stamped Book) and P. L., 1786).
Kraigie, John Kraighill.	Marysburgh	Soldier German Troops, p. Provision List, 1786, A. McL.
Kroukheit, Hercules	Ernest Town	Soldier R.R.N.York, P. (P. L. 1786).
Kroukheit, John	do	Soldier K. R. R. N. Y., P. Stamped Book, P.L. 1786.
Lake, Christopher	do	Soldier Loyal Rangers, O. C. 17th, Nov. 97 200.
Lake, Senr., John	do	M. C. 300 Gn out soldier,O. C., 8th Nov. 1797.
Lake, jun., John	do	Son of
Lake, James	do	
Lake, Thomas	J. D	By order in Council 23rd July, 1803, soldier Loyal Rangers.
Lake, Nicholas	Ernest Town	M. C. 750 to close claims, soldier in Col. Peters, L. B. M. 1790), O. C., 11th Nov. 1797.
Laird, John	E District, Augusta	

APPENDIX B. 203

NAMES.	RESIDENCE.	DESCENDANTS.
Lamb, Isaac, senr.....	Johnstown District....	O. C. 6th May, 1806, joined General Burgoyne in 1777.
Lambert, Corpl. Cornelius	H District............	B. Rangers, S. G. had a wife and one child. P. L. N., 1786. Stamped Book, Niagara.
Lambert, David	Fredericksburgh	R. R. N. Y., A.McL, P.L., 1786.
Lampman, Frederick..	H District............	New York, a wife and four children, P. L. N., 1786, Mathias, his son, I.S.
Lampman, Peter......	do	In New York, brought 8 children, P. L. N., 1786, says a wife and 2 children, Stpd. Book Niagara, I.S.
Lampson, John	E. Dist. Edwardsburgh	A Pensioner, served in 1777, under Gen. Burgoyne, self and family 600, received 200 acres at the Bay of Shaleure, which sold, L. B. L., 10 June, 1791.
Lampson, James......	Edwardsburgh........	Son of John Lampson.
Lampson, William....	E. Dist. Edwardsburgh	Ensign Loyal Rgrs., L.B.L.
Lamson, William	do Elizabeth Town	
Land, Abel	H. District...........	States to have served last war, say Indian Department and Engineers' Department at York Town.
Land, Robert........	do	Indian Department S. G. S. P. L. N., 1786, Stamped Book Niagara.
Landen, Asa..........	E. District...........	States p. Petition to have joined General Burgoyne.
Landen, Asa, Junr....	do	(Son of Asa) joined in 1777, bore arms a part of the war.
Landen, Heman	do Augusta..	Joined before the treaty of separation, E. Jessup.
Landen, Samuel	Augusta..............	Son of Asa Landon, Senr.
Landers, Jabez	E. District Yonge.....	
Lang, John	do do	Marine Department,his own information. Stamped Book Niagara.
Landrie, Mitchel......	Elizabeth Town	
Lanecty, John........ La Lumette.	Marysburgh	British Soldier, P. L. 1786, S. A.McL.
Lap, Jeremiah........	Kingston	Soldier Pennsylvania Loyalists, P.,L.B.M., 1791, 200 acres.
Larne, Henry	Yonge	A soldier formerly R.J.D.G.

APPENDIX B.

NAMES.	RESIDENCE.	DESCENDANTS.
Larne, William	Escott	
Larraway, Abraham	H. District	Soldier B. Rangers, Land completed, S.P.L.N.,1786. Stamped Book Niagara.
Larraway, Abraham	Fredericksburgh	Soldier 2d B. Royal Yorkers, 200 L.B.M. 1791, Bounty land refused, Stpd. Book.
Larraway, Harman	do	
Larraway, Jonas	H. District	M. C. Soldier Butler's Rangers, had a wife and four children P. L. N., 1786, Stamped Book.
Larraway, Senr. Isaac	Fredericksburgh	Soldier R.R.N.Y., Stamped Book, P.L.N. 1786.
Larraway, Jun. Isaac	do	R.R.N.Y., Stamped Book.
Laroway, Jonas	do	Soldier R.R.N.Y., A.McL.
Larroway, Peter	H. District	C.B.R. Soldier, 300 acres sold to Mr. Street, S. P. L. N. 1786, Stamped Book.
Larroway, Peter	Fredericksburgh	Soldier 1784, G. Haldimand, 100, R. R. N. Y., Stamped Book, A.McL.
Lawe, Mrs. Elizabeth	H. District	Daughter Owen McGrath, M.D., Expunged.
Laughlin, Alexander	Midland	Inserted by Order-in-Council 12th July, 1798, was 10 days a soldier in McAlpine's Corps, taken prisoner, &c.
Lawer, William	Fredericksburgh	Soldier R.R.N.Y.
Layer.		
Laurence, George	H. District	Soldier B. Rangers, C.B.N., 1794, a wife and one child, P. L. N., 1786, Stamped Book Niagara.
Laurence, Richard	do	Loyalist from N. Brunswick.
Laws, Samuel	Richmond	Soldier R. R. N. Y., Genl. Haldimand, 1784, 100, P. L., 1786.
Leaky, Abraham	E. District	Son of William Leaky.
Leaky, William	do	1789 L. Bd. Montreal 200, came to Canada in 1781 with his family p. P. one a soldier Loyal Rangers is dead, R.J.D.G.
Leaky, Jun. William	do Wolford	
Leaken, David	do Augusta	
Leech, Catherine, widow		O.C. 8th February, 1808.
Lee, David	Bastard	Soldier Loyal Rangers.
Lehincter, Nicholas	Marysburgh	

APPENDIX B. 205

NAMES.	RESIDENCE.	DESCENDANTS.
Leman, John	E. District, Lancaster.	Single, P.L. 2d, 1786.
Lemon.		
Lemons, senr, Joseph..	H. District	
Leonard, John.	Ernest Town........	1789 P. dated Eliza. Town, states a young man, had received 100 acres, 200 more granted in District of Lunenburg, had been in service.
Lerrock, Senr. Francis.	do	Soldier Loyal Rangers.
Lerrock, Junr. Francis	do	Soldier Loyal Rangers.
Lerrock, Peter........	do	Drummer in Loyal Rangers.
Lewis, Barent	Adolphus Town.......	Loyalist from New York, P. L., 1786, soldier Indian Department, P. L. B. M. A.McL.
Livingston, Daniel....	Johnstown District ..	Inserted by order-in-Council 26th July, 1798.
Livingston, John	Augusta.	
Livingston, John	E Dist., Charlottenb'gh	Sergeant R.R.N.Y. Muster Roll; who died in 1782; his son's petition in 1807.
Livingston, John ...	do	Late from the State of N. York. L. B. Grenville, 1793.
Livingston, Mary, ... alias Mutchmore	do Charlottenb'gh	Widow of Jonathan Muchmore, soldier R.R.N.Y.
Livingston, Neil......	do do ..	Son of a soldier—200 acres, Ld. Bd. L.
Livingston, Wm......	Augusta.	
Livingston, Wm......	E District, Osnabruck.	
Lightheart, Daniel....	M District............	Soldier in Jessup's.
Lindsey, John........	Ernest Town	and Lindsey, James, Fredericksburgh. Soldier King's Rangers, p. R. Roll. P.L. 1786.
Lippincott, Richard ..	H District...........	Captain Associated Loyalists.
Little, Senr., John....	W District	S.G. U.E. A wife and two children. P.L.D. 1786.
Livermore, Moses	Hawkesbury..........	O.C. 29th March, 1808. Soldier Loyal Rangers.
Livingston, John......	H District.	
Livingston, Neal......	do	
Loldel, Daniel........	M District............	Soldier R.R.N.Y.
Lobedell, Daniel......	Fredericksburgh.	
Lockhart, Wm........	Escott.	
Lockwood, Benjamin..	H District.	

APPENDIX B.

NAMES.	RESIDENCE.	DESCENDANTS.
Lockwood, David	Ernest Town	Son of a sergeant, who served in Genl. Burgoyne's, but died before the peace. David came in to settle in 1789. L.B.M.200. Bounty refused, Augt. 10, 1791. Step-son to Jeptha Hawley.
Lockwood, Josiah	H District............	Had two sons in the York Volunteers, and was himself within the British lines.
Lodwick, Frederick.. } Fredrick, Lodwick }	Marysburgh	M. C. (Stamped Book)—his name Lodwick Fredrick—had a wife and 3 children. P.L. 2d, 1786—R.R.N.Y. Muster Roll.
Loeney, Edward......	E District............	Son of John. J.B.
Loeney, John	Charlottenburgh	Dead—wife alive. J.B. R.R. N.Y. Muster Roll.
Loeney, Samuel ...... Loeney, Wm..........	E District } do }	Sons of John. J.B.
London, Barthol'w....	H District............	A settler in 1789 ; states, p. petition, to have suffered imprisonment.
Lorence, John........ Lawrence	E District........ ...	O.C.7th July,1802,corrected.
Lorimier, Chevalier ..	do	How U.E.? Son of Francis, a subaltern last war.
Losce, Cornelius......	Matilda	Soldier King's Rangers, p. R. Roll, or Jessup's Loyal Rangers.
Lossie, Wm	M District.	
Losee, Joshua, Senr...	....	See order - in - Council 17th March, 1807. Soldier Loyal Rangers.
Lott, Senr., John	Thurlow..............	A settler after the war. G. Harris.
Lotridge, Captn. Robt.	H District............	Indian Department. S. G. (Five in family), P.L.N. 1786. Niagara Stamped Book.
Lotz, John .... Lutes	Marysburgh	(Stamped Book.) German soldier—had a wife, P. L. N. 1786. A. McL.
Lovelass, Archi'd.....	Grand R., E District..	Sons of Lieut. Thomas Loveless, Lieut. Loyal Rangers.
Lovelass, Wm........	do ..	Who was hanged by the Rebels. A. McL.

APPENDIX B.

NAMES.	RESIDENCE.	DESCENDANTS.
Lovell, John	Marysburgh	Soldier 53rd Regt., 1791—L.B.M. 350 (& P.L.1786); a wife.
Louck, Abraham	E District, Augusta	1784, Genl. Haldimand, 100. Soldier R.R.N.Y. Muster Roll.
Loucks, George	Williamsburgh	Soldier R.R.N.Y. L.B.L. Muster Roll—a wife and 2 children, P. L. 2d, 1786 (Stamped Book).
Loucks, Nicholas	E District, Augusta	A soldier in Jessup's—by his widow, Eleanor Fiddler—a wife & 3 children. B.M.A.
Loucks, Richard	Williamsburgh	A wife and 6 children—P.L. 2d, 1786.
Loucks, Abraham	Fredericksburgh	Soldier K.R.R.N.Y. L.B. M. 1793—300, P.L. 1786.
Loucks, George	do	Soldier R.R.N.Y. L.B.M. 1793—300.
Loucks, Henry	do	Soldier K. R. Regt. N.Y. 1784, G. Haldimand, 100. Stamped Book.
Loucks, Jacob	do	Soldier R.R.N.Y. (& Catherine Loucks, his widow) Stamped Book.
Louckes, Joseph	E District, Osnabruck	Sergeant R.R.N.Y. Muster Roll A—P.L. 2d,1786. Restored before Reduction—Capt. M. McDonell.
Loyd, Daniel	Fredericksburgh	1785, Govr. Hamilton, 100. Loyalist, R.R.N.Y. P.L. 1786 (Weaver Stamped Book).
Loyd, John	Kingston	German soldier—Que.: German soldier.
Loyd, Richard	Fredericksburgh	1785, Govr. Hamilton—Loyalist—200. R.R.N.Y. P. L. 1786 (Laborer Stamped Book).
Loyd, Thomas	Marysburgh	Discharged British soldier. Stamped Book—A. McL.
Lucas, Amos	M District	P.L. 1786—King's Rangers —A. McL.
Lucas, George	do	Son of Amos (200).
Lutz, Sampson	H District	Indian Department, S. G. O.C. 21st July, 1796.
Lymburner, John	do	From New Brunswick—his father never was in this Province; son of Margaret.

APPENDIX B.

NAMES.	RESIDENCE.	DESCENDANTS:
Lymburner, Margaret.	of Caistor	Deceased, by O. C. 28th April, 1807.
Lymburner, Mathew..	H District	From New Brunswick—his father never was in this Province; son of Margaret.
Lynch, James	E District, Cornwall	Soldier R.R.N.Y. Muster Roll. P.L. 2d, 1786; and Linch, James, soldier R. R. N.Y. Muster Roll.
Lynk, John	do Cornwall	Soldier R.R.N.Y. Muster Roll A (single man), P.L. 2d, 1786.
Lynk, Mathias	do Cornwall	Soldier K. R. Regt. N. Y. Muster Roll. P.L.2d,1786.
Lyons, Benjn	H District	Son of William Lyons, who was a soldier in the 8th Regt.
Lyst, Andrew	Fredericksburgh	Soldier R.R.N.Y. L.B.M. 1791—300 acres.
Lyst, Henry Loyest	do	M.C. Soldier RoyalYorkers, Ld.Bd.certe.A.McL. P.L. 1786.
Moak, Philip	E District, Osnabruck	Six Nation Indian Department, p. discharge of Colonel Danl. Claws.
Maby, Frederick	H District	States having joined the Royal Stand'd before 1783.
Maby, Lavinia		Wife of Frederick Maby.
Maby, Sergt. Lewis	H District	M.C. B. Rangers—a wife & 5 children, P.L.N. 1786.
Main, James	E District	1792, late from Vermont, P. 4th article—a settler.
Main, Senr., Thomas..	do	Soldier 84th Regt.
Main, Mathew	do	
Main, Thomas, Junr..	do	Lately from Vermont — a settler.
Major, John	H District.	
Malcom, Finlay	E District	From New Brunswick.
Mallery, Enoch	of Yonge	A soldier in Jessup's—R. J. D. G.
Mallery, Nathaniel	Yonge	L. B. L. 1790. Emigrated from U. States.
Mandeville, Richard	E District, Cornwall	Soldier R.R.N.Y. Muster Roll.
Mandeville, Richard	Williamsburgh	Sergeant R..R.N.Y. M.Roll —at Montreal, B.M.A.
Manhart, David	Elizabeth Town	Did not join the Royal Standard before the Treaty of Peace; lost part of h s property on account of loyalty—a settler, S.S. O.E.

APPENDIX B.

NAMES.	RESIDENCE.	DESCENDANTS.
Maracle, Frederick....	H District............	Soldier B. Rangers, S. G. Niagara Stamped Book.
Maracle, Sergt. John..	do	B.R. S.
Maracle, James	do	Butler's Rangers. P.S. P.L. 1786.
Marbet, Michael......	Adolphus Town	Loyalist from New York— A. McL.
Marcelis, John Bapt..	H District............	Butler's Rangers, L.B. Nassau, 1794. Stamped Book Niagara.
Marcellis, Peter	do	B. Rangers, Niagara Stamped Book. S. P.L.N. 1786.
Marcellis, John	E District, W'msburgh	R.R.N.Y. M. Roll—had a wife and 7 children—P.L. 2d, 1786.
Marcellus, Sevares....	deceased, of Osnabruck	Soldier R.R.N.Y., O.C. 22d Feb., 1808.
Marier, John.........	Kingston.............	
Markland, Thomas.....	do	
Marlatt, John........	E. District	
Marlatt, Thomas.....	do	Settler.
Marsh, Abraham..... or Mash.	do	P. L. 2d, 1786.
Marsh, Benjamin.....	M. District...........	Soldier 84th Regt. Ld.Bd.L. Mash.
Marsh, Jeremiah......	do	Emigrant from the States, 1792, his parents here L. B.M. 200 acres.
Marsh, Mathias.......	do	
Marsh, Joseph........	Fredericksburgh	King's Rangers p. R. Roll, Corporal 1784, Gen. Haldimand, 100.
Marsh, Mathias.......	M. District.........	
Marsh, Samuel	do	Son of Col. Marsh.
Marsh, Wm..........	do	
Marsh, Senr., Wm....	do	A Pensioner, L.B.M., 1789, 1,050 acres in all.
Marsh, Junr., Wm....	do	Son of William Senr.
Marther, John........ or Martin.	H. District	Niagara Stamped Book.
Martin (Negro), Peter.	do	Butler's Rangers.
Martin, Wm.........	Augusta.............	Says that he aided and assisted the King's officers and subjects during the War—only came in after peace, not U. E.
Mathews, James......	H. District	New Jersey Volunteers.
Mathews, Jonathan...	do	Soldier B. Rangers S. G. Niagara Stamped Book, S.P.L.N. 1786.

APPENDIX B.

Names.	Residence.	Descendants.
Matlack, Caleb	H'District	
Mattice, William	Eastern	Was a soldier Butler's Rangers, by order-in-Council, 19th November, 1807.
Mattice, Adam	E. District	Son of Nicholas, Soldier Butler's R., Ld. Bd. Lunenburg.
Mattice, Abraham	H. District	Soldier B. Rangers, S. G., Niagara Stamped Book, S. P. L. N. 1786.
Mattice, John	E. District	Soldier R. R. N. Y., Muster Roll A. (P.L. 2d 1786), O. C. Restored 29th Jan. 1808.
Mattice, Nicholas	E. Dis. Elizabeth Tw'n	Soldier B. Rangers, had a wife and four children at the Peace of 1783, P.L. 2d 1786.
Mattice, Nicholas	Charlottenburgh	R. R. N. Y. Muster Roll A., Single man, P.L. 2d, 1786.
Mattice, John	Niagara District	Soldier Butler's Rangers, Order-in-Council, 7th March, 1807.
Mauk, Gasper / Mark, Gaspert.	Marysburgh	German soldier, C. Book and Provision list of 1786, L. B. A., 1794, 100 and 200, Stamped Book.
Mauk, Gotlip	do	German soldier, C. Book and Provision list, 1786, A. McL.
May, Wm	H. District	Soldier B. Rangers—had a wife and five children P.L. N. 1786. Niagara Stamped Book.
Maybe, Abraham	Adolphus Town	Capt. Associated Loyalists.
Maybe, John	Ernest Town	Butler's Rangers, S.P.L.N. 1786. Niagara Stpd. Book.
Medaugh, James	H. District	Indian Department, P.S., P. L.N. 1786. Niag. Stpd. Bk.
Medaugh, Stephen	do	R.R.N.Y. Muster Roll, has a wife and 3 children P.L. N. 2d, 1786.
Medaugh, Senr., John.	E. District Matilda	Soldier R.R.N.Y. L. Bd. L. Muster Roll, has a wife & 3 children P.L. 2d 1786.
Medaugh, Junr., John.	do do	Came to the Province in 1784, P. from U.S.
Meddough, Martin	do Osnabruck	R.R.N.Y., Muster Roll A., P.L., 2d, 1786.
Menske, John	Marysburgh	If Meisuke? German soldier C.B. yes.

APPENDIX B. 211

NAMES.	RESIDENCE.	DESCENDANTS.
Mercle, Christo'r......	E. Dist. Williamsburgh	
Mercle, Henry........	do do	R.R. N. Y. Muster Roll A., P.L. 2d 1786.
Mercle, Henry........	do do	
Mercle, John.........	Williamsburgh........	Soldier R.R.N.Y., L.B.L.& M. Roll, Single, P.L. 2d, 1786.
Mercle, John......... Mukle.	H. District...........	Sergeant Butler's Rangers S.P.L.N. 1786.
Mercle, Senr., Jacob..	E. Dist. Williamsburgh	R. R. N. Y. Muster Roll, R. R.N.Y. L.B.L. Stpd. Bk.
Mercle, Junr., Jacob..	do do	Single man, P.L. 2d, 1786.
Mercle, Michael......	Williamsburgh........	Soldier R.R.N.Y. L.B.L. & Muster Roll, Single, P.L. 2d, 1786.
Mercle, Henry........	E. District Osnabruck.	R. R. N. Y. M. Roll, a wife and one child, P.L. 2d 1786.
Merckle, John........	Marysburgh..........	German soldier p. Provision list of 1786.
Merkle, Jacob........	E. District Osnabruck.	Soldier R.R.N.Y., L.B.S.B. G. had a wife and 4 children, P.L. 2d, 1786.
Meredith, Charles.....	H. District...........	
Merit, Lt. Thomas....	do	Queen's Rangers Cavalry.
Metch, Jacob.........	Marysburgh..........	Stamped Book, German soldier, C. B. and Provision list 1786.
Meyers, Christr.......	Kingston.............	Soldier German Troops, Stamped Book.
Meyers, George W....	M. District...........	Son of John W. Meyers, P. L. 1786.
Meyers, John W	do	Captain Loyal Rangers, Stamped Book.
Meyers, Tobias W....	do	L.B.M. State Loyalist,1793. 300, Soldier Loyal Rangers A. McL.
Michel, Carlman......	E. District...........	
Michel, Hervey.......	do	
Middleton, Robert....	Marysburgh..........	Discharged British soldier, P. L. 1786, S. Stamped Book. A.McL.
Millard, Corpl. Dan...	H. District...........	85th Regt. S.G. had a wife, P. L. N. 1786, Stamped Book Niagara.
Millard, Jessee	do	84th Regt. S. G. had a wife and four children, P.L.N. 1786, Stamped Book Niagara.
Millard, Thomas...... Millar.	do	Sergt. Royal Regt. N. York, Muster Roll, S. P. L. N. 1786, Stpd. Bk. Niagara.

212   APPENDIX B.

NAMES.	RESIDENCE.	DESCENDANTS.
Miller, Andrew	H District	Niagara Stamped Book, S. P.L.N. 1786.
Miller, Andrew	Ernest Town	L.B.M. 1790, R.R.N.Y., P. L. 1786.
Miller, Andrew Moeller.	do	Soldier Loyal Rangers, Provision list 1786, Stamped Book.
Miller, Andrew	Marysburgh	Soldier German Troops, L. B. M. 1793, 300 and Provision list 1786.
Miller, Cornelius if not Conrade	Marys & Sophiasburgh	Soldier King's Rangers, A. McL. Provision list and King's Rangers, 1786.
Miller, Garret	M. District	Soldier or N.C.O. with Burgoyne came to Canada in 1777, O.C. 20 July 1797.
Miller, George	Home District	Found on original Roll, 1st Nov. 1804, S.P.L.N. 1786, Niagara Stamped Book.
Miller, George	Ernest Town	Son of Jacob Miller, Adjt. Associated Loyalists, &c. J. D.
Miller, Gilbert	M. District	Soldier Loyal Rangers, Stamped Book.
Miller, John	Marysb'g & Sophiasb'g	Soldier German Troops, p. Provision list 1786. Stamped Book. A. McL.
Miller, Jacob	Ernest Town	Soldier King's Rangers, p. R.Roll. Adjutant Associated Loyalists, 950, Ass. L.B.M. 1790, P. L. 1786, or Loyal Rangers L.B.M.
Miller, James	Elizabeth Town	An early settler, refuses a description, in General Haldimand's certificate stated unencorporated Loyalist.
Miller, Jonathan	Fredericksburgh	Soldier King's Rangers p. R. Roll L.B.M. 1791, asks for land as an officer.
Miller, Jonathan	Marys and Sophiasburgh	Volunteer King's Rangers, S.G. Soldier King's Rangers..A.McL.
Miller, Nicholas	Williamsburgh	Soldier R.R.N.Y. Muster Roll. L.B L. and one a soldier Indian Dept., P. O.E. Single P. L. 2d, 1786.
Miller, Peter	H District	Butler's Rangers—one son P. L. N. 1786. Niagara Stamped.

APPENDIX B.   213

NAMES.	RESIDENCE.	DESCENDANTS.
Miller, Stephen	Cornwall	⎫ Muster Roll. Corporal in the Royal Regt. New York, Pilot in the Loyalists and private in West Chester Refugees.
Miller, Stephen	E District	Supposed the same person, has lost an arm.
Miller, Thomas	H District............	Soldier B. Rangers, 300 Gr. out O.C. 28th March, 1797 —a wife and four children. P. L. N. 1786. Stamped Book Niagara.
Miller, Zebeda........ Zebulon.	E District, Lansdown..	Emigrant, New York State, L.B.M, 1789.
Mills, John	H District........	Suffered the Pillory, imprisonment and loss of property and was upon Staten Island. p. Certificate of John Petit.
Mills, John	Marysburgh	British Regiment, A.McL. O.C. 7th July, 1796.— Stamped Book.
Mitchel, Jehiel	Bastard	....
Mills-Church, Jona- ... than	E District	Entered as Church, Jonathan Mills—See,C.
Millross, Andrew	do.	Soldier R.R.N.Y. P.L. 2d, 1786.
Millross, John........	do.	⎫
Millross, Thomas	do.	⎬ Sons of Andrew. J.B.
Millross, Wm...	do.	⎭
Milson, John	do., Cornwall....	....
Merkle, Frederick	do., Williamsburg	Soldier R.R.N.Y. L.B. S. and G.
Mitchel, George	do.	Son of George, P. L. 2d, 1786.
Mitchell, George.........	Augusta..............	R.R.N.Y. Muster Roll. A.
Mitchell, Harvey	E District..............	Son of George Mitchell.
Mitchell, Zalmon	do.	Son of George, late from Vermont, 1793—a settler, P.
Mills, Henry .... Mittz	Fredericksburgh	Soldier R.R.N.Y. L.B.M. 1790, 200. 1793, 100. P.L. 1786.
Mills, John .... Moak, Mitts	do.	Soldier R.R.N.Y. L.B.M. 1790, 200. 1793, 100. P. L. 1786. Stamped Book.
Monger, Charles......	....	Deceased joined at Detroit in 1780. O.C. 17th March, 1808.

APPENDIX B.

NAMES.	RESIDENCE.	DESCENDANTS.
Monger, Wm.	W District	Soldier B. Rangers, W. List 1789.
Montgomery, Archid..	E District.............	Master of the Black Snake Privateer, L.B. Grenville, 1793—700 acres.
Montross, Peter	H District............	Loyal American Regt.
Montross, Silas	do.	Son of Peter Montross.
Moody, Walter	do.	Pilot last War.
Moott, Henry	E District	Soldier Loyal Rangers.
Mott Moor, John	Marysburgh	A Sergeant, Regt. 34th.— Genl. Haldimand. 100 and P.L. 1786—one in R.R.N.Y. Muster Roll, a soldier.
Moor, Dodley	E District, Augusta ..	Late from Vermont, 1793. L.B.L.
Moor, Mosa (Hosea) ..	do. Yonge	Was a Soldier in Jessup's, many years left the Province, R.J.D.G.
More, Sylvester (see below)	....	On Original Roll.
Moor, Thomas..........	Kingston	Stamped Book — Loyalist from N. York. B. M. A. A.Mc.L.
Moor, Wm.	Adolphus Town	S.G. foreman or overseer of Works,Engineers' Department—Loyalist P.L. 1786. A.Mc.L.
Morden, John	H District............	Soldier R. R. N. Y. P. L. 1786. A.M.L.
Morden, James	Sophias and Amelias-burgh	M. C. Royal Yorkshire—a soldier. 300 ac. Ld. Bd. Certr. Muster Roll. P.L. 2d, 1786.
Morden, Joseph	M District.............	....
Morden, Moses	H District............	N.C.O. Jersey Volunteers—P.
Morden, Ralph	do.	Deceased, condemned and executed by the Rebels in 1780, had 3 sons John, Ralph and James.
Morden, Richard	Sophias and Amelias-burgh	Mr. Cotlins, Book Stamped, son of Widow Forrest, P. L. 1786. A.Mc.L.
Mose, Sylvester	Edwardsburg	....
Morrison, David......	E District	....
Morrison, Henry	do., Augusta.....	....
Morrison, Mary	E District	Daut. of Capt. William Morrison.

APPENDIX B.

NAMES.	RESIDENCE.	DESCENDANTS.
Morrison, Capt. Wm.	E District, Lancaster...	S.G. R.R.N.Y.
Morrison, Wm........	do.	Son of Capt. W. Morrison.
Mosher, Lewis........	do., Augusta	Soldier Loyal Rangers.
Mosher, Nicholas	do.	S.G. Drew Land as Corporal Loyal Rangers—soldier.
Mosher, Rachael.......	do.	Daur. of Timothy Hodge, L. Board, 1793.
Mosley, George	Of York	Deceased O.C. 10 May, 1808 Served as an Artificer.
Moss, Samuel	do., Cornwall	S. G. Sergeant p. Muster Roll. R.R.N.Y. P.L. 2d, 1786.
Moss, John	H District...........	Soldier Butler's Rangers, W. List.
Most, John	Kingston	L.B.M. Soldier 53rd Regt. German Soldier, C. Book. Que. which? P.L. 1786.
Monsure, John	do.	Stamped Book—came with Capt. Grass from New York; first settler 100. P.L. 1786.
Mott, Reuben	E District, Augusta ..	Soldier Loyal Rangers.
Mott, Edward	Yonge	Emigrant from New York State 1792. P. Ld.Bd.
Muchmore, Jonathan..	....	E. D. Deceased inserted on the U.E. List by Order in Council, 20th June, 1807.
Mugel, Gadless	Sophias and Amelias-..burgh	Soldier R.R.N.Y. A.C.
Mulloy, Wm.	Marysburgh	Discharged Soldier.
Munro, Daniel........	E District, Yonge	
Munro, David........	Cornwall	Soldier R.R.N.Y. W.A.D. P.L. 2d, 1786.
Munro, Henry........	E District	Son of Capt. John. J. B.
Munro, Hugh Lt.	do.	Soldier R.R.N.Y. Muster Roll.
Munro, Hugh	do.	Lt. in Jessup's, 2100 in addition, but not under the Order in Council of 22nd Oct., 1780—Report Committee of Council, 16th Dec., 1791.
Munro, Hugh	do.	Lieutenant R. R. New York S.G. P.L.N.J. 1786.
Munro, Honl. John ..	Matilda	S.G. Captain R.R.N.Y.
Munro, John	E District, Yonge.....	R.R.N.Y. Muster Roll.
Munro, Junr. John ..	do.	Son of Capt. John, soldier R.R.N.Y. Muster Roll.

APPENDIX B.

NAMES.	RESIDENCE.	DESCENDANTS.
Munro, Samuel	Yonge	S. Sherwood, Esq. deposeth that Samuel Munro joined the Royal Standard before the Treaty of Separation, in 1783, 12th Feby., 1805.
Munro, Thomas	E District	P.L.N.J. 1786.
Munsal, Moses		Was killed by the Rebels on his way into Canada—Order in Council, 8th March, 1806, placed on U.E. List.
Munro, Thomas	do. Charlottenburg	
Munson, David		On Original Roll.
Murchison, Duncan	Lancaster	Was a son of William—Soldier R.R.N.Y. Muster Roll—had a wife and 2 children. P.L. 2d, 1786.
Murchison, John, Junr.	E. District Charlottenburgh.	A Soldier R.RN..Y, Muster Roll, P.L.,N.J.,1786.
Murchison, John, Senr.	do do	Soldier R.R.N.Y., in Capt. Angus McDonell's Company, p. Rev. A. McD.
Murchison, Keneth	do do	Son of John Murchison Sr., was a soldier in Capt. Angus McDonell's Compy R. R.N.Y., p. Rev. Alr. McD.,1808.
Murchison, Wm	do do	R.R.N.Y., M.R.M. & Son of Duncan, 200 acres L. Bd. L., one P. L. N. J., 1786.
Murdoff, Senr., George	Fredericksburgh	Sergeant R. R. N. Y., Genl. Haldimand 1784, 100, P. L. 1786, A.McL. Stamped Book.
Murdoff, Junr., George	do	Que.R.R.N.Y,.A. McL.,son of Geo. Murdoff, left the Province.
Murdoff John	do }	Son of George, is come of age. 1793, L.B.M. 200.
Murdoff, (John	do }	
Murdoff, James, Sergt.	do	P. K. Royal Regt. N.Y.L. B.M.1790,300 Genl.Haldimand 1784,100,P. L. 1786, Stamped Book.
Murdoff, Thomas	do	Son of George Murdoff Snr.
Murray, Lt. Duncan	H. District	84th Regt., had a wife and four children, P.L.N. 1786. Stamped Book.

APPENDIX B.

NAMES.	RESIDENCE.	DESCENDANTS.
Murray, Qr., Mr. John	H District.............	84th Regt. S.P.L.N 1786.
Mustard, John .... or Mutard	E. District.............	P.L.N.J. 1786.
Mutchemson, Ruggles	Yonge	
Myncher, Fredk. Jno. or Moenncke	Marysburgh, &c......	Soldier German Troops. Stamped Book.
Myncker, John	Marysburgh	Soldier Riedessel's Dragoons, L.B.M. 1790 & Provision List, 1786.
Myres, John..........	Elizabeth Town	From New York, L. B. L. 1790.
Myres, Michael.......	E. District	Soldier R.RN.Y, O. E.
McAlpin, Duncan	do	Sergeant Loyal Rangers, P. to L.B.L. 1793.
McArthur, Archibald...	E. District, Charlottenburgh	R.R.N.Y.
McArthur, Charles....	do Augusta...	Soldier King's Rangers, p. R. Roll.
McArthur, Donald ..	do Charlottenburgh	Rept. L.B. Stormont, stated U. E., R.R.N.Y., P.L.N. J., 1786.
McArthur, Duncan...	do	Sergt. K. Rl. Regt. N. Y., R.R.N.Y.,P.L.N.J.,1786.
McArthur, Duncan ...	do Charlottenburgh	R.R.N.Y., was son to Donald.
McArthur, Duncan ..	3rd, Charlottenburgh..	Original Roll,
McArthur, Junr., Jno.	E. District	Son of Donald, single, P.L. 2d, 1786, O. C. 5th January 1798, P.L.N.J. 1786.
McArthur, Senr., Jno.	Charlottenburgh	From Nova Scotia L.B.L., R.R.N.Y.
McArthur, John.......	Thurlow...............	Soldier Loyal Rangers,B.M. A.
McArthur, Peter	E. District............	Son of Donald.
McArtheren, Daniel	Augusta................	
McArtheren, Daniel	Elizabeth Town.......	
McAulay, Robert	Kingston...............	Captain of Loyalists, Carleton Island.
McBane, Gilles........	E. District, Cornwall ..	Soldier R.R.N.Y., L.Bd. & M. Roll (single, P.L. 2d 1786).
McBane, Richard	do	Emigrant from Scotland,L. Bd. L.
McBane, Isabella, alias McDonell	Charlottenburgh.......	Supposed wife of Giles.
McBeane, John.......	Marysburgh	Soldier 34th Regt. L. B. M. 1790, P.L. 1786, from New York State, wishes to become a subject and settler, L.B.L. 1792.

APPENDIX B.

NAMES.	RESIDENCE.	DESCENDANTS.
McCaffrey, John	E. District, Cornwall.	Soldier R.R,N.Y., L. Bd. & Muster Roll, P.L.2d, 1786.
McCall, Senr., Donald.	H. District	Of Montgomeries Highlanders, former war.
McCarbin, Benjamin..	E. District, Edwardsburgh.	
McCarger, Joseph	Marysburgh	Discharged soldier B., a weaver. Stamped Book.
McCarthy, James	do	A Soldier British Regt,84th S.G. 1789, L.B. Montreal, 200.
McCarthy, Michael...	do	84th Regt. discharged British Soldier, P. L. 1786, S. Stamped Book.
See McKarty for McCarty	Florance	R.R.N.J.
McCaulay, Ann	M. District	From U.E., daughter of Kirby of Lake Champlain.
McClellan, Wm	H. District	B. Rangers S.G. had six children, P.L.N. 1786,Niagara. Stamped Book.
McConnell, Hugh	Fredericksburgh	Soldier R.R.N.Y., Muster Roll, P.L. 1786.
McCool. Archd	H. District	Deceased.
McCool, Wm	do	Son of Margaret McCool, from Carolina, O.C., 21st July, 1796.
McCollom, James	Niagara District	Was a soldier in——. Inserted on U.E. List, O. C. 27th January, 1807.
McCready, David	E. District	
McCrimmon, Donald...	Marysburgh	Soldier 84th Regt. L.B.M. 1790, 350, (& P.L. 1786), a wife. Stamped Book.
McCue Wm	Escott	R.R.N.Y. Muster Roll A.
McCuin, Senr., David.	E. District, Cornwall...	R.R.N.Y., Muster Roll P.L. 2d, 1786.
McCuin, Jnr., David..	do	Son of David, Senr, J.B.
McCullock, Chas	Kingston	Discharged Artificer, from New York A.McL. Stamped Book.
McCurdy, James	Marysburgh	British Soldier,P.L.1786, A. McL. Cordwainer. Stamped Book.
McDonald, Allan	Gainsborough	O.C. 8th March, 1808, Sergeant Butler's Rangers.
McDonald, Christn. ..	H. District	B. Rangers S.G., a wife, one child, P.L.N. 1786. Stamped Book. Niagara.

APPENDIX B. 219

Names.	Residence.	Descendants.
McDonald, Donald ...	Ernest Town	P. 1794,says Loyalist, P. L. 1786.
McDonald, Donald ...	Kingston	
McDonald,Capt.Jno...	H. District	B. Rangers S. G.
McDonald, Sergt.Peter	do	S.G., B.R., P. Goreham's Corps.
McDonald, Sergt. Ronaldor Randall.......	do	Butler's Rangers, deceased, application by Christian, Niagara. Stamped Book, a wife and two children, P.L.N. 1786.
McDonald Wm	H. District	— Son of Randall, Sergt., B. R., Niagara. Stamped Book.
McDonell, Alexr........	Marysburgh......	Discharged British Soldier (P.L. 1786), a wife. Stamped Book, A.McL.
McDonell, Alexr......	do	British Soldier P.L, 1786,A. McL. S. Stamped Book. Another a British Soldier, P.L. 1786, S.
McDonell, Col. Alexr.	Charlottenburgh!......	Captain R.R.N.Y.
McDonell, Alexr.	E. District	Soldier Queen's Rangers, L. Bd., P.L. 2d, 1786.
McDonell, Alexr......	Cornwall	Soldier R.R.,N.Y. M. Roll, P.L.N.Y., 1786.
McDonell, Alexr.....	do	R.R.,N.Y.,MusterRoll,P.L. N.J. 1786.
McDonell, Alexr.... .	E. District............	Deceased Captain RoyalYorkers, P.L. 2d, 1786.
McDonell, Alexr......	do Charlottenburgh...............	N.I.S.,from R.R.N.Y.,Muster Roll, P.L. 2d 1786.
McDonell, Alexr......	Charlottenburgh	No. 9, R.R.N.Y., M. Roll, N.B. P.L.N.J., 1786.
McDonell, Alexr........	E. District, Cornwall	Knodirt Soldier 84th Regt. S., P.L. 2d 1786.
McDonell, Alexr......	do	One a Soldier Loyal Rangers, one of this name a Treasury Loyalist.
McDonell, Alexr.........	do	One an emigrant from U.S., one P.L.N.J. 1786.
McDonell, Alexr......	do	R.R.N.Y., P.L.N.J. 1786, Muster Roll.
McDonell, Alexr	do	R.R.N.Y., Muster Roll N. B., P.L.N.J. 1786.
McDonell, Capt. Allan	H. District	84th Regt. Stamped Book, Niagara.
McDonell, Allan.........	Kingston.............. ...	G. Haldimand 1784, 100.
McDonell, Allan.......	E. District	Captain R. Regiment, N. York, S.G.P.L. 1786.

APPENDIX B.

NAMES.	RESIDENCE.	DESCENDANTS.
McDonell, Allan	E District	R.R.N.Y. M. Roll, one of this name was a Commissary at Ozwigchie and Pensioner.
McDonell, Allan	do	Son of a Soldier L.Bd.L., one A.McD., a Loyalist, P.L.N.J. 1787.
McDonell, Allan	do	Son of a reduced soldier, L. Bd.L., one a British soldier, P.L. 1786, Kingston.
McDonell, Allan	Matilda	Single, P.L., N.J., 1786.
McDonell, Andrew	E District, Edwardsburgh	
McDonell, Angus	12th Con., Cornwall	P.L. 2d, 1786, one of this name a soldier 84th Regt.
McDonell, Angus	4th do do	P.L. 2d, 1786.
McDonell, Angus	5th do do	R.R.N.Y., P.L., N.J.,1786, one of this name a Corporal Jersey Volunteers, L. Bd.L., one a son of Duncan.
McDonell, Angus	E District	Captain R.R.N.Y., S.G.,P. L. 2d, 1786.
McDonell, Col. Archd.	do	Captain R.R.N.Y.
McDonell, Archd	Cornwall	84th, a soldier A. McPhee, P.L. 2d, 1786.
McDonell, Archd	Marysburgh	Lieut. 84th Regt., disbanded soldier, Provision list,1786 (British) S.(Stamped Book
McDonell, Daniel	E District, Augusta	Corporal R.R.N.Y., Muster Roll, P.L., N. J., 1786, & P.L. 2nd, 1786.
McDonell, Donald	5th Con., Cornwall	P.L., N.J., 1786.
McDonell, Donald	4th do do	P.L., N.J., 1786.
McDonell, Donald	6th do No 12 do	P.L., N.J. 1786.
McDonell, Donald	4th do No 22 do	P.L. 2d, 1786.
McDonell, Donald	5th do No 4 do	P.L. 2d, 1786, one a British soldier, P.L. 1786, Kingston, S.
McDonell, Donald	E District of Roxboro'.	Corporal 84th Regt. S.G.,P. L., N.J., 1786.
McDonell, Donald	do	Soldier R.R.N.Y., L.B.S. & G., p Muster Roll, P.L. N.J. 1786.
McDonell, Donald	do	Soldier 84th Regt. (single), P.L., N.J., 1786.
McDonell, Donald	do	A Loyalist, L.B. Stormont, P.L., N.J.,1786.
McDonell, Donald	Kingston	

APPENDIX B. 221

NAMES.	RESIDENCE.	DESCENDANTS.
McDonell, Duncan....	Cornwall	Soldier 84th Regt., P.L., N. J., 1786.
McDonell, Duncan....	do	One a sergeant B. Militia, Quebec, L.B. Stormont, 1790, P.L. 2d, 1786.
McDonell, Duncan....	Cornwall...............	One a soldier R.R.N.Y., p. Muster Roll, one of this name from New York, L. Bd.L., 1790 (P.L. 2d,1786)
McDonell, Farquer ...	E District of Williamsbargh	L.B. Stormont, soldier 84th Regt., Corporal R.R.N.Y. M. Roll, a wife and four children, P.L. 2d, 1786, 7th March, 1805, came to America with the 26th Regiment, was taken prisoner at Sorel. Joined Sir John Johnson at Johnson's Bush—his own information.
McDonell, Finnan	do	Stamped Book, Sergt. 84th U.E., A.Mc.L., P.L., N.J. 1786.
McDonell, Mrs. Helena	H District............	Her husband took up arms at the head of 200 Highlanders.
McDonell, Hugh......	Roxburgh...............	R.R.N.Y.
McDonell, Hugh........	Cornwall	Lieut. R.R.N.Y., P.L.. N. J., 1786.
McDonell, Hugh......	E District, No 45.....	North side River au Raisin, Charlottenburgh, R.R.N. Y., his son John drew No 10-4 Nepean, P.L., N.J., 1786.
McDonell, Hugh......	do	Soldier 84th Regt.
McDonell, Capt. John.	do	M.C. Cornwall, R.R.N.Y.
McDonell, Capt. John.	do	Son of Captain Alexander, R. R. N. Y., P. L. 2d, 1786.
McDonell, John	4th Con. No. 17, Cornwall................	R.R.N.Y. Muster Roll, P. L., N.J., 1786.
McDonell, John	4th do No 20 do	R.R.N.Y., Muster Roll, P. L., N.J., 1786.
McDonell, John	5th do No 7 do	R.R.N.Y., Muster Roll, N. B., P.L., N,J., 1786.
McDonell, John	5th do No 9 do	P.L., N.J., 1786.
McDonell, John	11th do " A " do	P.L. 2d, 1786.
McDonell, John	5th do No 11 do	P.L. 2d, 1786.
McDonell, John	9th do " A " do	P.L. 2d, 1786.

APPENDIX B.

NAMES.	RESIDENCE.	DESCENDANTS.
McDonell, John	5th Con. No. 10, Cornwall	One a soldier R.R.N.Y., P.L., 1786, one son of Capt. John McDonell of Cornwall.
McDonell, John	Edwardsburgh	R.R.N.Y., P.L.,N.J.,1786.
McDonell, John	E District, W½. No 17 Cornwall	One a soldier late 84th Regt. P.L. 2d, 1786.
McDonell, John	do	One of 84th Regt., a soldier by his widow, Isabella, P.L. 2d, 1786.
McDonell, John	E District	One a wife and six children, P.L. 2d, 1786. One of the name came in the Myrtle, T.L.
McDonell, John	do	No. 17 South side River aux Raisins. Settled in the Colonies before the war, drew lots 18 in 6th Con., 10-1, 20-3 and ½ No 13-3, Roxboro', P.L. 3d, 1786.
McDonell, John	Marysburgh	Stated to have been an Associated Loyalist (P.L. 1786, B. Soldier), S. Stamped Book, A.Mc.L.
McDonell, John	do	British soldier (P.L. 1786), A.M.L.,S.Stamped Book.
McDonell, John	Matilda	Stamped Book, has a wife and two children, P.L., N.J., 1786, came in after the war, was well known in Albany as a staunch Loyalist, N.McLean.
McDonell, John	E District	Sergeant of Roxboro' S.G., P.L., N.J., 1786.
McDonell, John Bane	do Charlottenburgh	R.R.N.Y. Muster Roll, P.L., N.J., 1786.
McDonell, John Due	do do	R.R.N.Y., P.L. 3d, 1786.
McDonell, James	Kingston	Captain R.R.N.Y.
McDonell, James	E District	Captain R.R.N.Y. (Stamped Book), P.L.,N.J.,1786. One a sergeant R.R.N.Y. Muster Roll.
McDonell, Keneth	Cornwall	R.R.N.Y. M. Roll, P.L.,N.J., 1786, a sergeant R.R.N.Y. Muster Roll,and one P.L. 2d, 1786, and McDonell Keneth, E District Charlottenburgh.
McDonell, Widow Nelly	E District, Charlottenburgh	

APPENDIX B. 223

NAMES.	RESIDENCE.	DESCENDANTS.
McDonell, Capt. Miles	E Dist., Charlottenb'gh	Ensign R.R.N.Y., by order in Council, 11th November, 1806.
McDonell, Esq. Ranald	Cornwall	Ensign 84th Regt. (P.L. 2d, 1786).
McDonell, Ranald....	E District	Lieutenant R.R.N.Y., P.L. N.J., 1786, one a sergeant R.R.N.Y., Muster Roll.
McDonell, Ranald....	do Charlottenburgh	In pensioner R.R.N.Y., L. Bd. Muster Roll, a wife and two children P.L., N. J., 1786.
McDonell, Ranald 4th.	Charlottenburgh	Original Roll.
McDonell, Roderick ..	E District, Charlottenburgh	Soldier R.R.N.Y., L.Bd. Muster Roll, P.L., N.J., 1786, his son James recommended for land, 1807, one of 84th Regt., P.L., N.J., 1786.
McDonell, Roderick E.	Charlottenburgh	Original Roll.
McDonell, Wm	Kingston	A drummer in 84thRegiment only (P.L., 1786), S.
McDonell, Wm	Cornwall	Son of Capt. John, J.B.
McDougall, John., ...	Home York	By order in Council, 4th Feb'y., 1807.
McDougald, John	E District, Augusta ..	Soldier in Jessup's, P. 1790, A.Mc.L.
McDougald, John.......	Ernest Town	Soldier Loyal Rangers, L. B.M., 1790, 300 (P.L., 1786).
McDougall, John	E District	R.R.N.Y., had a wife and two children, P. L. 2d, 1786.
McDougall, Peter	Ernest Town.........	Soldier Loyal Rangers, called Loyalist, P.L., 1786, A Mc.L.
McDuff, Chas	Marysburgh	Discharged B.Soldier, A.Mc. L., a carpenter, Stamped Book.
McFall, Lt. David....	H District:	M.C. not U.E.
McFall, David........	E District, Lancaster..	Lieutenant Jessup's, single P,L. 2d, 1786.
McFall, Lt. Neil......	H District............	
McFerson, Thomas....	Marysburgh	
McGaw, Patrick......	H District............	M.C. O.C., 7th Jan'y. 1797 and O.C. 6th Jan'y, 1797.
McGilles, Senr. Donald	E Dist., Charlottenb'gh	Sergeant R.R.N.Y., Muster Roll, P.L., N.J., 1786.
McGilles,Junr. Donald	do do	R.R.N.Y., Muster Roll, N. B. (P.L., N.J., 1786).

APPENDIX B.

NAMES.	RESIDENCE.	DESCENDANTS.
McGillies, Donald ...	E Dist., Charlottenb'gh	R.R.N.Y., Muster Roll. P. L., N.J., 1786.
McGilles, Hugh	do do	
McGilles, Duncan	do do	Emigrant from Scotland, L. B., 1790.
McGin, George	Ernest Town	M.L. Lieut. Indian Department, S.G., Stamped Book. P.L., 1786.
McGlocklon, David.. McGlocklon, Robert.	E District	Sons of William of Cornwall who was a soldier R.R.N. Y., and on the U.E. list by the name of McLaughlin.
McGowen, Thomas......	Marysburgh	Soldier 44th Regt. L. B. M. 1793, 300, & P. L. 1786. (Stamped Book and Sergt. Donald McIntosh's certificate.
McGrawth, Owen	Fredericksburgh	M. C. Gt. 300. Soldier (R. R.N.Y. P. L. 1786). O.C. 8th July, 1797. (Stamped Book).
McGregor, Donald......	E. Dist., Cornwall.....	R.R.N.Y. Muster Roll P.L. 2d, 1786.
McGregor Hugh.......	E Dist., Charlottenb'gh	Artificer L. B. L. Was settled on the Mohawk River before 17;—p. affidavit of Archibald McArthur,19th July, 1806; P. L. N. Y. 1786, and O. C. 7th April, 1807.
McGregor, John	do	Corporal R.R.N.Y. Muster Roll. R. R. N. Y. P. L. N. J., 1786.
McGregor James	do Cornwall ...	Sergeant R. R. N. Y. S. P. L. 2nd, 1786
McGregor Mary	do	Daughter of John McGregor J. F.
McGregor Peter	do Charlottenb'gh	R. R. N. Y. Muster Roll. R. R. N. Y. P. L. N. J., 1786.
McGruer Alexander....	do	Late an Emigrant from Scotland; Ld. Bd. L., 1790.
McGruer Christian ...	do	
McGruer Donald	do	Soldier 84th Regt.
McGruer John..........	do	Corporal R.R.N.Y. Muster Roll. P.L.N.J., 1786.

APPENDIX B. 225

NAMES.	RESIDENCE.	DESCENDANTS.
McGuin Ann, now Nanorile	M. District	Daughter of Capt. Daniel McGuin, P.L. 1786.
McGuin, Anthony	Kingston	Son of Captain Daniel McGuin
McGuin, Daniel	do.	Stamped Book. One of this name a Captain R. R. N. Y. S. G. L. B. M. 1789 P. L. 1786.
McGuire, Patrick	E District	S. G. Lands as a Corporal. Soldier, 84th Regiment. J. F.
McIlmoyle, Archibald	do Edwardsburgh	A settler. Not privileged R. J. D. G.
McIlmoyle, Hugh	Edwardsburgh	S. G. Land as Sergeant Loyal Rangers P.
McIlmoyle, John	E District	Late of Edwardsburgh. Reinstated by Order in Council, 26th June, 1807.
McIlmoyle, James	do Edwardsburgh	Soldier Loyal Rangers.
McIlmoyle, Thos	do do	Employed in Secret Service, O. C., 16th Feb., 1808.
McIntyre, Sen., Daniel	H. District, Grimsby	Soldier old French War. Re-instated U. E. list, July 11th, 1806.
McIntosh, Alexander	E. Dist., Edwardsburgh	
McIntosh, Benjamin	Charlottenburgh	Soldier 34th Regt., P.L.B.L.
McIntosh, Daniel	E. Dist., Edwardsburgh	
McIntosh, Donald	Marysburgh	One of this name a soldier's son—Land in E. D., 1789; this one was Sergeant 84th Regt. L. B. M., 1789, 550—P. L., 1786, a wife, 3 children. Stamped Book.
McIntosh, John	Thurlow	1791 only. Came of age and an apprentice to Alex. Chisholm, 200, L. B. M.
McIntosh, John	E. Dist., Edwardsburgh	Son of a soldier, L. B. L. (one R. R. N. Y., P. L. 2d, 1786).
McIntosh, Lauchlin	Marysburgh	Soldier 84th Regt., L. B. M. 1791. (P. L. 1786). S. Stamped Book.
McIntosh, Peter	Lancaster	R. R. N. Y. (had a wife and two children), P. L 2d, 1786.
McIntosh, Peter	E. Dist., Lancaster	
McIntosh, Daniel	do Charlottenburgh	If Donald, R. R. N. Y. Muster Roll.

APPENDIX B.

NAMES.	RESIDENCE.	DESCENDANTS.
McIntyre, Donald	E Dist., Lancaster	R. R. N. Y. Muster Roll. R. R. N. Y. P. L. N. J., 1786.
McIntyre, Sen., Duncan	do do	Soldier R. R. N. Y. (P. L. N. J., 1786).
McIntyre, Jun., Dunc'n	do do	Sergeant R. R. N. Y. Muster Roll. P. L. N. J., 1786.
McIntyre, John	do do	Sergeant R. R. N. Y. Muster Roll.
McIntyre, John	Williamsburgh	P. L. N. J., 1786.
McIntyre, John	E. Dist., Charlottenb'gh	Sergeant Royal R. R. N.Y., N. 41, front 300, 200, 200, Kenyon, P.L.N.J., 1786.
McIntosh, Jesse	do. Augusta	1793, late from State of New York, L. B. Grenville.
McKarty, Florence...	Matilda	McCarty, Soldier R.R.N.Y.
McCarty, McKay, Angus	E. District, Lancaster.	Soldier Royal Yorkers. R. R. N. Y. Muster Roll P. L. N. J. 1786.
McKay, Donald	do do	Soldier R. R. N. Y. Muster Roll, P. L. N. J, 1786.
McKay, Hugh........	do do	Soldier Royal Yorkers. R. R. N. Y. Muster Roll.
McKay, Hugh.	Charlottenburgh	From Nova Scotia. P.L.N. J. 1786.
McKay, John	H. District	Son of ——. Supposed R. R. N. Y., P. L. 2d., 1786.
McKay, John	Marysburgh	Soldier British Regt., 84th Regt., p. Sergeant McIntosh, N.J. 1786. Stamped Book.
McKay, John	E Dist., Charlottenb'gh	p. Muster Roll, R.R.N.Y., P. L. N. J., 1786.
McKay, John	do do	Sergeant, R. R. N. Y., L. B. L., P.L.N.J., 1786.
McKay, Samuel	Ernest Town	Stepson of Captain William Johnson. Soldier Loyal Rangers A. McL.
McKay, William	E. District, Lancaster	Soldier 53rd Regt., L.B.L., and one a soldier Queen's Loyal Rangers, P.L.N.J., 1786.
McKee, John.........	Osnabruck............	Sergeant R. R. N. Y. Muster Roll, M. B., P. L. 2d., 1786.
McKenzie, Sen., Colin	Ernest Town..........	Sergeant Loyal Rangers, called Loyalist — P. L. 1786, A. Mc. L.

APPENDIX B. 227

NAMES.	RESIDENCE.	DESCENDANTS.
McKenzie, Jun., Colin	Ernest Town	Drummer Loyal Rangers — son of Colin McKenzie, Sen. (P. L., 1786).
McKenzie, Duncan	E. District	R. R. N. Y. Muster Roll, P L. N. J., 1786.
McKenzie, John	Charlottenburgh	R. R. N. Y. M. Roll. P. L. N. J., 1786.
McKenzie, John	E. Dist., Edwardsburgh	A Soldier 84th Regt.
McKenzie, Lt. Keneth	Cornwall	S. G. R. R. N. Y.
McKenzie, Capt. John	Williamsburgh	S. G. R. R. N. York.
McKenzie, Wm.	Marysburgh	Soldier 84th Regt. L.B.M., 1791, 300, Stamped Book S.
McKim, James Sen.	Ernest Town	Sergeant in Jessup's A. Mc. L. (P. L., 1786).
McKim, James Jun.	do	Son of James.
McKim, Wm.	do	Son of James, Sen.
McKinny, John	do	Soldier Loyal Rangers, L. B. M., 1789.350, A. McL. (P. L., 1786).
McKinny, Amos	Midland	By Order in Council, 4th Dec., 1806.
McKitchie, John	E. Dist., Williamsburgh	Corporal R. R. N. Y.
McLaney, John	H District	Stepson to John Dennis.
McLaren, Archibald	E. District, Augusta	
McLaren, Hugh	do do	Soldier R. R. N. Y. L. Grant. P. L. N. J., 1786.
McLaren, Peter	do do	Lieutenant in Jessup's S.G.
McLaren, Peter	do Elizabethtown	
McLaughlin, Alexander	do Charlottenburgh	R. R. N. Y. Muster Roll. N. B., P. L. N. G., 1786.
McLaughlin, Edward	H. District	Served several campaigns last war.
McLaughlin, James	do Ancaster.	24 years service in 42nd Regt. from States, U. E.
McLaughlin, James	do	New Jersey. Joined Royal Standard at New York. R. Clench.
McLaughlin, Wm.	E. District, Cornwall	R. R. N. Y. Muster Roll P. L. 2d, 1786.
McLean, Alexander	do Elizabethtown	P. 1789, states a young man. Five years' residence and 100 acres. A settler. T. Smith.
McLean, Donald	H. District	From New York.
McLean, Donald	E. Dist., Charlottenb'gh	Soldier R. R. N. Y. Muster Roll. P. L. N. J., 1786.
McLean, Jun., Donald	do	Son of a Soldier. L. B. L.
McLean, Duncan	Augusta	

APPENDIX B.

NAMES.	RESIDENCE.	DESCENDANTS.
McLeane, John	E. Dist. of Elizabeth Town	T. Sherwood & A. Campbell certify to him having joined during the War. Restored 3rd March, 1806. W. E. E. Jessup.
McLean, John	W. District	S. G. Loyalist. Suffered imprisonment and loss of property. 600 acres, 1793.
McLean, Murdock	E. District	Sergt. R. R. N. Y. Muster Roll. N. B.
McLean, Robert	Elizabeth Town	P. 1789, A young man, has resided 5 years. A settler, son of Alexander. T. Smith.
McLean, Stephen	Kingston	Discharged artificer.
McLean, Wm.	E. District	Son of a Soldier. L. B. L.
McLelan, John	Cornwall	Soldier 84th Regiment.
McLeland, Sen., John	E. Dist. Charlottenburg	R.R.N.Y.,P.L., N.J., 1786.
McLeland, Jun., John	do do	Son of John.
McLeland, Kenith	do do	Soldier Carolina Regiment. L.B.L.
McLeod, Widow Isabella	do	Is she the widow of Sergeant John, late 84th? Had 3 children. P.L. 2d, 1786.
McLeod, Thomas	do	Son of a Soldier. L.B.L. A settler.
McLeod, Wm.	do Charlottenburg	M.C. Sergeant Sir J. Johnson's S.G., L.B.L. Sergt. R. R. N. Y. Muster Roll. P.L.N.J. 1786.
McLeod, Wm.	do	S.G. Land as sergeant or son of a soldier. L.B.L.
McMartin, Malcomb	Williamsburgh	Lieutenant R. R. N. York, S.G. Single. P.L.2d,1786.
McMartin, Malcom, Sr.	E.Dist. Charlottenburg	Father to Lt. McMartin, an artificer. P.L.N.J. 1786.
McMartin, John	do do	S.G. Land as Sergt. Served in King's works. J. Clark. P.L., N.J., 1786.
McMasters, John	Adolphus Town	James on the Original Roll.
McMichael, Edward	H. District	Lieutenant Guides & Pioneers, S. G.
McMichael, Isaac	do	
McMicking, Peter	do M.C.	Butler's Rangers, soldier. O. C. 25th Feb. 1797. A wife and 3 children. P.L.N. 1786.

APPENDIX B. 229

NAMES.	RESIDENCE.	DESCENDANTS.
McMicking, Thomas..	H District............	Indian Department, S.G. A wife and one child. P.L. N. 1786. Niagara Stamp'd Book.
McMillan, Donald....	E. District, Cornwall..	1787, Collins' 200. Loyalist. Employ'd on King's works. Miles McD.
McMullen, Daniel....	Fredericksburgh.....	A wife and child. P.L. 2d, 1786. A. McL.
McNabb, Alex........	H. District............	Not privileged, S. P. L. N. 1786.
McNabb, John	do	Joined the Royal army at the commencement of the war, and served in different capacities.
McNabb, James......	H. District	Deceased. Not privileged.
McNairn, John	E. District, Cornwall..	S.G. Land as sergeant. Supposed R.R.N.Y. P.L. 2d. 1786. One a private in Captain Herchmer's company Batteaumen. A.McL.
McNaughton, Donald.	do Charlottenburg	R.R.N.Y Muster Roll. P. L., N.J. 1786.
McNaughton John....	do do	R.R.N.Y. Muster Roll. P. L., N.J. 1786.
McNeal, Archibald ...	do Elizabeth Town	From Vermont. Lost property to the amount of £3,000, P. 1794.
McNeal, John........	do do	O.C. 1806, Feb. 26th. Restored to U. E., soldier in McAlpin's corps. A son of William. See Christian Hossack's petition, 1797.
McNeil, Archibald....	do Edwardsburg..	Soldier Loyal Rangers.
McNeil, John	H. District	
McNeil, Wm.........	Elizabeth Town	Son of John McNeal.
McNight, Thomas .... Knight.	E. District	Soldier Loyal Rangers.
McNish, James	do Augusta....	Joined the Royal Standard at Fort; only one.
McNish, James	do Elizabeth T'n	Stanwix in 1777, p. certificate of Gideon and Samuel Adams.
McNish, Joseph	Elizabeth Town	With General Burgoyne at Lachine in 1783. Employed on Secret Service under the name of *Corn Cob.*

APPENDIX B.

NAMES.	RESIDENCE.	DESCENDANTS.
McNut, James	Fredericksburgh	Came into this Province in 1779 or 1780 ; his son's affidavit.
McPhee, Allan	E. District	84th Regiment.
McPherson, Alexr	do	R.R.N.Y. Muster Roll. P. L., N.J. 1786.
McPherson, John	M. District .... M.C.	Soldier Loyal Rangers. L. B.M.1789,500. L.B.Certe. A. McL.
McPherson, John	Ernest Town	John of E. Town, S. L. Rs. P.L. 1786.
McPherson, Peter	do	Soldier Loyal Rangers. L. B.M. 1789, 300. P.L. 1786.
McPherson, Murdock.	E.Dist. Charlottenburg	Sergeant R.R.N.Y. Muster Roll. P.L., N.J. 1786.
McPherson, James	Charlottenburg	On Original Roll. Sergeant 2nd Battalion R.R.N.Y.
McQuin, Senr., Alex	H. District	18 years in the service ; was in the battle of Fontenoy ; had been wounded ; came into this Province after the war.
McRobert, Mary	do	
McTugget, James McTagart.	Fredericksburgh	M. C. McTagart, Corpl. S. G., L.B.M. 1793, 300. R. R.N.Y., P.L. 1786. Stp'd Book.
McVee, John McFee.	Elizabeth Town	1787, J. McDonell, ½ No. 21. 1789, Chewitt No. 22, 23, 12 Township. A labourer in Forage Department. P. L., B.G.
McWilliams, John	E. District, Osnabruck	R.R.N.Y. Muster Roll ; had a wife ; P.L. 2d, 1786.
Napping, John	Kingston	Soldier King's Rangers.
Naughton, Andrew	Grand River, E. Dist	S.G. Captain Pioneers.
Naughton, Philander	E District	
Naulton, Thomas	Elizabeth Town	
Neil, George	H District	Loyal Militia, South Carolina ; bore arms at sixty-six.
Nebling, Ernest	M.C. of Marysburgh	Soldier 53rd Regiment, L.B. M. 1790, 100, and in 1792, 200. L.B. Certe, and P. L. 1786 ; Stamped Book.
Neher, John Nehrr.	Fredericksburgh	Soldier R.R.N.Y.,P.L.1786, A. McL. Stamped Book.
Nellis, Abraham	H. District	Son of Captain W. Henry Nelles.

APPENDIX B. 231

NAMES.	RESIDENCE.	DESCENDANTS.
Nellis, Warner........	H District............	Son of Captain W. Henry Nelles.
Nellis, Lieut. Robert..	do	Indian Departme't. Niagara Stamped Book.
Nellis, Wm...........	do	Son of W. Henry Nelles.
Nellis, Capt. W. Henry	do	Indian Department ; a wife and 5 children , P. L. N. 1786. Niagara Stamped Book.
Nettleton, Amos......	Augusta..............	Petition of 1798 ; states no service but eight years' residence ; served part of the war in the Continental service ; a common settler. Oliver Evarts.
Nettleton, Daniel	E District............	Admitted as a settler. 200 L. B.L. 1791. Soldier in Jessup's L. Rangers.
Neville, Edward.....	W. District	New settlement, Lake Erie, B.R. ; a Corporal B. Rangers, W.L.
Newalt, Frederick .... Neuwald	Marysburgh	Soldier German Troops, p. provision list, 1786.
Newberry, Sergt. Wm.	H. District	Sergeant Butler's Rangers.
Newkirk, James	do.	B. Rangers S. G. Stamped Book Niagara, S. P.L.N. 1786.
Nicholson, Alex	Fredericksburgh	Soldier Loyal Rangers, L. B. M. 1789—300.
Nicholson, Archibald..	do.	Loyal Rangers. A. McL. Called Loyalist. P. L. 1786.
Nicholson, Robert	H. District	Gen. Haldimand's certificate. 1784, 100 acres, No. 4, 1 con. Augusta ; told so. Simon Covill.
Nicholson, Robert	E. District, Augusta	
Nickerson, Elihud	Hamilton	O.C. 5th March, 1808 ; served as sergeant.
Noble, Wm	Lancaster	A private in Capt. Herchmer's Batteaux Company. A. McL. A wife. P. L. 2d, 1786.
North, James	Marysburgh..........	Sergeant ; discharged from 53rd Regiment ; not U.E. 400 acres ; his widow Winnifred North, 200 bounty. L.B.M. 1791.
North, Reeds	do	British Soldier (P.L. 1786). A. McL. Stamped Book.
North, Thomas	H. District	Soldier New Jersey Volunteers. O.C. 7th July, 1796.

APPENDIX B.

NAMES.	RESIDENCE.	DESCENDANTS.
Nudale, Adam........	E. District	Soldier R.R.N.Y. T. Weager.
O'Brien, John	Marysburgh	Soldier 60th Regt. Report L.B. Stormont.
O'Conelly, James	H. District	Soldier Butler's Rangers, L. B. Nassau, 1794.
Ogden, John	Marys & Sophiasburgh	Soldier R.R.N.Y. Muster Roll A, 2, gts. 300, all he has a claim to—see L. B. M. 1789; nevertheless on the 26th Augt., 1794, he again states his desire to become a settler, and the L. B. A. order him 200 acres.
Ogden, Junr., John ..	do do	
Oliver, Aaron	Richmond	Soldier Indian Department, L.B.M. 1791.
Oliver, Cornelius......	do	L. B. Mecklenburgh state Loyalist, 1791. Son of Frederick.
Oliver, Frederick	do	Soldier Indian Department; L.B.M. 1790, 550 (P.L. 1786)—a wife & six children.
Oliver, John..........	do	L.B.M. state Loyalist, 1791. Son of Frederick.
Olker, Elisha	....	By order-in-Council 13th Novr., 1797.
O'Neale, Widow Eliza.	Kingston	of Lt. O'Neal, Jessup's or Roger's—L. B. M. 1790— 1,200 (P.L. 1786).
Orser, Arthur	do	Loyalist from New York (Stamped Book), P. L. 1786.
Orser, Gabriel	M District............	Loyalist from New York (Stamped Book), P. L. 1786.
Orser, Isaac	do	Loyalist from New York— P.L.1786—Stamped Book.
Orser, Solomon	Kingston	Loyalist from New York— A. McL. — M. Collins' Book. P.L. 1786.
Orsier, Wm..........	do	
Ornal, Conrad .... Orbel	do	German soldier — Collins' Book. P.L. 1786.
Osterhout, Wm.......	H District............	Soldier B. Rangers, O. C. 21st July, 1796. S. P.L.N. 1786.

APPENDIX B. 233

Names.	Residence.	Descendants.
Otto, Gotlet	E District	German soldier — Collins' Book. See order-in-Council, reinstated 17th March, 1807. Soldier Butler's Rangers.
Outhouse, Nicholas	H District	Joined the Royal army at Fort Montgomery—was a guide.
Overholt, Abraham	do	Pilot to New York army— S. G.
Overholt, Miss Elizabeth	do	
Overholt, Stols	do	Stamped Book, Niagara.
Ozburn, James	Markham	O.C.19th April,1808. Joined in 1776 ; raised a volunteer company.
Page, Joseph	H District	Butler's Rangers—S.G. Niagara Stamped Book. P. L.N. 1786.
Painting, Timothy	Augusta	P. states from Nova Scotia.
Pantan Palmer, Caleb	M District	Son of David, p. Petition, 1797.
Palmer, David	do	Corporal King's Rangers, p. R.Roll—L.B.M. 1790,700.
Palmer, David	H District	A settler from New Jersey in 1788 ; much persecuted —P.
Palmer, John	M District	34th Regiment — S. G. B. M. A.
Palmer, Silas	Kingston	Loyalist from New York— A. McL. Stamped Book. Called Loyalist, P.L.1786.
Palper, Gustus	Marysburgh.	
Pannal, Abraham	E District	If Parnel, a soldier during the war.
Papts, Adam	do	Soldier Butler's Rangers, p. affidavit R.P.
Parepoint,negro,Richd.	H District	Pioneer Butler's Rangers— Niagara Stamped Book— P.L.N. 1786.
Parish, Ezekiel	E District	L.B.L., a settler, 1791. Sergeant Peters' militia—by his widow, Mary.
Parish, Wm	Yonge	Asks to be admitted as a settler, 1790, L.B.L. Son of Ezekiel.
Parks, Robert	E District, Cornwall	S.G. Land as corporal, R.R. N.Y. P.L. 2d, 1786.

O

NAMES.	RESIDENCE.	DESCENDANTS.
Parker, Robert	E District	A settler—came to this Province in 1784. O.E.
Parker, John	H District	A Loyalist during the war—S.G.; an old soldier, p. P., if of E District. Soldier R.R.N.Y. M. Roll.
Parks, Cyrenus Escreynos	Fredericksburgh	Soldier King's Rangers, p. R. Roll. L.B.M. 1790,400. P.L. 1786.
Parks, James	do	Sergeant King's Rangers, p. R. Roll. L.B.M. 1790,400. One Stamped Book, Niagara—I. Depart. one—P. L. N. 1786.
Parks, Nathaniel	do	Drummer King's Rangers,p. R. Roll—P.L. 2d, 1786.
Parks, Senr., Nathan	E District	1784, Genl. Haldimand, 100 as. A soldier King's Rangers—P.L. 1786.
Parks, Junr., Nathan	do	Son of Nathan Parks, Senr.
Parlow, John	do at Matilda	Ld. Bd. L.—his father was a pensioner. An artificer at Carleton Island.
Parrott, James	Ernest Town	Lieutenant Loyal Rangers, A. McL. (P.L. 1786.)
Parsons, Thomas	W District	S.G. B. Rangers.
Palter, Philip	Matilda	Soldier Butler's Rangers—L.B.L.
Pattingall, Jacob	Fredericksburgh	German soldier. C.B.Stamped Book.
Pattingall, Samuel	do	R.R.N.Y. B.M.A.
Pattison, Daniel	Yonge	Lame; came in a settler after the peace—W. Chewitt.
Pawling,Captn. Benjn.	H District	B. Rangers, Niagara Stamped Book. (Single.) P.L.N. 1786.
Pawling, Qr.-Mr. Jesse	do	B. Rangers—has a wife and servant, P.L.N. 1786.
Peak, James	Sophias&Ameliasburgh	
Pearse, John	Williamsburgh	In petition for land, 1792, expects an equal right with strangers—L.B.L.
Peebles, Charles	E Dist., Edwardsburgh	} Served in the waggon Department. P. 1789.
Peebles, Charles	do	
Peek, Caleb	do	Soldier R.R.N.Y. Muster Roll, at Montreal. B. M. A.
Peet, David	do	Son of David Peet, Senr., deceased — a loyal man. L.B.L.

APPENDIX B. 235

NAMES.	RESIDENCE.	DESCENDANTS.
Pierce, Patrick	Marysburgh	A sawyer, p. Stamped Book.
Pell, Jonathan	H District	Son of Joshua.
Pell, Joseph	do	Son of Joshua.
Pell, Joshua	do	Son of Joshua.
Pember, Philip	Kingston	M.C. Corprl. R.R.N.Y. L. B.M. 1790. 3 Gl. I. O.C. 25th Jan'y, 1797. 2 June does not appear entitled to the bounty—P. L. 1786—Stamped Book—lived with Mr. Steedman before the war.
Pemberton, James	H District	Stamped Book, Niagara—P.L.N. 1786.
Pennick, Samuel	Elizabeth Town	Lieut. in Col. Peters' Militia —L.B.L.
Pennock, Philimon	E District	Prays to be admitted as a settler, 6th July, 1790—L B.L.
Pepst, Rudolph	do	
Perrigor, James	do	A sergeant R.R.N.Y. Muster Roll.
Perry, Daniel	Ernest Town	Son of Robert Perry.
Perry, John	do	Soldier Loyal Rangers.
Percy, John	do	Soldier Loyal Rangers—A. McL.
Perry, Senr., Robert	do	Soldier—a sergeant Loyal Rangers—Ld. Bd. Ce. (P. L. 1786.)
Perry, Junr., Robert	do	Son of Robert Perry.
Perry, Senr., William. Parry	do	Soldier Loyal Rangers—L. B. M. 1791, 400 acres (P. L. 1786).
Perry, Junr., William	do	Son of William, Senr.—200 as. L.B.A. 1793.
Peters, Bensley	Kingston	Captain of Associated Loyalists, in the Ann.
Peters, John	Marys & Sophiasburgh	Ensign Loyal Rangers (ensign, P.L. 1786).
Peters, Thomas	E District	A volunteer, L.B. Grenville, 1793—did duty in Montreal.
Peterson, Abraham	Sophias&Ameliasburgh	Loyalist—P. L. 1786—from New York; A. McL.
Peterson, Christian	Fredericksburgh	L.B.M. says Loyalist, 1790 —400 as. A. McL. P.L. 1786.
Peterson, Conrod	E District	S. G.—land as a sergeant.
Peterson, Conrodt	do	Sergeant Loyal Rangers—L.B.L.

APPENDIX B.

NAMES.	RESIDENCE.	DESCENDANTS¶
Peterson, Nicholas, Senr.	Adolphus Town	1790 L.Bd.M.State Loyalist 400. A.McL., P.L. 1786. Servd. 1793, 27 Augt. L. B.A. States—100 received and Grants 200.
Peterson, Nicholas, Junr.	do	Loyalist P.L. 1786—Son of
Peterson, Paul	Fredericksburgh	A soldier in the Refugees. L. B. M. 1790—450. P. L. 1786.
Peterson, Nicholas, Senr.	Sophias and Ameliasburgh	Genl. Haldimand — 100.— Loyalist from New York. P.L. 1786.
Pettit, Daniel	Marys and Sophiasburgh	Associated Loyalist, a native of Long Island.
Pettit, John	H District	New Jersey Volunteers— S.G.
Pettit, Nathaniel	do	Active Loyalist.
Petry, John Jost Petrie.	do	Niagara Stamped Book.
Petry, Sergt. Joseph	do	M.C. B. Rangers. Stamped Book Niagara—a wife and one son. P.L.N. 1786.
Petty, Margery, formerly Widow Foster	do	
Phelps Elijah	do	Butler's Rangers. S.G. Niagara Stamped Book.
Philips, John	do	Say King's Rangers, p. R. Roll. Stamped Book.
Phifer, Frederick, Philer or Pieper.	Marysburgh	34th Regt., a soldier. P.L. 1786, a smith. Stamped Book.
Philips, Elisha	Fredericksburgh	Soldier King's Rangers, p. R. Roll, 1789. G. Haldimand, 100—as Sergeant 100, in right of his father, a soldier—do. L. B. M., 1792.
Philips (now Merrits), Mary.	M District	
Philips, Michael	Ernest Town	Genl. Haldimand's Certificate for 200—Called Loyalist. P.L. 1786.
Phillips, William	Osnabruck	Joined in 1778. O. C. 22nd Febry, 1808.
Philips, Peter	Fredericksburgh	Soldier R.R.N.Y. L.B.M. 1790. 350. P. L. 1786. Stamped Book, 1784.— Genl. Haldimand, 100.

APPENDIX B. 237

NAMES.	RESIDENCE.	DESCENDANTS.
Phillips, Ziba	Formerly of Augusta	O. C. 5th January, 1808. Sergeant King's Rangers
Pickard, Benjn.	H District	Soldier Butler's Rangers. S.G.
Pickard, James	do	Soldier Butler's Rangers, S.G.
Pickard, Wm.	do	Soldier B. Rangers. Stamped Book Niagara. O. C. 11th March, 1797.
Pickle, Senr., John	Fredericksburgh	P.K.R. Regt., N.Y. Soldier L.B.M. 1790, 550, 1784. Genl. Haldimand, 100. J. F. Bickle should be Pickle. P.L. 1786. Stamped Book.
Pickle, Junr., John	do	Son of John Pickle, Senr., 200. Soldier King's Rangers. p. R. Roll.
Pilchard, Stephen	Marysburgh	Discharged British Soldier. A.McL. Stamped Book.
Piller, Michael	Williamsburgh	R.R.N.Y. Muster Roll.
Pine, Chase	E District	
Pitman, Cary	do	A Fifer in Jessup's Corps. Ld.Bd.L.
Pilman, Russell or Pitman.	Fredericksburgh	Ld.Bd. Certe. Described Soldier Loyal Rangers, L. B.M. 1792. 450. A.Mc.L. P.L. 1786.
Place, William Simmon.	Osnabruck	O.C. 8th March, 1808. Soldier, King's Rangers.
Plate, Christian	H District	B. Rangers. S.G. Niagara Stamped Book.
Plater, George	do	{ One person. Pilot to the
Plater, George	do	{ Philadelphia Army.
Plato, Peter or Plant.	do	A Discharged Soldier.— Stamped Book and Niagara do.
Platt, John	E District, Montreal	Employed in Secret Service. J.F.
Papst, Rudolph	Osnabruck	Original Roll. Soldier R.R. N.Y. by I. Chrysler.
Porter, Timothy	Marysburgh and Sophiasburgh	Soldier Loyal Rangers— had drawn 100. L. B. A. 1794. 200. P.L. 1786.
Post, Jacob	H district	A Soldier Butler's Rangers.
Post, Frederick	Fredericksburgh	Was a Soldier Orange Rangers. P. of his son, 1797.
Potreg, Thomas	E District	

APPENDIX B.

NAMES.	RESIDENCE.	DESCENDANTS.
Potten, Richard......	Marysburgh	Discharged British Soldier. P. L. 1786.
Pother, John	Augusta..............	Fifer Loyal Rangers. S. G. p. Discharge.
Powell, Abraham	London District	By Order in Council 13th January, 1807.
Pound, Daniel........	H District............	
Powell, Capt, John ...	do.	Indian Department—a wife and 3 children. P. L. N. 1785. Niagara Stamped Book.
Powell, John	E District, Lancaster	Single, P.L. 2d, 1786.
Powell, William Dummer.	H District............	One of the Judges, U.E.
Powiss, Edward	Marysburgh	Soldier, 84th Regt., L.B.M. 1791, 450.—and P.L. 1786, a wife and 2 children. Dead B.M.A.
Powley, Francis	Kingston	First Settler—called Loyalist. P.L. 1786.
Powley, Jacob.........	do.	Son of Francis Cotlins Booth P. L. 1786. Order in Council, 28th February, 1805—replaced on U. E. List.
Prentice, Daniel ......,	E District............	Soldier K.R. Regt., N.Y. P.L.N.J. 1786.
Prentice, Richard	do	1785—Called Loyalist by G. Hamilton, 100. A.Mc.L. a Blacksmith. Stamped Book.
Prescod, Senr., John... Piscod	do Prescott, ... Cornwall	S.G. Lands as Sergeant R. R.N.Y, P.L. 2d, 1786. M. Roll.
Prescod, Junr., John.. Piscod	do	Son of a soldier, 200 acres. Ld. Bd. L. Pescod.
Price, Christian	H District............	B. Rangers. S.G. Had a wife. P. L. N. 1786. Niagara Stamped Book.
Price, David	do	Indian Interpreter—had a wife and one child. P.L. N. 1786.
Price, Thomas..........	Marysburgh..........	Soldier King's Rangers. p. R. Roll — and one of this name 84th Regt. S.— British soldier. L. B. M. 1791. P. L. Stamped Book.

APPENDIX B. 239

NAMES.	RESIDENCE.	DESCENDANTS.
Prindle, Doctor	Fredericksburgh	Soldier King's Rangers. p. R. Roll. L.B.M. 1790—300.
Prindle, Joel	do	Soldier King's Rangers.—Gov. Hamilton, 100.
Prindle, Joseph	Fredericksburgh	King's Rangers, by Order in Council, 13th January, 1807.
Prindle, Timothy	do	Soldier King's Rangers, p. R. Roll.
Pringle Prindle, William	do	King's Rangers by Order in Council, 13th January, 1807.
Proctor, Joseph	Yonge	Late from South River.
Prout, Sherman	H District	Butler's Rangers, Niagara Stamped Book. S. P.L. N. 1786.
Pruyn, Matthew	Marysburgh	Joined at N. York, O.C. 22d Febry., 1808.
Prunner, Senr., Peter	E District	Genl. Haldimand, 100. Soldier R.R.N.Y. P.L. 2d, 1786.
Pruyne, Herman	Midland	Order in Council, 17th February, 1807.
Prunner, Junr., Peter Brunner	E District	
Purdy, David	Ernest Town	Sergeant 19th, 400 — from New York. Stamped Book. P.L. 1786. A.McL.
Purdy, Joseph	New Castle	See Order in Council, 11th March, 1807. Guide to the Army.
Purdy, Gilbert	Kingston	Died with Genl. Howe's Army—Chesepeake. Left a widow. P.L. 1786.
Purbus, John	Niagara District	Order in Council, 21 Febry., 1807. Joined Butler's Rangers.
Putman, Cornelius	Ernest Town	Genl. Haldimand, 1784, 100. R. R. N. Y. P.L. 1786. Stamped Book.
Purdy, Jesse	Elizabeth Town	O.C. 8th March, 1808—Soldier Col. Emerick's Cavalry.
Putman, Effron Ephraim	E Distric t	Soldier R. R. N.Y. Muster Roll. B.M.A.
Purdy, Mary		O.C. 16thJune,1807. Widow of Gilbert Purdy.
Putman, Henry	H District	B. Rangers. Niagara Stamped Book—a wife P.L.N. 1786.

APPENDIX B.

NAMES.	RESIDENCE.	DESCENDANTS.
Quant, Frederick	H District	
Quant, Jacob	W District	Soldier B. Rangers. W List. 1789.
Quarry (a Negro) Joseph	H District	
Quick, Benjamin	H District	
Quick, Solomon	do.	A soldier, Niagara Stamped Book.—A wife and one child. P.L.N. 1786.
Quin, Michael	do.	R.R.N.Y. Muster Roll.
Quinn, Christopher	E District, Augusta	Received Genl. Haldimand's Certificate for 100 acres.
Quin, John	do. Cornwall	Soldier R.R.N.Y., Muster Roll, P.L. 2d, 1786.
Quin, Michael	do. do.	R. R. N. Y., supposed J.F. P.L. 2d, 1786
Rambouch, Wm	Fredericksburgh	S.G. A private R.R.N.Y. 100. McD. & 200. E.D. P.L. 1786.
Rambough, Amos	E District	Soldier R.R.N.Y. P.L.1786.
Rambough, David	do. Osnabruck	Son of a soldier, 200 acres, Ld.Bd.L.
Rambough, John	do. do.	Soldier R.R.N.Y. Ld. Bd. L. P.L. 2d, 1786.
Rambough, Jacob	do. do.	Soldier R.R.N.Y. P. 1796.
Ramsay, Henry	Willoughby	Soldier B. Rangers, discharged in 1779. O.C. 13th March, 1807.
Ramsay, David	H District	
Randolph, Benjamin	Yonge	A settler in 1795. O. Everts —If Ranolds, a soldier R. R.N.Y. M. Roll.
Rankin, James	M District	Son of Colonel Rankin.
Ransier, George	H District	Butler's Rangers. S. G.— had a wife and one child. P. L. N. 1786. Niagara Stamped Book.
Ransier, William or Ransler	Kingston	M.C. R.R.N.Y. M Roll. O. C. 16th Nov. 1797. Stamped Book.
Rattan, Senr., Peter	Adolphus Town	S.G. Captain Jersey Volunteers. P.L. 1786.
Rattan, Junr., Peter	do.	Son of Peter, Senr., L.B. M. 1793, 100 and 200 Bounty. P.L. 1786.
Rattan, Wm.	do.	S.G. Lieutenant Associated Loyalists and L. B. M. P.L. 1786.
Reddick, Adam	E District, W'msburg.	Son of Christopher Reddick, L.B.M. 1793.

APPENDIX B. 241

NAMES.	RESIDENCE.	DESCENDANTS.
Reddick, Christor	E District, W'msburg .	A Loyalist, L.Bd.L. Soldier R. R. N. Y. J.F.— Had a wife and 3 children. P.L. 2d, 1786.
Reddick, George.........	Williamsburg	R.R.N.Y. Muster Roll.
Redick, John	E District, Osnabruck.	R.R.N.Y. Muster Roll A: A wife. P.L. 2d, 1786.
Ruddock		
Reddie, Philip........	M District	Emigrant settler from U.S. 1792. L.B.M. 200.
Redins, Francis	Ernest Town	Discharged soldier R.R.N. Y. Ld.Bd. Certe. P.L. 1786.
Reide, George	H District............	Butler's Rangers, S. G.— Has a wife and one child. P. L. N. 1786. Niagara Stamped Book.
Reede, Moses	Elizabeth Town	1789. P. States residence since 1788—no service - a settler. E. Jessup's.
Reide, Wm.	H District............	Soldier Butler's Rangers, was taken prisoner (himself).
Reide, Wm.	Yonge.................	Capt. of Militia, South Carolina—last from Nova Scotia, P.
Reely, Sergt., John ..	H District............	B. Rangers, Niagara Stamped Book. O. C. 17th March, 1797—a wife and five children. P. L. N. 1786.
Reynolds, Lt. Caleb...	do.	B. Rangers, S.G. Niagara Stamped Book. S. P.L. N. 1786.
Reynolds, Benjamin ...	Home District.........	By Order in Council, 13th October, 1807. Soldier R. R.N.York.
Riceley, Corpl. Christr.	do.	S.G. B. R. Niagara Stamped Book, S. P.L.N. 1786.
Richards, Christr.....	do.	B. Rangers, S. G. Niagara Stamped Book, S. P.L.N. 1786.
Richards, Daniel......	Marys & Sophiasburg .	Son of John Richards.
Richards, John	do. do. .	S. G. Lieutenant Indian Department. Interpreter L.B.M. 1791. 2000. Stamped Book. P.L. 1786.
Richards, Junr., John	do. do. .	Son of John Richardson, P. 1794. A boy, discharged. A Sergeant, but never did duty. O.R.

NAMES.	RESIDENCE.	DESCENDANTS.
Richards, Owen	Marys & Sophiasburg .	Son of John Richardson—a boy, was discharged as a Sergeant, 2d Battn. R.R. N. Y.—never did duty. O.R.
Richardson, Asa........	Fredericksburgh	S.G. Que.? Loyal Rangers. P.L. 1786. A.McL.
Richardson, Henry....	do.	Son of Asa.
Richardson, Thomas..	M District	Treasury Loyalist.
Richardson, Thomas ..	Fredericksburgh	Son of Asa Richardson, L. B.M. 1790. 200 only.
Richardson, Wm.	do.	Son of Asa, Provisional list. King's Rangers, 1786.
Rickerman, Edward .. Rykman	Sophias & Ameliasburgh	Stated Loyalist, L. B. M. 1793. 300.
Ryckerman, Tobias ...	do. do.	..
Rickley, Andrew ..... Rightly	Fredericksburgh	Soldier King's Rangers, p. R. Roll. P.L. 1786. L.B. M. Sergt. 1790—500.
Ridman, Nicholas	Matilda	
Ridner, Henry..........	Adolphus Town, now of Ameliasburgh	L.B.M. 1791—stated Loyal, 200. Soldier Jersey Volunteers. Ordered to be reinstated on U.E. List, 1805, 23rd February.
Ridner, Junr., Henry	do.	Son of Henry Ridner, Senr.
Rimmerman, Henry ... Roemerman	Marysburgh	German soldier. C. B. and Provisional List, 1786.— Brunswick Troops, L.B. M. 1791, 300. Stamped Book.
Ritchie, John	Ernest Town	This is John Richards, Jnr. —son of John Richards, Senr.
Roberts, Thomas	Marysburgh	Discharged British soldier, P.L. 1786, E., one a soldier R. R. N. Y. Muster Roll. A.McL.
Robertson, James	H District	Soldier Butler's Rangers. W. List, 1789—one a soldier Loyal Rangers—a wife P. L. N. 1786. Stamped Book Niagara.
Robertson, Daniel .... Donald	E District, Cornwall..	Daniel was a soldier 44th Regt. P. L. N. J. 1789— Daughters Jane and Barbara—This a Loyalist who joined in 1777—S. A.

APPENDIX B. 243

NAMES.	RESIDENCE.	DESCENDANTS.
Robertson, Joseph	E Dist., Edwardsburg	Stamped Book Niagara—a wife and two children, P. L.N. 1786—one a soldier Butler's Rangers, P.
Robertson, Joseph	do. do.	Soldier Loyal Rangers.
Robertson, Prince	H District............	S.G. B.R.
Robertson, Lt. Neil ..	E District	S. G. R.R.N.Y.
Robertson Thomas.....	do. Cornwall	P,L. 2d, 1786.
Robertson, Wm.	do. Edwardsburg	
Robins, James	Kingston	Lieut. Loyal Rangers. P.L. 1786.
Robins, Richard	Ernest Town	} Sons of James Robins.
Robins, Richard	Kingston	
Robins, Wm.	do.	Son of James.
Robins, Wm.	E District, Charlottenburg	Soldier R. R. N. Y. Muster Roll. P. L. N. J. 1786—one of this name, P. L. 1786, Kingston.
Robinson, Christopher	Kingston	Ensign Q. Rangers.
Roblin, John	Adolphus Town	Son of Philip L.B.A. 1794, 200.
Roblin, Owen P.........	do.	Son of Owen, Senr., is 21 years of age—L. B. M. 1793, 200.
Roblin, Senr., Owen ...	do.	Loyalist L.B.M. 1793—unassigned S.B. Certificate States U.E. P.L. 1786—A.McL. Genl Haldimand 200, entitled to 700.
Roblin, Junr., Owen..	do.	Son of Philip.
Roblin, Philip........	do.	Govr. Hamilton,200—Loyalist. A.McL. P.L. 1786.
Roblin, Stephen	Sophias & Ameliasburg ..	Served in Major Ward's Block-house—information. M. Clark.
Rodney, Sergt. Geo... Bridges	H District.............	Died in New Brunswick.
Roe, Coleman	W District	S.G. Provincial Navy; came from England in a ship of War to Quebec, during the American War—his son-in-law, Ananias Ogden's information, 20th Oct., 1807.
Rogers, David M.	Marys & Sophiasburg .	Son of Major James, King's Rangers. P.L. 1786.
Rogers, John	Ernest Town	
Rogers, Col. James ..	Marys & Sophiasburg .	S. G. Major Commandt. P. L. 1786.

NAMES.	RESIDENCE.	DESCENDANTS.
Rogers, James.........	Marys & Sophiasburg.	Son of Major James, King's Rangers. P.L. 1786.
Rogers, Wm.............	Ernest Town	Soldier Loyal Rangers, L.B. M. 1790. Cutlins, 200—P. L. 1786. A Hatter Stamped Book.
Roice, Senr., Evan.... or Roye	E District, Cornwall...	Soldier R. R. N. Y. Muster Roll.
Roice, Junr., Evan ...	do.	Soldier R. R. N. Y. Muster Roll.
Rorison, Bazil	Elizabeth Town	Had been Lieut. Orange Rangers and resigned. W.E.
Rooreback, Capt. Bennet	....	Not resident in the Province.
Road, Wm. .... Rood,	E District, Augusta ..	Not privileged—R.I.D.G.
Rose, Aaron...........	do Edwardsburg	Son of Samuel Rose, U.E.
Rose, Alexr.....	do Charlottenb'g	Soldier R.R.N.Y. L.B.L. & Muster Roll N.B. (P.L. 2d, 1786.)
Rose, Alexr...........	do	Son of a soldier—Ld. Bd. L.
Rose, Charles.........	do Charlottenb'g	Soldier R.R.N.Y. Muster Roll.
Rose, William	Charlottenburg	On Original Roll.
Rose, David	E Dist., Edwardsburg.	Late of Vermont—L. B. L. 1792.
Rose, Daniel...........	Ernest Town	Late of Jessup's—left his wife, Eleanor, and seven children—500 as. (P. L. 1786.)
Rose, Donald	H District............	Indian Department (a wife and four children)—P. L. N.1786—Niagara Stamped Book.
Rose, Ezekiel	E District............	Came into this Province beginning of the War—L. B. L.
Rose Mathias	Ernest Town	Ld. Bd. Ce.—described soldier Loyal Rangers—P.L. 1786.
Rose, Junr., Mathias..	do	Soldier Loyal Rangers—L. B. M. 1790- 500. (P, L. 1786.)¶
Rose, Moses..........	Bastard	The old man dead—the one alive about 26 years old, 1808. Came in on commencement of the War—L. B. L.

APPENDIX B. 245

NAMES.	RESIDENCE.	DESCENDANTS.
Rose, Samuel	E Dist.,Edwardsburg.	Late of Vermont—1792, L. B. L—is son of Samuel Rose, mentioned below; was a boy, and not entitled to more than as S. U.E.
Rose, Samuel	do	Joined General Burgoyne. Aaron Rose, David Rose, Susannah Morrison, his children. *J. Fraser, letter.*
Rose, Samuel	do Yonge.	
Rosenbarg, Jacob .. } Rosenbourg	do Williamsburg.	Soldier in Jessup's Corps— P. L.B.L.
Ross, Alexr.	Marysburgh	L. B. M. states Loyalist— 1793, 200, and recommended for 200 more (Stamped Book)—one a British soldier—P.L. 1786; a wife & child. A.McL.
Ross, Alexr.	E. Dist., Charlottenb'g	A Loyalist—L. B. report, Stormont.
Rose, Alexr.	do Williamsburg	Drummer R.R.N.Y. J.F.
Ross, Alexr.	do Lancaster	One an emigrant from Scotland – L. Bd. L.
Ross, Colin	Marysburg	Soldier British Regt. – A. McL. Gone to Montreal. B.M.A. Stamped Book.
Ross, Donald	E Dist., Lancaster	Of Captn. Watts' comp'y— P.L.N.J. 1786.
Ross, Donald	do do	Son of a soldier—200 acres, L. Bd. L.
Ross, Donald	do do	Came in with Sir J. J. in 1776—R.R.N.Y. Muster Roll.
Ross, Finlay	do Charlottenburg	Soldier R.R.N.Y.—Ld. Bd.
Ross, George	do Lancaster	Son of a soldier—200 acres, Ld. Bd. L.
Ross, John	do do	P.L.N.J. 1786.
Ross, Jacob	do Osnabruck	R.R.N.Y. Muster Roll A— P.L. 1786.
Ross, Philip	do Charlottenburg	R.R.N.Y. P.L.N.J. 1786. One do., P.L.N.J. 1786.
Ross, Thomas	do Cornwall	Soldier R.R. N.Y. Muster Roll (P.L.N.J. 1786).
Ross, Thomas	do Lancaster.	
Ross, Thomas Ben.	do do	Had a wife & five children— P.L. 2d, 1786.
Ross, Thomas Taylor.	Lancaster	Had a wife & three children —P.L. 2d, 1786.

NAMES.	RESIDENCE.	DESCENDANTS.
Ross, Walter	Marysburg	Sergeant 84th Regt.—drew land in E District. British soldier, P.L. 1786; a wife—Stamped Book.
Ross, Wm	do	N.C.O. 84th Regt. L.B.M. 1790 (P.L. 1786)—A.McL. Stamped Book.
Ross, Wm	do	Soldier British Regt.— A. McL.—P.L.N.J. 1786.
Ross, Zenus	Fredericksburg	Soldier K. Rangers—Genl. Haldimand, 1784, 100—his widow.
Rowe, Corpl. Fr.derick	H District	Butler's Rangers—S.G. Niagara Stamped Book.
Rowe, Sergt. John	do	Sergeant Butler's Rangers—Niagara Stamped Book; O.C. 25th April, 1797. S. P.L.N. 1786.
Roweshorn, John Rosahorn	Kingston	M.C. Sergt. Captn. Damar's troop (Stamped Ld. Bd. Certe.) S. P.L.N. 1786.
Rudderbuck, John	E Dist.,Edwardsburg	Soldier Jessup's corps of Loyal Rangers.
Rudderbuck, Simeon	do do	
Runnion, Henry	do Cornwall	Soldier R.R.N.Y. Muster Roll A (P.L. 2d, 1786).
Ruport, Podar } Peter	do Osnabruck	R.R.N.Y. Muster Roll A., B.M.A.
Rush, Martin, Senr.	M District	Engineer Department. O.C. 12th June, 1798.
Rush, Martin, Junr.	do	
Rush, Andrew or Rusk	Ernest Town	Soldier King's Rangers, p. R.Roll—L.B.M. 1790,100.
Russell, James	H District	A settler from England.
Russell, Michael	E Dist., Matilda	(Deceased). Soldier R. R. N.Y.—N.M.L. Has wife. P.L. 2d, 1786.
Russell, Rosewell	do Charlottenburg	1790, L. B. L. Admitted a settler.
Russell, Wm.	do Matilda	Corporal R.R.N.Y. Muster Roll — single — P. L. 2d, 1786. One a drummer Loyal Rangers—Niagara Stamped Book.
Rutter, Senr., George	Adolphus Town	Loyalist from New York. A. McL.
Rutzenstine, G. B. De	Marysburg	S.G. Captain Prince Frederick's Germans.
Ryckman, Lt. John	H District	Indian Department, S. G. Niagara Stamped Book.

APPENDIX B. 247

NAMES.	RESIDENCE.	DESCENDANTS.
Ryckman, John	Adolphus Town	Loyalist, P. L. 1786, from New York. A. McL.
Ryerse, Lt. Joseph	H District	M.C. Lt. Jersey Volunteers O.C. 21st Augt., 1797.
Ryerse, Capt. Samuel	do	Captain Jersey Volunteers.
Sacheverell, Mrs. Jane	do	Widow of John Sackerville, volunteer, Indian Department.
Salvester, Levy	E Dist.,Elizabeth T'wn.	
Sanders, Henry	do Yonge	P. L. 1786. One a soldier Loyal Rangers.
Saunders, Abraham	do Edwardsburg	Soldier Ll. Rangers—son of Wm. Saunderson—R. J. D. G.
Saunders, Henry	Marysburg	Soldier King's Rangers, p. R. Roll (Stamped Book) 53rd — one a discharged British soldier—P.L.1786. S. O.C. 30th Augt., 1797, 300.
Saunders, Wm.	E Dist.,Edwardsburg	Is dead ; was a soldier in Jessup's—E.J. R.J. D.G.
Saunderson, Thomas	Fredericksburg	P., 1794, states Loyalist, and wish to become a settler.
Saupe, Gotlep	Marysburg	Soldier German troops, Gen. Haldimand, 100 — P. L. 1786—A. McL.
Saver, John	Matilda	R.R.N.Y. Muster Roll.
Scaret, John	Lancaster.	
Scaffer, Nicholas Schaffer	E District	Corporal Butler's Rangers —himself.
Schermerhorn, John	Fredericksburg	Son of Wm. Schamerhorn.
Schermerhorn, Wm.	do	Provision List 1786—King's Rangers—A. McL.
Schneeider, Abraham	Ernest Town	Soldier Loyal Rangers—A. McL. Called Loyalist P. L. 1786.
Schneeider, John	do	L. Bd. M. Soldier Loyal Rangers—450 (P.L. 1786), A. McL.
Schneider, Isaac	do	Soldier Loyal Rangers, L.B. M. 1792, 300 (P.L. 1786)— A. McL.
Schneeider, Simon	do	Soldier Loyal Rangers—called Loyalist P.L. 1786.
Schram, Corpl. Frederick	H District	B. Rangers, S.G. (had a wife and 3 children), P.L.1786. Niagara Stamped Book.

APPENDIX B.

NAMES.	RESIDENCE.	DESCENDANTS.
Schram, Frederick....	Louth................	Soldier Butler's Rangers, O. C. 24th Febr'y, 1808—one of Col. Butler's corps—p. Discharge.
Schram, John	do	One of Col. Eaton's corps—a wife and 3 children—P. L.N. 1786. L.B. Nassau, 1794. Niagara Stamped Book.
Schram, Jeremiah	do	Butler's Rangers, S. G. S. P. L. N. 1786 — Niagara Stamped Book.
Schram, Valentine....	do	B. Rangers, S. G.—had a wife and one child—P.L. N.1786. Niagara Stamped Book.
Schriver, George...... Sohiver	Fredericksburg	Drew 200 as. in Matilda—E. D. & L. B. M. 1793. States Loyalist-200, bounty. Single. P.L. 2d, 1786.
Scott, Arch'd	H. District	R.R.N.Y., P.L. 2d, 1786.
Scott, Senr., John	E. District	M.C., Yonge, Soldier Loyal Rangers, and for Neal Scott, his late son, Soldier Loyal Rangers, L.B.L.
Scott, Francis	E. District Augusta ..	Sergeant Loyal Rangers.
Scott, John	do	Soldier Loyal Rangers.
Scovils, Samuel	Bastard	
Scratch, Leonard	New Settlement L.Erie	Soldier Butler's Rangers, W. List.
Sea, Harmanns	Ernest Town	Soldier Loyal Rangers.
Seager, Frederick.....	H. District	Soldier Butler's Rangers,had a wife and four children, P. L N., 1786, Niagara Stamped Book.
Seager, Jacob	do ....,	S.G., B.R., Soldier Butler's Rangers, W. list.
Sealye, Augustus	Lancaster	Had a wife and nine children P.L. 2d, 1786.
Sealye, James	E. District, Lancaster.	
Segar, Adam	Richmond............	Soldier Indian Department, L.B.M. 1790, 300.
Segar, Staatz, Senr ...	do	R.R.N.Y., Muster Roll A, in Canada B.M.A.
Segus, John	Marysburgh	Discharged British Soldier, P. L., 1786, S. Stamped Book.
Sealey, Joseph........	Augusta......	Sol. Loyal Rangers, L.B.L.
Sealey, Joseph........	Elizabeth Town......	Original Roll.

APPENDIX B. 249

NAMES.	RESIDENCE.	DESCENDANTS.
Sealey, Justus........	Elizabeth Town	A Drummer Loyal Rangers, L.B.L.
Sealey, Justus.... ...	E. District Augusta...	R.R.N.Y., Muster Roll, one a soldier Loyal Rangers.
Secord, Daniel........	H. District	Indian Department, S.G., had a wife and 5 children, P. L. N., 1786, Niagara Stamped Book.
Secord, Senr., David..	do	N.C.O., B. Rangers, a wife and two children, P.L.N., 1786, Niagara Stpd. Book.
Secord, Senr., John ...	H. District	Sergeant New York Volunteers, a wife and 2 children P.L.N., Niag. Stpd. Bk.
Secord, Junr., John ..	do	Butler's Rangers, S. G., Niagara Stamped Book.
Secord, Senr., James...	do	Deceased Lieutenant B. Rangers, S. G.
Secord. Senr., Peter ..	do	Volunteer B. Rangers, S.G. S.P.L.N., 1786, Niagara Stamped Book.
Secord, Junr., Peter ..	do	Son of Peter Senr., Stamped Book.
Secord, Sergt. Silas. ..	do	B. Rangers, S.G., had a wife and one child, P.L.N., 1786, Niagara Stpd. Book.
Secord, Lt. Solomon...	do	B. Rangers, S.G. S. P.L.N., 1786, Niagara Stpd. Book.
Secord, Sergt. Stephen.	do	B. Rangers, S.G. O.C. 25th April, 1797, Niagara Stpd. Book.
Sencebaugh, Sergeant Christian.	Niagara District......	By Order-in-Council, 2nd December, 1806.
Scerman, Henry......	Fredericksburg	
Service, John, Junr...	E. District, Matilda ..	John Service, R. R. N. Y., Muster Roll, P.L. 2d,1786.
Service, Mary		Widow of Philip Service, R.R.N.Y., who died at Lachine, O.C., 29th January, 1808.
Servos, Christopher ...	E. District, Osnabruck.	Soldier R.R.N.Y., Muster Roll.
Servos, Lt. Daniel	H. District	Indian Department, S G., 2 women and 3 children, P. L.N. 1786, Niag. Stpd.Bk.
Servos, Lt. Jacob.....	do	Indian Department, S.G.S. P. L. N. 1786, Niagara Stamped Book.
Servos, Philip	E. District, Matilda ..	Royal Yorkers.

P

APPENDIX B.

NAMES.	RESIDENCE.	DESCENDANTS.
Servos, Peter, Senr....		See Order-in-Council, 17th March, 1807, Soldier R.R. N.Y.
Shaffer, Ferdinand....	Marysburgh..........	British Soldier, A. McL., Laborer, Stamped Book.
Shank, Capt. David ..	H. District..........	Queen's Rangers.
Shannon, David......	Ancaster	O.C. 19th April, 1808, joined in 1777, on secret service.
Sharpe, Cornelius	Adolphus Town	L. B. M., states Loyalist, 1793, 300, Loyal Rangers, A.McL., P.L., 1786.
Sharpe, Junr., John G.	Ernest Town	M. C., Soldier, son of Lt. Guesbard, Loyal Rangers, p. his father's certificate O.C. 17th Nov. 1797, P.L. 1786.
Sharpe, Senr., John ..	do	Late of Adolphus Town Loyalist, L.B.M.300, 1790, G. Haldimand, P.L. 1786, A.McL.
Sharpe, Gusbord...... Guysburg.	do	Lieutenant Loyal Rangers, A.McL., P.L. 1786.
Sharp, John..........	E. Dist. Edwardsburg.	Soldier Loyal Rangers.
Shatford, Moses	do Augusta......	L.B.L., had drawn 100, 1791, 100 more.
Shatford, Thomas.....	do do	⎫
Shatford, Thomas	do do	⎬ Settlers.
Shatford, Thomas	do do	⎭
Shaver, John	Osnabruck	See Order-in-Council 17th March, 1807, Soldier Butler's Rangers.
Shaver, Adam........	E. District Matilda ...	Corporal R.R.N.Y., Muster Roll, had a wife and one child, P.L. 2d, 1786.
Shaver, Adam............	do do	Son of Philip, single, P. L. 2d, 1786.
Shaver, Conradt	do do	Son of Philip.
Shaver, John	do do	R.R.N.Y., M.Roll, one with a wife and one single, P.L. 2d, 1786, one a wife and 4 children, P.L. 2d 1786.
Shaver, John	do do	R.R.N.Y., M. Roll, had a wife and 6 others in family, P.L. 2d, 1786.
Shaver, John	Williamsburgh	R. R. N. Y., M. Roll, had a wife and 3 children, P. L. 2d, 1786.
Shaver, Jacob	E. District, Matilda ..	R.R.N.Y., Muster Roll, had a wife, P.L. 2d, 1786, his widow, Esther Shaffer, N. McL.

APPENDIX B. 251

NAMES.	RESIDENCE.	DESCENDANTS.
Shaver, Senr., Philip...	Matilda	Soldier R.R.N.Y., M. Roll, had a wife and 7 children, P.L. 2d, 1786.
Shaver, Junr., Philip..	E. District, Matilda ...	1793 had drawn 100 acres L. B.L., son of Philip.
Shaw, Col. Æneas	H. District	Captain Queen's Rangers.
Shaw, Michael........	do	Soldier Butler's Rangers.
Shaw, Wm., Esq......	W. District	1 gt. 400, Sergeant 5th Regt.
Shaw, Wm.	Fredericksburgh	A Corpl. R.R.N.Y., Stamped Book, O. C. 8th July, 1797, P.L. 1786, A.McL.
Sheck, Christian......	E. District Cornwall ..	Dead, J.B., supposed R. R. N. Y., P. L. 2d 1786, Stamped Book.
Sheck, David........	do do	Son of Christian, as a Magistrate, 1,200 acres, 12 July, 1798.
Shehan, Walter B	H. District	Lieut. 34th Regt. S.G.
Sheets, George........	E. District Cornwall..	Soldier R. R. N. Y., Muster Roll, P.L. 2d, 1786.
Sheets, Senr., Jacob ..	do do	Soldier R. R. N. Y., Muster Roll P.L. 2d, 1786.
Sheets, Samuel	E. District Augusta...	Son of Jacob Sheets, Junr.
Sheets, Wm	do Cornwall ..	R.R.N.Y., Muster Roll A, Single man, P.L. 2d, 1786.
Shell, Benjamin	Matilda	Son of John.
Shell, Daniel	Williamsburgh........	Son of John.
Shell, John	E. Dist. Williamsburgh	R. R. N. Y., Muster Roll, a Loyalist, L. B. L., had a wife and four children, P. L. 2d. 1786.
Sheriff, Wm.........	Kingston.............	Soldier 29th Regiment.
Sherwood, Abel.......	Niagara District......	By Order-in-Council 4th February, 1807.
Sherrard, Wm........	M. District	Soldier Loyal American Regt. L.B.M., 1790.
Sherman, Simon	Hawkesbury...........	See Order-in-Council 11th March 1807, Soldier Loyal Rangers, sons William and Jonathan.
Sherwood, Samuel	Thurlow..............	Lieut. Loyal Rangers, P. 1789, 500 acres L. B. M., 1791, A.McL.
Sherwood, Esq., Justus	E. District	S.G. Captain Jessup's.
Sherwood, Samuel	do	Son of Justus, soldier Loyal Rangers, one a Sergeant supposed of Butler's Rangers, P.L., 1786.

NAMES.	RESIDENCE.	DESCENDANTS.
Sherwood, Thomas....	E District............	M. C., Subaltern Ensign Jessup's O.C. 28th Jany., 1800.
Sherrwood, Ruben....		By Order-in-Council of 11th June, 1789.
Shew, Junr., Ezekiel..	E. District, Augusta..	Said on U. E. Roll, not entitled U.E.
Shibbarn, Charles.....	do do ...	
Shebley John.........	Ernest Town	G. S. Corporal in Jessup's L.B.M. 1790, 650. A.McL. P. L. 1786.
Shibley Jacob	do.	Loyal Rangers.
Shipman Daniel	Elizabeth Town	A settler ; did not join Loyal standard before 1783. I Dillon.
Shoeman, Baultis	Fredericksburg	Son of William.
Shoeman, Martin	do	Son of William ; a soldier R.R.N.Y., L.B.M. 1792, 200.
Shoeman, Wm........	do	Soldier R.R.N.Y., L.B.M., 1790, 500 ; P. L. 1786. Stamped Book.
Shorey, Sen., David ..	Ernest Town	M. C. Loyal Rangers. A. McL., 2 Certe, 400. P.L. 1786.
Shorey, Junr., David..	do	Son of David, Sen., P. 1794.
Shorey, Rufus........	do	Son of David Shorey, Sen.
Shorp, Augustus......	Adolphus Town	
Shorts.		
Shoults, John	E District, Augusta ..	
Showers, Sen., Mich'l.	H District............	Deceased ; B. Rangers, soldier, S. G. A wife and 4 children. P.L.N. 1786.
Shawder, Magnus	Ernest Town	Soldier Loyal Rangers, C. 200, A. McL. P.L. 1786.
Schrader.		
Shuther, Andrew	do	M. C. 1 Gt. 200. Soldier 34th Regt. ; L.B.M. 1791. 300 and P.L. 1786. Stm'd Book.
Shwertfeger. John A..	Williamsburg	R.R.N.Y.
Silk, Daily	E. Dist. Edwardsburg.	Soldier Loyal Rangers.
Sills, Conrad	Fredericksburg	R.R.N.Y. A. McL. 1784 ; General Haldimand, 100. P.L. 1786, of R.R.N.Y. Stamped Book.
Sills George	do	Sons of Conrad, R.R.N.Y., B.M.A.

APPENDIX B.   253

NAMES.	RESIDENCE.	DESCENDANTS.
Sills, John	Fredericksburg ..	*Stamped Book.* They had been mustered as soldiers, though the oldest in 1790 was only 22 years old, and the youngest 16 years of age. They resided with their father and were thought deserving of 100 acres each only. L.B. M. 24th March, 1790 ; but L. B. A. 1793, grant 200 more to Lawrence.
Sills, Lawrence	do ..	
Silmeser, Martin	E. District, Cornwall..	A soldier in Jessup's corps, L.B.L. P.L. 2d, 1786.
Silverthorn, Sr., Thos.	Stamford	Deceased. O.C. 9th April, 1808 ; resided in New Jersey ; joined the Royal Standard.
Silmeser, Nicholas	do Cornwall ...	Son of Martin ; supposed R.R.N.Y. P.L. 2d, 1786.
Silvester, Levy	....	Original Roll.
Simmerman, Henry ..	Marysburgh	A soldier 53rd Regiment, P. P.L. 1786.
Simmerman, Mathias, Senr	of Clinton............	O.C. 30th August, 1797, 300. Stamped Book. A wife and child.
Simmonds, Daniel	Ernest Town	See Order in Council 17th February, 1807 ; sergeant. P.L. 1786.
Simmonds, Henry	do	Lieutenant Loyal Rangers, S.G. A. McL. P.L. 1786.
Simmon, David	Marysburgh	Sons of Henry, 200 acres. L.B. A. 1794.
Simonds, Henry	Thurlow	Soldier Loyal Rangers. L. B.M. 1790. A. McL.
Simonds, John	Ernest Town	Son of Lieutenant Hy. Simmons ; called Loyalist. P. L. 1786.
Simmons, Caleb	E. Dist. Elizabe'h Town	Emigrant from U. S. Ld. Bd. L. 1790.
Simmons, Moses......	Mary's & Sophiasburg.	Son of Lieutenant Henry Simons ; called Loyalist. P.L. 1786.
Simmonds, Nicholas ..	Ernest Town	Ld. Bd. certe. Loyalist Loyal Rangers, Que. A. McL. P.L. 1786.
Simmonds, Nicholas ..	M. District	L.'B. A. 1794 ; had drawn 100 ; grant 200 more.
Simons, Sen., Titus...	H District...........	S. G. Qr. Master.

APPENDIX B.

NAMES.	RESIDENCE.	DESCENDANTS.
Simson, William........	....	See Order in Councill 11th March, 1807. Artificer in the King's works.
Simpson, John.......	Marysburgh..........	Son of Israel. L.B.A. 1794, 200.
Simpson, Alex........	Kingston	Loyalist. A. McL. Schoolmaster. Stamped Book. P.L. 1786.
Simpson, Alex........	do.	
Simpson, Daniel......	Fredericksburg	Sergt. 24th Regt. 2 grants, 500. The L. B. A. 1794. only granted 200 acres as a settler.
Simpson, Israel.......	Marysburgh..........	S. G. Sergeant ; discharged from British Regiment. P. L. 1786. A. McL. Stamped Book.
Simpson, Obadiah	Adolphus Town	Joined in North Carolina in 1796, and served in Delaney's corps ; affidavit, 1803.
Sims, Sergt. John .... Sim.	H District............	Butler's Rangers. Niagara Stamped Book.
Singleton, George	Thurlow	S. G. Captain R. R. N. Y. Stamped Book. P.L. 1786.
Sipes, Andrew........	Matilda	Butler's Rangers ; has a wife and one child. P. L. 2d, 1786.
Sipes, Jacob..........	H District............	S.G. B.R. Niagara Stamped Book—S. P.L.N. 1786.
Sipes, Jonas............	do	B. Rangers, S. G. S.P., L. N.J., 1786.
Sirwall, Christopher ..	Marysburg	
Skinner, Timothy	H District............	Expunged U. E. list. Order in Council 24th May,1808. Children. P. L. N. 1786. Did not join the Royal Standard before peace. Niagara Stamped Book.
Slack Joseph	E District, Bastard...	Nov. 10th, 1794. P. from New York State lately ; wishes to become a subject and settler.
Slouser, Rudolph	Sophias & Ameliasb'g	
Sleaphy, Bartholomew	Marysburgh	Discharged soldier (British)
Slieneman, Henry	do	
Slighter, John........	H District............	In Barton's regiment.
Slingerland, Anthony.	do	Plundered and a prisoner ; a wife and 6 children. P.L. N. 1786. Niagara Stamped Book.

APPENDIX B. 255

NAMES.	RESIDENCE.	DESCENDANTS.
Slingerland, Garret ...	Niagara	Of Butler's Rangers. O.C. 22nd February, 1808.
Slingerland, Richard ..	H District	Butler's Rangers, S.G. L.B. Nassau, 1794. Niagara Stamped Book.
Sloot, Michael	Adolphus Town	S. G. officer. Lieutenant Associated Loyalists. P. L. 1786.
Slouter, Cornelius .... Slotor.	do	L. B. A. 1794 ; had drawn 100 ; 200 more ordered; an emigrant settler.
Slusenburg, Henry .... Schlussenburgh, Henrick	}Marysburgh	Soldier 53rd Regiment. L. B. M. 1791, and P.L.1786, S.StampedBook. A.Mc.L.
Smades, Joel	E District, Wolford ..	Residence since first settlement ; not privileged. R. J.D.G.Petition 1808,states a pilot between New York and Montreal and Niagara.
Smith, Col. Samuel ...	H District	
Smith, Benoni	E District, Augusta ...	Soldier in McAlpin's corps. L. B. L.
Smith, Comfort	Fredericksburgh	Soldier King's Rangers, p. R. Roll, 350 acres.
Smith, Daniel	do	p. Regimental Roll. Soldier King's Ragrs. ; had drawn 200 acres ; L. B. A. 1794, 200 more. Stamped Book.
Smith, Daniel	E District, Cornwall ..	Son of a soldier, Ld. Bd. L. Soldier R. R. N. Y. P. L. 1786.
Smith, Dennis .... Smith, Dennis	do Augusta } do Edwardsbgh	Soldier Loyal Rangers. L. B. L.
Smith, Elias	H District	Had Governor Tryons' protection ; enlisted him for the Loyal Americans ; 27 at one time.
Smith, Elias, Esq	Newcastle District, } Elizabeth Town	By Order in Council, 17th June, 1806.
Smith, Encrease	E District	Settler from Vermont. L. B.L. 1790.
Smlth, Frederick	Marysburgh	B. Ranger's, S.G.; had four children. P. L. N. 1786. Niagara Stamped Book.
Smith, George	Elizabeth Town	A settler from Vermont, 1790, L. B. L. ; one a soldier R. R. N. Y. Muster Roll ; one of this name unencorporate Loyalist. Genl. Haldimand—200.

NAMES.	RESIDENCE.	DESCENDANTS.
Smith, Hart............	H District............	New Jersey Volunteers,S.G.
Smith, Henry	H District..............	King's Rangers. 'P.L. 1786. (Stamped Book); had a wife; P.L. 1786. Butler's Rangers — himself 25th Apl., 1808. Niagara Stp'd Book.
Smith, Henry .... Schmitt.	Marysburgh	Soldier Col. Barnet's corps. P.L. 1786. Schmitt B. soldier, S. Corporal L.B. M., 1791—700 acres. A. McL.
Smith, Senr., John ...	G. River, H District..	Daughters Eleanor, Hannah, and Elizabeth, U. E.
Smith, John..........	H District............	Soldier 78th Regiment at taking of Quebec, and in 84th Regt. U.E. Stamped Book Niagara.
Smith, Nicholas	do	Found on original Roll, 1st Nov., 1804; was a soldier Butler's Rangers.
Smith, John..........	do	Who died at Brunswick.
Smith, John..........	do	Head of the lake; a settler in 1788; had three sons, Benjamin, Stephen and John. Magistrate's certe. 28th September, 1793.
Smith, John..........	Fredericksburg	Soldier King's Rangers, p. R. Roll
Smith, John..........	Kingston	(Dead). States B.M.A.
Smith, John..........	E District, Augusta ..	Sergeant in Jessup's.
Smith, Senr., John ...	do Cornwall ..	Soldier R. Regt. N. York Muster Roll; Collins', 1787 —200. P.L. 2d, 1786.
Smith, Junr., John ..	do do ..	Died in Ireland; not married.
Smith, John George ..	Fredericksburg	Son of Jacob Smith, Senr.
Smith, Senr., Jacob ...	H District.......... ..	Was a soldier in the Jersey Volunteers, J.S.; his sons Lewis, Amos, Edmund, Jacob and Joseph.
Smith, Jacob	E District, Cornwall ..	
Smith, Jacob, Senr ...	Fredericksburg	Soldier R.R.N.Y., 350 acres including family land. L. B.M.1790. Stamped Book. P. List 1786. A. McL.
Smith, Junr., Jacob ...	do	Son of Jacob Smith, Senr.
Smith, James.........	M District............	A sailor M. Department. O. C. 17th March, 1797.
Smith, James.........	E Dist.,Elizabeth T'wn	P.L., N.J. 1786.

APPENDIX B. 257

NAMES.	RESIDENCE.	DESCENDANTS.
Smith, James.........	E. Dist.,Charlottenb'gh	84th Regiment; from the States. D. Murchison.
Smith, Michael	Fredericksburg	Soldier R. R. N. Y. (dead). P.L. 1786.
Smith, Peter	Kingston	Sergeant B. Rangers, S. G. Niagara Stamped Book.
Smith, Senr., Peter...	E. District,Charlottenburgh	R.R.N·Y. P.L.N.J. 1786. Smith Stamped Book.
Smith, Junr·, Peter ..	do do	84th Regt., P.L.N.J. 1786.
Smith, Peter J.	Mary's & Sophiasburgh	Lieut. King's American Regt.
Smith, Philip	Fredericksbnrgh	1787 Collin's 200. Loyalist. Soldier R.R.N.Y. Stamped Book.
Smith, Richard.	M. District	
Smith, Richard	Osnabruck	R.R.N.Y. Muster Roll.
Smith, Robert........	E. District, Elizabeth Town	Soldier R. R. N. Y. Muster Roll & one soldier Loyal Rangers.
Smith, Samuel........	Kingston	Soldier LoyalRangers. U.E.
Smith, Col. Samuel ..		Coll.
Smith, Stephen	E. District, Elizabeth Town	Soldier R.R.N.Y. O.E.
Smith, Terence	do do	Dead. Son of the late Geo. Smith, Esq., late of St-John's.
Smith,Thomas........	Kingston	500, order-in-Council, 19th February, 1807. O.C. 2d, August, 1797.
Smith, Esq., Thomas..	L'Assomption	Came to Niagara in 1776, with a plan of Fort Stanwix.
Smith, Esq., Thomas..	E. District, Yonge....	Ensign Royal Regt.of York. Lieut. L.B.L.
Smith, Esq., Thomas..	Yonge	Son of the late George Smith, Esq. Single. P.L. 2d. 1786.
Smith, Wm...........	Fredericksburgh	Volunteer Loyal Rangers, L.B.M. 1790, 350, P.L. 1786. One of Sidney, a common settler in 1787,his own information.
Smith, Wm...........	Mary's & Sophiasburgh	M.C. King's Rangers, A.Mc L., L.Bd. Certe.P.L.1786.
Snetsinger, Mathias ..	E. District, Cornwall..	Soldier R.R.N.Y. Muster Roll A. P.L. 2d. 1786.
Snider, John.........	H. District	Butler's Rangers P.
Snider, Tobias........	Marysburgh, M.C.....	Soldier 53rd Regt (& P. L. 1786). S. L.Bd. certificate. Stamped Book.

APPENDIX B.

NAMES.	RESIDENCE.	DESCENDANTS.
Snyder, Adam	E. District, Cornwall	Soldier R.R.N.Y. M. Roll; had a wife and 3 children. P. L. 2d. 1786.
Snyder, Conradt	do do	R.R.N.Y. M. Roll; had a wife and 3 children, P. L. 2d. 1786.
Snyder, John	Augusta	Settler E. J.
Snyder, John	E. District, Lancaster¹	Soldier Royal Rangers.
Snyder Jacob	do do	S.G. Loyalist, came to Canada in 1780. Had a wife and 8 children. P. L. 2d. 1786.
Snyder, Jeremiah	do do	R.R.N.Y. Muster Roll A. Had a wife and 1 child. P.L. 2d. 1786.
Snyder. Marcus	Ernest Town	M.C. Loyal Rangers, a sol-(550 as.) in all. G. Hamilton's Certe., P.L. 1786.
Snyder, Mathew.	E. District, Elizabeth Town	
Snyder, Senr., Wm.	do do	Ensign Jessup's—S.G.—L. B. L. L.B. Montreal 200, 1789.
Snyder, Junr., Wm.	do do	A Soldier Loyal Rangers.
Snyther, Corpl. Jacob.	H. District	
Soper, Samuel	do	Butler's Rangers, P.
Sowils, John	E. District, Matilda	Son of Wm. Soules, senr, p. Mr. Paterson's Certe., 27th December, 1804.
Sowils, Senr., Wm.	Matilda	W. Soles, 200 acres as a settler, 1790. L.B.L. Soldier Loyal Rangers.
Souls, Daniel	H. District	Joined Royal Standard in New York, 1778; p. Certe. of Major Millage.
Sowils, Jnr., Wm	E. District, Matilda	
Sparam, Doctor	do. Augusta	Hospital mate reduced—had served in war of 1763. P. L. 1786.
Sparam, Thomas	Kingston	Son of Doctor Sparam.
Spencer, Andrew	Sophias & Ameliasburgh	
Spencer, Benjamin	do do	Soldier King's Rangers, ; p. R. Roll.
Spencer, Augustus	Marys & Sophiasburgh	1787, Atkins, 200, P.L.1786.
Spencer, Hazelton	Fredericksburgh	S. G. Lieut. R.R.N.Y. A. McL., P.L. 1786. Stamped Book.
Spencer, Henry	Sophias & Ameliasburgh	
Spencer, John	do do	Emigrant from Vermont, L. B.M. 1793, 200.

APPENDIX B. 259

NAMES.	RESIDENCE.	DESCENDANTS.
Spencer, John	Marys & Sophiasburgh	
Spencer, Junr., John	Sophias&Ameliasburgh	
Spencer, Robert	H. District	Soldier Butler's Rangers ; a wife and 5 children. P.L. N. 1786, Niagara Stamped Book.
Spicer, Daniel	E. District	A Soldier L. Rangers ; his father was of Jessup's Corps, R.J.D,G.
Spicer, Ezekiel	do Augusta	Soldier in Jessup's Corps, L.B.L.
Sporbeck, Jacob	Niagara District	Deceased, Order-in-Council 24th February, 1807. Soldier Butler's Rangers.
Springer, David	H. District	Deceased, if Daniel, soldier B. Rangers, S.G.
Springer, Richard	do	B. Rangers,S.G.; had a wife and 5 children, P. L. N. 1786. Niagara Stamped Book.
Springfield, Joseph	W. District	B. Rangers, U. List, 1789.
Springstien, Stoats	H. District	B. Rangers,S.G.; had a wife and 2 children. P. L. N. 1786.
Spurgin, Wm	do	From North Carolina.
Stacey,John	do	Artificer S. G. Dock yard, Detroit p. A wife and 4 children, P.L.N. 1786.
Staker, Elizabeth	Kingston	O.C. 10th May, 1808. Widow of Nathan Staker.
Stanes, Job Stains, Joab	Fredericksburgh	British Soldier,P.L. 1786, A. McL. Stamped Book.
Stamp, Giles	E. District, Williamsburgh	Private Soldier 44th Regt.
Stamp, Guillies	do Augusta	Soldier British Regiment.
Stanford, Wm	do Matilda	1793. had drawn 100 acres, L.B.L. Soldier, R.R.N.Y.
Stansfield, John	Crowland	O.C. 10th May, 1808, from Pennsylvania; served on board a 74 until 1783.
Stark, James	Elizabeth Town	Suffered imprisonment ; a Baptist Preacher, L.B.L.
Starrs, George Starr	E. District, Yonge	Now of Hawkesbury, O.C. 17th May, 1788. Soldier Loyal Rangers.
Starts, Jacob	Marysburgh, B.R.	B.R. Soldier 53rd Regt., L. B.M. 1790,100 acres only.
Stata, Henry Stait	E. District, Williamsburgh	Soldier Royal Regt. N.York Muster Roll.

APPENDIX B.

Names.	Residence.	Descendants.
Stater, Philip or Stoats	E district, Osnabruck	Stoats, Philip, a soldier in Crustyberg's Regt. Statay, Philip, R.R.N.Y.
Stealy, Martin	do Matilda	R.R.N.Y. Muster Roll. Had a wife, P.L. 2d. 1786.
Steel, Mathew	Sophias&Ameliasburgh	Loyalist from New York, A. McL. Loyalist. P. L. 1786.
Steel, Wm.	H. District	Soldier Jersey Volunteers, J.S.
Steely, Tobias	Fredericksburgh	Soldier R.R.N.Y. L.B.M¶ 1793, 300, P. L. 1786. Stamped Book.
Stephens, Abel	Bastard	Did not join the Royal Standard—A settler, R. S. D. G. O.C., 4th December, 1806 ; to be continued on the U. E. List.
Stephens, Pennuel	do	A Settler.
Stephenson, Francis	Niagara District	O.C. 6th May, 1806. Captain Queen's Rangers.
Stevens (Comy), Aaron	H. District	M. C. Issuing Commissary, Indian Department, O C. 4th February, 1797.
Stevens, Elisha	E. District, Leeds	Settler.
Stevens, Senr., John	H. District	B. Rangers S.G., or Forrester's Interpreter, Niagara Stamped Book. Had a wife and 4 children, P. L. N. 1786.
Stevens, Roger	E. District, Augusta	Came after the Treaty of Peace.
Stevens, Roger	E. District	Ensign King's Rangers, L.B. L. Dead.
Stewart, Lt. Alex.	H. District	M.C. Col. Thomson's Regt,
Stewart, John	Marysburgh	Soldier 84th Regt. L.B.M.. 1791, 200 (P. L. 1786). S. Stamped Book, A.McL.
Stewart, James	W. District	S.G. Loyalist in many Scouts —Loyalist List, W.D.
Stewart, Robert	Marysburg	Discharged British Soldier. P. L. 1786, A. McL. S. Stamped Book.
Stewart, Thomas	H District	M.C. a driver, Royal Artillery—P.O.C. 8th October, 1796.
Stiles, Selah Silas.	do	Genl., Haldimand, 100, Soldier, R.R.N.Y. Muster Roll A.

APPENDIX B. 261

NAMES.	RESIDENCE.	DESCENDANTS.
Stine, Sergt. John	H. District	Sergeant New Jersey Volunteers.
Stinson, John	Marys & Sophiasburg	Captain King's Rangers, S. G. & L.B.M., 1790—P.L. 1786.
Stinson, Junr., John..	do	Son of Captain John.
Stofle, John	H District............	M.C. Soldier in B. Rangers, Niagara Stamped Book, S. P.L.N., 1786.
Stone, John	do	King's A. Dragoons, O.C., 17th March, 1797; has a wife and 3 children—P.L. N., 1786; Niagara Stamped Book.
Stone, Joel	Leeds	Original Roll Captain of Loyalists.
Stoneburner, John.... Stonebrander.	E District, Osnabruck	And Stoneburner, Jacob, E District, P.L. 2d, 1786, Drumr., R. R. N. Y. M. Roll, Soldier, R.R.N.Y. Muster Roll A.
Stoneburner, Joseph ..	do do	A Corporal R.R.N.Y. Muster Roll P.L. 2d, 1786.
Stoneburner, Leonard.	do do	Soldier, R. R. N. Y. Muster Roll P.L. 2d 1786.
Stoneburner, Junr., .. Jacob	Cornwall	On Original Roll Soldier, R. R.N.Y.
Stoner, John	H District............	Soldier B. Rangers, S.G.
Stooks, Edward	do	R.R.N.Y. Muster Roll A; has a wife and 5 children; P.L. 2d, 1786.
Stooks, Mrs. Hannah, formerly widowSykes	do	
Stockwell, John	W District	S.G. Loyalist, U. L.
Storen, Jeremiah ..... Storms.	Marysburg	British Soldier, P.L.,1786,S.
Storey, Simon	E District, Elizabeth Town.	1794, from Vermont, wishes to be-come a subject & settler, P.
Storin, George........	Williamsburg	On Original Roll — George Storing, of Midland District, was a Soldier, R.R. N.Y., A.McL., 1805.
Storm, John..........	do	Soldier, R. R. N. Y., a wife two children; P.L., 1786. Muster Roll.
Storens, Gilbert	Ernest Town	Soldier in Jessup's A. McL., P.L., 1786.

APPENDIX B.

NAMES.	RESIDENCE.	DESCENDANTS.
Storens, Henry	Ernest Town	Had drawn 200 L.B.M., O. C., 17th Nov., 1797, and L. B. A., 1794 ; 200 acres as son of Gilbert—states to have drawn none before— P.L., 1786.
Storens, Jacob	do	Son of Gilbert Storens.
Stover, Martin	do	Served during the War S.G. Loyal Rangers, A.McL., P.L., 1786.
Stowood, John	do	
Staats, Sylvester	Niagara	O.C. 16th June, 1808, Sergt. Butler's Rangers.
Strada, Henry	E District, Williamsburg	R.R.N.Y. Muster Roll, has a wife and 2 children, P. L. 2d., 1786.
Strader, John	do Matilda	R.R.N.Y. Muster Roll, has a wife and one child .P.L. 2d., 1786.
Strader, Simon	do Matilda	R.R.N.Y. has a wife and 2 children. P.L. 2d., 1786.
Strader, William	do Matilda	R.R.N.Y, has a wife. P.L. 2d., 1786.
Street, Senr., Samuel	H District	A Loyalist.
Strenth, Peter	Marysburg	Discharged British Soldier.
Striker, Sampson	Marys & Sophiasburg	Petition states—Sergeant in Delaney's Corps, L.B.M., 1790; L.B.M. 1793. 400.
Strope, Gaspe	Kingston (yes)	A Soldier in Col. Barnet's Corps—GermanChasseurs.
Stuart, George	H District	Soldier in Butler's Rangers, P. Niagara Stamped Book.
Stuart, George	E. District	Single man, P.L. 2d, 1786. ⎫
Stuart, Gilbert	do Osnabruck	do P. L. 2d, 1786. ⎬ Sons of James J.B.
Stuart, Henry	do	do P. L. 2d, 1786. ⎭
Stuart, James	do	S.G. Surgeon's Mate, R.R. N.Y., P.L., 2d, 1786.
Stuart, Rev. John	Kingston	S.G. Chaplain R. R. N. Y. Stamped Book. P.L. 1786.
Stull, Latham	H District	Soldier, Butler's Rangers p. Petition ; and P. McMeekin.

APPENDIX B.

NAMES.	RESIDENCE.	DESCENDANTS.
Summers, Andrew....	E District, Charlottenburg	R.R.N.Y. Muster Roll. P. L.N.J. 1786.
Summers, David......	do Osnabruck..	Son of a reduced Soldier. L,. Bd, Lunenburg.
Summers, Jacob	do Charlottenburg	Soldier R.R.N.Y. Muster Roll A. P.L.N.J., 1786.
Surplet,[Robert	W District	Indian Department, U.E. Loyalist; came in with Mr. McKee.
Sutherland, Alex.....	E District, Lancaster..	Soldier Royal Regt. New York; supposed to be son of Joseph Sutherland, formerly supposed of 26th Regt.
Sutherland, George ...	do Lancaster ..	Soldier R.R.N.Y. Ld. Bd. L., single. P.L. 2d, 1786.
Sutherland, John.....	Marysburg	Soldier R.R.N.Y. Stamped Book.
Sutherland, John Johnson	E District, Lancaster..	Son of Lieut. Walter.
Sutherland,JohnStuart	do Charlottenburg	Son of Lieut. Walter.
Sutherland, Thomas ..	do Lancaster.....	Soldier O C. 5th Jan., 1798; single, P.L. 2d, 1786.
Sutherland, Esq.,Walter	do do	Lieutenant R.R.N.Y.; was not settled in America before the War; belonged to a British Regt., supposed the 26th Regt.
Sutherland, Walter ...	do Charlottenburg	Had a wife and 2 children, P.L., 2d, 1786.
Swan, Esq., Thomas..	do Cornwall	
Swart, Simon.........	Ernest Town	M.C.P., R.R.N.Y., M Roll and P.L., 1786.
Swartfeger, Frederick.	Mary's & Sophiasburg	P.K.R. Regt., N.Y.—a Soldier; Genl. Haldimand's Corps, 1784. 100, A.McL. Stamped Book, P.L. 1786.
Swayze, Senr., Caleb..	H District........ ...	Killed.
Swayze, Caleb........	do	Son of Caleb Swayze, Senr.
Swayze, Isaac	do	Pilot to the N. York Army.
Sweet, Charles........	E District, Augusta ..	
Sweet, Oliver.........	do	S. G. Land, as Corporal, Royal Rangers.
Sweet, Philip	Thurlow.............	Soldier German Troops.
Swiney, Hugh........	Marysburg	44th Regt., Gov. Hamilton, 1785. 100, and P.L. 1786. Stamped Book.
Switzer, Philip	Ernest Town	Corporal Rangers; Soldier Loyal Rangers, L.B.M., 1791. 500 P.L. 1786, A. McL.

APPENDIX B.

Names.	Residence.	Descendants.
Taylor, Christina......	M District............	
Taylor, John.........	Thurlow..............	Loyal Rangers one—A. McL. Corporal King's American Regt.; P. M. C. & F. 500.; one of this name a Sergt. 34th Regt., L.B. M., 1790, P.L., 1786.
Taylor, Michael......	Kingston	Associated Loyalist. Stamped Book. Shoemaker, A. McL.
Taylor, William......	do	Called Loyalist, P.L., 1786. Stamped Book.
Taylor, Junr., Wm...	do	Son of Sergt. Taylor, 34th Regt.
Tederick, Sergt. Jacob	H District	
Tederick, Lucas......	do	Corporal Butler's Rangers.
Teeple, Peter.........	do	Sergeant.
Ten Brœck, Capt. P...	do	B. Rangers S.G. Eleven in family; P.L.N., 1786. Niagara Stamped Book.
Ten Eyck, Andrew ...	Kingston	Soldier Jersey Volunteers.
Terry, Parshal........	do	S. G. B. Rangers. A wife and three children, P.LN. 1786. Niagara Stamped Book.
Terry, Paul	Elizabeth Town	Joined at Sotocket on Long Island in 1777, belonged to Lieut.-Col. Hulet's Refugee Corps. Served in the King's works.
Teynick, Samuel......	E District, Lancaster	
Thacker John	H District............	Soldier Jersey Volunteers.
Thicle John .... Thicly	Ernest Town	Soldier Loyal Rangers. A. McL. Called Loyalist, P. L. 1786.
Thomas, Jacob	H District............	Colonel Barton's. Niagara Stamped Book.
Thomas, Jacob	E District, Elizabeth.. Town	Soldier Loyal Rangers.
Thomas, Peter	Ernest Town	Soldier Loyal Rangers. A. McL.
Thomas, Peter	E District, Elizabeth.. Town	Called Loyalist. P. L. 1786.
Thompkins, Israel....	do Augusta ..	Soldier of Jessup's Corps. R. A. D. G.
Thompson, Capt: Aw.	H District............	B. Rangers. S. G.
Thompson, Archid....	do	Indian Department, a wife and two children. P.L.N. 1786. O. C. 21st July, 1796. Niagara Stamped Book.

APPENDIX B. 265

NAMES.	RESIDENCE.	DESCENDANTS.
Thomson, Archid......	H District............	Employed as a Master Carpenter ; Niagara Stamped Book ; 1200 acres. L.B.M. 1790 ; closed his claim with 500 acres ; a wife and 3 children. P. L. 1786.
Thomson, Daniel	E District, Augusta ..	Certified by Lt. Campbell to have been a Guide, and to have furnished Provisions. P. L. N. J. 1785.
Thompson, Mrs. Elizth.	H District............	
Thompson, George....	do	Lieutenant King's Rangers. S. G.
Thompson, George....	Matilda...............	Corporal R. R. N. Y. Mus-Roll A. ; has a wife. P. L. 2d, 1786.
Thompson, John......	E District, Yonge	R. R. N. Y. M. Roll, B. M. A. ; one a soldier Loyal Rangers.
Thompson, Peter	H District............	B. Ranger's S. G. ; had a wife and one child. P.L. N.1786. Niagara Stamped Book.
Thompson, Robert....	Marysburg	Sergt. 44th Regt. L. B. M. 1791. 450, P. L. 1786, a wife.
Thompson, Samuel....	H District............	
Thompson, Timothy ..	Fredericksburg	Ensign R.R.N.Y. Stamped Book. P.L. 1786.
Thompson, William ..	do	Soldier King's Rangers. p. R. Roll.
Thresser, Ladock .... Zadock	M District............	Emigrant from U. S., 1790. L. B. M. 200.
Throop, Daniel	Augusta...............	1794—Lately from Connecticut ; suffered imrisonment and loss of property, as certified by Capt. Joel Stone.
Tice, Capt. Gilbert....	H District............	Indian Dept. ; a wife and 4 servants. P.L.N. 1786. Niagara Stamped Book.
Tillebough, Christian.. alias Tilleback.	E District, Matilda ..	Soldier R. R. N. Y. J. F. P. L. 2d, 1786.
Tillebough, Jnr. Chrisn.	Williamsburg	
Tillebough, Martin.... or Dilleback.	E District, Matilda ..	SoldierRoyal Foresters; restored toU.E. O.C., 29th January, 1808.
Tillebough, Peter	Williamsburg	Son of a Soldier, 200 acres, L. Bd. L.; his name *Delebough*.

Sons of Chrst.

Q.

APPENDIX B.

NAMES.	RESIDENCE.	DESCENDANTS.
Tendall, Robert	Kingston	Discharged Soldier from Regt. not U. E., on 31st. P. L. 1786.
Tipple, John	Osnabruck	Land as Sergeant R.R.N.Y.
Tuttle, Solomon	E District	
Toosler, William or Dusler.	do Cornwall	
Topp, John	Malden	A Soldier in Butler's Rangers. Q.
Tousack, Gasper	H District	Soldier Butler's Rangers.
Tracey, Timothy	do	
Trainer. John	do	S. G. Soldier.
Tredwell, John	do	
Turnbull, William Trambell	do	Soldier Royal Forresters. O. C. 21st July, 1796.
Turner, Edward	W District	Came in in 1778 ; two children. P. L. N. 1786. Niagara Stamped Book.
Trompeau, John	Sophias and Ameliasburg	A Loyalist within the British lines at New York. L.B.M. 1790.
Trompeau, Paul	Adolphus Town	S. G. Lieut. Delany's Brigade. P.L. 1786. A.M.L.
Trumble, Peter	Augusta	An Irishman, 26 years of age in 1796 ; cannot be U. E. Signed P.R. on U.E. List
Tuttle, Jonathan	E. District, Yonge	P. 1790 ; did not join the British Standard; suffered imprisonment and loss of property.
Tuttle, Nathan	do do	Soldier Loyal Rangers. L. B. L.
Tuttle, Peter	do Augusta	
Tuttle, Samuel	do do	
Twohy, John		Deceased O. C., 11th Feby., 1808 ; Soldier R.R. N.Y.
Tyler, Gerrard. Tiler.	Fredericksburg	Ld. Bd. Certe. SoldierLoyal Rangers; Kingston Rangers. P.L. 1786.
Urquhart, Alexander.	E District, Lancaster	
Urquhart, William	do do	Soldier R. R. N.Y. Ld. Bd., a wife 5 children. P. L. N. J. 1786.
Ulleman, Francis		See Order in Council, 17th March, 1807. Soldier R. R. N.Y.
Vallian, Peter	Midland District	By Order in Council, 22nd June, 1799.

APPENDIX B. 267

NAMES.	RESIDENCE.	DESCENDANTS.
Valentine, Benjamin..	Kingston	A labourer. Stamped Book.
Valentine, Widow C..	E District...	Widow of Adjutant John Valentine, R.R.N.Y.
Valentine, John	Yonge.............	A settler, R.J.D.G.
Vallop, John	Marysburg	British Soldier P.L. 1786. Stamped Book.
Van Allen, Jacob......	Matilda	R.R.N.Y. Muster Roll A.; has a wife and one child. P.L. 2d, 1786.
Van Alstine, Alexander	Adolphus Town	Son of Peter. L.B.M, 1793, 200.
Van Alstine, Cornelius	do do	Son of Peter.
Van Alstine, Jacob ..	H District............	O.C. 24th Jany., 1797. B. Rangers. Niagara Stmpd. Book. S.P.L. 2d. 1786.
Van Alstine, Jonas ..	Richmond	1787, Collins 100. Fifer R. R. N.Y. 1786. Stamped Book.
Van Alstine, Isaac....	do	R.R.N.Y.; a Soldier R.R. N.Y.,L.B.M. 1790 ; 200 ; Genl. Haldimand, 100. Stamped Book. P.L.1786.
Van Alstine, Peter....	Adolphus Town	Cuyler's Captain J.D.
Van Alstine, Lidia....		Deceased Widow of James Van Alstine, who died in His Majesty's service, O. C., 16th Feby., 1808.
Van Alstine, Lumber.. Lambert.	Richmond	Soldier R.R.N.Y. M. Roll. L.B.A. 1791, 200 ; a wife and one child. P.L. 1786.
Van Camp, John	E District, Matilda..	Soldier in Jessup's Corps. L. B.L., single. P.L. 2d, 1786.
Van Camp, Jacob	Matilda	Soldier R.R.N.Y. M. Roll; had a wife and 4 children. P.L. 2d, 1786.
Van Camp, Peter	E District, Matilda..	Soldier in Jessup's, P.
Vancleft, John	Fredericksburg	O.C. 10th Feby., 1808 ; joined Royal Standard at New York in 1801.
Vandebarrich, Garret..	Richmond	Van Deberg, L.B.M 1790 ;
VanDeberg, or Vande Berick.		Soldier R. R. N. Y., 600, Muster Roll A. ; a wife 3 children. P.L.1786.
Vanderbozart, Francis	Fredericksburg	Soldier King's Rangers, p. R. Roll, 300 acres. L.B. M. 1791.
Vanderheyden, Adam	Ernest Town	Old Tickets of Draft Soldier Loyal Rangers. P.L.1786.

APPENDIX B.

NAMES.	RESIDENCE.	DESCENDANTS.
Vanderlip, Miss Elizth.	H District............	Daughter of Frederick Vanderlip.
Vanderlip, Frederick..	do	Deceased was a Soldier in Butler's Rangers.
Vanderlip, Miss Mary	do	Daughter of Frederick.
Vanderlip, William ..	do	S. G. Soldier. Niagara Stamped Book. S.P.L.N. 1786.
Vandervart, Michael..	Adolphus Town	S. G. Lieutenant in Guides and Pioneers.
Vandresser, Peter	H District............	Soldier Butler's Rangers.
Vandercar, John......	Ernest Town	UuincorporateLoyalistGenl.
Vandecaf.		Haldimand, 100. P. L. 1786. K. R's. A.McL.
Vanducar, Ralph	do	Secret Service, a Pensioner
Vandecaf Roelfe.		with Jessup's Corps. L. B.M. 1790, 300. P.L. do. Stamped Book.
Vanduzen, Casparus ..	Adolphus Town	L.B.M. 1790, Loyalist, 350, from New York A.McL.
Vanduzen, Conrod....	do do	Loyalist P.L. 1786, from New York A.McL.
Van Every, Sergeant David...............	H District............	B. Rangers, S. G. Had a wife and 3 children. P.L. N., 1786. Niagara Stamped Book.
Van Every, Samuel ..	do	B. Rangers, P. Niagara Stamped Book.
Van Every, Wm......	do	B. Rangers, S. G.
Van Every, McGregor	Flamboro'	By Order in Council, 13th April, 1802.
Van Horne, Coms,....	Adolphustown	of the Commissary General's Department, L. B. M., 1790—350. P. L., 1786.
Van Hoosen, Richard..	H District............	Had a wife and 2 servants. P. L. N., 1786. Niagara Stamped Book.
VanKleeck,Sen.,Simon	Hawkesbury	O. C., 5th March, 1808. Served as an artificer.
Vankoughnet, Mickle..	E District, Cornwall..	R. R. N. Y.
Vanorder, Isaiah......	Kingston	
Vanorder, Matthew ..	do.	
Van Pellen, Arent.....	H District............	
Van Koughnet, John..	E District, Cornwall..	
Vardy, Thomas........	....	By Order in Council, 12th July, 1798.
Van Skiver, John	Adolphus Town.......	Loyalist, had drawn a lot L.B.A., 1794. 200 more. P.L., 1786. A.Mc.L.

APPENDIX B. 269

NAMES.	RESIDENCE.	DESCENDANTS.
Van Skiver, Peter	Marysburgh	A Loyalist. L. B. M., 1790 —350. P.L., 1786. A.Mc. L.
Vanoolkenburgh, Chloe	E District, Augusta ..	
Vent, Adam...........	Ernest Town	Gov. Hamilton, 1785. Loyalist—100. A wife and 5 children. P.L., 1786. Soldier in Jessup's. A.Mc.L.
Vent, Mary	M District	Daughter of Adam Vent ...
Vincent, Ensign, Elijah	H District	Guides and Pioneers.. ....
Viger, Gasper	Marysburgh	German Soldier. P.L., 1786.
Vizeir		S. Stamped Book. No U. E. List. Says German Soldier.
Vogley, John	do	Soldier 53rd Regt. L.B.M., 1791. 350 (P.L., 1786). Stamped Book and Sergt. McIntosh's certificate.
Vollick, Isaac	H District...........	M. C. Soldier, Butler's Rangers. Had a wife and 5 children. P.L.N., 1786.
Vollick, Sturn........	do	Soldier Butler's Rangers. O. C., 11th March, 1797.
Vrooman, Sergt. Adam	do	B. Rangers. S. G. Had 2 women and 2 children. P. L. N., 1786. Niagara Stamped Book.
Vullicar Conrad	Marysburgh	Discharged British soldier. P.L., 1786. Stamped Bk.
Wager, Everhard	Fredericksburgh	R.R.N.Y. A.McL. Soldier
Weager		Loyal Rangers. (100, G. Haldimand). P.L., R.R. N. Y., 1786. Stamped Book.
Wager, Thomas	do	Stamped Book. Son of Everhard. R.R.N.Y. P.L., 1786.
Wager, Wm.	do	P. L., 1786.
Waggoner, Henry.....	E District, Cornwall..	R. R. N. Y. Muster Roll F, has a wife and two children. P. L. 2d., 1786.
Waggoner, Henry.....	Matilda	Son of Jacob. J.B. Son of a soldier. 100 acres L. B. L.
Waggoner, Sen., Jacob	E. District, Cornwall...	M. C., R. R. N. Y. Muster R ll. O. C., 15th Jan., 1798. P. L. 2d., 1798.
Waggoner, Jun., Jacob	do do	Son of Jacob J. B.

APPENDIX B.

NAMES.	RESIDENCE.	DESCENDANTS.
Waicoff, John	Yonge or Elizabeth Town	Loyal Rangers.
Wait, George	E District, Cornwall	Tailor. Soldier R.R.N.Y., Muster Roll. E.
Waite, Joseph	do do	Corporal R.R.N.Y. Muster Roll.
Walker, Sen., Daniel	Ernest Town	Gov. Hamilton, 1785—100—1789. Atkins—200. (Loyal Rangers). A.Mc.L. P.L. 1786.
Walker, Jun., Daniel	do	Son of Daniel. I.G,, 200. L.B.A., 1794.
Walker, Jacob	H District	Deceased. B. Rangers. Had a wife and one child. P. L. N., 1786. Niagara Stamped Book.
Walker, James	E District, Augusta	Surgeon Jessup's S. G.
Walker, Weiden	Ernest Town	From Vermont; did not join the Royal Standard, tho' stated Loyal. L. B. M., 1790.
Walker, Wm.	do	Emigrant settler, 1789. L. B. M., 200.
Walker, Wm.	H District	Loyalist from North Carolina.
Waldroff, Martin, Sen.		See Order in Council, 17th March, 1807. Widow and sons, John and Martin.
Wall, Edward	do	Deceased; Indian Department.
Walliser, Anthony	E District, Matilda	Soldier Royal Regt. N. Y., L. B. L. Has a wife and two children. P. L. 2d, 1786. R. R. N. Y. Muster Roll.
Walliser, Jun., Anthony	do do	Son of Anthony.
Walliser, John	do do	R. R. N. Y. and son of Anthony.
Walliser, Martin	do do	Soldier R.R.N.Y. Muster Roll. Single. P. L. 2d, 1786.
Walsh, Samuel	Fredericksburgh	See Samuel Welch. P. L., 1786.
Walter, Martin	E District, Matilda	Soldier R.R.N.Y. A wife. P. L. 2d, 1786.
Walter, Philip	do do	R. R. N. Y. Muster Roll. Single. P. L. 2d, 1786.
Wanomaker, Peter	Adolphustown	A Sergeant in Jersey Volunteers. L. B. M., 1791.

APPENDIX B. 271

NAMES.	RESIDENCE.	DESCENDANTS.
Ward, Charles........	E District, Augusta...	Son of Sergeant John Ward, Loyal Rangers.
Wardle, Cornelius	H District............	Soldier 2d B. Jersey Volunteers.
Wardle, Michael......	do.	M. C. Sergt. New Jersey Volunteers. P. O. C., 8th Oct., 1796.
Warner, Sergt. Chris..	do	Sergeant B. Rangers. J. S. Had a wife and four children. P.L.N. 1786. Niagara Stamped Book.
Warner, Conradt......	E District, Osnabruck	
Warner, George	do do.	Son of Michael. J.B.
Warner, Godfrey	do Cornwall .	
Warner, John .... Waner	Kingston	Soldier King's Rangers or Associated Loyalist. A. McL. P. L. 1786.
Warner, Sen., Michael	E. District, Cornwall..	Royal Yorkers. R.R.N.Y. P. L. 2d, 1786.
Warner, Jun., Michael	do do ..	Son of Michael Warner, Sen.
Wartman, Abraham ..	Kingston	1785. Called Loyalist by Gov. Hamilton. 100acres. A.McL. P. L., 1786.
Wartman, Barnabas..	do	Son of Abraham. Loyalist. P.I., 1786.
Wartman, John	do	Son of Abraham. Stated Loyalist; L.B.M. 1790—300, and by Gov. Hamilton, 1785. 100 (P. L., 1786). Stamped Book. A.McL.
Wartman, Peter......	do	A. C., 16th Nov., 1807, Sergeant. Capt. Herckmer's Company. Stamp-Book. Loyalist. P. L. 1786.
Washburn, Ebenezer..	Fredericksburgh	S. G. Sergeant Loyal Rangers. A. Mc L. P. L., 1786.
Watson, Major ...... (Vide Suspended List).	E District, Augusta ..	Formerly an American soldier—was taken prisoner by our Indians, and afterwards in the Indian Department. R. J. D. G.
Weart, Conradt	do Osnabruck	R. R. N. Y. Muster Roll. Young man. P. L. 2d, 1786.

APPENDIX B.

NAMES.	RESIDENCE.	DESCENDANTS.
Weart, George........	E District, Williamsburgh	R. R. N. Y. Young man. P.L.2d, 1786.
Weast, John.......... Whart	Sophias and Ameliasburgh..............	Soldier R.R,N.Y. L.B.S. & G. 200 E. D. Young man. P.L.2d, 1786. Muster Roll.
Weatherhead, Samuel	E District, Augusta..	Settlement under orders of 1783. Soldier Loyal Rangers.
Weaver, Francis......	H District............	Soldier in Butler's Rangers. O. C. 21st July, 1796.
Weaver, Frederick....	E District, Cornwall..	Soldier R.R.N.Y. L.B.L., 1791 Muster Roll. Three children. P.L.2d, 1786.
Weaver, John.	E District, Cornwall..	R. R. N. Y. Muster Roll at Montreal. B.M.A.
Weaver, Peter........	do do ..	Soldier R.R.N.Y. O.E.
Weiger, Jacob........	do Williamsburgh	Sergeant R.R.N.Y.
Welch, Samuel	Ernest Town	Soldier King's Rangers, p. R. Roll.
Welch, Quartermaster Thomas	H District............	Maryland Loyalists.
Welch, Wm...	E Dist., Edwardsburgh	Naval Department, S.G.— one had a wife and one child. P. L. N, 1786. Stamped Book Niagara.
Wellery, Henry	Williamsburgh........	On original Roll.
Wellkank, Thomas....	Kingston	Quartermaster to Philadelphian Troop of Horse raised by J. Galloway. O.C., 7th March, 1797— 600 as.
Wells, Wm...	do	Incorporated Loyalist. A. McL. Shipwright. Stamped Book.
Wemp, Barnabas .... Wimpel	do	Soldier in Col.GuyJohnson's Foresters. Owen Robbin's affidavit, 1807. L. B. M., 1791. G. H., 1785—100. P.L. says R.R.N.Y.,1786. Stamped Book.
Wert, Andrew........	E District, Osnabruck	R.R.N.Y. Muster Roll.
Wert, Jun., John	do do	Soldier R.R.N.Y. J.F.
Westbrook, Anthony..	H District............	Indian Department. S. G. Foresters. A wife and four children. P. L. N., 1786. Stamped Book, Niagara.

Names.	Residence.	Descendants.
Wesley, George	Kingston	
Weston, George or Wenston	do	Currier. Stamped Book.
Whaling, Michael or Whelane	Charluttenburgh	Soldier R. R. N. Y. Muster Roll. P.L.2d, 1786.
Whealer, David Whelin	E Dist., Charlottenb'gh	R. R. N. Y. Muster Roll. P.L.N.J, 1786.
Wheaton, John	W District, S.G.	McAlpin's Corps. Was an artificer in that corps.
Wheeler, Ephraim	H District	Major McAlpin's Corps—Joined at Boston. Augusta R.J.D.G.
White, John	Augusta	A settler of 1786. L.B.L.
White, Sen., Joseph	E District, Augusta	Volunteer in Jessup's. Alex. Campbell, Esq., certifies that he joined the Royal Standard.
White, Junr. Joseph	E District, Augusta	Was married and at St. John's during the war. S. Sherwood's cereificate. Employed on secret service, Order in Council. Restored to U.E.3rd,Mar. 1806.
Whiteman, David	Kingston	Discharged soldier, Loyalist A.Mc.L. (Stamped Book, P.L., 1786.
Whitley, John	E Dist.Elizabeth Town	1787, Collins 200, R.R.N.Y. Muster Roll, E.
Whitley, John	do do	Soldier Jessup's Corps, R.J. D.G.
Whitmire, John	H District	
Whitney, Elijah	Elizabeth Town	Emigrant settler, L.B. E.D. 1793.
Whitner, Henry	H District	Soldier Butler's Rangers.
Whitsell, Andrew	do	Soldier Barton's or Jersey volunteers S.G.
Whitsell, Nicholas	Kingston	Soldier in the Hessian troops L.B.M., 1791.
Whittle Richard	do	A tailor, served in Butler's Rangers, O.C. 22nd Feb., 1808.
Wickwise, Jonathan Wickwise, Jonathan	E District do Augusta }	Soldier Loyal Rangers.
Wickwise, Lewis	do do	1789, Lebins Wickwise was a drummer King's Rangers, P.
Wickwise, Philip	do do	Soldier Loyal Rangers.
Wilcox, Senr. Elisha	New Settlement Lake Erie	Butler's Rangers, W. list, 1789.

APPENDIX B.

Names.	Residence.	Descendants.
Wilcox, Hagned Hazard	E District, Augusta	Son of Hazard Senr.
Wilcox, Senr. Hagned. Hazard	do do	Certified to have commanded a company in Canada, and to have been killed in battle at New York, his son Wm. O'Hazard apply.
Wilcox, Leberry	do do	
Wilders, Daniel	M District	British soldier P.L. 1786, S. Stamped Book.
Wilkins, Isaac	H District	
Wilkins, Martin	do	
Wilkinson, Capt. R...	E District	M.C. 1050, completes Mc.C. and family land grant out, P.L. N.J., 1786.
Willard, Levy	do Cornwall	
Willkey, Wm. Williekey	Marysburgh	British soldier (P.L. 1786), S. Stamped Book.
Wollery, Henry	E District	Soldier.
Williams, Albert	Fredericksburgh	Soldier R.R.N.Y., L.B.M., 1789, in all 350 (P.L. 1786, Stamped Book).
Williams, Armstrong	Ernest Town	Soldier Loyal Rangers, L. Bd.M. 1791, 350, A.Mc.L. P.L. 1786.
Williams, Senr. David.	do	L.Bd. certificate, sergeant in Jessup's L.Bd.M. 1790, 700 P.L. 1786, A.Mc.L.
Williams, David	do	Son of David Williams Sr.
Williams, Elijah	do	Son of David Williams Sr., p. L.Bd. certificate, 200 L.Bd.M. 1790.
Williams, Fredk	H District	M.C. a soldier Engineer Department, O.C. 25 April, 1797. L.Bd. Nassau, 1794, a wife and five children, P.L. N. 1786.
Williams, Henry	Sophias & Ameliasb'gh	
Williams, Senr. John..	Ernest Town	M.C. soldier Jessup's Loyal Rangers, A.Mc.L. (P.L., 1786).
Williams, Junr. John.	do	Son of John Williams Senr. Loyal Rangers, P.L. N., 1786, A.Mc L.
Williams, James	do	Son of John Williams, soldier Loyal Rangers,L.Bd. M., A.Mc.L.
Williams, Joshua	do	Son of John Williams Senr. a boy.

APPENDIX B. 275

NAMES.	RESIDENCE.	DESCENDANTS.
Williams, Rachel	H District............	Widow of Frederick Vanderlip, daughter of N. Petitt, 450, had three children, P. L. N., 1786.
Williams, Robert.....	Ernest, Town	L.Bd. certificate, described Loyalist, L.Bd.M., 1793, 300, P.L. 1786, of Adolphustown, had drawn 100 L.Bd.M.19th March,1793, 200, Loyal Rangers, A.Mc. L.
Williams, Robert.....	Kingston	A seaman, not U.E., O.C., 20th July, 1797.
Williams, Samuel.....	H District............	Associ'td Loyalist in Ward's Block House.
Williams, Moses......	Lancaster	Corporal King's Rangers. Order in Council, 29th January, 1808.
Williams, Samuel......	Ernest Town	One of this name Lieutenant of Artillery in Major Ward's Loyalists, S.G.
Williams, Thomas.....	W District	S.G. blacksmith Indian Department.
Wilson, William......	E District, Augusta...	
Wilmot, Allan.........	H District............	Son to Captain Wilmot of Delaney's.
Wilsey, Benona.......	E District, Augusta ...	Loyal Rangers, p. L.Bd. certe. Joseph, his son, Govr. Haldimand's certificate says sergeant, a wife and two children.
Wilsie, James	Yonge	A soldier Loyal Rangers.
Wilson, Bathsheba, formerly widow Soper.	H District............	
Wilson, Benjamin	do	Came in as a settler in 1787. See Petition in 1797.
Wilson, Sergt. John ..	do Thorold....	B.R., a sergeant, a wife and six children, P.L.N. 1786, Stamped Book, Niagara.
Wilson, Irish John...	do	Aided to recruit men, concealed officers and party, suffered imprisonment, p. certificate of N. Petitt, O. C. 13th March, 97, land made up 1200 acres.
Wilson John Senr	do	From Staten Island. Came in a settler in 1878 with three sons, one in Crowland.

APPENDIX B.

NAMES.	RESIDENCE.	DESCENDANTS.
Wilson, John Junr.....	Home	Son of John Senr., by Order in Council,11th November 1806. Associated Loyalist.
Wilson, Jacob	H District	Sergeant in the Jersey Volunteers, P. 1796.
Wilson, Joseph	do	Barton's Jersey Volunteers, R. Clinch.
Wilsie, John............	Yonge..................	Was in 1777 a soldier Loyal Rangers,but owing to sickness after the capitulation of Saratoga, remained and came in after the war.
Wiltsey, Junr. Benoni.	E Dist, Elizabeth Town	S.L.R. soldier Loyal Rangers. Discharge.
Windecker, Henry....	H District............	S.G. B. Rangers, a wife and four children, P. L. N., 1786. Niagara Stamped Book.
Wing, Gersham	Elizabeth Town	1789, P., no service stated. A settler R.J. D.G. O.C. 4th February, 1807. Reinstated on W.E. list.
Winney, Corpl. Corn'ls	H District.............	B. Rangers, Stamped Book Niagara, S. P.L. N.,1786.
Winter, Henry	E District, Osnabruck.	Soldier R.R.N.Y., a wife, P. L. 2d., 1786.
Winter, Peter	do do	Soldier R.R.N.Y., L.Bd., single P.L. 2d, 1786.
Winterbottom, Samuel	M District............	Royal Artillery and Marine Department,Lake Ontario S.G.
Wintermute, Corpl. Abraham...............	H District.............	S.G. B. Rangers, a wife and one child, P.L. N., 1786, Niagara Stamped Book.
Wintermute, Benjn....	H District.............	A soldier B. Rangers. Niagara Stamped Book, O.C. 17th March, 1797. S. P.L. N., 1786.
Wintermute,Corpl. Jno	do	M.C.B. Rangers, a wife and five children,P.L.N.,1786. Niagara Stamped Book.
Wintermute,Mrs.Mary	do	
Wintermute, Corporal Peter	do	M.C. B. Rangers, a corporal L.Bd. certe., a wife and four children,P.L. N.1786. Niagara Stamped Book.
Wintermute, Philip ..	do	S.G. B. Rangers. Niagara Stamped Book. S. P.L. N., 1786.

APPENDIX B. 277

Names.	Residence.	Descendants.
Wist, David Wuist	Ernest Town	Soldier Genl. Haldimand, 1784, 100, Loyal Rangers, A.Mc.L.
Wist, John Wuist	do	Soldier R.R.N.Y., General Haldimand, 1784, 100, P. L., 1786, and Capt. Myer's letter.
Wist, Junr. John	do	Soldier Loyal Rangers. Muster Roll, P.L., 1786.
Wood, Benjamin	E Dist, Charlottenb'h.	Son of Jonas Senr., J. B. Soldier Butler's Rangers, L.Bd, Lunenburg.
Wood John	do Cornwall	Son of Jonas Senr., J. B. Soldier R.R.N.Y. Muster Roll, P.L. 2d., 1786.
Wood, Jonas	Williamsburgh	Soldier R.R.N.Y. Muster Roll. P.L. 2d, 1786.
Wood, Junr. Jonas	E District	Son of Jonas Senr. J. B. Indian Department.L.Bd.L.
Wood, Josiah	do Cornwall	
Wood, Nathan	do	Que. ; if not son of Jonas— Yes, son of Jonas Senr.— a boy.
Wood, Roger	do	Son of Jonas Senr. J.B. Son of a soldier, 200 acres, L. Bd.L. Soldier R.R.N.Y. I.C.
Wood, Stephen	do	Son of Jonas Senr. J.B. S. and G., a boy.
Wood, Thomas	do ElizabethTown	Soldier Loyal Rangers, p.E. Jessup's Certificate.
Wood, Wm	do	
Wood, Wm	do Cornwall	Son of Jonas. Soldier R.R. N.Y., L.Bd.L., P.L. 2d., 1786.
Woodcock, Abraham	Fredericksburgh	Soldier R.R.N.Y., L.BdM., 1791, 300, A.McL., P. L., 1786.
Woodcock, John	Fredericksburg	R. R. N. Y., P. L. 1786, Stamped Book, B.M.1790, Loyalist, 350 acres 1784— G. Haldimand, 100 ; 1785, Govr. Hamilton's certificate, Loyalist, 1793. He did not join the British Standard before the Treaty of Separation—in con sequence, those of his daughr. Katharine's petition was rejected, 19tb March, 1793. A. McL.

APPENDIX B.

NAMES.	RESIDENCE.	DESCENDANTS.
Woodley, George	H District	Delaney's.
Woolly, John	Elizabeth Town	Emigrant settler from U. States in 1788.
Work, James Warrick	Ernest Town	Negro soldier in Loyal Rangers. Muster Roll.
Wormwood, Mathew	H District	Soldier Butler's Rangers, R. Clinch's certificate. S. P. L. N. 1786. Niagara Stamped Book.
Wragg, John	E District	Son Richard — an ironmonger in Montreal—R. J. D.G.
Wragg, Richard	do	Resident in Montreal.
Wragg, Thomas	do	Joined in 1779. N. McL.
Wright, Amos	do	
Wright, Amos	Augusta	Original Roll.
Wright, Asel	do	Soldier 84th Regt. Ld. Bd. P.L. 2d, 1786.
Wright, Daniel	Marysburg	Sergt. 53rd Regt. L.B.M. 1791, 750 acres, and P.L. 1786. Had nine children born before 1789. Stamped Book — p. certificate of Archd. McDonell, J.P,
Wright, Daniel	E District, Cornwall	Son of a soldier. Ld. Bd. L. P.L. 2d, 1786. Joined the Royal Standard 1777. S. Anderson's certificate.
Wright, Gabriel	H District.	
Wright, James	Marysburg	Soldier 53rd Regt. L.B.M. 1791, 300, and P. L. 2d, 1786. S. Stamped Book.
Wright, James	E Dist., Elizabeth T'wn	Soldier 84th Regt.—enlisted at Nova Scotia.
Wright, Jesse	do Matilda	Sergeant R. R. N. Y. M. Roll. Has a wife & two children. P.L. 2d, 1786.
Wright, Joseph	Marysburg	Stamped Book. Loyalist, tailor, and one of the first settlers, p. Collins' book. A soldier 84th Regt. L.B. M. 1791, 700 acres, and P. L. 1786. A wife, five children.
Wright, Robert	M District.	
Wright, Samuel	Sophias & Ameliasburg	Soldier B. Rangers.
Wright, Samuel, Senr.	Elizabeth Town	O.C. February, 1805, ordered to be inserted on U.E. list.

APPENDIX B. 279

NAMES.	RESIDENCE.	DESCENDANTS.
Wright, Samuel, Junr.	E Dist., Elizabeth T'wn	Son of Samuel, Senr. L.B. L. Suspended U.E. list.
Wright, Sylvester	do do	P. states son of a Loyalist; does not state the name of his father. L.B.L.
Wright, Waite........	M District............	Was a soldier King's Rangers. J. Vanyant. Provision List King's Rangers 1786.
Wright, Widow Mary.	Kingston............	Loyalist from New York. P.L. 1786. A. McL.
Wright, William......	Marysburg..........	Discharged from 53rd Regt. Not a U.E.
Wright, Wm.	E Dist., ElizabethT'wn.	
Wrong, John	H District............	Belonged the Marine Department at Quebec and district. P. L. N. 1786. Stamped Book Niagara. Petition 1797. Was discharged by Commodore Grant.
Wickoff, Peter........	do	Stamped Book Niagara. S. P.L.N. 1786.
Yates, John..........	Bastard	A settler. Came in after the War, 1788, from Connecticut. P.
Yoemans, Arthur	Kingston............	Mr. Dorlands says that he saw him at Sorel in 1783. A son, David.
Yorks, John..........	do	Son of Isaac Yorks.
Young, Abraham.....	H District.	
Young, Senr., Adam..	do	Deceased. S. G. Indian Department. Stamped Book Niagara. A wife. P.L.N. 1786.
Young, Sergt. Daniel..	....	S. G. Indian Department. Stamped Book Niagara. A wife and two children. P.L.N. 1786.
Young, Daniel........	Marys & Sophiasburg..	R.R.N.Y. L.B.M. 1791. A. McL. Stamped Book. P. L. 1786.
Young, George........	H District............	In this Province and Newfoundland since 1774. Served under Col. Pringle of the Engineers. S.G.
Young, Henry........	H District............	S. G. Indian Department— Rangers, L.B.N. 1784— Stamped Book Niagara; a wife; P.L.N. 1786.

APPENDIX B.

NAMES.	RESIDENCE.	DESCENDANTS.
Young, Senr., Henry	Fredericksburg	Soldier R.R.N.Y. P.L.1786.
Young, Junr., Henry	do	Son of Henry; 200 acres; L.B.M. 1791.
Young, Henry	Marys & Sophiasburg	Lieutenant Royal Regt., N. York. P.L.1786. Stamped Book.
Young, Junr., Henry	do	Son of Henry.
Young, Lt. John	H District	S.G. Indian Department. S. P.L.N. 1786. B.R. Six in family — Stamped Book Niagara.
Young, Sergt. John	do	B.R. A wife & six children; P. L. N. 1786; Stamped Book Niagara.
Young, Junr., John	do	
Young, Sergt. Jacob	do	Deceased — Sergt. King's Rangers.
Young, Jacob	do	
Young, James	E District, Lancaster	Had a wife and six children —P.L. 2d, 1786.
Young, Senr., Peter	Fredericksburg	Soldier R.R.N.Y. Stamped Book. P.L.1786—A.McL. F. Thompson.
Young, Junr., Peter	do	Drummer R.R.N.Y. Stamped Book. P.L. 1786. F. Thompson.
Young, Philip	H District	Sergeant Butler's Rangers.
Young, Stephen	Fredericksburg	Labourer—Stamped Book.
Younglove, Ezekiel	H District	Soldier Jersey Volunteers.
Zufelt, Henry	Hallowell	O.C. 10th February, 1808— Loyal Rangers.

Names inserted on U. E. List by order of the Honourable the Executive Council.

NAMES.	WHEN INSERTED.
Peter Valeau, Lt.....	22nd June, 1799, M.C. On Provision List 1786, A. McL. Loyalist. Stamped Book.
Philleback, Chris'n....	Entered on the U.E. list, Pillebug.
Moybe, Lavinha......	O.C. 27th June, 1798. Wife of Frederick. Not on record in C.O.
Jones, Sarah..........	O.C. 3rd July, 1798.
Sherwood, Thomas....	Entered before, in his proper place, O.C. 11th June, 1798.
Kintner, George	Already entered in his proper place.
Jacocks, David	Entered in proper place.
Hoskins, Abiel	O.C. 26th May, 1807. See his daughter, Tabatha Livingston's petition.

A true copy from the U.E. list in the Council Office.

ALEXR. McDONELL,
Confidential Clerk.

Doyle, Sarah	O.C. 20th June, 1798. Not on record in C. Book.
Hill, Thomas	O.C. 28th Febr'y, 1798.
Smith, Col. Samuel ...	O.C. 11th June, 1798.
Sherwood, Reuben....	O.C. 11th June, 1798. Soldier Loyal Rangers.
Livingston, Daniel....	E.D. O.C. 11th June, 1798.
Claus, Captn. Wm. ...	O.C. 11th June, 1798. Lieut. R. R. N. Y. Son of Colonel Daniel Claus.
Hils, Joseph..........	O.C. 16th April, 1799. How? His father was never in this Province—came in with grandfather.
Olker, Elisha	O.C. 13th November, 1797.
Chryster, Peter.	
Dill, Barsnett, Senr.	
Freeman, John.	

JOHN SMALL, *C.E.C.*

Van Every, McGregor	O.C. 13th April, 1802.
Huston, Elijah	Son of Lieut. Huston. O.C. 5th July, 1798. Suspended 5th Novr., 1804.
Vardy, Thomas	O.C. 12th July, 1798.
Bedford, Jonathan....	24th Augt., 1802, page 127.
Stephenson, Francis...	Capt. Queen's Rangers. O.C. 31st December, 1805.
Flack, Richard	H District. Came to Canada when a boy, with his father. O.C. 2nd August, 1797—his name to be put on U.E. list.

R

SUPPLEMENTARY LIST.

NAMES.	REMARKS.
Armstrong, Jonathan	I. Soldier R.R.N.Y. M.R.
Alt, Conrad	A. " " "
Argassinger, Philip	A. " " "
Austin, Isaac	A. " " "
Archer, Edward	A. " " "
Aston, Jacob	A. " " "
Arkland, Dedrick	Soldier 60th Regt.
Aikin, William	" 29th Regt.
Aners (or Aneas), Cors	An old soldier. L.B. Nassau, 1794.
Almis, Christian	German soldier last war. do.
Allen, John	Soldier Loyal Rangers.
Andrew, John	" "
Andrew, Jacob	" "
Ayres, Daniel B	" "
Allen, Andrew	" 84th Regt. J. F.
Atherton, Phenias	A captain in the service.
Algire, Philip	Soldier R.R.N.Y. J. F.
Algire, John	" " "
Alexander, David	" 84th Regt. From Scotland to Quebec.
Atkinson, William	Soldier Butler's Rangers. S. G.
Anderson, Thomas (and one child)	Provisioned Cataraqui.
Arnold, James	S.
Avory, William	Came in 1785. O. E. See page 64, Capt. John Jones list of Loyalists provisioned.
Allan, Mrs. (and six children).	
Aspy, William	S.
Anderson, Jane	S. P. at Detroit.
Acher, Lodwick	Absent. Johnstown. R.R.N.Y. M. Roll.
Abril, Robert	Enlisted in 53rd Regt. Absent.
Austin, John	His father killed in the service at Wilmington.
Austin, Jonathan	Soldier in Captn. Barnes' Holfictos Company last war.
Able, Henry	Soldier K. R.
Adams, William	" "
Allan, Henry	" "
Alsworth, Ezra (deserted)	" "
Anthony, John	" "
Anthony, Richard	" "
Ash, Peter	" "

APPENDIX B.

NAMES.	REMARKS.
Allen, Ebenezer	Sergeant Butler's Rangers.
Austin, Doctor Charles	Surgeon R.R N.Y.
Ashburn, John	Corporal 84th Regt. Matilda.
Anguish, John	Soldier B. Rangers.
Arner, Jacob	" "
Arnold, Frederick	Loyalist--with Mr. McKee.
Arnold, John	Soldier B. Rangers.
Ashworth, Thomas	King's, or 8th Regt.
Antonee, Richard	Soldier R.R.N.Y. Que.
Aber, John	Served last war.
Adams, Joseph	Marine Dept. (Ad——.)
Ainise, Sally	A principal Indian woman.
Ammon, John Godfrey	A reduced soldier.
Allan, Hugh	Soldier 31st Regt.
Ayres, Thomas	T. Loyalist, 1792. Stepson of Thos. Richardson, trader in Lower Canada in 1780.
Alemger, William	B. Rangers.
Arnold, Jacob	"
Ashford, John	8th Regt.
Arnold, Oliver	Soldier Butler's Rangers.
Brook, James	S. Provisioned at Cataraqui.
Bartlemass, Peter	S. Soldier Loyal Rangers (Lt. —— certe.)
Booth, Jesse	S.
Bevins, James	S.
Bliss, John	A wife and two children.
Barber, Abraham	A wife. Soldier Loyal Rangers.
Blaw, Robert	S.
Beebe, Peter	A wife and two children.
Barnes, Godlup	S.
Bone, William	S.
Baker, John, Senr.	
Baker, John, Junr.	Jersey Volunteers.
Bangard, Conradt	A wife and three children.
Butler, George	S.
Brien, John	S. British soldier.
Ball, Widow (and one child)	Provisioned at Johnstown.
Bringman, Christopher	S. Provisioned at Johnstown.
Burk, Patrick	A wife. Soldier R.R. N.Y. Muster Roll.
Ball, Jacob	S. Soldier Loyal Rangers.
Boket, Dallows	A wife. Soldier Loyal Rangers.
Brownhill, Stephen	S. R.R.N.Y.
Brownhill, Joseph	Emigrant from the States. J.F.
Bright, Lewis	S. Soldier.
Burton, John	S. Emigrant from Ireland since the peace.

APPENDIX B.

NAMES.	REMARKS.
Benn, Luke	A wife and four children.
Bruce, Peter	A wife and three children.
Bueley, David	A wife and three children.
Bogart, Martin	S.
Brant, John	S. German soldier J. F. list, 8th Decr., 1803.
Bowman, Luke	S.
Beauhart, John	A wife and three children.
Buttsher, Elias	S.
Burhouse, Isaac	S. 30 years ⎫ Settlers. Came into Canada March, 1785. See Capt. Jones' list — date, 15th April, 1785.
Boys, Joseph	60 yrs. of age ⎬
Burhouse, Simon	56 " ⎭
Benn, Thomas	Provd. at Niagara. Or, Bayne, Thos.
Bowen, Joseph	A wife.
Bradt, Christian	A wife.
Bradt, Adrian	A wife.
Bellinger, Elijah	S.
Buzeer, Jacob	S.
Brown, Henry	And wife.
Berger, Frederick	S. Fort Erie. Soldier 34th Regt.
Brown, Elijah	S.
Brook, Benjamin	S.
Boyle, Ann	S. Provisioned at Detroit.
Bertlay, Michael	Fredericksburg. Entered U. E.
Berry, William	S. Gone to the States.
Bower, Wm., Junr.	" "
Bode, Christopher	Quitted his land.
Bird, Jonathan	Montreal.
Breda, Frederick.	
Beberwine, ———	Gone to the States.
Bradford, John Burnet	Never Joined. Soldier Jessup's Loyal Rangers.
Brooks	Widow of John Sorel. Soldier Loyal Rangers.
Boukes, John	R. R. N. Y.
Bradley, Price	Soldier King's Rangers.
Barlow, Abner	Corporal "
Barnhart, Joseph	Soldier "
Barnum, Levi	Sergeant "
Bennet, Ephraim	Soldier "
Billings, Joseph	" "
Bristol, Daniel	" "
Brooks, Samuel	" "
Brown, Charles	" "
Brown, David	" "
Brown Joseph	" "
Brown, William	" "
Buck, Isaac	

APPENDIX B. 285

NAMES.	REMARKS.
Boger, Lodwick	Soldier B. Rangers.
Brown, John	" " or 60th Regt.
Burke, Patrick	Surgeon mate B. Rangers.
Burton, Thomas	8th Regt.
Best, Harmanus	Lieut. Jessup's, or Rogers', Ensign.
Blake, Doctor Charles	Surgeon 34th Regt.
Baro (or Barone), Joseph	Detroit Volunteers, and Gov. Hamilton's. (Sergeant.)
Barrit, P.	84th Regt.
Beaubein, C.	Gov. Hamilton.
Beaubein, J. B.	Siege of Quebec.
Bigras, I. B.	Corporal Detroit Volunteers.
Blazens, Laurence	B. Rangers.
Bonde, Joseph	Lieut. Indian Department.
Bonsack, Christopher John	29th Regt. 8 years and a three years' man. p. discharge.
Boulanger, C.	Gov. Hamilton.
Butler, Edward	B. Rangers. Irish.
Benville, Francis	W. D. Served during the War.
Betton, David	Commodore Naval Department.
Baker, William	Marine Department. Served since '73.
Barth, Lewis	Master-mate, Marine Department, Lakes Erie and Huron.
Boyne, John	Storekeeper, Fort St. Phillip, Minorca.
Bryant, John the late	Lake Ontario 20 years, lastly a master.
Burns, David	Surgeon 71st Regiment.
Barnhardt, Widow	Que. : If the military lands of Sergt. George Barnhart.
Bender, Laurence	Soldier R. R. N. Y.
Bunbury, Joseph	5th Regiment.
Barbo, John	Soldier 84th Regiment. W. D.
Blake, Martin	Soldier, Cruitzbury. German soldier.
Barton, Stephen	Loyalist U. E.
Bewther (or Beuter), John	German Soldier.
Brown, Neil	Soldier 71st Regiment.
Brown, Robert	Treasury Loyalist, 1792. Had been in America.
Burney, James	Treasury Loyalist, 1792.
Burton, John	" "
Benson, Jonas	" "
Benson, Christina	" " from England.
Buker, John	" "
Brown, Gasper	Brought in a prisoner. N. privileged.
Bass, Thomas	Soldier.
Burns, John	
Bell, Daniel	
Bryan, Pat	

APPENDIX B.

NAMES.	REMARKS.
Buffeland, James	
Bowse, John	
Bradt, Ryan	
Besil, Jabish	
Brust, Matthew	
Bacchuster, John	
Brozie, Gabriel	
Bacchers (or Brachen), John	R.R.N.Y. Muster Roll.
Bouslale, Luke	
Barnhardt, David	
Binsell, John	
Bolson, Evans	
Batty, Michael	
Bradburn, Francis	
Bradley, Abraham	
Baderly, William	Soldier.
Brinker, Henry	
Burns, Peter	
Beetle, Barnabas	
Burns, Matthew	
Brown, Aaron	
Brenvell, John	
Barnes, Thomas	
Bolton, Abraham	A soldier in Jessup's Corps.
Brown, William	Soldier 10th Regiment.
Black, Jacob	A. soldier R.R.N.Y. Muster Roll.
Becker, Adam	A. " " "
Bonk, David	A. " " "
Blood, John	J. " " "
Burns, Garret	A. " " "
Bratt, Elisha	A. " " "
Black, Cato	A. " " "
Brooks, Donald	A. Drummer R.R.N.Y. "
Baxter, Roger	A. soldier R.R.N.Y. Muster Roll.
Bangell, Henry	A. " " "
Bangell, Peter	A. " " "
Bangell, Adam	A. " " "
Bangell, William	A. " " "
Bangell, John	A. " " "
Becker, Conradt	A. " " "
Brathower, John	A. " " "
Beverly, David	A. " " "
Berry, George	E. " " "
Brahower, Francis	A. " " "
Benneway, Ezekiel	A. " " "
Bents, Joseph	G. Served in German Corps. U.D.
Burke, John	Corporal Loyal Rangers.
Bigelow, Jesse	Late from Vermont. L.B.L., 1790.
Baxter, David	Discharged from the King's service. L.B.N., 1794.

APPENDIX B.

NAMES.	REMARKS.
Best, Conrad	Ensign Loyal Rangers.
Balster, William	Soldier Loyal Rangers.
Bennit, Charles	" "
Brownson, John	" "
Beagle, Daniel	" "
Bonisteel, Philip	" "
Bobbit Elkanah	" "
Brownson, James	" "
Bull, Aaron	His widow was a U. E.
Bell, Enos	Soldier Loyal Rangers.
Bolton, Henry	" "
Betts, Benjamin	" "
Burgarr, Alexander	" "
Blashar, Lozo	" "
Beaty, David	" "
Beckman, Samuel	" "
Boltwood, John	" "
Burrows, Thomas	" "
Bratt, Abraham	" "
Brisbin, John	" "
Blockley, John	" "
Brisbie, Robert	" "
Brisbin, Samuel	" "
Brisbin, James	" "
Bustard, William	" "
Brown, James	" " died in Dec., 1782.
Barnhardt, Jobest	" "
Bell, Francis	" "
Benninger, Isaac	" "
Baker, Jacob	German soldier. J.F.
Brinkman, Christopher	" "
Brady, Luke	No description.
Burke, Peter	Soldier R.R.N.Y. Entered before.
Becksted, Alexander	A settler in 1793.
Brougner, Jacob	Son of John, Sen., Niagara District.
Beby, Richard	Soldier 29th Regiment, p. Sergeant McIntosh's certificate.
Bowen, Wm. C.	Soldier R.R.N.Y., p. certificate of Rev. J. Stuart.
Browning, Joseph	Common settler. N.McL.
Bickle, Jacob	" "
Becket, Peter	Negro. No description. O.E.
Brown, Rhoda	Daughter of John Wiltsie; served under Gen. Burgoyne. O.E.
Boulton, George	Joined in 1777. On U.E. O.E.
Begford, Henry	Common soldier. O.E.
Battes, Abigal	Her husband was hanged by the rebels.

APPENDIX B.

Names.	Remarks.
Bocker, John	Soldier R.R.N.Y. 2nd Bat. Lieut. Spencer.
Boiseau, Joseph	Soldier 84th Regiment.
Boyle, George	Col. Barton's Corps. Deserted from Staten Island; information of Asahel Ward, 6th Dec., 1811.
Billett, Francis	S^rgt. Artillery Detroit Volunteers.
Coonshoon, Christopher	S. Pd. at Cataraqui.
Connor, Lieutenant	
Cronkhite, Abraham	A wife.
Cronkhite, Wm	S.
Cronkhite, Widow	
Clock, Adam	A wife and child. Corporal.
Christie, Simeon	S.
Colder, John	A wife, Jannet and child. Soldier R.R.N.Y. N. McL.
Calder, Christian	"
Coons, Simeon	A wife and 6 children. 2ndBatn.R.R. N.Y. M. Roll.
Catchbar, Christopher	S.
Conger, David	S.
Clark, George	S.
Crankshore, Moses	S. British Soldier.
Caffard, John	A wife and child. Provd. at N. Johnstown.
Cameron, Widow	3 children. " "
Curry, Moses	S.
Christy, George	A wife and 4 children.
Chambers, Robert	S. Soldier R.R.N.Y. M. Roll.
Campbell, Robert	S. Soldier 60th Regt., S.G.
Chitick, Henry	S.
Coons, Widow	A child.
Castleman, Adam	S.
Cattum, William	S. R.R.N.Y. M. Roll. Cottom.
Canute, Henry	Provd. at Niagara.
Cocket, John	S.
Cocket, Widow	2 children.
Chrysler, Henry	A wife and 7 children.
Cassady, George	S.
Campbell, Thomas	S. Soldier Butler's Rangers.
Chambers, Francis	S. Soldier B. Rangers.
Clowes, Peter	A wife and 4 children. Came to this Province in 1785.
Cline, Joseph	S.
Conway, Patrick	S. Soldier B. Rangers.
Cummins, Peter	A wife and 2 children. Pd. at Detroit
Coldwell, William	A wife and child.
Corr, Ralph	
Cornish, John	At Montreal.

APPENDIX B. 289

NAMES.	REMARKS.
Corney, Alexander............	Quitted his land.
Cramer, John.....................	In Canada. Soldier R.R.N.Y. M. Roll.
Cook, John, Senr..	Quebec.
Cramer, Peter	In Canada.
Croydon, Harmanus.................	Montreal.
Cook, Phillip	Sorel, Corporal R.R.N.Y. M. Roll.
Courtney, Dennis	Canada Soldier " "
Carrier, John......................	Of Jessup's Corps.
Campbell, John....................	60th Regt.
Campbell, Robert..................	42nd Regt.
Carn, Nathaniel...................	B. Rangers,.
Canis, John	8th Regt., John Carris.
Cassada, John.....................	B. Rangers.
Carn, Mathias	N. C. off. ? B. Rangers.
Collard, Elijah	Pilot to the New York Army.—S.G. —No it was his brother John.
Crumb, Jacob.....................	B. Rangers.
Cereps, John	34th Regt. or Corps.
Calder, Frederick ......,..........	King's Rangers.
Campfield. Skim..................	"
Carkner, John	"
Catchapaw or Catchfoot, Henry	"
Carrigan, Wm	"
Chapel, Henry	"
Clemmens, John	"
Calhonmer, Conrod	"
Connolly, John	"
Colner, George..	"
Colhamer, George.................	"
Codner, Ishmael...................	"
Cross, John.......................	R·R.N.Y. Soldier, M. R.
Crotter, Peter.....	King's Rangers.
Curties, Christopher..............	"
Carrigan, Paul..	Soldier Loyal Rangers.
Clark, Paul..................... ...	Osnabruck.
Clark, Thomas	Sergt., Charlottenburgh.
Curere, Peter ....,.....	Corpl. Matilda.
Christie ——	Corpl., Fredericksburgh.
Clock, Adam..	" "
Cameron, Duncan.................	Soldier 84th Regt. (W.D.).
Cameron, John.....................	" B. Rangers "
Campeau, R.	Govr.. Hamilton.
Casity, Luke	B. Rangers.
Chabert, I. de....................	Govr., Hamilton.
Chalmers ——	W. D. Loyalist.
Chesne, P........................	Govr., Hamilton.
Chicot, I. B.	Minute man—Lieut.
Clearwater, John	B. Rangers.

APPENDIX B.

Names.	Remarks.
Coffee, Samuel, Ensign..................	B. Rangers.
Coppas, John........................	34th Regt.
Comcodle, John.....................	B. Rangers.
Crawford, Wm	2nd Batln. Delaney's.
Crone, H.	British Navy.
Chatterton, John	Soldier Delaney's Refugees; lost his left arm.
Cozens, Daniel	Capt. New Jersey Volunteers.
Crookshank, Patrick	Royal Artillery.
Curry, Widow.......................	Que.; if the Military land of Corporal Ephraim Curry.
Clark, Thomas Alexr.	A millwright from England.
Connor, James	Surgeon (Hospital mate).
Cowan, David	Lieut., Naval Department.
Collon, Abraham	German Soldier.
Claick, Gasper	"
Chriten-de-Fitzienstin	"
Cushion, James....................	1792, T.L., wife and 4 children. Served in Engineers' Dept. in America,
Cox, John, 1792....................	T. L.
Clark, John........................	84th Regt., W.D.
Clark, Thomas	Loyalist, W.D.
Coons, David......................	
Clark, Adam	
Cock, Henry	
Clavenstine, Hermon	
Castiller, Lawrence	
Coamoner, Frederick	
Cotton, Abraham	
Cramp, Benjamin..................	
Carner, Mattice....................	
Chuvinil, John	
Carr, James	
Cox, Alexander	
Case, John.........................	
Clement, John P.	
Cogdon, John.....................	Soldier R.R.N.Y. Muster Roll.
Clink, Thomas	
Cummings, Robert	
Culp, Tulmon.....................	
Coklin, James	
Countryman, John.................	Detroit Vols. (or Joseph D.W.S.).
Crouse, Peter	F. Corporal R.R.N.Y. Muster Roll.
Campbell, Wm....................	A. Soldier " "
Cornelius, Henry..................	A. " " "
Calder, James	N.B. " " "
Callegan, Charles....	I. " " "
Carr, Hugh........................	I. " " "
Clyne, Jacob	A. " " "

APPENDIX B. 291

Names.	Remarks.
Crassley, Nathaniel	E. Soldier R. R. N.Y. Muster Roll.
Connolly, William	I. " " "
Cain, Henry	A. " " "
Crightoof, John	A. " " "
Cline, Phillip	A. " " "
Case, Elijah or Elihue	A. drummer " "
Cryderman, Thomas	A. soldier " "
Crawford, David	A. " " "
Claw, Francis	F. " " "
Carrier, Martin	F. " " "
Crabtree, John	A. " " "
Cousins, John	E. drummer " "
Caldwell, Thomas	Son of Capt. Wm. Caldwell, W. D.
Cray, John	Ireland, Major Close's list, 1788.
Clengenberner, Nicholas	German " "
Connor, John	Volunteer Queen's Rangers.
Cralinger, Nicholas	Soldier 34th Regiment.
Corbin, Micah	Late from New York State. L.B.L., 1790.
Conroy, Michael	Soldier 8th Regiment. L.B.L., 1791.
Capleman, John	An old soldier. L.B. Nassau. 1794.
Cressey, William	Soldier 29th Regiment. "
Cole, Henry	Soldier Loyal Rangers.
Cox, Edward John	" "
Cossens, Jacob	" " died in July, 1783.
Carpenter, Beloved	" "
Cameron, Hugh	" "
Clark, William	" "
Coons, Mathias	" "
Castle, Eliphalet	" "
Choudy, Jacob	" "
Costelow, James	" " died in 1782.
Crisedell, Thomas	" "
Carpenter, John	" " died in July, 1783.
Curtis, Uriah	" "
Crawford, George	" "
Crawson, Abraham	" "
Coleton, Daniel	" "
Conner, Thomas	" "
Copeland, William	" "
Conner, Michael	" "
Coon, Abraham/	" "
Clum, Henry	" "
Carpenter, Jacob	" "
Cotlard, James	" "
Conklin, Abraham	" "
Cole, George	" "
Cole, Francis	" R.R.NY. J.F.
Carr, John	" " "

APPENDIX B.

Names.	Remarks.
Clunes, John	Clerk Engineer Department.
Castleman, Martin	Son of a Loyalist. J.F.
Chrysler, Henry, Sr.	Indian Department.
Carley, Abraham	An old soldier—Mr. Adam's Certificate says secret service.
Clark, Daniel or Donald	Emigrant from Scotland. J.F.
Carley, Isaiah	N. P. in the States. O.E.
Coleman, Abel	A settler 1788. O. E.
Campbell, Phœbe	Daughter of John Booth. O.E.
Caine, Peter	Came to Canada in 1803. O.E.
Cyler, Valentine	Loyalist. Major Close's list.
Cook, John	Of Camden ; an active Loyalist. Bore arms in Carolina, p. Col. Balfour's Certificate, sett,ed in 1785.
Countryman. Joseph	Soldier Butler's Rangers. M. Elliott's Certificate.
Carnèr, George	Soldier Jersey Volunteers,. p. P. 1799.
Clendennan, Walter	Soldier B. Rangers.
Clock, Jacob ....—	2nd Batt. R.R.N.Y. Deserted ; information of Jonathan Hart, Oct. 1811.
Daniel, George	S. Prov'd. Cataraqui.
Dalmage, Jacob	S. son of David Dalmage, U.E.
Dafoe, Widow	And one son.
Deane, Moses	A wife.
Dyre, John	S.
Davis, Joseph	S.
Dodge, Thomas	A wife and 2 sons. Prov'd. Johnstown soldier R.R.N.Y. N.McL.
Drew, Paul	A wife and 5 children. Common settler. N.McL.
Dobins, Henry	L. 44th Regiment.
Davis, John	A wife. Soldier Loyal Rangers.
Dixon, Widow, and	3 children.
Dowling, John	A wife.
Duckler, Andrew	S,
Dutcher, Derrick	55 years of age ; a settler. Came to Canada in March, 1785. Capt. John Jones' list.
Davis, John	S, N.C.O. Butler's Rangers. S. G.
Doughedy, Samuel	Carleton Island.
Dennys, Nicholas	Waiting to bring up his Crop. R.R. N.Y. M. Roll.
Darron, Conrod	At Montreal.
Dusler, Andrew	" Soldier R.R.N.Y. M.Roll
Dusler, William	" " " J.F.
Darkness, Adam	Loyalist ; much persecuted.
Davis, John	Soldier R.R.N.Y. M. Roll.
Donaldson, John	55th Regiment.

APPENDIX B. 293

Names,	Remarks.
Daley, John	84th Regiment
Dogstader, George	Sergeant, Marysburg.
DeGray, —	Sergeant, Charlottenburg.
Daly, Patrick	Captain R.R.N.Y. Paymaster.
Darey, Thomas	" " "
Delaney, Peter	Ensign " "
Depenciere, Theodore	Lieutenant German Troops. Regt. Prince Frederick.
Dalton, Walter	Sergeant 47th Regiment and King's; draft to 8th.
Drummond, —	Ensign British Regiment.
Dequindre, Antonie	Lieutenant Indian Department.
Dequindre, Fonteney	" " "
Dequindre, Francis	" " "
Dequindre, William	"
Doyle, Dennis	Official Service, 84th Regiment.
Dermond, Timothy	84th Regiment.
Dice, Charles	Loyalist.
Dean, Jonathan	Detroit Volunteers.
Dugan, William	8th Regiment.
Dequindre, Dagnis	Lieutenant Indian Department.
Dafoe, Abraham, Jun.	King's Rangers.
Dafoe, Jacob	" "
Dafoe, Martin	" "
Dafoe, William (deserted)	" "
Davis, Abel	" "
Derrick, Philip	" "
Dibble, Asa	" "
Dimors, Jacob, Sen.	" "
Dimors, John	" "
Davis, Jonathan	" "
Dennis, Jacob, Jun	Senior Soldier R.N.N.Y. M. Roll.
Dandoist, John Henry	German soldier.
Darder, Martin	" "
Demoree, David	Soldier associated Loyalist.
Dawson, Solomon	Soldier 44th Regiment.
Deserontyo John	Captain Mohawk Chief.
Demont, William	Captain T.L., 1792.
Dougherty, Edward	T.L. 1792, from Ireland.
Darley, John	T.L. 1792, from England.
Dalton, John	B. Rangers.
Donaldson, James	Sergeant 8th Regiment.
Dodemead, John	" "
Desmond, John	Soldier 8th Regiment.
Decker, Jacob	
Deil, T	
Devis, David or Davison	Soldier Butler's Rangers.
Daily, George	
Dennis, Nathaniel	

294　　　　　　　　APPENDIX B.

NAMES.	REMARKS.
Dtzcernian, Henrick...............	
Deal, Adam........................	Soldier R.R.N.Y.
Dogstader, Pompey	
Dantz, John.......................	
Dunberry, John....................	Soldier R.R.N.Y. Muster Roll.
Dish, Henry	
Doclimicle, John	Sergeant 8th Regiment.
Daly, William	I. Soldier R.R.N.Y. Muster Roll.
Dopp, John........................	A.　　　"　　　"
Dopp, Adam	A.　　　"　　　"
Dure, John........................	N.B.　　"　　　"
Dougherty, John	I.　　　"　　　"
Daily, Philip	A.　　　"　　　"
Devan, Cornelius	I. Corporal "　　　"
Deckins, George	A. Major Close's list, 1788.
Dyce, George	German (or Dyer　"
Disc, Jacob.......................	Loyalist　　　　　"
Donahooe, James	Ireland　　　　　"
Douglas, Thomas	Artificer, P. to L.B.L. 1790.
Dame, Capt. George	Butler's Rangers.
Duberry, John	Soldier 50th Regiment; discharged June 24th, 1784.
Davis, James	Soldier Loyal Rangers.
Duntan, Levi	"　　　"
Dunham, Samuel	"　　　"
Davis, Benjamin	"　　　"
Dunham, Solomon	"　　　"
Dawson, John	"　　　"
Drake, Benjamin	"　　　"
Davis, Daniel.....................	"　　　"
Dodge, Peter	Soldier R.R.N.Y. J.F.
Dugan, Cornelius	"　New York Volunteers.
Dunmead, William	"　Jersey Volunteers. Petition.
Dougharty, Anthony..............	Bore Arms in North Carolina. U.E.
Dugan, Thomas	Clerk and Storekeeper, Indian Department. O.C., 96.
Drew, Francis	Sergeant 34th Regiment.
Donnelly, Henry	Common settler (deceased). A.McL.
Dykes, Thomas	Soldier Butler's Rangers. W.D.
Deer, John	Soldier 53rd Regt. A. Campbell's certificate.
Doole, John.......................	Soldier 29th Regiment. Petition 1809. Transferred 200. Clerk to H. Spencer.
Elsworth, Henry	A wife and child. Provisioned at Cataraqui.
Ellison, Joseph	S.
Elmer, John......................	And Wife.
Eamer, Peter	A wife and child.

APPENDIX B. 295

Names.	Remarks.
Eamer, Philip.....................	A wife.
Evickhouse, Henry	A wife. Soldier R.R.N.Y. J.F.
Elliot, John.......................	A wife and ten children. A settler, came in March, 1785.
Elliot, Juda......................	S. Son of John. A settler, came in March, 1785.
Elliot, Samuel	A wife and six children. Settler, p. P. to L.B.L., 1791. Came in in March, 1785. Capt. John Jones' list.
Erling, Frank, } absentees .... Erling, John,	to Johnstown.
Empson, Robert.................	6 years in the Rangers. W.D.
Earp, Richard	8th Regiment.
Elliot, John.......................	B. Rangers.
Empson, John	"
Ellice, John.......................	Soldier 84th Regt.
Eddy, Daniel	King's Rangers.
Egleton, Eliab	" "
Estdo, Jacob	German Soldier.
Eustace, —	Lieut. T. L., 1792.
Embry John - Embra	84th Regt. Say ship carpenter. H. Ellott, 1805.
Enderdier, Christopher	
Ellis, Henry	
Ellsworth, Alexander	
Egar, Lambert	
Espie, William	
Essling, Garret	A. Soldier R.R.N.Y. Muster Roll.
Elloms, John	A. " "
Earhart, Simon	Soldier R.R.N.Y.
Ekins, Moses	Soldier Loyal Rangers.
Ernest, Anthony	" "
Eustman, Amherst	" a Loyalist. J.F.
Every, William	A settler in 1785. O.E. Came in March, 1785.
Estell, Daniel.....................	Joined Lord Cornwallis in 1782. Soldier. Capt. Leeman's.
Faddle, John	S. Provisioned at Cataraqui.
Ferguson, Jonathan	A wife and two sons.
Friar, Mr. J.	And child.
Ferguson, Widow.................	Two sons and two daughters.
Fraser, Collin....................	
Farling, John....	Wife and one child.
Fikes, Daniel	A wife, three sons and one daughter.
Foster, Adam......................	S. Soldier R.R.N.Y. Muster Roll.
Freist, John	A wife and six children.
Fundy, Janone or Tanno............	Fonda—a black soldier. J.F. Batteaux Service. Herckmer.

Names.	Remarks.
Finlayson, John	A wife.
Franks, Widow	And one child.
Fridt, Deborah	And son.
Frier, Mrs.	And child – absent.
Fuster, Andrew	At Cataraqui.
Fusow, Andrew	Niagara.
Freeze, Jacob	Gone to the States. R.R.N.Y. Muster Roll.
Flumberry, William	Gone to the States.
Fearman, William	Soldier 29th Regiment.
Foryea, John	B. Rangers.
Frelick, Abraham	"
Frelick, Clement	"
Frelick, Jacob	"
Fredenburgh, Mathias	"
Freeman, Francis	84th Regiment.
Ferris, William	King's Rangers.
Fleming, Patrick	B. Rangers.
Facer, Harry	Seige of Quebec, and engaged smith to Marine Department.
Fancher, P.	84th Regiment.
Ferre, Andrew	B. Rangers.
Filplay, C.	44th Regiment.
Finlay, Samuel	B. Rangers.
Forsyth, William	60th Regiment.
Fraser, Alexander	Guards and Nova Scotia Volunteers.
Fry, Joseph	B. Rangers.
Frehery, Lawrence	Marine Department, Lake Erie.
Ferhan, William	Discharged sailor, Marine Dept.
Finch, John	Called a good Loyalist.
Fowler, Jonathan	Ensign.
Foye, Lewis	44th Regiment.
Freil (the late), by Deborah	In His Majesty's service.
Friot, Isaac	(Lieut.) Cuyliers.
Fraser, Jean	Que: If the military land of Corp'l. Wm. Fraser.
Filfield, John	King's Rangers.
Filo, Samuel	" "
Filo, Thomas	" "
Fisher, James	" "
Fitzgerald, William	" "
Fosborough, John	Soldier Loyal Rangers.
Frost, James	
Fortiere, Pierre	Mate, Marine Department.
Falconer, Thomas	Soldier 84th Regiment.
Futreal, John	" 60th "
Fleming, John	Out-pensioner. Sergt. 53rd Regt.
Fisher, John	Niagara German soldier.
Freeman, Richard	Soldier R.R.N.Y. Muster Roll.

APPENDIX B. 297

NAMES.	REMARKS.
Forbes, Nicholas	B. Rangers.
Forsyth, I. T. & Robert	Sons of William, 60th Regiment.
French, John	British seaman.
Furlow, Jacob	B. Rangers.
Furlow, Cornelius	"
Fournier, Andrew	A sailor.
Fagan, Arthur	Soldier, 53rd Regiment.
Fridel, Ignace	German soldier.
Faulstroth, Henry	" "
Fairfax, Christian	T. Loyalist, 1792. From England.
French, Frederick	"
Fagan, Thomas	T. Loyalist, from Ireland.
Fauscett, Silas	
Fairel, John	
Frowman, John	
Fotlick, Adrian	
Ferguson, John	Soldier Loyal Rangers.
Le Forrest, Abraham	
Fidget, James	
Ford, Jacob	
Fulton, Michael	I. Soldier R.R.N.Y. Muster Roll.
Frats, David	A. " " "
Fragstorm, Michael	F. " " "
Freeland, John	A. " " "
Fries, Abraham	A. " " "
Finknor, John	A. " " "
Fares, Thomas	Loyalist. Major Close's List, 1788.
Fares, Joseph	" " "
Fisher, Frederick	" " "
Fyke, Francis	" R.R.N.Y. J.F.
Fulman, Nicholas	A soldier 62nd Regt. p. Mr. Patterson's certificate.
Farrel, Patrick	Soldier 31st Regt. P. to L.B.L.
Francis, John	A discharged soldier 34th Regt. S.G. L.B. Nassau, 1794.
Ferguson, John	Quartermaster Loyal Rangers.
Ferrel, Amherst	Soldier Loyal Rangers.
Falterer, John	" "
Falteroth, John	" "
Falkner, John	" "
Ferris, England	" "
Frink, Andrew	" "
Fraser, James	" "
French, Andrew	" "
Fredick, Dedrick	" "
Francis, Jeremiah Wm.	" "
Ferguson, James	Soldier R.R.N.Y. J.F.
Fraser, Alexander	Roxboro'. A common settler. N. McL.

S

APPENDIX B.

Names.	Remarks.
Fitzimmon, Barney	Soldier 60th Regt. N.McL.
Flynn, David	Loyalist. J.Fd.
Fraser, Peter	Son of Simon, who died in prison, 1777. N.McL.
Fock, John	Son of Henry Focks, or Fykes, R. R.N.Y. N.McL.
Faddle, George	Incorporated Loyalist. Gen. Haldimand's certificate.
Fisher, Duncan	Of Montreal; served with General Burgoyne.
Farrell, Patrick	Soldier 31st Regt. at Coteau du Lac.
Fields, Nathan	Sergeant B. Rangers.
Gibson, Widow and 1 daughter	Provis'd at Cataraqui.
Gathaway, John	S. " "
Grosse, Edward	" "
Grout, Henry	" "
Gronber, Paul	S. " "
German, John Jun	S. Soldier Loyal Rangers.
Grant, Widow and 3 children	Provis'd at Johnstown.
Gorman, John	S.
Goff, Joseph	S.
Gaskin, Charles	S.
Grout, Theodore	S. Son of Mr. Grout, Issuing Commissary Loyalist. J.F. N.McL.
Gibson, Andrew	S. Soldier. R.R.N.Y. J.F.
Griffin, Samuel	S. Came to Canada March, 1785. A settler. Capt. John Jones' list.
Going, Francis	A wife and 3 children. Provi'sd at Niagara.
Graves, John	Wife and child. Not come up.
Grass, Charles	to Canada.
Grevase, Asa	Jessup's.
Gleeson, Daniel	Soldier 84th Regiment.
Glenn, Jacob	Lieut. R.R.N.Y.
Graves, George	Lt. from the Southward.
Gummersall, Thomas	Capt. R.R.N.Y.
Garrett, Daniel	Loyalist and Express in the War.
Gill, Robert	103rd Regiment.
Granger, Zacharias	King's Rangers.
Gleeson, Thomas	" " deserted.
Goshee Peter (the late)	By Daniel Gleeson, 84th Regiment.
Girty, George	Partisan all the War. U.E.
Godfrey, G.	Governor Hamilton.
Goodnight, John	Butler's Rangers.
Grubb, Thomas	Loyalist.
Guin, Nicholas	Lieut. Minute men.
Grindstone, Jacob	Seaman on Lake Ontario.
Glinger, George	8th Regiment.

APPENDIX B.

NAMES.	REMARKS.
Guthrie, Robert	Surgeon B. Rangers.
Gilchrist, John	Sergt. Elizabethtown, Loyal Rangers.
Grant, Alexander	" Charlottenburgh.
Grant, Allan	" Elizabethtown.
Gill, John De Courcy	Hospital mate of Canada.
Goose, John	Soldier. W.D.
Grant, Archibald	Lieut. 84th Regiment.
Gahagan, Edward	Marine Department.
Gamble. John	Hospital mate last war.
Garner, the late Matthew (by John)	Soldier American War.
Gibson, George	Ship Carpenter and Ordnance Service, Gibraltar.
Grant, Alexander	Commodore Naval Depart. Lake Erie
Graves, Adam	Captain " " "
Grout, John	R.R.N.Y.
Green, Caleb	Ensign King's Rangers.
Green, Roger	Soldier " "
Gamlin, Widow	Their husbands both served his Majesty. Gowin—son—an officer, was killed.
Gowin, Widow	
Grichel, John	German soldier.
Gerhart, Ernette	" "
Gorman, Sigismond	" "
Giles, Thomas	Treasury L., 1792. Had been a soldier in H. M. service in America.
Goode, William	Treasury L., 1792. Emigrant from England.
Girbig, Carl Wilhelm	
Grendel, Francis	
Grant, Thomas	
Grum, Elijah	
Golden, John	
Goned, John	
Green, Charles	
Goon, John	Soldier 84th Regiment.
Grant, Hugh	N.B. Soldier R.R.N.Y. Muster Roll.
Gray, Philip	F. " " "
Gordon, George	Soldier in McAlpine's Corps. L.B.L., 1791.
Griffin, Charles	Soldier in Jessup's Corps. L.B.L., 1791.
Gay, Jane	Widow of Peter Foster—a soldier, drowned in 1780.
Gaven, Thomas	Soldier Loyal Rangers.
Gillet, Adonijah	" "
Goodwilly, Joseph	" "
Gilles, John	" "
Gordineer, Robert	" "
Garhard, Mathew	" "

APPENDIX B.

NAMES.	REMARKS.
Gervey, John	Soldier Loyal Rangers.
Gallermoult, Baptiste	" "
Gilbert, Josiah	" Non-Commissioned Officer King's A. Regiment.
Green, Peter	Soldier of Delaney's Corps.
Gorin, Francis	Quartermaster General's Department at Quebec in 1776.
Grant, George	Osnabruck. A common settler. N. McL.
Goulden, Thomas	Soldier Butler's Rangers. L.B.L.
Houff, or Huff, Christian	S. A soldier in a German Regiment.
Hoffman, Josiah	A wife and one child.
Ham, John	S.
Hagadoorn, Jacob	A wife and two children.
Harns, Thomas	S.
Hicks, George	S.
Hainer, Barnett	S.
Howell, Widow	S.
Hailman, Peter	S. Soldier, German Troops.
Huniman, Henry	A wife and child.
Huffnegle, Widow	and four children.
Harkmer, Mathew	S.
Hicks, Thomas	S.
Haveline, Mathew	S. German soldier, J. F.
Hoxey, Samuel	S.
Hinman, John	S.
Hetherington, C.	S.
Huckey, John	S.
Hopper, Conrad	Soldier R. R. N. Y., J. F.
Hayne, Henry	A wife and son soldier R. R. N. Y., Muster Roll.
Hynes, Adam	Wife and seven children.
Haislip, James	A wife, Butler's Rangers, L.B.N.
Hutchison, Wm	S.
Hammon, John	S.
Houghlang, James	S.
Hoff, Hans and wife	Soldier R. R. N. Y. Muster Roll.
Hilton, Lawrence	S. Coteau du Lac.
House, Conrod	Corpl. Sophiasburg.
Heyser, Frederick	
Heysick, John	
Hendider, Christopher	Quitted his land.
Harley, Christopher	Niagara.
Hicks, James	
Huntsinger, Jacob	Gone to the States.
Hattingbrant, Jacob	" " Soldier R.R. N. Y. Muster Roll.
Houghtail, Joseph	Gone to the States for his family.

APPENDIX B. 301

NAMES.	REMARKS.
Hay, Joseph	Lt.-Govr. of Detroit.
Hay, Henry	Lieut. R. R. N. Y.
Hilliard, Nathaniel	Lieut. Indian Dept.
Holland, John Frederick	Lieut. R. R. N. Y.
Hannah, Samuel	Soldier King's Rangers.
Heron or Herring Elliot	" "
Henderson, Archibald	" "
Henderson, James	" "
High, William	" "
Hericks, John	" "
Hix, George	" "
Huffman, Conrod	" "
Hall, Thomas	King's or 8th Regt. 3 years' man.
Harboth, Frederick	Regt. of Brunswick, Lunenburgh..
Harness, Michael	B. Rangers.
Harpur, Thomas	" "
Hill, Patrick	" "
Hobbs, John	U. E.
Hainer, Zechariah	B. Rangers.
Hamilton, John	" "
Hamilton, Robert	" " Soldier R.R.N.Y. M.Roll.
Hamilton William	" " " R.R.N.Y. M.Roll.
Hambro, John	Carpenter's mate in several ships.
Haffy, William	Surgeon.
Harkimar, John	Soldier B. Rangers.
Harrow, Alexander. Esq	Naval Dep't Lake Erie.
Haywood, James	M. Claimant.
Heron, Owen	Sergt.-Major 84th Regt.
Hutchings, John	Served during the whole war.
Hamilton, Colin	Corpl. Cornwall or Roxborough, 84th Regt.
Hay, John	Sergt. Charlottenburg.
Henly, Thomas	" Hawkesbury.
Holmes, Thomas	" Oznabruch.
Hurd, Thomas	" Fredericksburg.
Hoff or Huff, Andrew	8th Regt.
Hogedone, Harmanus	B. Rangers.
Humphrey, Emanuel	N. C. officer, Butler's Rangers.
Herns, John	Soldier R. R. N. Y.
Herring, John	" "
Holmes, James	Col. or Lt. Col. from the Southward.
Hoppenad, Frederick	German soldier.
Hock, George	" "
Hock, Godfrey	" "
Haner, David	" "
Hill, Isaac	Captain, Mohawk Chief.
Hill, Aaron	" " "
Hewitt, John, no privilege	Treasury L. 1792, Emigrant E.
Hewitt, Thomas, "	" " Emigrant E.

302   APPENDIX B.

NAMES.	REMARKS.
Howell, William.................	Son of John, senr..................
Howell, John....................	Served in time of the French war in America.
Howell, John, Junr...............	Treasury L. 1792, son of John, Senr.
Holmes, Charles....	" "
Herchfield, Frederick	" " of German Troops.
Holdford, William................	" " Emigrant from Eng.
Horsfall, Joseph	" "
Herner. Frederick................	" " Soldier, Ger.Troops.
Humphreys, Thomas	" " had been in America.
Holmes, Joseph	" "
Hill, Patrick	B. Rangers, W. D.
Holmes, Hugh	Loyalist, W. D.
Hazard, John....................	" " U. E.
Hill, Jacob	" "
Hanger, Frederick................	
Hogerman. Andrew	
Henrick, William	
Hanington, Cornelius	
Helmick, George.................	
Horn, Frederick	
Humbleman, John	
Houfman, Frederick..............	
Hearse, Andrew..................	
Hoks, Joseph	
High, John	
Hart, Jonathan	
Hons, John	
Henderson, John	
Haly, George	Soldier 44th Regt.
Hooste or Huest, John	Served in Refugees at New York, W. List.
Hartly, David	Loyalist Major Close's List, W. D., 1788.
Haston, Izrail....................	A. Soldier R.R.N.Y. Muster Roll.
Hubor, Adam....................	F. " " "
House, Chroust	A. " " "
Heith, John.....................	F. " " "
Howell, Griffith..................	A. " " "
Hales, John	I. " " "
Hope, Richard	E. " " "
Henning, Henry	F. " " "
Havilin, Benjamin	A. " " "
Holland, David	E. " " "
Hylard, Nicholas	A. " " "
Herring, Nathaniel...............	A. " " "
Herring, Henry..................	A. " " "
Haines, Henry	A. " " "
Hinmand, Benjamin	A. " " "
Horner, William.................	A. " " "

APPENDIX B. 303

Names.	Remarks.
Hyatt, Cornelius	Soldier Loyal Rangers.
Hamerla, John	Hessian soldier.
Havens, John	A settler in 1787. See P. 1794.
Hagan, Samuel	Soldier 57th Regt., P. L. B. L.
Hyde, Ephraim	Settler from Vermont, P. to L. B. L. 1790.
Holowager, George Godfrith	Sergt., German Troops, P. to L.B.L. 1790.
Hilliker, John	Sergt. Loyal Rangers.
Harris, Jonathan	Soldier "
Harris, Richard	" "
Hard, Limon	" "
Hewet, Henry	" "
Haath, Phineas	" "
Hiens, Godfrey	" "
Holland, John Andrew	" "
Hiclle, Andrew	" "
Huttinger, Adam	" "
Hogelen, Henry	" "
Helliker, Abraham	" "
Hard, Elisha	" "
Hoyt, Abraham	" "
Hubbel, Isaac	" "
Hunter, Moses	" "
Hill, Timothy	" "
Hand, John	" "
Hoffman, Jabest	" "
Holstead, Emas	" "
Hutchison, George	" "
Hervey, David	" "
Huntly, John	" "
Harman, Valentine	" "
Hoy, Alexander	" "
Hyatt, Gilbert	" "
Hogle, John	" "
Hawly, Eli	" "
Hogle, George	" "
Hogedale, Christopher	" "
Hogedale, John	" "
Huddleman, John Andrew	" "
Hoeman, John	" "
Hagerdoon, Peter	" "
Hogan, Edward	" "
Heymond, John, (died Sept., 1783)	" "
Hosier, Joseph	" "
Haines, George	A soldier Butler's Rangers J.F.
Hartle, Henry	Son of a Loyalist, J. F.
Harman, Henry	Soldier German Troops.
Hustis, Lieut. James	Of Col. Emrick's Corps.

APPENDIX B.

Names.	Remarks.
Hope, Richard	Soldier R.R.N.Y., I. F.
Hough, George	Soldier 2nd Batt. R.R.N.Y., H.Spencer's Certificate.
Harris, David	Soldier King's Rangers, T. Bell's Certificate.
Hall, Isaac	Cornwall, joined in 1777, A. McL.
Hesford, Joseph	R.R.N.Y. "
Ham, Malachi	Soldier Butler's Rangers ; after the reduction he removed to New Brunswick, from whence he has lately returned p. letter from R. Clench, 24th January, 1807.
Hevett, Thomas	Soldier 31st Regt., p. Petition, 1809.
Howley, Zadoc	Soldier King's Rangers, L. Bd, M.D.
Hetlar, Adam	Soldier 2nd Batt. R.R.N.Y., Certificate of Andrew Kimmerly.
Hainer, Henry	Soldier Butler's Rangers, R. Clench's affidavit.
Ilard, James	Of Jessup's.
Iredale, Abraham	Lieut. of Guides and Pioneers.
Johnson, Judah	Prov'd at Cataraqui.
James, Daniel	S.
Jinks, Joseph	A wife and nine children, Incorporated Loyalist.
Johnson, John	S. prov'd at Johnstown, R.R.N.Y., J. F.
Johnson, Samuel	A wife and two children.
Johnson, Jacob	S.
Jago, Henry	S. Soldier B. Rangers.
Jacob, Christian	Wife and 1 child, soldier B. Rangers.
Jacks,	Widow and three children
Jones, William	Absent, soldier Loyal Rangers.
Jacobs, James	" to Johnstown.
Jones, James	Sergt. of Oznabruck.
Jacobs, George	Said to have been employed.
Johnson, Patrick	B. Rangers.
Jones, J., or John	" and Seige of Quebec.
Jones, John	Sergt. 60th Regiment.
Joes, Isaac	King's Rangers.
Jones, John	Treasury L. Emigrant fromEngland..
Jarden, Peter	Not privileged. Frenchman.
Jones, David	H. D. Settler in 1787.
Jack, William	
Jost, Christopher	
Johnson, Charles	I. a soldier R.R.N.Y. Muster Roll.
Johns, Daniel	Resided in the States after the War P. 1797.
Jones, Ephraim	Soldier Loyal Rangers.

APPENDIX B. 305

Names.	Remarks.
Jadscheak, John	Soldier Loyal Rangers.
Johnson, Jonathan	" "
Jackson, John	" "
Jackson, William (died March, 1783.)	" "
Innice, Gilbert	" "
Jacobs, John	" "
Jobear, Francis	" "
Jackson, Edward	Soldier 29th Regt.
Johnson, Jacob	Son of Conrad Johnson. T. Dix.
Johnson, David, of Cornwall	Cornwall, settler from England J. F.
Jones, Elpheus	Son of Elisha who joined in 1775, and after the Peace of 1783 went to Nova Scotia. O. E.
Johns, Edad	Common settler in 1786. O. E.
John, Hugh	" " 1786. O. E.
Koughnett, Michael	A wife and four children, Sergeant, Fredericksburg.
Kerr, Robert	A wife and one child, Surgeon, R.R.N.Y.
Keif, Francis	S. soldier 53rd Regt., O.C., 30th August, 1797, 300.
Kizer, John	S. soldier R.R.N.Y. Muster Roll.
Knave, John	" " "
Kentner, John	" " p. Genl. Haldimand's Certificate.
Kelsey, John	Settler, came into Canada, March 1785. Capt. John Jones' Certe.
Kilman, Philip	A wife, prov'd at Niagara.
Kippas, John	" P. Fort Erie.
Knapp, George	" and two children, P. Detroit.
Koughnott, John	S. gone to the States, soldier R.R.N.Y.
Knave, Adam	S. gone to the States, soldier R.R.N.Y. Muster Roll.
King, Patrick	Lachine, soldier R.R.N.Y. M. Roll.
Kilburne, Charles	of Jessup's—not in.
Keller, Daniel	Lieut.
Ketler, Lewis	Lieut. Brunswick's Corps.
Ketler, William	Soldier King's Rangers.
Knight, Charles	Sergt. Williamsburg.
Knought,	Sergt. Sophiasburg.
Killing, or Keeling, Luke	Provincial Marine Department.
Kind, Thomas	8th Regt.
Kahmann, I. H.	Said to have been a Sergt. in Col. Creutzberg's Chasseurs.
Kettle, Jeremiah	
Kenner, Thomas	Discharged seaman from L. Erie.
Klengenbrummer, Nicholas	do from Col. Bryman's Grenadiers of Brunswick, 1783.

APPENDIX B.

NAMES.	REMARKS.
Klenzmann, Daniel	German soldier.
Koeing, John	" "
Krickel, Nicholas	" "
Ketler, Henry	Soldier R.R N.Y.
Kerlin, John	Y. Loyalist, emigrant from England.
Kidden, Thomas	8th Regt.
Kelly, Thomas	84th "
Kennedy, Andrew	
Korunme, Dingmund	
Kersy, William	
Kelly, Mathew	
Keese, Hendrick	
Kappas, Daniel	
Kelly, Joseph	
Kilman, John	A soldier R.R.N.Y. Muster Roll.
Kisker, Donald	N. B. " "
Kyser, Michael	A. soldier R.R.N.Y. Muster Roll.
Karn, Jacob	A. " "
Ketchum, David	A. " "
Kelly, John	Soldier 84th Regimeet.
Kelly, Martin	Sergeant Loyal Rangers.
Ketchum, Ephraim	Soldier " "
Keith, Cornelius	" " "
Kingsheart, Elisha	" " "
Knar, John,	" " "
Ketch, Cornelius	" " "
Kingsberry, Joseph	" " "
Kniskarn, Henry	Soldier Butler's Rangers.
Kilmire, Nicholas	A settler E. J.
Kayne, Michael	Soldier R.R.N.Y., J. F.
Kilmire (alias Byrne), Philip	" " J. F.
Kanabensten, George	Soldier 34th Regiment, W. Dickson.
Lancette, James	Soldier Prov'd. at Cataraqui 34th Regt.
Levings, Jedediah	S.
Lindsay, James, Senr	S.
Lucky, Samuel	A soldier R.R.N.Y. Certe. H. Spencer.
Laughya, William	S.
Loft, David	S. soldier R.R.N.Y.
Loyd, Henry	S.
Long, Conradt	S.
Lawray, John	S. R.R.N.Y. M. Roll.
Lewis, Frederick	A wife and two children, a settler, J. F. Came to Canada, March 1785. Captain John Jones' list.
Leahy, Lodowick	S. Prov'd. at Niagara.
Lawrence, James	S.
Leikee, Conrad	S.

APPENDIX B.

NAMES.	REMARKS.
Long, Philip	S.
Lansingh, P. P	Lieutenant R.R.N.Y.
Lundergan, Cornelius	On board of King's vessel.
Louks, Peter	Montreal soldier R.R.N.Y. M. Roll.
Low, Nicholas	States for his family.
Lake, Israel	Soldier Loyal Rangers.
Lampman, Abraham, Senr	" "
Lampman, Abraham, Junr	" "
Leatch, William	" "
Lent, Elias	" "
Liddle, Andrew	" "
Losee, Pompo	" "
Lucas, Daniel	" "
Lummis, Ezekiel	" "
Long, Peter	8th Regiment.
Lyons William	"
Langan, Patrick	Lieutenant R.R.N.Y.
Lipscombe, Patrick	Captain "
Lamotte, William	Gov. Hamilton, Capt. Indian Dept.
Laws, Jacob	German Troop.
Lawler, J	Siege of Quebec.
Lebrete, Alexis	Governor Hamilton.
Lepage (dit Amont), J. B	84th Regiment.
Lewis, Nathaniel	B. Rangers.
Lisbourne, John	"
Lickemburg, Michael	60th Regiment.
Little, James	Loyalist U. E. by Major Mathews.
Long, Phili	Loyalist.
Lucas, Conrod	8th Regiment.
Lyons, George	U. E.
Lawe, George	Captain 84th Regiment.
Lamaire, Christopher	Sergeant.
Lemoine, Henry	Ensign 84th Regiment.
Link or Lynk, Benjamin	Soldier R.R.N.Y.
Livingston, Benjamin	Officer 2nd Battalion R.R.N.Y.
Lindsay, Samuel	Captain Guides and Pioneers.
Long, Edward	Boatswain.
Linch, Frederick	German soldier.
Lemon, Jacob	Settler in 1789.
Loyd, William	T. Loyalist had been in America.
Loyd, John	" son of William.
Loyd, Edward	" " "
Lindsay, Edward	"
Lewis, Nathan	B. Rangers.
Lakey, Henry	
Lutes, John	A settler.
Lang, Philip F	
Louks, Adam	
Landregan, Cornelius	

APPENDIX B.

Names.	Remarks.
Londers, James	
Lensing, David	
Lickemburner, Nicholas	Soldier 60th Regiment W. List.
Lans, Jacob	German soldier, taken prisoner in Virginia.
Loveless, Ebenezer	Served in Burgoyne's Expedition.
Lessley, John	Soldier R.R.N.Y. Muster Roll.
Lockwood, James	" " "
Lockwood, Peter	" " "
Lewis, John	" " "
Lubdel, James	" " "
Lawyer, John	" " "
Langden, Richard	" " "
Loveless, Jeremiah	Emigrant settler.
Loveless, James	Son of Thomas, a subaltern in the late Queen's Rangers, p. P. to L.B. L. 1790, 200 granted for himself.
Loveless, Thomas	Soldier Loyal Rangers.
Lamphear, William	" "
Lamphear, Samuel	" "
Light, Benjamin	" "
Loughy, William	" "
Lonsow, Joseph	" "
Leib, John	" "
Logan, David	" "
Lean, John	" "
Lightheart, John	" "
Lester, Thomas, Senr	" "
Leonard, Baldoff	" "
Lebarge, Jean	" "
Loucks, William	Son of Richard Loucks.
Lewis, Frederick	A settler.
Lauden, Benjamin	A settler.
Lonsburry, Isaac	Soldier Butler's Rangers.
Loucks, John	Oznabruck a common settler N.McL.
Leonard, John	Major Holland's guides one year.
Link, Jacob	Son of Mathias, Senr. N.McL.
La Forge, Vincent	Interpreter to Six Nation Indians.
Lee, William	A Black, volunteer with Capt. Bird, 8th Regiment.
Morey, John	A wife and four children. Prov'd at Cataraqui.
Miller, Conradt	S.
Miller, Elisha	S.
Miller, Justice	S.
Mabee, Abraham	A wife and four children. Capt. Incorporated Loyalists.
Mathews, Thomas E	S. A settler.

APPENDIX B. 309

NAMES.	REMARKS.
Martin, Emas	A wife and three children. Prov'd at Johnstown.
Maxfield, John	A wife.
Malone, William	S.
Munroe, Alexander	A wife and five children.
Matice, Henry	S. Soldier Butler's Rangers, see Mary P.'s P.
Mahanes, John	S.
Morden, Daniel	S. Soldier R.R.N.Y. Muster Roll.
Mott, Joseph	S. Soldier R.R.N.Y. M. Roll.
Mines, George	S. of German Troop. N. McL, and two children.
Morrison, Widow	
Mercle, Catherine	S.
March, Thomas	A wife and child, soldier 84th Regt. p. discharged, came Sept. 24, 1807.
Medaugh, Peter	A wife and son, a settler.
Mitchell, Agnes	One other woman and child.
Mount, Moses	S. Sergt. Butler's Rangers.
Money, Michael	S. Abst. from Cataraqui.
Morland, John	A wife and child, gone off.
Marland	
Miller, Samuel	Quebec.
Morvin, Daniel	Montreal.
Marcelius, Sevories	Gone to the States,R.R.N.Y. M.Roll.
Meilly	Canada.
Mitchell, Winard	Soldier R.R.N.Y., M. Roll.
Moor, Francis	Soldier King's Rangers.
Morehouse, John	Corpl. "
Morehouse, William	Drummer "
Mosher, Benjamin	Soldier "
Munro, Elijah	" "
Murison, Jonathan	" "
Miller, Jeremiah	" B. Rangers.
Midaugh, George	" "
Mitchell, Gilbert	" "
Muirhead, James	Surgeon Mate 60th Regt.
Maun, Isaac	Lieut. R.R.N.Y.
Maun, John	Ensign "
Miller	Capt. King's Rangers.
Margaon, Thomas	Sergt. Marysburgh.
Miller, Nathaniel	Detroit Volunteers and Pro. Navy.
Moor, Laurent	" " "
Murphy, John	Soldier R.R.N.Y., M. Roll.
March, Josiah	Soldier R.R.N.Y.
Maisenville, Alexis	Capt. with Gov. Hamilton.
Martin, John	Firm Loyalist.
Martin, Thomas	Near five years in the Navy.
Myers, Michel Andrew	1st Bat. 60th Regt. 25 yrs. N.C.Officer.
Melvin, Meredith	Lieut. Marine Dept.

APPENDIX B.

NAMES.	REMARKS.
Miles, James	Loyalist, served during war.
Minzies, James	Soldier.
Margan or Morgan, William	Sergt. Oznabruck 53rd Regt.
Mitchell, John	Drum Major, Williamsburgh.
Mosher, Hezekiah	Augusta settler, R.J.D.G.
Miller, Ulrich	German Soldier.
Moenneke, John Fredk.	"
Miller, John	84th Regt.
Milton, Thomas	Treasury Loyalist.
Milton, Thomas, Jr	"
Mansfield, Martin	" Emigr't from Irel'd.
Mariner, Barrett	Wife and 5 children, Treasury Loyalist, Emigrant from Ireland.
Mompesson, Capt	Treasury Loyalist.
Morris, William	1792.
Morris, Nathaniel	ɩ "
Morton, Alexander	Seaman, Emigrant 1792.
Martine, Robert	
Mulloy, James	Indian Department.
Moody, Jonathan	
Marks, Christopher	
Monier, John	
Mirvay, James	
Milliard, Isaac	
Miglebury, Peter	
Misener, Leonard	
Mickler, Godfry	
Myers, Christian	Of Mountain, son of Michl. Myers, N. E., N.McL.
Myers, George	A soldier in German Corps,W.D.1788.
Messamore, John	Loyalist Major Close's list, "
Mellott, Peter	" "
Murray, Patrick	Soldier R.R.N.Y., Muster Roll.
Mills, Cornelius	" " and one Loyal Rangers.
Massey, James	Soldier R.R.N.Y., Muster Roll.
Martial, John	" "
Mechison, John	" "
Morrison, Angus	" "
Marsellis, Garret	" "
Muirhead, John	T.Loyalist, had been a sol. in America.
Mann, William	Soldier R.R.N.Y. Muster Roll.
Mann, Edward	" "
Mitchell, Hugh	" "
Mantle, John Baptiste	" "
Miller, David	" "
Munro, Cornelius	" "
Mosier, John	" "
Miles, Thomas	" "

APPENDIX B. 311

NAMES.	REMARKS.
Mullen, John	Soldier R.R.N.Y. Muster Roll.
Murray, George	" "
Mindor, John	" "
Mallory, Ephraim	Settler from Vermont, L.B.L., 1790.
Mallory, Elisha	Drummer in Jessup's.
Mallory, Jeremiah	Soldier in Jessup's.
Munro, Israel	Late from New York, L.B.L., 1790.
Mires, Jacob	" " State " "
Mace, John	Soldier 8th Regt., L.B.L., 1790.
Mahan, Hugh	Soldier 60th Regt.
Mann, Thomas	Ensign Loyal Rangers.
Miller, Ralph	Soldier Loyal Rangers.
Maynard, Henry	" "
Moore, Jasper	" "
Michel, David	" "
Mead, James	" "
Mock, John	" "
Mitchel, David	" "
Mott, Henry	" "
Maxwell, William	" "
Millers, John	" "
Mosier, Christopher	" "
Moffit, William	" "
Mitchel, John	" "
Myers, Philip	Son of Michael Myers, U.E., J.F.
Mulroy, John	Soldier 84th Regt.
Mukle, Richard	Soldier R.R.N.Y.
Murchison, Murdo	" "
Morgan, Kinzie	Drummer 29th, 34th or 53rd.
Mengis, James	Soldier 26th and 29th Regiments.
Murphy, John	Drummer Butler's Rangers.
Monk, William	Soldier "
Millon, John	Soldier German Troops.
Mitchell, John	Lancaster soldier 44th Regt., N.McL.
Mott, Joseph	Soldier R.R,N.Y., J.F.
Mathews, Pompey	Black soldier, R.R.N.Y.. J.W.
Moore, Patrick	Soldier 44th Regt., p. Discharge.
Mabee, John	States that he remained in Sussex County till the close of the war.
Moor, William	Soldier 84th Regt.
Mills, John	Soldier 31st Regt.
Merwin, Elnathan	Served under Gen. Burgoyne, not resident, O.E.
Myers, Godfrey	Soldier R.R.N.Y., O.E.
Miller, Nathan	From Scotland, W.D.
Marchand, Francis	Soldier 84th Regt.
Mosley, George	Served in the Engineer Department.
Miller, Samuel	Incorporated Loyalist—at Ward's Block House.

APPENDIX B.

NAMES.	REMARKS.
Maracle, Henry	Soldier Butler's Rangers, S.G.
Miller, Jacob	" " "
Muirhead, James	Surgeon 60th Regt.
Moor, John	Soldier 8th Regt., p. discharge.
McAulay, James	Surgeon's Mate, Q.R.
McAlpine, the late, by Elizabeth	Captain,
McBride, Peter	Soldier 34th Regt.
McBride, John	Sergt. Q.R.
McCoye, Squire	Corpl. King's Rangers.
McKinnon, John	Captain Butler's "
McMichen, John	B. Rangers.
McNabb, Colin	Ensign Nova Scotia Volunteers.
McDonell, Angus	Lieut. 71st Regt.
McDonell, James	Ensign 84th "
McCarthy, Francis	Ensign R.R.N.Y., as McKenty.
McGiven, ——	Lieut. Delaney's.
McKay, William	" R.R.N.Y.
McKenzie, Alexr.	" "
McKenzie, Alexander	Ensign "
McLean, Allan	Lieut. 29th Regt.
McLean, Hector	" 84th "
McCarty, Edward	" 84th "
McDunach, ——	Loyalist, W.D.
McFarson, James	B. Rangers.
McGillies, Randall	do Sergeant.
McLaughlin, John	8th Regt.
McPherson, Daniel	84th "
McGregor, Gregor	Service at Detroit.
McCann, Andrew	Lieut. Q. Rangers.
McColgan, Adam	Soldier
McClellan, James	Soldier B. Rangers.
McDonell, Alexr.	Corpl. Q. "
McDonell, Patrick	Soldier R.R.N.Y. Muster Roll.
McFall, the late, by his daughter	Killed in the King's service.
McFarlane, John	Boat bldr. Served in various situations.
McMillan, Alexr.	Lieut. Delaney's.
McNabb, Allan	" Q. Rangers.
McTavish, Alexr.	Soldier in 74th Regt.
McKillop, Daniel	Sergt. in B. Rangers.
McGowin, Stephen	Soldier R.R.N.Y.
McMahon, John	
McGill, John	Qr. Master Q. Rangers.
McCarthy, Duncan	Corpl. Charlot'nb'g. R.R.N.Y.M.Roll.
McCaghey, John	" Williamsb'g. " "
McClure, John	" "
McNight, James	Sergt. Elizabeth Town.
McLean, Neal	Lieut. 84th Regt.
McArty, John	Soldier R.R.N.Y. M. Roll.
McKay, Francis	42nd Regt.

APPENDIX B. 313

Names.	Remarks.
McDonell, Henry or, James	Treasury L. English emigrant.
McGraugh, Garrett	Lieut. do.
McAlpine, and children	Treasury do.
McMullan, Neil	" do. from Staten Island.
McClay, Mrs.	"
McMullan, John	" do. Emigrant from Ireland.
McMullan, Alexr.	" do. " "
McMullan, Angus	" do. " "
McMullan, Catherine	do. " "
McMullan, Patrick	do. " "
McMullan, John	do. " "
McMullan, Hugh	do.
McCarthy, Timothy	1792. Emigrant from England.
McCrea, Thomas	Came up as a sailor, Marine Dept. M. Elliott.
McPherson, Kenneth	S.
McKay, James	S.
McLean, Hector	British soldier.
McKain, Samuel, and wife	Provisioned at Johnstown. R.R.N.Y M. Roll.
McIntosh, Donald.	
McBean, Donald	Wife and five children.
McKenzie, Widow	S.
McKercher, Donald	S. A soldier R.R.N.Y. J.F.
Daniel	
McCallum, Donald	S.
McGregor, Margaret, and child.	
McLeod, Daniel	A wife and four children.
McLean, Neil, and wife.	
McKinly, William	At Montreal.
McGregor, Philip	A wife and five children. Prov'd at Niagara.
McMasters, Samuel	Removed.
McHern, John	Coteau Du Lac.
McClougady, James	Lachine. Soldier R.R.N.Y. M. Roll.
McCosson, John	Coteau Du Lac for his family.
McCue, James	States for do. Soldier R.R.N.Y.M.Roll.
McMullen, Michael	To Johnstown. " " "
McDowell, Ronald	"
McDonell, John.	
McIntee, Barn's.	
McLeod, Norman.	
McBee, Lewis.	
McMean, John.	
McLeod, John.	
McCarfrae, Dennis.	
McDonald, Donald.	
McLean, John	Native of Ireland. Major Close's list, 1788.

T

APPENDIX B.

NAMES.	REMARKS.
McKinty, Francis	Sergt.-Major R. R. N. Y. Muster Roll.
McLawren, Evan	Soldier " "
McCarter, Donald	" " "
McDonell, Evan	" " "
McDougall, Peter	" " "
McCarty, Caleb	Corporal " "
McVicar, Dougal	Soldier " "
McKellup, Alexander	" " "
McCormiss, William	" " "
McMurdy, James	" " "
McKenvin, Charles	Soldier 31st Regt. L.B.L. 1790.
McCartney, James	" 84th " L.B.Nassau,1794.
McDonald, James	" 71st "
McGregor, Duncan	Sergeant Loyal Rangers.
McKenzie, John	Drummer "
McKenzie, Thomas	" "
McNeil, Alexander	Soldier "
McSheehy, Eugene	" "
McNeil, James	" " Died in 1782.
McGillivray, Daniel	" "
McKenzie, Alexander	" "
McMullan, John	" "
McDonald, Michael	" "
McKenzie, John	" " Died in 1783.
McDonell, Randy	R. R. N. York.
McIntosh, Alexander	A soldier.
McKendrick, John	" 97th Regt.
McLaughlin, Archibald	Soldier.
McArthur, Jenny	Daughter of John Hogart, who joined in 1779. N. McL.
McDonell, Colquhan	Soldier in 84th Regt. J. F.
McGuire, Donald	Son of Patrick. J. F.
McDonell, Hector	Son of Farquhar. (Deceased.) J. F.
McDonell, Catharine	Daughter of Wm. Cameron of Charlottenburg. Soldier R. R. N. Y. Joined in 1777.
McPhee, John	Common settler—N. McL.—and one was a soldier 73rd Regt. Discharged in Britain.
McDonell, Finlay	Common settler (deceased). N. McL.
McPhee, Duncan	" "
McKenzie, Roderick	Joined in 1777. 22-12 Lancaster. "
McCew, Patrick	Soldier 84th Regt.
Near, Charles	Soldier King's R.
Nicholl (or Nichorlas), John	" "
Noys, Nathaniel	" "
Newkirk, William	" "
Nicholson, William	Sergt. Fredericksburg. R. R. N. Y.

APPENDIX B. 315

NAMES.	REMARKS.
Newkirk, E.	Soldier B. Rangers.
Newman, Arthur	Called a good Loyalist.
Neighton, John	Soldier 5th Regt.
Nappin, Widow	and one child. Prov'd. at Cataraqui.
Nicholl, Robert.	A wife and one child.
Neddo, Lewis	A wife and one child. Prov'd. at Johnstown. U. Canadian. Not privileged.
Neder, Luke	A wife and four children.
Newkirk, John	A wife. Prov'd. at Niagara.
Newark, John	
Neibour, John	
Nail, Frederick	Soldier R.R.N.Y. Muster Roll.
Newton, John	" "
Newton, Thomas	" "
Nicholas, James	" "
Nanamaker, Jacob	" "
Night, Charles	Soldier 53rd Regt., L.B.L., 1790.
Northrop, Elihu	Sergt. Loyal Rangers.
Northrop, Azer	Soldier "
Nelson, Caleb	" "
Nicholas, John	" "
Nix, John	" "
Nunn, John	" Jersey volunteers. J.F.
Nettleton, Timothy	Son of Amos, a settler. O.C.
Oakley, Benjamin	Soldier King's R.
Orra, Philip	" "
Oflaharty, Patrick	" 8th Regt.
O'Carr, Peter	Said to have been on the Lakes a Petty Officer.
O'Neal, John	Lieut. Jessup's or Roger's.
Orser, Widow	and child. Prov'd. at Cataraqui.
Ostrom, Ralph	
O'Hara, Catherine	and son. Prov'd. at Johnstown, widow of a Royalist, J.F., widow of Kean O'Hara, soldier R.R.N.Y. N.McL.
Ostrander, Andrew	Wife and child. Prov'd, at Niagara.
O'Brien, Widow	and two sons.
Osliger, Hen	A. Quitted his land.
Oyler, Valantine	Loyalist Major Close's list, 1788.
O'Bryan, Timothy	Soldier R.R.N.Y. M. Roll.
Orchard, Donald	" "
O'Harra, Kain	" "
O'Bryan, John	" "
Orchard, William	" "
Oatman, Henry	Soldier R.R.N.Y., L.B.L., 1791.
Osburn, Nathaniel	Soldier Loyal Rangers.
Okes, John	" "

APPENDIX B.

NAMES.	REMARKS.
Ostrander, Evert	Soldier Loyal Rangers.
Ostrander, Abraham	" "
O'Kief, Cornelius	" "
Orr, Thomas	Soldier 84th Regt., N.McL.
Patterson, Ebenezer	Soldier King's Rangers.
Patterson, George	" "
Patra, John	" "
Persons, Christopher	Corporal "
Pells, Henry	Soldier "
Phils, Thomas	" "
Phils, Samuel	" "
Poickle or Pike, Jonathan	" "
Pickle, perhaps Christopher	" "
Pickle, Jacob	" "
Phillips, Almon	" "
Phillips, Seth	" "
Pritchard, Azariah	Captain "
Pritchard, Azariah	Volunteer "
Purkins, Jonathan	Soldier King's Rangers.
Palmer, Joseph	Sergeant 8th Regiment.
Palmer, Joseph Junr	Soldier 34th Regiment.
Parker, John	Soldier R.R.N.Y. M.R.
Powell, Joseph	Soldier B. Rangers.
Price, Joseph	" "
Pomeroy, —	Capt., an apothecary from the S. ward.
Pratt, John	Corpl. of Osnabruck. Soldier R.R. N.Y. M. Roll.
Prust, —	Sergeant Fredericksburg.
Pardo, John	8th Regiment.
Philiply, Charles	Ten years in 44th Regt., and volunteer all the war.
Pike, John	A settler after the war, M. Elliott.
Pomainville, J	Gov. Hamilton.
Powell, Joseph	Indian Department.
Prince, John	B. Rangers.
Parks, Rolland	Cornet.
Paxton, Thomas	Marine Department.
Pollard, Richard Esq	Borne arms in 1775.
Pilkington, Robert	Lieut. Royal Engineers, not privil'gd.
Porter, Richard	Capt. 60th Regiment, "
Porty, Christian	German soldier.
Palmerston, James	Volunteer Indian Department.
Pruin, William	Treasury Loyalist. Emigrant from England.
Peirce or Pearson	
Purkess, William	" " "
Parker, William	" " Was in His Majesty's service in America.

APPENDIX B. 317

NAMES.	REMARKS.
Phillips, John........................	Treasury Loyalist. Called a Jew from Philadelphia.
Pike, Robert.......................	Loyalist, W.D.
Piercy, John	A wife and two children. Prov'd. at Cataraqui.
Peters, Joseph	A wife and three children.
Parsalls, John.................	and wife.
Prippin, Augustus.................	S. John Justus Prippin, soldier 34th Regiment.
Paterson, Elias......................	S. Prov'd at Johnstown. Drummer R.R.N.Y. M.R.
Painter, George.....................	A wife and child. Soldier R.R.N.Y. M. Roll.
Potter, William....................	A wife. Soldier R.R.N.Y. M. Roll.
Pickle, James......................	S.
Prosser, Richard	S. Soldier R.R.N.Y. M. Roll.
Perry, Edward.....................	S. Soldier 8th Regiment.
Putnam, Nathaniel	S.
Pescod, David....................	S.
Paddock, John	S. Soldier R.R.N.Y. M. Roll.
Plaus, John.......................	S.
Plaus, Richard	S.
Prime, Cato.......................	S. Soldier R.R.N.Y. M. Roll.
Picket, William....................	A wife and four children.
Price, William	" "
Pritchard, John....................	S.
Parks, John	S.
Philips, Nicholas	and two children.
Philips, Nicholas Junr.............	and wife.
Pattengell, C.....................	Gone to the States.
Price, Patrick......................	
Preter, John	At Quebec.
Pfaudt, Frederick..................	At Montreal.
Pervisus, John	To Johnstown.
Pecking, James	
Plasse, John	
Pea, Charles	
Predget, John.....................	
Playges, Laurence..................	
Ploss, Henry	
Pitcher, Laurence..................	
Patten, Robert	
Pangart, Conrade	German Soldier.
Peppers, John	
Partness, Adam...................	In many years much persecuted. W.D.
Pimricais, Joseph	A drummer R.R.N.Y. M. Roll.
Plantz, John	A soldier " "
Perch, Robert....................	A. " " "
Palmer, John	A. Sergt. " "

APPENDIX B.

Names.	Remarks.
Perch, Nathaniel	A. Soldier R.R.N.Y. M. Roll.
Prime, Francis	A. " " "
Putnam, Francis	A. " " "
Price, Jacob	A. " " "
Plant, John	I. Corporal " "
Parlmis, John	Loyalist Major Close's List, 1788.
Parlmis, George	" "
Pennick, Joseph	Son of Captain James Pennick, of Peter's Corps. P. to L.B.L. 1790; states from Vermont lately.
Parish, Joel	From Vermont, P.L.,L.B.L.,1790.
Putman, Robert	Soldier 29th Regt.
Pettit, Jonathan	An old soldier. L.B. Nassau, 1794.
Pritchard, Stephen	A Soldier 29th Regt. "
Poyer, Nicholas	German Soldier, Regt. of Spink.
Parnel, Abraham	A solder during the war.
Parker, Wm	Soldier Loyal Rangers.
Preston, Wm	" "
Plinter, Christopher	" "
Persons, Chalwell	" "
Proctor, Ephraim	" "
Plass, Peter	" "
Pest, John (died in January, 1783)	" "
Poor, Augustus	" "
Parthlow, John	" "
Portague, Baptiste	" "
Peters, Andrew	" "
Pettit, Dunham	" "
Phelps, Jonathan	" "
Prosser, Richard	" R.R.N.Y. J. F.
Papts or Babst, John	Son of Adam Papst, U.E.
Park, James	Volunteer, Indian Dept.
Putman, Nathan	Emigrant from the States. J.F.
Phillips, John	Soldier 2nd Batln. R.R.N.Y. H.
Quig, Patrick	S. Prov'd. at Johnstown. Soldier 84th Regt.
Ryan, Cornelius	Lieut. T. Loyalist.
Roggie, John	A wife and 4 children. T. Loyalist— German Soldier.
Rampler, Henry	T. Loyalist.
Road, Wolf Gang	"
Robinson, Benjamin	"
Ruhart, Jacob	B. Rangers.
Redin, Edward	8th Regt. W.D.
Ronon, John	84th Regt. W.D.
Ruff, James	"
Ruport, Peter	Soldier R.R.N.Y., also one named Peder Rupert, R.R.N.Y. I.C.

APPENDIX B.

NAMES.	REMARKS.
Robertson, David	Sergt.. Cornwall and Roxboro'.
Ruiter, Henry	Captain R. Rangers.
Ruiter. John	Lieut. " or Loyal Rangers.
Ruiter. Henry	"
Ross, John	Major 34th Regt.
Rancier, Joseph	Butler's Rangers.
Reynolds, Samuel	Soldier R.R.N.Y. M. R.
Rozacrantz, Nicholas	Volunteer Butler's Rangers.
Reynolds, Thomas	Commiss'y. of Provisions.
Rivard, F.	Govr.. Hamilton.
Roberte, François	Detroit Volunteers.
Roberte. Joseph	"
Roe, Walter	Warrant Officer, Marine Dept.
Rose, John	B. Rangers.
Rudhest or Ruhart G. & J	Loyalists and B. Rangers.
Ross, John	Sergt. 26th Regt.
Rough, James	His Majesty's Navy ; last war.
Rummerfield, Anthony	Called a good Loyalist.
Ruth, Richard	Entered the service in 1758.
Ryter, John	A discharged soldier.
Rogers, James	Long prisoner ; attached to us.
Ross, Lewin Ralph	Lieut. 5th Regt. (not privileged).
Raimond, Widow	One child. Prov'd. at Cataraqui.
Reynolds, John	S. Soldier King's Rangers, L. B. L. 1791.
Redford. Thoms	S.
Roat, George	S.
Rochell, John	S.
Ridley, Wm	S.
Ryckman, Widow	and 3 children.
Reynolds, Daniel	S.
Ross, Charles	S. Prov'd. at Johnstown. Sergeant Loyal Rangers.
Roach, John	A wife and child. Soldier Loyal Rangers.
Richardson, George	S.
Read, Duncan	S.
Ruport, Francis	S. Soldier R.R.N.Y. M. Roll.
Ruport, John	S. R.R.N.Y. Joined in 1776. N. McL.
Ruport, Adam	A wife, 3 sons and 3 daughters.
Ruport, Hans	S.
Rose, James	S. Soldier R.R.N.Y. M. Roll.
Rose, Henry	A discharged German soldier—One of this name came in in March. Capt. John Jones.
Richardson, Edward	and Wife. prov'd. at Niagara.
Ramsay, James	and 2 women.

APPENDIX B.

NAMES.	REMARKS.
Ransier, Ann	and 1 Man. Provd. at Fort Erie.
Reid, Michael	Niagara.
Royser, Michael	Montreal.
Roach, James	Canada. Soldier R.R.N.Y. M. Roll.
Roland, Lewis	
Roing, Iosare } Rhuart, Jacob }	Soldiers, Butler's Rangers.
Ramser, Adam	
Rawsom, Christr	
Raw, John	
Reynolds, Solomon	
Reynolds, Reuben	
Ramsay, James, Jr	
Reynoll, Wm.	Soldier Loyal Rangers.
Ritchie, John	Scotland, Major Close's, 1788.
Rose, Wm	N.B. Soldier R.R.N,Y. M. Roll,
Riley, David	I. Sergeant " "
Robinson, Robert	E. Soldier " "
Rose, Finlay	N.B. " " "
Rice, Frederick	A. " " "
Rawlins, Grant	Barbs. Sergeant " "
Reid, Alexander	I. Soldier " "
Robinson, James	N.B. " " "
Rowstoun, George	E, " " "
Reynolds, John	
Reynolds, George	} Mjr. Close's List, 1788—Loyalists.
Rassely, Julions	
Rassley, Frederick	
Randall, David	A Settler, 1790.
Renna, John	Soldier Col. De Bernard's Hessian.
Reynolds, Ephraim	A Settler, L.B.L., 1790.
Reynolds, John	Soldier King's Rangers.
Rily, Thomas	" 24th Regt.
Robins, Joshua	An old Soldier, L.B.N., 1794.
Rouse, George	Sergeant Loyal Rangers.
Robertson, Duncan	" "
Richardson, Timothy	Soldier "
Refenburg, Abraham	" "
Radiker, Henry	" "
Russel, Elisha	" "
Robins, Wm.	" "
Row, Alexander	" R.R.N.Y. J. F.
Row, James	Soldier R.R.N.Y. J.F.
Resh, Philip	Soldier German Troops.
Robinson, Joseph	Soldier Butler's Rangers.
Ren, Anthony	German soldier, N.McL.
Richardson, William	Son of Asa, employed on Secret service, and died therein. O.E.
Reynolds, Samuel	Volunteer Butler's Rangers. S.G,

APPENDIX B. 321

NAMES,	REMARKS.
Ricely, Christian	Soldier Butler's Rangers.
Smith, Joseph	Sergt. Edwardsburg L. Rangers. S.G.
Scrambling, ——	" of Fredericksburg.
Scetterly, Joseph	Soldier K. Rangers.
Shank, Jacob	" "
Slengerline, Philip	" "
Smith, Eliphilcete	" "
Snyder, Christian	" "
Speed, George	" "
Spencer, Thomas	" "
Stuart, Solomon	" "
Stevens, Simon	" "
Sweet, Nicholas	" "
Shwarts, Frederick	R.R.N.Y. or King's Rangers.
Sutton, Isaac	" "
Shunck, Martin	A soldier.
Shilders, John	B. Rangers.
Skeaws, John	"
Slain, George	"
Slingerland, Tunis	"
Smith, Adam	"
Smith, Robert	Naval Dept.
Stevens, Nicholas	Interpreter Indian Dept.
Stewart, George	B. Rangers.
Stout, Martin	"
Stout, Richard	"
Saint Endre, I.B.	Detroit Volunteers.
Schefflin, Jonathan	" " Lieutenant.
Scott, William	Loyalist, private Detroit Volunteers.
Elizabeth, his daughter.	
Speak, Simon	B. Rangers
Shaver, Michael	Hesse Hanam.
Shoick, Peter	B. Rangers.
Siebetslie, George	German Corps and Provincial Navy.
Simmonds, James	8th Regt.
Smith, John	84th " and at taking of Quebec.
Smith, I. or J.	" "
Smith, Thomas	Marine Dept.
Soweracrito, I. B.	Detroit Volunteers (sergeant).
Souraint.	
Spackman, J.	Royal Artillery.
Stoaly, John	B. Rangers.
Shippy, Zebulon	Called a good Loyalist.
Small, George	Served under Sir John Johnson, Corporal. R.R.N.Y. M. Roll.
Smith, William	German Marine Dept.
Stapleton, the late (by Elizabeth)	Master Carpenter Engineers' Dept.
Staggman, John	Lieut. Hessian Corps.

APPENDIX B.

NAMES.	REMARKS.
Sutherland, David....	Lieut.
" William..............	B. Rangers.
" William..............	His father fell in service of the King.
Swerdfager, Rev. William..........	Much persecuted, came in in 1790.
Steadman, Philip	Not privileged.
Schel, Anthony..................	German soldier.
Schudlett, James	"
Schnitter, Nicholas	"
Semler, John	"
Swartfager John	R.R.N.Y.
Shaw, Hugh	Sergt. 25th Regt.
Sheler, John	29th Regt.
Staylor, William	Corps of Rangers.
Shabash, Peter	Green Yagur.
Stark, Henry Bethune.............	Capt. 63rd Regt.
Shuman, George	A soldier German Regt.
Schutz, George	A soldier.
Slingerland, Walter	B. Rangers
Shepherd James	Sergt. K. A. Dragoons.
Smades, Joshua..................	Joined at New York, 1778, Secret service.
Spragus, Jonathan	Came in 1794 ; lost his property.
Scarlett, George..................	His father's house and barn burnt in Carolina.
Stewart, Francis	A settler in 1794.
Stafford, Abel....................	" 1795.
Spinks, James....................	Marine Dept.
Stapleton, Elizabeth.	Widow of William Martin, Corporal, Niagara.
Shouk, Patrick	B. Rangers. W. D.
Segon, Jacob	"
Stratton, Thomas	Ship Carpenter. Lake Champlain.
Scott, William	Sergt. Detroit Volunteers.
Steel, Margaret Scott	Daughter of Jacob Huett, a settler.
Stephenson, James	Treasury Loyalist ; had been a tavern keeper in New York.
Scott, Catherine	Treasury Loyalist.
Spalden, Catherine	" " emigrant from England.
Stretch, Daniel	" " "
Stephinson, Richard..............	" " "
Sibley, Gilbert	" " son of the widow Sarah.
Sibley, Sarah	" " from Nova Scotia, a widow, and is returned there.
Selby, Thomas	Treasury Loyalist.
Swartze, Peter	Butler's Rangers. W.D.
Sinpless, Robert..................	Loyalist, W.D., Butler's Rangers.
Seek, Nicholas	" " a child not privileged, 180-.
Skeetel, Jacob	" "

APPENDIX B.

NAMES.	REMARKS.
Skittle, Jacob	Loyalist, W. D.
Smith, Thomas	" " Marine Dept.
Spiers, John	S. prov'd at Cataraqui.
Scout, John	A wife and one child ; soldier Loyal Rangers.
Simmon, widow	and two children "
Swope, Stephen	S. soldier Loyal Rangers
Sangerhausen, George	S. " "
Schnyder, Peter	S. " "
Schnyder, Zachariah	S. "
Seager, John	A wife and seven children.
Sinnet, Peter	S.
Sample, Hugh	S.
Staples, Ebenezer	S.
Sopher, Joseph	S.
Shoultz, Peter	S. soldier 29th Regt. p. discharge.
Surwatt, Christian	S. " 53rd Regt. (or Sowerwort).
Spratley, Thomas	S. Provincial at Johnstown, soldier R.R.N.Y. Muster Roll.
Stout, John	S.
Somers, Laney	S.
Smith, Conrod	S. son of John of Cornwall U.E. J.F.
Spencer, Barnard	S. Sergt. R.R.N.Y. Muster Roll.
Sagus, Henry, or Segar	Soldi Loosburg Hessian Regt.
Stoneburner, James	One child.
Streets, James, Junr.	S.
Serey, Richard	S. soldier R.R.N.Y. Muster Roll.
Stickman, John	A wife and child.
Stoly, Jacob	S.
Schrout, Henry	S.
Soper, Sarah	S.
Seron, Christopher	A wife and five children ; emigrant from the States. J.F.
Shaver, Nicholas	A wife and two children.
Shyers, Jacob	S. soldier R.R.N.Y. Muster Roll,
Swanson, George	S.
Snow, John	S.
Sewest, ——	Six children.
Segar, John	A wife and two children, prov'd at Niagara.
Schram, James	A wife and five children.
Schram, Abraham	A wife.
Song, Peter	S.
Smith, Mathias	S.
Sheverland, John	And wife.
Stawple, Jacob	And wife. Prov'd at Fort Erie.
Steaty, John	A wife and child.
Springstin, Gasper	S.
Simmonds, James	S.

Names.	Remarks.
Stringer, John	And wife. Gone off to the States.
Scrambling, David.	S.
Sutton, Samuel	At Montreal. Soldier R.R.,N.Y. M. Roll.
Scanlin, John	At Montreal.
Stotlick, Philip	do.
Smith, Hugh	Terrebonne. Soldier R.R.N.Y., M. Roll.
Slingerland, Dennis	
Skinner, Isaiah	Son of Timothy.
Schequet, Jacob	
Stedman, William	
Springer, Margaret	
Steby, John	
Stoffle, Jacob	
Scuss, John	
Shoart, Michael	
Sitnoff, Jacob	
Springsteen, George	
Stringer, Andrew	
Showman, Conrade	
Secord, Magdalen	
Steishoff, John	
Snider, Luke	
Snider, Saul	
Smith, Fticke	
Shotice, John	
Simson, Robert	Sergeant Loyal Rangers.
Sons, Bott Samuel	
Sewert, Jacob.	
Shivington, Francis	
Sturuat, Christopher	
Soy, Anovy	
Singer, John	
Shortcrop, Christopher	
Scheffre, Michael	Soldier German corps. Major Close's list, 1788.
Shepley, John	Loyalist.
Speckman, Joseph	do.
Sherman, Henry	German soldier.
Schelsted, George	A German.
Stoutmyre, Adam	Served as boatswain on Lake Erie.
Showls, John G.	F. Soldier R.R.N.Y., Muster Roll.
Shaver, George	A. 25 years soldier R.R.N.Y. Muster Roll.
Shaver, George	A. 20 years soldier R.R.N.Y. Muster Roll.
Smith, William	E. Soldier R.R.N.Y. Muster Roll.
Sheveritt, John	E. " "

APPENDIX B. 325

Names.	Remarks.
Seymour, Henry	E. Soldier R.R.N.Y. Muster Roll.
Spratly, Thomas	E. " "
Syphert, Joseph	F. " "
Shades, Adam	A. " "
Sullivan, Dennis	I. " "
Schamerhorn, Peter	I. " "
Siver, Henry	F. " "
Stoneberg, Stephen	A. " "
Shaver, Maurcus	A. " "
Sullivan, Cornelius	I. " "
Stats, Casper	F. " "
Solomon, Jeremiah	A. " "
Slieneman, Henry	Soldier in the German Troops.
Shirelant, John	Corporal do.
Shirts, John	Soldier Loyal Rangers, L.B.L. 1791.
Sturges, William	do. 29th Regiment.
Smith, Henry	Soldier King's Rangers.
Smyth, George	Surgeon Loyal Rangers.
Summervill, John	Sergeant Loyal Rangers.
Skinkle, Henry	Soldier "
Simmon, Balster	" "
See, James	" "
See, John	" "
Sole, Timothy	" "
Sharor, Thomas	" "
Still, John	" "
Stafford, Joseph	" "
Sastera, Joseph	" "
Stone, James	" "
Stever, Peter	" " (died June 1783).
Scott, David	" "
Slater, William	" "
Scott, David, Junr.	" "
Scott, Neil	" "
Stenson, Elnathan	" " (died July, 1783).
Scott, Daniel	" "
Stone, Simon	" "
Sampson, Aaron	" "
Sampson, Theophilus	" "
Sewseth, Henry	" "
Sulfrage, John	" "
Sutherland, James	" "
Sharp, Philip	" "
Scott, Abraham	" "
Saffara, Joseph	" "
Simmons, Jonas	" "
Snurr, Peter	" "
Sherer, Thomas	" "
Sanders, William, Junr	" "

NAMES.	REMARKS.
Sailmon, John	Soldier Loyal Rangers.
Scherbert, Augustus	" "
Shoughnessy, Wm. Henry	" "
Sayer, Henry	German soldier.
Seager, John	A settler of 1784. J.V.A.
Speck, Philip	Soldier Butler's Rangers.
Sweatman, Isaac	" "
Staughmill, Henry	German soldier.
Shell, David	Son of ———— ; a Loyalist. J. F.
Stauty, Jacob	Soldier Butler's Rangers. Jac. Slonob.
Slingerland, Walter	Butler's Rangers ; son of Anthony R. Clinch.
Stansfield, John	Served on board the Magnificent, 74 gun.
Sloch, Peter	Soldier 29th Regiment.
Shaffer, Esther	Widow of Jacob Schafer, soldier R. R.N.Y. N. McL.
Smith, Donald	Son of John, sergeant R.R.N.Y N. McL.
Schrider, Simon	Soldier R.R.N.Y. N. McL.
Smades, Abraham	Came in 1803 or 1804. O. E.
Swarts, Michael	Soldier R.R.N.Y. O. E.
Snyder, John	A smith and armourer. W.D.
Steel, John	Soldier 84th Regiment, p. Col. McDonell's certe.
Sencebaugh, John	Sergeant Jersey Volunteers. See petition of 1806.
Swartz, Henry	Soldier Butler's Rangers, p. discharge.
Schultz, Peter	Soldier 29th Regiment, p. discharge.
Snyther, Michael	Kingston. Soldier Incorporated Loyalists.
Shafford, Conurt	Soldier R.R.N.Y. Capt. J. Anderson's certificate.
Smith, William	Adjutant B. Rangers, S. G.
Smith, Frederick	Soldier do. "
Sheldon, John	do. do. "
Springer, Daniel	do. do. "
Tracy, James	4th Regiment, 10 years.
Taylor, John	Sergeant 34th Regt. Ernest Town.
Taylor, Peter	Soldier R.R.N.Y. Muster Roll.
Tuffie, Samuel	B. Rangers.
Thomas, John	8th Regiment.
Turny, George	B. Rangers.
Turney, John, Senr.	Lieut. B. Rangers.
Turney, John, Junr.	Volunteer B. Rangers.
Thorn, William	Provincial Navy.
Tyler, William	Lieut. K. Rangers.
Thomas, James	Soldier R.R.N.Y.

APPENDIX B. 327

NAMES.	REMARKS.
Tip, William	Gen. Riediesel's Regt.
Troop, John	(By Esther Ross.) Lieut.
Trump, Charles	Gunner to *Onondago*, L. Ontario N. Dept.
Thiery, Mr.	Of Yonge. Indian interpreter.
Tully, Thomas	A wife and child. Treasury Loyalist. Emigrant from Ireland.
Tully, Thomas, Junr.	Treasury Loyalist. Emigrant from Ireland.
Thureson, Lawrence	Lieut. Treasury Loyalist. Emigrant from Ireland.
Turner, John	Treasury Loyalist.
Tinbrook, Thomas	A negro. Provisioned at Cataraqui.
Thorn, John	S.
Turner, Richard	S. Soldier Loyal Rangers.
Turner, John	S. British soldier.
Trelow, John	A wife. Provisioned at Johnstown.
Thimbler (Templer), Christopher	S. German soldier. J. F.
Thomas, William	S.
Tilabough. John	S.
Truman, Francis	S.
Thomson, John	A wife.
Thomson, James	S.
Tounsend, James	S.
Tredenburg, Mathew	S.
Tarrell, John	S.
Thomas, James	A wife and two children. Soldier Butler's Rangers. J. F.
Taylor, Lewis	Not entitled to land.
Thezer, Mathew	At Montreal.
Trickey, John	A settler. P. to L.B.L. 1791.
Tryar, Samuel.	
Tuffard, Conrad.	
Taylor, Charles	A Canadian. Maj. Close's List, 1788.
Timberman, John	Loyalist. Maj. Close's List, 1798.
Tipperaine, Christopher	F. Soldier R.R.N.Y. M. Roll.
Trapp, Richard	E. Drummer " "
Thrumbell, Robert	A. Soldier " "
Tolback, Bolsor	A. Soldier " "
Thompson, Thomas	I. Soldier " "
Tibbet, John	Late from N. York State. L.B.L.1790.
Thompson, Mathew	Adjutant Loyal Rangers.
Tall, Simon	Soldier Loyal Rangers.
Tuttle, John	" "
Tuttle, William	" "
Tuttle, Stephen	" "
Tramble, Asahel	" "
Tuttle, Joseph	" "
Truman, Peter	" "

APPENDIX B.

Names.	Remarks.
Talhammer, David	Soldier Loyal Rangers.
Trip, Robert	" "
Thielie, Laurence	" "
Tuchout, James	" "
Tinkney, Abraham	" "
Twifle, John	Died in Dec., 1782. Soldier Loyal Rangers.
Tarlouse, John	German soldier. J. F.
Tufflemire, Martin	Settler. W.D.
Turneaux, Jean Baptiste	Sergt. of artillery, under Gov. Hamilton.
Ulman, Henry	S. Soldier R.R.N.Y. M. Roll.
Udle (or Uddle), John	25th Regt.
Umpey, Amherst	Soldier K. Rangers.
Upton, William	" "
Understone, James	Provincial Navy.
Urquart, Roderick	Mil'y claimant.
Ulse, Andrew	Loyalist Maj. Close's list, U.D. 1788.
Utler, Isaac	Soldier Loyal Rangers.
Van Cure, Benjamin	Provisioned at Cataraqui.
Van Duser, Jac.	A wife & two children at Johnstown.
Vrooman, Isaac	S. Provisioned at Niagara. Soldier B. Rangers. S.G.
Van Every, Benjamin	A wife, four sons and one daughter. Soldier B. Rangers.
Vanderheyden, David	Absent. 2nd Batt. R.N.N.Y.
Vanduwort, Peter	Gone to the States.
Vanalstine, Lemuel	To Detroit.
Vanalstine, James	To Ireland.
Vanalstine, the late	By Catherine.
Vernon, Gedion.	
Van Aller, Lawrence	Lieut. B. Rangers.
Valantine	Ensign R.
Valantine. John	Adjutant R.R.N.Y.
Vanvost, Yallas Vandict, Peter Vagler, Evert Vosbury, John	Soldiers King's Rangers.
Van Every, Peter	Soldier B. Rangers.
Vallade, I. B.	Gov. Hamilton's Volunteers.
Vallade, Francis	Detroit Volunteers.
Van Camp	R.R.N.Y. W. D.
Van Camp, Junr.	" "
Visceneaux, Lewis	Siege of Quebec, and Marine Dept.
Van Scott, John	Soldier R.R.N.Y.
Vandyke, Gradus	An old soldier. L. B. Nassau, 1794.
Vanderlip, John.	
Vansize, Joseph.	

APPENDIX B. 329

NAMES.	REMARKS.
Van Volkinburg, Laurence.	
Valentine, James	I. Soldier R.R.N.Y. Muster Roll.
Vrooman, Thomas	A. " "
Veeder, Lucas	F. " "
Vernor, Michael	F. " "
Vansnell, John	F. " "
Vansalsburg, Cornelius	A. " "
Van Colz, John	" "
Voss, Christopher	Soldier Loyal Rangers.
Vanvost, John	" "
Voluntine, Isaac	" "
Velie, Andrew G.	" "
Van Camp, Jacob	" "
Voluntine, Gabriel	" "
Van Camp, Tunis	" "
Van Snell, Frederick	" R.R.N.Y.. JF.
Wade, Elijah	Williamsb'g. Soldier R.R.N.Y. *M.R.*
Westley, Joseph	Sergeant. Kingston.
White, Alexander	Capt. from the Southward.
Welch, John	Naval Dept.
Wemp, Andrew	Lieutenant Butler's Rangers.
West, John	B. Rangers.
Willice, Abel	"
Wood, John	8th Regt.
Wynn, John	N.C. officer Butler's Rangers.
Winney, Peter	Corpl. King's Rangers.
Warner, Levit	Soldier
Wamer, John	Soldier "
Waters, John	Loyalist. W. D.
Wayland, Leonard	"
West	Perhaps sergt. 52nd Regt. W. D.
Weston, Amos	Blacksmith. Many years with Stedman N. P.
Weston, Samuel	52nd Regt.
Whittle, Richard	Volunteer to Port St. Vincent with Gov. Hamilton.
Williamson, John	B. Rangers.
Winter, Christopher	"
Wood, James	"
Wormwood, John	"
Wright, John	"
Wright, Henry	Loyalist.
Wilcox, Hezekiah	U.E. Loyalist.
Wallis, John	Soldier King's Rangers.
Wakley, Stephen	" "
Warder, Thomas	" "
Watson, Ralph	" "
Wemp, Aaron	" "

U

APPENDIX B.

NAMES.	REMARKS.
Wheeler, Samuel	Soldier King's Rangers.
Whitman, George	" "
Winer, Joseph	" "
Westbrook, Andrew	Son of Anthony.
Wilkins, Robert	Loyalist.
Weishuhn	Sergt. 60th Regt.
Wray, John	Soluier 1st Batt. 60th Regt.
Wright, Edward	Quartermaster cavalry, Q. Rangers.
Wright, Thomas	Surgeon 1st Batt. 60th Regt. Hospital mate during the war.
Ward, George	Sergt. 24th Regt. W. D.
Witzell, Nicholas	B. Rangers.
Wilson, George	Treasury Loyalist. Emigrant settler.
Wilson, James	" "
Webster, Elizabeth	" " from England.
Wooding, John	Wife and child. Treasury Loyalist. Emigrant from England.
Wycott, Francis	Treasury Loyalist. Englishman. Emigrant settler.
Wolfington, John	Treasury Loyalist.
Williams, John	" Emigrant from England.
Wheeler, James	Treasury Loyalist.
Wilcox, Elick	Soldier B. Rangers.
Windall, Joseph	8th Regt.—W. D.—and a 3 yrs. man.
Winter, Joseph	84th Regt. W. D.
Winter, Butler	84th Regt. W. D.
Wilcox, Morris	Loyalist. W. D.
Wilcox, Isaiah	" "
Wytzell, Nicholas	A wife and five children. Provisioned at Cataraqui. Not U.E.
Walters, Humphrey	Wife & child. Prov'd at Cataraqui.
Wanack, James	S.
Williams, Nathan	S.
Williams, William	A wife and seven children.
Warners, Levi	S.
Wright, Semion	A wife.
Wormly, Jacob	S.
Woodcock, Peter	A wife and child.
Wills, John	S. British soldier.
Wagaline, George	S. Provisioned at Johnstown. German soldier. Afterwards in 60th Regt. N. McL.
Winzell, Adam	A wife and three children. A settler. N. McL.
Willoby, William	S.
Watson, James	A wife & three children. Soldier 34th Regt.

APPENDIX B.

NAMES.	REMARKS.
Wilkison, Daniel	S.
Walden, Jack	A wife and seven children.
Walker, Alex	S.
Willoby, John	S.
Whart, Andrew	A wife.
Winter, Jacob	S. Soldier R.R.N.Y. J. F.
Waldrof, John	A wife & child. Son of Martin, Senr. Son of Mrs. Lenny Woldroff.
Wright, John	S.
Wolsey, Abel	A wife.
Winter, Janet	S.
Warner, John	A wife and five children.
Watson, John	S. To Coteau Du Lac.
Waldradt, Jacob	S. To the States. Soldier Loyal Rangers.
Waunamaker, Jacob	Gone to the States.
Weatherwat, William	In the States. Of Jessup's Loyal Rangers.
Wickie, John	Never joined. Of Jessup's.
Wilson, James	
Woodcock, William	
White, Jesse	Volunteer in Jessup's, p. daughter's P. to L.B.L. 1791.
White, Christ'r	
Wadman, William	
Westbrook, Alex	
Webster, Abraham	
Willoc, Samuel	
Willse, Abraham	
Wyley, Wyndel	German, Major Close's list, 1788.
Walter, Martin	F. Soldier R.R.NY. Muster Roll.
Wesseck, George	F. " "
Weaver Nicholas	F. " "
Worth, George	A. " "
Wolf, Christian	F. and one a soldier L. Rangers.
Wall, James	I. Soldier R.R.N.Y. Muster Roll.
Wearly, Peter	A. " "
Wormwood, William	A. " "
Wade, Abijah	" " J.F.
Wing, Ichabod	Late from N. York State, L.B.L.,1790.
Wing, Jedediah	" " " 1790.
Winter, John	" " " 1790.
Whiting, William	Soldier 84th Regt., L.B.L., 1791.
Ward, John	Sergeant Loyal Rangers.
Whitman, Maxwell	Soldier "
Ward, Abel	" "
Wainawright, John	" "
Whitman, Robert	" "
Wray, Roswell	" "

332   APPENDIX B.

NAMES.	REMARKS.
White, William	Soldier Loyal Rangers.
Williston, William	" "
Williston, William, Junr.	" "
Watson, Aaron	" "
Webster, Milo	" "
Weymore, George	" "
White, Samuel	" "
Warwick, James	" "
Webb, George	" "
Wyott, John	" "
Williams, Richard	Died in Sept., 1786. Soldier Loyal Rangers.
Wearing, Frederick	Soldier Loyal Rangers.
Woolf, Lodowick	" "
Waggoner, Hermanus	Soldier R.R.N.Y., J.F.
Wills, William	Soldier 29th Regt.
Wintermute, Abraham	Soldier Butler's Rangers.
White, Derrick	A Loyalist from Maryland, O.C.,1796.
Watson, James	Private 34th Regt. N.McL.
Wayett, Daniel	Joined in 1777. N.McL.
Waldroff, Widow Lenny	Of Martin Woldroff, Soldier R.R.N.Y. N. McL.
Weaver, Christy	Soldier R.R.N.Y. O.E.
Wright, Malcolm	Sergeant King's A. Dragoons.
Wade, Arthur	Corpl. 44th Regt. p. discharge, 1783.
Wilson, John	Col. Barton's Corps, deserted from Staten Island, information of Ashael Ward, 6th Dec., 1811.
Yeurex, William	S. Prov'd. at Cataraqui.
Young, Isaac	S.
Yeurex, Isaac	S.
Yearns, William	B. Rangers.
Youngs, David	King's Rangers.
Yager, Helmes	Butler's
Yager, William	" "
Young, Andrew	Was a gun-carriage maker.
Zilly, Ludowick	
Zeinger, John	

YORK, 22nd September, 1803.

Major Green informs that the men belonging to the 29th and 34th Regts. were discharged in 1787, when the regiments went home.

That the 53rd went home in 1789, when some men were discharged.

That the 44th Regt. went home at the peace, when some men were discharged.

That the men belonging to the 8th Regt. were discharged.

Mr. Hamilton's Information, Oct. 21st, 1803.

That Colonel De Peyster and the 8th Regt. left Upper Canada in the summer of 1785.

That he believes that the 34th went down in the summer of 1787.

The land located by John Grant of Strathspay, now of Pittsburg—

E½ 28, U.S. R.R. .... 55 acres.
W½ 29, do. .... 100 "
E½ 35, 7th con. Charlottenburg .... 100 "

255

$\left.\begin{array}{c}36\\37\end{array}\right\}$ 7th con. do.—granted to others .... 400 "

James Grant, his father—
  W½ 23, U.S. R.R.
  W½ 35, 7 do.

Catherine Leech, her children—
  John Munroe.....................⎫
  Jannet   "   ....⎪ Their father, dur-
  Robert   "   ....⎬ ing the war, in
  Daniel   "   ....⎪ the new States.
  Kitty   "   now married to Proctor⎭

APPENDIX B.

Mary Leech, now Britain, illegitimate.
Sarah Ward, now Patterson, illegitimate.
Trulove Golden, now Adams, illegitimate.

December 20, 1811.

Benjamin Babcock, of Kingston, a list of his children as sworn by his brother, David Babcock, 25th Jan'y, 1804, before A. Wood, Esq.—

Richard is 14 years.
David 12 "
Peter 10 "
Sarah 7 "
Jacob 5 "
John 3 "
Elizabeth 1 "

(Signed)   DAVID BABCOCK.